ELI-UNIDROIT MODEL EUROPEAN RULES OF CIVIL PROCEDURE

ELI-UNIDROIT MODEL EUROPEAN RULES OF CIVIL PROCEDURE

FROM TRANSNATIONAL PRINCIPLES TO EUROPEAN RULES OF CIVIL PROCEDURE

European Law Institute (ELI)
International Institute for the Unification of Private Law (UNIDROIT)

OXFORD
UNIVERSITY PRESS

OXFORD
UNIVERSITY PRESS

Great Clarendon Street, Oxford, OX2 6DP,
United Kingdom

Oxford University Press is a department of the University of Oxford.
It furthers the University's objective of excellence in research, scholarship,
and education by publishing worldwide. Oxford is a registered trade mark of
Oxford University Press in the UK and in certain other countries

First Edition published in 2021
Impression: 2

Published in the United States of America by Oxford University Press
198 Madison Avenue, New York, NY 10016, United States of America

British Library Cataloguing in Publication Data
Data available

Library of Congress Control Number: 2021936021

ISBN 978-0-19-886658-9

DOI: 10.1093/oso/9780198866589.001.0001

Printed and bound in the UK by
TJ Books Limited

FOREWORD

In 2004, UNIDROIT, together with the American Law Institute (ALI), published the ALI-UNIDROIT Principles on Transnational Civil Procedure. The Principles provided a model of balance between different legal families and traditions, but they were not adapted to the requirements of particular regions of the world, notably not to the specificities of European legal systems. This is why the European Law Institute (ELI) and UNIDROIT joined forces to develop these ELI-UNIDROIT Model Rules of European Civil Procedure. The idea was to reach out beyond the formulation of Principles and to develop more detailed rules, considering existing legal instruments at EU level, European legal traditions, and current legal developments in Europe, in order to produce a framework of reference and source of inspiration for a broad range of actors, notably legislators and policymakers. That ambitious idea flourished into the text we have the honour of presenting.

The project originated in an international workshop organised in Vienna in October 2013, at the initiative of former UNIDROIT Secretary-General José Angelo Estrella Faria and Christiane Wendehorst, then Vice-President of ELI and one of the authors of this foreword. During over seven years of hard work, around fifty international experts from Europe and beyond, as well as representatives of numerous institutions and organisations, were involved in this intense, collective endeavour, covering the entire spectrum of civil procedure, from service of documents to appeals, including -quite innovatively- certain types of collective proceedings.

In the midst of the Covid-19 pandemic as one of the most traumatic health, economic and social crisis our continent has lived through in generations, the ELI and UNIDROIT have continued their activities in pursuit of higher unification and modernisation of legal rules. The ELI Council, on 15 July 2020, the ELI Membership, on 5 August 2020, and a bit later, UNIDROIT's Governing Council on 24 September 2020, formally approved the ELI-UNIDROIT Model Rules on Civil Procedure, successfully concluding a common project which represents an excellent example of the cooperation between ELI and UNIDROIT and shows the potential for new projects in the future.

It is our pleasure to express our profound gratitude and admiration for the excellent work done by all participants. Perhaps it is only fair to start with the members of the Steering Committee, composed by representatives of both organisations (Remo Caponi and John Sorabji for ELI, Rolf Stürner for UNIDROIT) and ably chaired by Diana Wallis, former ELI President, and Anna Veneziano, UNIDROIT Deputy Secretary-General. A special word of appreciation is also owed to the Structure Group Co-Reporters, to Co-Reporters and, generally, to Members of the nine Working Groups who contributed with the research and the drafting of the Rules and Comments. Since this is a bilingual text, *un grand merci* goes to the "French Task Force", whose members ensured consistency with the French version of the black-letter Rules. Naturally, all experts involved would deserve a special mention, but, for obvious reasons of space, we must confine ourselves to making express reference to the complete list of names and affiliations of participants that opens this publication. Granting them the opening of the publication does not only acknowledge their invaluable work, but it is also a testament to the calibre of the experts we were fortunate enough to attract to this project. Finally, our gratitude goes to the representatives of the Observer Organisations and to the Advisers who lent their specialised knowledge to the project.

We would further like to extend our appreciation to those who supported the project team within our Secretariats over the years, and, particularly: at UNIDROIT Valentina Viganò, who was the focal point for the project organisation, and Isabelle Dubois, as well as Françoise Ghin; at ELI, Alina Lengyel, Adi Bikić, Ala Krinickytė and Tomasz Dudek. A special word of thanks to Unidroit's Lena Peters for the editorial work on the project and Frédérique Mestre and Marina Schneider for the translation of the comments into French.

Concluding this project is merely the end of the first step: these Model Rules must now start a new journey, a fascinating incursion into the modernisation of a more harmonised, user-friendly procedural law in Europe, one which allows for a better understanding and improved use of procedural rules, an objective especially relevant in a time when extreme circumstances are likely to put procedural systems to the test. While the *draft* Model Rules had already influenced the debate on law reform and the development of harmonised rules, we are confident that the finalised instrument will enjoy further dissemination and implementation as best practices in the field of civil procedure for national legislators and international policy makers, within Europe and beyond.

Vienna / Rome, January 2021
Prof. Christiane Wendehorst, ELI President
Prof. Maria Chiara Malaguti, Unidroit President
Prof. Ignacio Tirado, Unidroit Secretary-General

INTRODUCTION

An introduction is normally written by the authors, a role we do not claim for the ELI-UNIDROIT Model European Rules of Civil Procedure. What we can perhaps say is that we have acted as constant points of reference, respectively representing each of our institutions from start to finish, and it is in this capacity that we write these words of introduction.

When this project began over seven years ago, neither of us could have foreseen the depth and scope to which this publication would arrive. From the initial idea of turning the ALI-UNIDROIT Principles of Transnational Civil Procedure into rules pertinent to the European continent, the instrument, while purposefully not representing a model Code, has grown into an impressive number of pages of Rules and Comments, starting from general provisions and covering first instance proceedings (co-operative case management by parties and court, pleadings, service of process and due notice, *lis pendens*, proceedings preparatory to a final hearing, access to information and evidence-taking, judgments and their effects). It also addresses provisional and protective measures, appeals, collective redress and costs.

We would like to echo the UNIDROIT Secretary-General's and the UNIDROIT and ELI Presidents' words of admiration and thanks to our fellow members of the Steering Committee and to all the authors of this instrument. We would also wish to express gratitude to all those who, in one capacity or the other, participated in the discussions, seminars and workshops, sharing their comments and knowledge, including the institutional observers and the ELI and UNIDROIT institutional organs (ELI Council and Advisory Board, UNIDROIT Governing Council). Finally, we could never have achieved completion of the instrument without the dedicated assistance of the UNIDROIT and ELI staff over the years.

It has been quite a journey, and we have developed certain working methods and perhaps even, one might say, certain traditions within the team along the way. A highlight for all participants were the biannual meetings organised by UNIDROIT at its seat in Villa Aldobrandini in Rome and by ELI in Vienna and in cooperation with other organisations (particularly ERA in Trier). There have been many engaging discussions, some quite passionate, forcing us to reach compromises or better understand the value of the different approaches between legal systems.

The result of such discussions, the ELI-UNIDROIT Model European Rules of Civil Procedure, are perhaps unlikely to be read from cover to cover; different readers will be interested in different parts specific to their own practice, research or needs. It is our hope, however, that the amazing scholarship and wealth of practical experience that has gone into this instrument will be both an inspiration and a provocation to academics, policy makers and practitioners, across the European continent and beyond, to the extent that this may represent a milestone rather than an end point in the quest for modern, efficient, and fair rules of civil procedure.

January 2021
Diana P. Wallis
Anna Veneziano

PARTICIPANTS IN THE PROJECT

STEERING COMMITTEE AND WORKING GROUPS

STEERING COMMITTEE

Co-Chairs

José Angelo ESTRELLA FARIA — then UNIDROIT Secretary-General (co-chair until July 2018)
Anna VENEZIANO — Deputy Secretary-General, University of Teramo (co-chair since August 2018)
Diana WALLIS — then President of ELI, Solicitor & Mediator, University of Hull

Members representing the ELI

Remo CAPONI — University of Florence
John SORABJI — then Principal Legal Adviser to the Lord Chief Justice and the Master of the Rolls; University College London

Members representing UNIDROIT

Rolf STÜRNER — University of Freiburg; former Judge of the Courts of Appeal Stuttgart and Karlsruhe and former Co-Reporter for the ALI/UNIDROIT Principles
Anna VENEZIANO — UNIDROIT Deputy Secretary-General, University of Teramo

WORKING GROUPS*

ACCESS TO INFORMATION AND EVIDENCE

Reporters

Neil ANDREWS — University of Cambridge; former ALI/UNIDROIT Working Group member (co-reporter until 2017)
Fernando GASCÓN INCHAUSTI — University Complutense of Madrid

Members

Laura ERVO — University of Örebro
Frédérique FERRAND — University Jean Moulin Lyon 3; former ALI/UNIDROIT Working Group member
Victória HARSÁGI — Pázmány Péter Catholic University, Budapest
Michael STÜRNER — University of Konstanz; Judge of the Court of Appeal Karlsruhe

PROVISIONAL AND PROTECTIVE MEASURES

Reporters

Neil ANDREWS — University of Cambridge; former ALI/UNIDROIT Working Group member (co-reporter until 2016)

* Chronological order of formation, except for the overarching Structure Group (whose members are listed on page 6).

Gilles CUNIBERTI — University of Luxembourg (co-reporter until 2016)
Xandra KRAMER — Erasmus University, Rotterdam (reporter from August 2016)

Members

Torbjörn ANDERSSON — University of Uppsala
Remo CAPONI — University of Florence (co-reporter from September 2016)
Fernando DE LA MATA — ESADE Law School Barcelona; Baker & McKenzie
John SORABJI — then Principal Legal Adviser to the Lord Chief Justice and the Master of the Rolls; University College London (from September 2016)
Alan UZELAC — University of Zagreb

SERVICE OF DOCUMENTS AND DUE NOTICE OF PROCEEDINGS

Reporters

Astrid STADLER — University of Konstanz
Eva STORSKRUBB — University of Uppsala

Members

Marco DE CRISTOFARO — University of Padua
Emmanuel JEULAND — University Paris 1 Panthéon-Sorbonne
Wendy KENNETT — Cardiff University
Dimitrios TSIKRIKAS — University of Athens

LIS PENDENS AND *RES JUDICATA*

Reporters

Frédérique FERRAND — University Jean Moulin Lyon 3 (Co-Reporter); former ALI/UNIDROIT Working Group member
Burkhard HESS — Director of the Max Planck for International, European and Regulatory Procedural Law, Luxembourg

Members

Neil ANDREWS — University of Cambridge; former ALI/UNIDROIT Working Group member
Alexander ARABADJIEV — Judge, European Court of Justice
Marco DE CRISTOFARO — University of Padua
Tania DOMEJ — University of Zürich
Fernando GASCÓN INCHAUSTI — University Complutense of Madrid
Kalliopi MAKRIDOU — Aristotle University of Thessaloniki
Jarkko MÄNNISTÖ — Lawyer in Finland
Karol WEITZ — University of Warsaw

OBLIGATIONS OF THE PARTIES AND LAWYERS

Reporters

C.H. (Remco) VAN RHEE — Maastricht University
Alan UZELAC — University of Zagreb

Members

Emmanuel JEULAND — University Paris 1 Panthéon-Sorbonne

Bartosz KAROLCZYK — DZP, Warsaw
Walter H. RECHBERGER — University of Vienna
Elisabetta SILVESTRI — University of Pavia
John SORABJI — then Principal Legal Adviser to the Lord Chief Justice and the Master of the Rolls; University College London
Magne STRANDBERG — University of Bergen

JUDGMENTS

Reporters

Chiara BESSO — formerly University of Turin; Judge, Italian Supreme Court
Christoph A. KERN — Heidelberg University

Members

Laura ERVO — University of Örebro
Natalie FRICERO — University of Nice
Andrew HIGGINS — Oxford University
Thomas SUTTER-SOMM — University of Basel

PARTIES AND COLLECTIVE REDRESS

Reporters

Emmanuel JEULAND — University Paris 1 Panthéon-Sorbonne
Astrid STADLER — University of Konstanz

Members

Vincent SMITH — British Institute for International and Comparative Law; ESCP
Ianika TZANKOVA— Tillburg University
Istvan VARGA — ELTE Faculty of Law
Stefaan VOET — KU Leuven

COSTS

Reporters

Paul OBERHAMMER — University of Vienna
Eva STORSKRUBB — University of Uppsala
Wendy KENNETT — Cardiff University (co-reporter from 2018)

APPEALS

Reporters

Frédérique FERRAND — University Jean Moulin Lyon 3; former ALI/UNIDROIT Working Group member
Christoph A. KERN — Heidelberg University

Members

Fernando GASCÓN INCHAUSTI — University Complutense of Madrid
Magne STRANDBERG — University of Bergen

STRUCTURE GROUP

Reporters

Loïc CADIET — University Paris 1 Panthéon-Sorbonne; then President of the International Association of Procedural Law (IAPL)

Xandra KRAMER — Erasmus University, Rotterdam

Members, Final Drafting Team

John SORABJI — then Principal Legal Adviser to the Lord Chief Justice and the Master of the Rolls; University College London

Rolf STÜRNER — University of Freiburg; former Judge of the Courts of Appeal Stuttgart and Karlsruhe and former Co-Reporter for the ALI/UNIDROIT Principles

French Task Force

Loïc CADIET — University Paris 1 Panthéon-Sorbonne; then President of the International Association of Procedural Law (IAPL)

Frédérique FERRAND — University Jean Moulin Lyon 3; former ALI/UNIDROIT Working Group member

Emmanuel JEULAND — University Paris 1 Panthéon-Sorbonne

OBSERVERS

American Law Institute (ALI)
Asociación Americana de Derecho Internacional Privado (ASADIP)
Association for International Arbitration (AIA)
Court of Justice of the European Union (CJEU)
Council of Bars and Law Societies of Europe (CCBE)
Council of the Notariats of the European Union (CNUE)
European Commission (EC)
European Parliament
European Network of Councils for the Judiciary (ENCJ)
Hague Conference on Private International Law (HCCH)
International Association of Lawyers (UIA)
International Association of Young Lawyers (AIJA)
International Bar Association (IBA)
IBA Litigation Committee
IBA Arbitration Committee
International Association of Procedural Law (IAPL)
International Union of Judicial Officers (UIHJ)
Max Planck Institute Luxembourg

ADVISORY COMMITTEE MEMBERS*

Teresa Arruda ALVIM WAMBIER — Professor at the Pontificia Universidade Catolica of São Paulo (PUC-SP); Partner in the firm Wambier & Arruda Alvim Wambier from Brazil
Alexander ARABADJIEV — Judge, Court of Justice of the European Union
Stefania BARIATTI — Professor of International Law, Università degli Studi di Milano, Milan (Italy); UNIDROIT Governing Council Member
Núria BOUZA VIDAL — Professor of Private International Law, Pompeu Fabra University School of Law, Law Department, Barcelona (Spain); former UNIDROIT Governing Council Member
Anna ENGELHARD-BARFIELD — Attorney at Law in Germany (Hamburg) and the US
Michael ELMER — Vice-President, Maritime and Commercial High Court, Copenhagen; Co-founder and Vice-President of the Association of European Competition Law Judges; former UNIDROIT Governing Council Member
B. Bahadır ERDEM — Professor of Law, Istanbul University; Lawyer, Istanbul (Turkey); former UNIDROIT Governing Council Member
Antonio GIDI - Professor, Syracuse University College of Law
Peter GOTTWALD — Professor of private law, private international law and civil procedural law, University of Regensburg
Geoffrey C. HAZARD Jr. † - Professor, University of Pennsylvania Law School, former Director of ALI
Christopher HODGES — Professor, Centre for Socio-Legal Studies, Oxford University; Erasmus University
Samuel ISSACHAROFF — Professor of civil procedure and constitutional law at NYU; practitioner
Ole LANDO †— Professor emeritus of Copenhagen Business School in Frederiksberg (Denmark); founder and Chairman of the Commission on European Contract Law (CECL); former member of UNIDROIT Working Group on International Commercial Contracts
Richard (Rick) MARCUS — Professor University of California, Hastings College of the Law
Paul MATTHEWS — Master of the High Court, Chancery Division, in England and Wales; co-author of the leading English text on disclosure; part-time Professor at King's College, London
José Antonio MORENO RODRÍGUEZ — Professor of Law; Attorney, Asunción (Paraguay); Member of the International Chamber of Commerce Arbitration Court; UNIDROIT Governing Council Member
Andras OSZTOVITS — Head of the Faculty of Law, Károli Gáspár University of the Reformed Church in Hungary, Budapest (Hungary)
Eduardo OTEIZA — President of the Instituto Iberoamericano de Derecho Procesal
Monika PAUKNEROVÁ— Professor at Charles University, Prague; UNIDROIT Governing Council Member
Thomas PFEIFFER — Professor of private law, international private law and civil procedural law, Heidelberg University
Judith RESNIK — Professor, Arthur Liman Professor of Law at Yale Law School
Marco Antonio RODRIGUES — Professor at Rio de Janeiro State University

* Please note that the list contains the affiliations of advisers at the time of their appointment.

CONTENTS

Abbreviations xviii

Preamble **1**

I. Project History 1
II. Architecture and Development of the Project 2
III. Project Methodology 3
IV. Model Rules Rather than a Complete Code 4
V. Coherence and Consistency of Terminology 5
VI. General Remarks on the Scope of the Model European Rules of Civil Procedure 8
1. Civil and Commercial Matters 8
2. Uniform Flexible Rules for First Instance Proceedings 9
3. Flexible Application of the Uniform Rules and Early Final Judgments 9
4. The Integration of Complex Cases into the Rules 10
5. The Significance of the Rules for Lawyers and Court Case Management 10
6. Integrating Consumer Cases into the Rules 11
7. Settlement as an Integral Part of the Rules concerning First Instance Proceedings 14
8. Particular forms of Procedure in Special Parts of the Rules 15
VII. The *Acquis Communautaire* and the Rules 17
1. General Remarks 17
2. Rules on Jurisdiction, Recognition and Enforcement 19
3. Small Claim Proceedings and Proceedings for Payment Orders 21
4. *Acquis Communautaire* and the Case Law of the Highest European Courts 21
VIII. Modern Communication and Recording, Artificial Intelligence and the Rules 22
1. Appropriate Use of Electronic Communication and Recording 22
2. Artificial Intelligence and the Rules 23

MODEL EUROPEAN RULES OF CIVIL PROCEDURE

PART I - GENERAL PROVISIONS **27**
Section 1 - Scope 27
Section 2 - Principles 28
A. Co-operation 28
B. Proportionality 34
C. Settlement 37
D. Right to be heard 40
E. Representation and assistance 44
F. Oral, written and public Proceedings 48
G. Languages, interpretation and translation 56

Section 3 – Proceedings 58
A. Commencement, termination, Concentration and scope 58
B. Facts, evidence and applicable law 63
C. Sanctions for non-compliance and relief from sanctions 72

PART II - PARTIES 77
Section 1 – General Part 77
Section 2 – Special Part 81
A. Multiple Parties 81
B. Substitution and Succession of Parties 87
Section 3 – Cross border issues 87

PART III - CASE MANAGEMENT 89

PART IV - COMMENCEMENT OF PROCEEDINGS 96
Section 1 – Pre-commencement procedural duties 96
Section 2 – Commencement and pleadings 98
A. Statement of claim 98
B. Joint application for party agreed proceedings 106

PART V -PROCEEDINGS PREPARATORY TO A FINAL HEARING 109

PART VI - SERVICE AND DUE NOTICE OF PROCEEDINGS 120
Section 1 – General part - Service, Due Notice and the Right to be Heard 120
Section 2 – Responsibility for and methods of service 122
A. General Provisions 122
B. Methods of Service 124
Section 3 – Cross border issues 133
A. In the European Union 133
B. Outside the European Union 135

PART VII - ACCESS TO INFORMATION AND EVIDENCE 136
Section 1 – General part 137
A. General Provisions on Evidence 137
B. Management of Evidence 142
C. Presentation and Evaluation of Evidence 147
Section 2 – Access to evidence orders 150
Section 3 – Types of evidence 158
A. Documents 158
B. Testimonial Evidence 160
C. Examination of Parties 163
D. Expert Evidence 164
E. Judicial Inspection 169
Section 4 – Cross-border issues 171
A. In the European Union 171
B. Outside the European Union 172

PART VIII – JUDGMENT, *RES JUDICATA* AND *LIS PENDENS* **174**
Section 1 – General Part 174
Section 2 – Special Part 181
A. Default Judgment 181
B. Judicial Settlements 185
Section 3 – Effects of Pendency and Judgments 187
A. *Lis pendens* and related actions 187
B. *Res judicata* 193

PART IX – MEANS OF REVIEW **198**
Section1 – General Part 198
Section 2 – Appeals 200
Section 3 – First Appeals 206
Section 4 – Second Appeals 211
Section 5 – Review of procedural error and miscellaneous appeals 214
Section 6 – Extraordinary Recourse 216

PART X – PROVISIONAL AND PROTECTIVE MEASURES **219**
Section 1 – General part 220
Section 2 – Special part 228
A. Asset Preservation 228
B. Regulatory Measures 232
C. Evidence Preservation 233
D. Interim Payment 235
Section 3 – Cross border issues 237

PART XI – COLLECTIVE PROCEEDINGS **240**
Section 1 – Collective Interest Injunctions 241
Section 2 – Collective Proceedings 243
A. General Part 243
B. Admissibility of Collective Proceedings 249
C. Case Management of Collective Proceedings 255
D. Settlements in Commenced Collective Proceedings 257
E. Judgments in Collective Proceedings 261
F. Collective Settlements outside Collective Proceedings 262
Section 3 – Cross Border Issues 265
Within the European Union 265
Section 4 – Costs, Expenses and Funding 268

PART XII – COSTS **270**

ANNEX: ELI – Unidroit Model European Rules of Civil Procedure 285

ABBREVIATIONS

INTERNATIONAL ORGANISATIONS

URUGUAY ROUND OF MULTILATERAL TRADE NEGOTIATIONS

TRIPS Agreement	1994 Marrakesh Agreement Establishing the World Trade Organization, Annex 1C, Trade-Related Aspects of Intellectual Property Rights

UNITED NATIONS ECONOMIC COMMISSION FOR EUROPE

CMR	Convention on the Contract for the International Carriage of Goods by Road (CMR) (Geneva 1956)

HAGUE CONFERENCE ON PRIVATE INTERNATIONAL LAW

HCCH 1965 Service Convention	Convention of 15 November 1965 on the Service Abroad of Judicial and Extrajudicial Documents in Civil or Commercial Matters (the HCCH 1965 Service Convention)
HCCH 1970 Evidence Convention	Convention of 18 March 1970 on the Taking of Evidence Abroad in Civil or Commercial Matters
HCCH 1980 Access to Justice Convention	Convention of 25 October 1980 on International Access to Justice
HCCH 2005 Choice of Court Convention	Convention of 30 June 2005 on Choice of Court Agreements
HCCH 2019 Judgments Convention	Convention of 2 July 2019 on the Recognition and Enforcement of Foreign Judgments in Civil or Commercial Matters

UNCITRAL

UNCITRAL Model Law	UNCITRAL Model Law on International Commercial Arbitration 1985 with amendments as adopted in 2006

COUNCIL OF EUROPE

European Convention on Human Rights	1950 Convention for the Protection of Human Rights and Fundamental Freedoms
1968 Information on Foreign Law Convention	European Convention on Information on Foreign Law (of 7 June, 1968, Council of Europe, European Treaty Series-No. 62)
Recommendation R (84)5	1984 Recommendation No. R (84)5 Principles of Civil Procedure designed to improve the functioning of Justice
Recommendation R (2000)21	Recommendation No. R(2000)21 of the Committee of Ministers to member States on the freedom of exercise of the profession of lawyer

EUROPEAN UNION

1. Conventions

1950 European Convention on Human Rights	1950 Convention for the Protection of Human Rights and Fundamental Freedoms
1968 Brussels Convention	1968 Brussels Convention on jurisdiction and the enforcement of judgments in civil and commercial matters
2000 European Charter of Fundamental Rights	2000 Charter of Fundamental Rights of the European Union
2007 Lugano Convention	2007 Lugano Convention on jurisdiction and the recognition and enforcement of judgments in civil and commercial matters
2012 European Union Treaty	2012 The Treaty on European Union
2012 Functioning of the EU Treaty	2012 Treaty on the Functioning of the European Union
2013 Unified Patent Court Agreement	2013 Agreement on a Unified Patent Court

2. Regulations

ESR Regulation	Council Regulation (EC) No 1348/2000 of 29 May 2000 on the service in the Member States of judicial and extrajudicial documents in civil or commercial matters
Brussels I Reg. (recast) or Brussels Ibis Reg. or Jurisdiction and Enforcement Regulation	Regulation (EU) No 1215/2012 of the European Parliament and of the Council of 12 December 2012 on jurisdiction and the recognition and enforcement of judgments in civil and commercial matters (recast)
Brussels IIbis Regulation	Council Regulation (EC) No 2201/2003 of 27 November 2003 concerning jurisdiction and the recognition and enforcement of judgments in matrimonial matters and the matters of parental responsibility, repealing Regulation (EC) No 1347/2000
Evidence Regulation	Council Regulation (EC) No 1206/2001 of 28 May 2001 on cooperation between the courts of the Member States in the taking of evidence in civil or commercial matters
EEO Regulation	Regulation (EC) No 805/2004 of the European Parliament and of the Council of 21 April 2004 creating a European Enforcement Order for uncontested claims
EOP Regulation	Regulation (EC) No 1896/2006 of the European Parliament and of the Council of 12 December 2006 creating a European order for payment procedure
European Small Claims Regulation or ESC Regulation	Regulation (EC) No 861/2007 of the European Parliament and of the Council of 11 July 2007 establishing a European Small Claims Procedure

Rome II Regulation	Regulation (EC) No 864/2007 of the European Parliament and of the Council of 11 July 2007 on the law applicable to non-contractual obligations (Rome II)
Service Regulation	Regulation (EC) No 1393/2007 of the European Parliament and of the Council of 13 November 2007 on the service in the Member States of judicial and extrajudicial documents in civil or commercial matters (service of documents), and repealing Council Regulation (EC) No 1348/2000
Rome I Regulation	Regulation (EC) No 593/2008 of the European Parliament and of the Council of 17 June 2008 on the law applicable to contractual obligations (Rome I)
EAPO Regulation	Regulation (EU) No 655/2014 of the European Parliament and of the Council of 15 May 2014 establishing a European Account Preservation Order procedure to facilitate cross-border debt recovery in civil and commercial matters
General Data Protection Regulation	Regulation (EU) 2016/679 of the European Parliament and of the Council of 27 April 2016 on the protection of natural persons with regard to the processing of personal data and on the free movement of such data, and repealing Directive 95/46/EC (General Data Protection Regulation).

3. Directives

Directive 98/5/EC	Directive 98/5/EC of the European Parliament and of the Council of 16 February 1998 to facilitate practice of the profession of lawyer on a permanent basis in a Member State other than that in which the qualification was obtained
IP Enforcement Directive	Directive 2004/48/EC of the European Parliament and of the Council of 29 April 2004 on the enforcement of intellectual property rights
Mediation Directive	Directive 2008/52/EC of the European Parliament and of the Council of 21 May 2008 on certain aspects of mediation in civil and commercial matters
Injunctions Directive	Directive 2009/22/EC of the European Parliament and of the Council of 23 April 2009 on injunctions for the protection of consumers' interests (Codified version)
ADR Directive	Directive 2013/11/EU on alternative dispute resolution for consumer disputes
Competition Damages Directive	Directive 2014/104/EU of the European Parliament and of the Council of 26 November 2014 on certain rules governing actions for damages under national law for infringements of the competition law provisions of the Member States and of the European Union
Trade secrets Directive	Directive (EU) 2016/943 of the European Parliament and of the Council of 8 June 2016 on the protection of undisclosed know-how and business information (trade secrets) against their unlawful acquisition, use and disclosure

4. Recommendations

Recommendation 2013/396	Commission Recommendation of 11 June 2013 on common principles for injunctive and compensatory collective redress mechanisms in the Member States concerning violations of rights granted under Union Law (2013/396/EU)

5. Rules of Procedure

2015 Draft Unified Patent Court Rules	2015 Rules of Procedure of the Unified Patent Court

6. Proposals

The 2018 Proposal	Proposal for a Directive of the European Parliament and of the Council on representative actions for the protection of the collective interests of consumers, and repealing Directive 2009/22/EC

INTERNATIONAL CHAMBER OF COMMERCE

ICC Arbitration Rules (2017)	ICC Rules of Arbitration (2017)

INTERNATIONAL BAR ASSOCIATION (IBA)

IBA Rules of Evidence'	IBA Rules on the Taking of Evidence in International Arbitration (2010)
IBA Principles Conduct Legal Profession	IBA International Principles on Conduct for the Legal Profession (2011)

INTERNATIONAL LAW ASSOCIATION

Helsinki Principles	1996 ILA Principles on Provisional and Protective Measures in International Litigation

CCBE (Council of Bars and Law Societies of Europe)

CCBE Code of Conduct	The Code of Conduct for European Lawyers, issued by the Council of Bars and Law Societies of Europe Charter of Core Principles of the European Legal Profession and Code of Conduct for European lawyers, (2019)

NATIONAL LEGISLATION

Austrian CCP	Austria Code of Civil Procedure (*Zivilprozessordnung (ZPO)*)
Belgium CCP	**Belgium** Code of Civil Procedure (*Code de procédure civile*)
Bulgarian CCP	**Bulgaria** Code of Civil Procedure (*Граждански Процесуален кодекс*)
Cyprus CPR	**Cyprus** Civil Procedure Rules (*Θεσμοί Πολιτικής Δικονομίας*)

Czech Republic CPC	**Czech Republic** Civil Procedure Code (*Občanský soudní řád*)
England CPR	**England** Civil Procedure Rules
Estonia CCP	**Estonia** Code of Civil Procedure (*Tsiviilkohtumenetluse seadustik*)
Finland CJP	**Finland** Code of Judicial Procedure (*Oikeudenkäymiskaari*)
France CCP	**France** Code of Civil Procedure (*Code de procédure civile*)
France CCon	French Consumer Code (*Code de la Consommation*)
Germany CCP	**Germany** Code of Civil Procedure (*Zivilprozessordnung (ZPO)*)
Germany UCA	Unfair Competition Act (*Gesetz gegen den unlauteren Wettbewerb (UWG)*)
Germany KapMuG	Act on Model Case Proceedings in Disputes under Capital Markets Law (*Gesetz über Musterverfahren in kapitalmarktrechtliche Streitigkeiten (KapMuG)*)
Greece CCP	**Greece** Code of Civil Procedure
Hungary CCP	**Hungary** Code of Civil Procedure (*Törvény a polgári perrendtartásról*)
Ireland District Court Rules	**Ireland** Order 101 of the District Court Rules
Ireland Superior Court Rules	Order 86A of the Rules of Superior Courts
Italy CCP	**Italy** Code of Civil Procedure (*Codice di Procedura Civile*)
Netherlands CCP	**Netherlands** Code of Civil Procedure (*Wetboek van Burgerlijke Rechtsvordering*)
Netherlands NCC	Rules for the International Chambers of the Amsterdam District Court and Court of Appeal (NCC).
Netherlands WCAM Dutch WCAM	Act on Collective Settlements of 2005 (*Wet collectieve afwikkeling van massaschades*, 2005)
Norway DA	**Norway** Dispute Act (*Lov om mekling og rettergang i sivile tvister (tvisteloven)*)

Spain LCP	**Spain** Law of Civil Procedure (*Ley de Enjuiciamiento Civil (L.E.C)*)
Sweden CJP	**Sweden** Code of Judicial Procedure (*Rättegångsbalken*)
Switzerland CCP	**Switzerland** Federal Code of Civil Procedure (*Zivilprozessordnung, ZPO*)
United States of America	
28 U.S. Code § 1782	28 U.S. Code § 1782. Assistance to foreign and international tribunals and to litigants before such tribunals
28 U.S. Code § 1407	US Judicial Panel on Multi-district Litigation (28 USC section 1407)
ALI/UNIDROIT Principles	ALI/UNIDROIT Principles of Transnational Civil Procedure
The Transnational Rules of Civil Procedure (Reporters' Study), Rules	Reporters' Study, *Rules on Transnational Civil Procedure, Introductory Note*, in ALI/UNIDROIT Principles of Transnational Civil Procedure (2006) (The Transnational Rules of Civil Procedure (Reporters' Study) Rules
The Storme Report.	Marcel Storme (ed.), Rapprochement du Droit Judiciaire de L'Union européenne/Approximation of Judiciary Law in the European Union, Dordrecht/Boston/London: Martinus Nijhoff Publishers 1994 (The Storme Report).
ECtHR	European Court of Human Rights
ECJ	European Court of Justice
CJEU	Court of Justice of the European Union

PREAMBLE

I. PROJECT HISTORY

1. In 2004, the American Law Institute (ALI) and the International Institute for the Unification of Private Law (Unidroit) adopted the ALI/Unidroit Principles of Transnational Civil Procedure.[1] They were intended to help reduce the impact of differences between legal systems in lawsuits involving transnational commercial transactions. Their purpose was to propose a model of universal procedure that followed the essential elements of due process of law. They were accompanied by a set of "Rules of Transnational Civil Procedure", which were not formally adopted by either Unidroit or the ALI but constituted a model implementation of the Principles, providing greater detail and illustrating how the Principles could be implemented in procedural rules. The Rules were to be considered either for adoption "or for further adaptation in various legal systems", and along with the Principles could be considered as "a model for reform in domestic legislation".[2]

2. On 18–19 October 2013, the European Law Institute (ELI) and Unidroit held an exploratory Workshop in Vienna (Austria), which aimed at an initial analysis of a series of different topics, ranging from service of process to enforcement, with a view to identifying the most promising issues and the most appropriate methodological approach to develop a common project in the area of procedural law.[3] In 2014, both organisations decided to cooperate on the development of European Rules of Civil Procedure based on the ALI/Unidroit Principles, considered in the light of other sources like the 1950 Convention for the Protection of Human Rights and Fundamental Freedoms (the European Convention on Human Rights), the 2000 Charter of Fundamental Rights of the European Union, the wider *acquis* of binding EU law, common traditions in the European

1 *ALI/Unidroit Principles of Transnational Civil Procedure* (Cambridge University Press) (2006) and <https://www.unidroit.org/english/principles/civilprocedure/ali-unidroitprinciples-e.pdf>

2 Reporters' Study, *Rules on Transnational Civil Procedure, Introductory Note*, in ALI/Unidroit Principles of Transnational Civil Procedure (2006) (The Transnational Rules of Civil Procedure (Reporters' Study) Rules, at 99.

3 The output of that exploratory workshop was published in the Uniform Law Review Vol.19 No. 2, 2014, 171-328 as follows: D. Wallis, *Introductory remarks on the ELI-Unidroit project*; G. Hazard, *Some preliminary observations on the proposed ELI/Unidroit civil procedure project in the light of the experience of the ALI/Unidroit project*; S. Prechal & K. Cath, *The European acquis of civil procedure: constitutional aspects*; T. Pfeiffer, *The contribution of arbitration to the harmonization of procedural laws in Europe*; X.E. Kramer, *The structure of civil proceedings and why it matters: exploratory observations on future ELI-Unidroit European rules of civil procedure*; N. Trocker, *From ALI-Unidroit Principles to common European rules on access to informaion and evidence? A prelminary outlook and some suggestions*; L Cadiet, *The ALI-Unidroit project: from transnational principles to European rules of civil procedure: Public Conference, opening session, 18 October 2013*; N. Andrews, *Fundamentals of costs law: loser responsibility, access to justice, and procedural discipline*; M. Kengyel, *Transparency of assets and enforcement*; R. Stürner, *Principles of European civil procedure or a European model code? Some considerations on the joint ELI-Unidroit project*; and also in Uniform Law Review Vol.19 No.3, 2014, 329-364: I. N. Tzankova, *Case management: the stepchild of mass claim dispute resolution*; E. Storskrubb, *Due notice of proceedings: present and future.*

ELI-Unidroit Model European Rules of Civil Procedure. ELI & Unidroit, Oxford University Press.
 DOI: 10.1093/oso/9780198866589.003.0001

countries, the Storme Commission's work,[4] and other pertinent European and International sources, be they binding or non-binding. A joint ELI/UNIDROIT project on this topic was seen as the means to provide a useful tool to help promote the increasing procedural coherence of European civil procedural law.[5] At the same time, from UNIDROIT's perspective, the project not only sought to implement the ALI/UNIDROIT Principles, but was an important first step towards the wider development of regional projects, each of which could then seek to adapt those Principles to the specificities of regional legal cultures. Following the decision to embark upon the project, ELI and UNIDROIT established a Steering Committee, co-chaired by the former ELI President and the former UNIDROIT Secretary-General and composed of representatives of both organisations.

II. ARCHITECTURE AND DEVELOPMENT OF THE PROJECT

3. Drafting the Rules and their accompanying Commentary was entrusted to several Working Groups (WGs), each of which was asked to develop regional rules for the main topics covered by the ALI/UNIDROIT Principles. Additionally, the Steering Committee decided to develop rules on appellate proceedings. Eight Working Groups were thus established: in chronological order, "Access to information and evidence"; "Provisional and protective measures"; "Service of documents and due notice of proceedings"; "*Lis pendens* and *res judicata*"; "Obligations of the parties and lawyers"; "Parties and collective Redress"; "Judgments"; "Costs"; and "Appeals".[6] In order to ensure that the project functioned efficiently and to enable members of those Working Groups that started working in the initial waves of the project to join further Groups and lend their experience to them, from 2014 to 2019, the Working Groups worked in successive waves. Each Group was representative of a wide variety of different European legal traditions.

4. The Working Groups were asked to prepare draft Rules and supporting comments. Drafts were considered at Annual Plenary Meetings of the Steering Committee and the Working Groups' Reporters and Members, which were hosted by the two sponsoring organisations.

5. Finally, an overarching "Structure Group" was established with the task of consolidating the Working Groups' texts, to oversee the framework and overall structure of the ultimate Rules and Commentary, and to ensure coherence and avoid gaps where aspects might not be covered by the designated Working Groups. It was also asked to produce a French translation of the Rules, in order to ensure that parallel texts were available.

6. From the outset, the project's Plenary Meetings benefited from the participation of a number of institutional Observers, particularly the Hague Conference on Private International Law (HCCH), European Institutions (the European Commission, the European Parliament, and the Court of Justice of the European Union), various professional associations and research associations and institutions, such as the Max-Planck-Institute for European Procedural Law, as well as the American Law Institute (ALI).

7. Moreover, a list of advisers was drawn both from academia and the legal professions, among which were members of the UNIDROIT Governing Council. ELI in its turn constituted a specific

4 Marcel Storme (ed.), Rapprochement du Droit Judiciaire de L'Union européenne/Approximation of Judiciary Law in the European Union, Dordrecht/Boston/London: Martinus Nijhoff Publishers 1994.

5 The scope of the project focused on European civil procedural law and not European Union civil procedural law.

6 For the complete list of participants see Participants in the project above.

Members' Consultative Committee (MCC) and appointed two Assessors for the project (Raffaele Sabato, Italian Supreme Court and European Court of Human Rights (ECtHR), and Matthias Storme, University of Leuven, Chair of the MCC).

III. PROJECT METHODOLOGY

8. The project adopted a common working methodology across the Working Groups. Its primary working language was English, although Working Groups were free to prepare drafts in other languages.[7] A number of Groups prepared drafts in French and Italian.[8] It was anticipated that in addition to the completion of English and French drafts, the completed Rules and Commentary would be translated into a wide range of European languages. Simultaneous drafting was also pursued in order to improve clarity, as this highlighted linguistic ambiguity and thus helped the Working Groups to prepare Rules and comments that were as clear as possible.

9. The methodological approach taken to devising the Rules themselves was determined by the Steering Committee from the outset. The aim was not to devise a set of rules articulating common practices, i.e. a "restatement" of European civil procedure, nor was it to devise a set of rules based on the predominance of approaches across European jurisdictions, or based on compromise. The project's aim was to devise a set of best practice rules for the future development of European civil procedure.[9]

10. Consequently the Working Groups, taking as their starting point the ALI/Unidroit Principles, considered the different approaches present in different European legal traditions through consideration of European countries' procedural codes and rules, both as stated in the written law and as produced in their courts. In doing so they took into account relevant European Union legislation. They also examined, where relevant, other legislative sources, such as those of inter-governmental organisations like the HCCH. Consideration was also given, where relevant, to the Storme Commission's work,[10] the European Convention on Human Rights, and Council of Europe Recommendation (84) 5,[11] the Charter of Fundamental Rights of the European Union. In the light of these surveys of existing provisions, the Working Groups determined the optimum approach to be taken, and accordingly prepared draft Rules and Commentary. Drafts were then subject to discussion at the project's Plenary meetings, a number of open conferences,[12] and

7 See further on the methodology, J. Sorabji, *The ELI-Unidroit Project—An Introduction and an English Perspective*, in A. Nylund & M. Strandberg (eds), *Civil Procedure and the Harmonisation of Law*, (Intersentia, 2019) at 46–50.

8 Drafts in Spanish and Polish were also prepared by some Working Groups.

9 See R. Stürner, *Principles of European civil procedure or a European model code? Some considerations on the joint ELI-Unidroit project*, (2014) Uniform Law Review 322, 324.

10 Marcel Storme (ed.), Rapprochement du Droit Judiciaire de L'Union européenne/Approximation of Judiciary Law in the European Union, Dordrecht/Boston/Londen: Martinus Nijhoff Publishers 1994 at 61 (The Storme Report).

11 1950 Convention for the Protection of Human Rights and Fundamental Freedoms and Council of Europe Committee of Ministers Recommendation (84) 5 on the Principles of Civil Procedure designed to Improve the Functioning of Justice, adopted by the Committee of Ministers on 28 February 1984 at the 367th meeting of the Ministers' Deputies.

12 Such as those held in conjunction with The Academy of European Law (ERA) in 2015 (Building European Rules of Civil Procedure, Trier, 26 November 2015) and 2018 (From Transnational Principles to European Rules of Civil Procedure, Trier, 26 November 2018).

meetings with the European Union institutions[13], as well as during sessions of the UNIDROIT's Governing Council and ELI Annual conferences, each of which provided valuable input for the work. The finalised Working Group drafts were then considered by the Structure Group, which in 2017 prepared a preliminary consolidated text of the output of the first three groups, presented to the UNIDROIT Governing Council and the ELI Annual Conference that year. In preparing the final consolidated draft, which was considered by both the ELI and UNIDROIT in 2019, the Structure Group sought to integrate the various texts into a consistent whole. Where Working Groups had produced overlapping rules (e.g., a number of the Working Groups had prepared draft general principles), these were consolidated to produce a single rule. The Structure Group had also to determine which draft could be considered the optimum solution where there was inconsistency of approach amongst the Working Groups. Additionally, the Structure Group adopted the same best practice approach in devising rules and comments to fill any gaps in the Working Groups' draft Rules and Commentary, and also in preparing the overarching principles that form the initial Part of the consolidated final text.

11. Each of the Rules identifies, where relevant, the ALI-UNIDROIT Principle, or Principles, from which it was developed. They also identify any relevant rules in the Reporter's study in the ALI/UNIDROIT project.[14] Other significant international and domestic law sources, such as HCCH Conventions, the UNCITRAL Model law on International Commercial Arbitration, Recommendations of the Council of Europe, the *acquis communautaire* of the European Union, provisions of national laws, the Draft Rules of Procedure of the Unified Patent Court,[15] and the Storme Report, are referred to in the comments only where they specifically influenced the Working Groups' solutions. The Structure Group, following a decision of the Steering Committee and in line with the usual practice of UNIDROIT, did not in the Commentary reproduce all the preparatory comparative studies conducted by the Working Groups with lists of all the specific provisions that could conceivably be relevant to the contents of the individual rule to be drafted. Comments refer to the variety of solutions chosen by different legal families or groups of national laws, with a final and succinctly reasoned conclusion why the Structure Group preferred to either follow or modify the approach taken by a particular procedural tradition, or combine elements of various such traditions.

IV. MODEL RULES RATHER THAN A COMPLETE CODE

12. A first attempt to develop common European Rules of Civil Procedure was the set of rules drafted by the Storme Commission. This Commission did not aim at drafting a complete code because, according to its analysis, convergence and the trend towards harmonisation differed remarkably in the various fields of civil procedure. It decided, therefore, to only draft a set of rules in fields where a move towards harmonisation and approximation was likely to be met with a sufficient degree of acceptance to motivate European and national legislatures to take the proposed rules as a basis for an innovative harmonising legislation.[16] Though many observers criticised the

13 In 2015 and 2017, as noted in J. Sorabji (2019) at 51 and 54.

14 See fn 2 above.

15 See the 2013 Agreement on a Unified Patent Court. And see its Rules of Procedure, 18th draft of 19 October 2015 with amendments until 15 March 2017 (the Draft Rules of Procedure of the Unified Patent Court) (2015 Draft Unified Patent Court Rules).

16 The Storme Report, General Introductory Report, pp. 37, 58 and following.

fragmentary character of this set of rules, the decision to proceed step by step in this early phase of European harmonisation of law has turned out to be a wise choice.

13. Today, convergence and the trend towards harmonisation have markedly increased. Whilst taking national specificities into account still remains important, there is room for a pragmatic and focused approach directed at key fields of civil procedure. Such an approach pays particular attention to those fields where harmonisation proposals have a good prospect of being welcomed and acted upon by national legislatures due to the fact that they are already considering national approximation or harmonisation projects, or due to an actual need for coherent and innovative development. Mass litigation intended to provide an effective means to secure consumer protection and compensation for harm, to give one example, exemplifies the latter. Less promising areas for complete harmonisation are, for instance, those of a very technical nature, which are often determined by regional or national peculiarities concerning the administration of justice specific to a legal culture. A pragmatic choice of specific fields for proposed harmonisation should also take account of the growing *acquis communautaire* of the European Union, and the fact that the *acquis* is not itself the result of systematic codification, as that may provide guidance on the reasonable limits that may constrain further harmonisation. In any case, in developing best practices the *acquis* itself should not necessarily be excluded from proposals for improvement.[17]

14. Compared with Model Codes, a major advantage of Model Rules is that they enable users to set different priorities according to the attractiveness of the chapters chosen. Model Codes require a consistent, continuous degree of detailed regulation. Model Rules, by way of contrast, enable the degree of detailed regulation to vary between different parts of the instrument, taking account of the prevailing degree of convergence and the feasibility of future detailed regulation in those different parts. The ELI/Unidroit Model European Rules of Civil Procedure attempt to strike the right balance in terms of focusing on the most important areas of civil procedure while, at the same time, adopting differing degrees of regulation where such differences appear justified. Consequently, the degree of detailed regulation is relatively high in all the parts of the Rules that address the interaction between the court and parties and among parties (Parts III-V) and in the part that concerns access to information and evidence (Part VII). Conversely, and not without good reason, it is relatively low in the parts on means of review (Part IX) or on costs (Part XII).

V. COHERENCE AND CONSISTENCY OF TERMINOLOGY

15. According to a well-accepted and often addressed requirement, model rules, even if they are not model codes, should be coherent. They should contain no contradictions and should use consistent terminology. However, it is also the case that national codes do not always really fulfil the requirements of transparency, coherence, avoidance of contradiction and consistency of terminology. Codes are drafted by commissions or groups, the membership of which often includes a wide range of representatives drawn from the legal profession each of whom has differing interests. They have to cooperate with each other, and often have to strike compromises in respect of content and terminology. Parliamentary intervention during the legislative process thereafter often results in changes or additional insertions that do not fully cohere with other parts of the text. Moreover, even in national legal cultures the same term may have differing meanings

17 For the relationship between these Rules and the *acquis communautaire* and its particular difficulties see below, Preamble VII. 4.

depending on the context where it is used. A good example is the term "cause of action", which in many jurisdictions has a different meaning in the context of *lis pendens*, and in respect of the preclusive and the positive effects of *res judicata*.[18] Nevertheless, attempts to replace this term by a better terminology have failed.

16. In international projects like the present one, the challenges of ensuring full coherence in content and terminological consistency are greater than in national codifications. In such projects, in addition to the factors relevant for national codifications, the internal debate within Working Groups, the influence of advisers and institutional representatives of the ELI and UNIDROIT, as well as the input of observers of other important legal institutions or organisations, all have to be taken into account in trying to secure a coherent and consistent approach. Differing perspectives from the different actors in the process render consensus all the more difficult to reach. In the present project, the Steering Committee and the Structure Group discussed issues with the Working Groups in order to secure a coherent and consistent approach, in terms of both the style and content of the Rules. In doing so, they also had to ensure that especially general rules could be modified in appropriate circumstances, while making provision for other specific rules to operate as exceptions to rules of general applicability.

17. Harmonised sets of rules are often criticised on the basis that they contain too many exceptions, too many contradictory elements or an unclear terminology, despite numerous attempts having been made to secure a clear and uniform of definition of terms used within them. This is true for many international provisions such as the ones contained in European Regulations or Directives, or innovative Rules of Procedure like the Draft Unified Patent Court Rules.[19] The present Rules are themselves unlikely to be exempt from such inevitable criticism.

18. Rigid authoritarian decisions to further transparency and coherence are not, however, generally to be recommended. Too rigid an approach may, for instance, produce negative consequences in other parts of a model set of rules. As a consequence, lack of complete coherence or consistency in a legal text can also stem from a desired need for a pluralistic approach, and one that reflects an appropriate respect for a competition of ideas. It can therefore be beneficial for legal texts to provide some leeway for flexible interpretation and application in different contexts. This is true for many such harmonising endeavours, including the present Rules.

19. The first Part of the Rules contains some very general principles relating to justice and civil procedure. They are designed to provide interpretative guidance for the detailed and more specific Rules in the other Parts. They are thus intended to provide a properly transparent and clear structural design of the Rules and civil proceedings as a whole. In many respects, this Part has been formulated according to the example provided by the first chapter of the First Book of the French *Code de procédure civile* with its "*Principes directeurs*".[20] Most national codes only refer to

18 The consequences of lacking clarity of terminology of national law in the fields of *lis pendens* and *res judicata* for harmonising the Rules are discussed in Part I, Rule 22 comments 1 and 2; Part VII, Introduction comments 2 and 3; Rule 142 comments 2 and 3; Rule 149 comments 2 and 3.

19 See the 2015 Draft Unified Patent Court Rules, *op. cit.*, above, Preamble, III.

20 See French Code of Civil Procedure (CCP) (*Code de procédure civile*), Arts. 1 to 24.

a limited number of procedural principles, often doing so in order to highlight those that are of particular importance due to innovative elements of a new or revised version of the code.[21] The French Code, however, contains a careful selection of principles that are of particular importance to any well-functioning, fair and efficient procedure. Individual rules in the various other parts of codes not only implement such general principles, but they can also modify or restrict their scope of application. In doing so, they often introduce contradictory elements into the code. If a strictly logical approach were taken, each such modification or exception to a general principle or rule should be spelt out in the context of those principles or rules. Such an approach is not, however, taken in the present Rules. The Rules' drafters concluded it was self-evident that broad, general rules could, potentially, properly give rise to exceptions taking into consideration that in the absence of modification, application of general rules could produce a perverse or otherwise unwarranted consequence.

20. A typical and often criticised feature of model codes and model rules is the existence of repetitive provisions. This is especially true of provisions formulated in a general context, e.g., in a part with general principles or rules, which are then repeated later on either with or without some minor variation in wording, in a specific context. Such repetition is often considered to be superfluous. Notwithstanding such potential criticism, repetitious drafting has survived in the history of legislation and codification in all legal cultures, codes and rules. That it has done so is often not without good reason. Repetitious provisions can make excessive reference to other parts of a code or set of rules unnecessary. This has a clear benefit for the reader and user of the instrument. It means that they can read a full coherent text without the need to constantly refer back and forth to other provisions. It can thus facilitate ease of use, understanding and interpretation.

21. Exactness and consistency in terminology developed in harmonisation projects must be considered on the basis of a functional approach, one that has a realistic prospect of being accepted by various legal cultures, each of which uses differing terms for similar concepts, which often, considered in their context, do not always operate in the same way. It is, consequently, not always possible or recommendable to use traditional terms drawn from specific procedural systems for procedural instruments or mechanisms the aim of which is to produce harmonised rules. To reduce the possibility of misconceptions arising from diverging legal terminology or the influence of national legal cultures, it is generally necessary to either use neutral terms[22] or, if that is not possible, national terms with an explanatory comment. If the latter approach is taken, the explanatory comment ought to explain how the meaning used in the harmonising text differs from its national use.[23]

21 See, e.g., for other codes with similar structure the English Civil Procedure Rules (CPR) Part 1 (overriding objective); § 128 German Code of Civil Procedure (CCP) (*Zivilprozessordnung (ZPO)*) (orality); Italian Code of Civil Procedure (CCP) (*Codice di procedura civile*) Arts. 99 to 101 (party disposition of commencement of proceedings and notice to the opponent), Arts. 115 and 116 (party disposition of the means of evidence and free evaluation of proof), Art. 128 (public hearing), Art. 180 (oral proceedings of the instructing judge) etc.

22 See, e.g., the term 'early final judgment' that replaces the common law term 'summary judgment' because of its special structural context (see Rule 65 comment 1); or the term '*pourvoi final*' for second appeal in the French version replacing the national term '*pourvoi en cassation*' (see Rules 155 and following).

23 See, for instance, 'cause of action' in Rule 22 comment 2, Part VIII, Section 3, Introduction comment 3 and Section 3 A, Introduction, comments 1 and 2, Rule 149, comment 2 and 3.

22. The approach ultimately taken in the present Rules sought to provide the maximum amount of terminological coherence and consistency, while at the same time recognising that it is necessary in some cases to read and understand individual rules in their context and by reference to the explanatory comments. The Rules ought therefore to be considered as an attempt to realise a feasible level of coherence and consistency, and thus to present a significant step towards the harmonisation of differing European procedural cultures. In this respect, each Rule should be read and interpreted in the light of its explanatory Comment as well as in the general context of the entire instrument.

VI. GENERAL REMARKS ON THE SCOPE OF THE MODEL EUROPEAN RULES OF CIVIL PROCEDURE

1. CIVIL AND COMMERCIAL MATTERS

23. Rule 1 defines civil and commercial matters by reference to Regulation (EU) No 1215/2012 of the European Parliament and of the Council of 12 December 2012 on jurisdiction and the recognition and enforcement of judgments in civil and commercial matters (recast) (the Jurisdiction and Enforcement Regulation or Brussels Ibis Regulation)[24] and the corresponding 2007 Lugano Convention.[25] The list of excluded areas of civil matters covers mainly status proceedings, family and matrimonial matters, succession cases, insolvency matters and arbitration. These fields of civil justice are either completely, or in part, governed by special procedural regimes in most European legal cultures. It is, therefore, reasonable to exclude these aspects of civil justice systems from the core area of applicability of these Rules.

24. Employment, or labour law, disputes also form a particular field of civil justice, albeit they are not excluded from the applicability of the Jurisdiction and Enforcement Regulation and the 2007 Lugano Convention.[26] In nearly all European legal cultures such disputes fall within the subject-matter jurisdiction of special tribunals or within the competence of specific judicial bodies in courts of general jurisdiction, and the procedural rules governing such matters either form a special part of the general civil procedure code or are codified in a special code for employment and labour law matters. The basic structure and most elements of such proceedings are taken from the regular civil procedure, to which their individual rules demonstrate a close relationship. Differences between regular civil procedure and employment or labour law procedure tend to reflect the particular history and strong social impact of the latter form of civil justice, which are not of particular importance in terms of their relationship or effect on the considerations that underpin these Rules.

25. However, it should be generally noted that European or national legislation could adopt these Rules in part or with modifications to fields of civil justice which are not the core areas of their applicability. For model rules in general, and these Rules in particular, the definition of applicability describes only the core of their coverage. Legislatures or arbitral organisations are free, and are invited, to adopt parts or modified versions of these Rules not only in areas within their stated scope of application, but equally more broadly. It is, therefore, neither necessary nor helpful to place too great an emphasis on the exact definition of the Rule's scope of application in relation to specialised areas of civil procedure

24 Also known as the Brussels I Regulation (recast).

25 2007 Lugano Convention on jurisdiction and the recognition and enforcement of judgments in civil and commercial matters (Lugano Convention).

26 See Art. 20 *et seq.* Brussels Ibis Regulation and Lugano Convention, Art. 18 *et seq.*

2. UNIFORM FLEXIBLE RULES FOR FIRST INSTANCE PROCEEDINGS

26. Parts III-VIII contain detailed rules for first instance proceedings: co-operative case management by parties and court, pleadings, service of process and due notice, *lis pendens*, proceedings preparatory to a final hearing, access to information and evidence-taking, judgments and their effects. These Rules comprise a full procedural programme covering all conceivable eventualities. They provide adequate and necessary procedural tools. They also divide the structure of proceedings into three phases: the written pleading phase, the interim phase designed to clarify less serious or less complex issues and to identify issues that need to be dealt with in depth in a final hearing, and the concentrated final hearing followed by rendition of judgment and, if appropriate, appeal.[27] The Rules do not abstractly differentiate between more complex and simple cases[28] by creating formal procedural tracks. Consequently, they apply to all first instance proceedings, independently of whether individual European countries have established courts of first instance with differing subject-matter jurisdiction according to any longstanding, albeit now partially diminishing, procedural traditions. The choice of uniform rules, however, does not mean that all cases need to utilise the full programme; the Rules should be applied to match the process to the case.[29]

3. FLEXIBLE APPLICATION OF THE UNIFORM RULES AND EARLY FINAL JUDGMENTS

27. Many disputes are concluded by an early final judgment in simplified proceedings. The present Rules are flexible, and parties and the court are expected to apply them according to the necessities of the individual case. For instance, if a defendant argues that the court lacks jurisdiction or that the claimant did not put forward such facts as support their claim, the court, having asked the claimant to make a satisfactory amendment to remedy any such defect and none being made, must render an early final judgment dismissing the claim without any evidential considerations or evidence-taking.[30] A defendant may, initially, limit their defence to arguments concerning the alleged lack of jurisdiction or the absence of pertinent facts so that they need not necessarily exhaust all the other conceivable arguments available to them, e.g., contesting facts, making offers of adverse evidence, or setting out an affirmative defence, if the defence chosen is reasonably well-founded and the court does not invite the defendant to amend their approach in the light of doubts it has about the strength of the defence as it had been presented.[31]

27 See ALI/Unidroit Principle 9. The Draft Unified Patent Court Rules utilise this structure too, in part with identical wording; see Rules 10 and 85 and the corresponding division of the rules into adequate chapters.

28 For small claim proceedings and payment order proceedings see below Preamble VII. 3.

29 See, especially Rule 61, comments 1 and 2.

30 See Rule 65(2)(a) and (b) with comments 1 to 3 for the similar cases of withdrawal or admission of the claim (Rule 65(2)(c), comment 4) and for the simplified proceedings applying comment 5. If the court finds the arguments of the defendant not convincing it may render an appealable judgment on preliminary procedural issues or on legal issues on the merits, or go on without preliminary judgment running the risk to be challenged on appeal based on the issue addressed by the defendant; see Rule 66 with comments 1 to 9.

31 For the court's duty to ask for amendment before sanctioning lacking sufficient pleading see Rules 54(2), 53(2), 53(3) sentence 1, 49(9), 47 with comment 4, 27(1) sentence 2 with comment 3 (regarding clear refusal of unreasonable pleading 'eventualiter') and 55(1).

4. THE INTEGRATION OF COMPLEX CASES INTO THE RULES

28. In more complex cases, claimants or defendants may apply for a judgment on a preliminary procedural issue, such as the competence of the court, party capacity to litigate etc. on legal issues concerning the merits of their dispute, e.g., a judgment on liability, or they may apply for a judgment for a part of the claim. The court may also take such steps on its own motion (*ex officio*).[32] In such circumstances the court may permit pleadings to be developed in stages, i.e., so as to initially give particulars and specified offers of evidence solely for the purpose necessary for the issue at hand and then to permit amendment on a continuing step-by-step basis as necessary for the determination of the next issue. The court will generally take such an approach following a common application by the parties or on the application of one of them. It will, depending on the circumstances of the case, generally do so at the early management conference where the arguments for such a step-by-step approach to pleadings is seen to be both reasonable and convincing.[33] The Rules explicitly encourage parties to provide each other with information about contested or admitted facts during the pre-commencement phase.[34] Where a party communicates to the court, or specifies in the pleadings that individual facts or entire parts of the dispute's factual basis are uncontested, in the absence of specific reasons such as a later disagreement on the matter between the parties, the court will not require the pleadings to be amended.[35] The Rules further allow parties to limit the court's discretionary power to particular issues that were not clarified in the pre-commencement phase, and to make an agreed joint application that can bind the court[36] to limit use of the full procedural programme. The latter provision is of particular utility in complex cases, where the parties are both legally represented.

5. THE SIGNIFICANCE OF THE RULES FOR LAWYERS AND COURT CASE MANAGEMENT

29. The foregoing does not mean that the significance of the function of the full programme provided by uniform rules of proceedings should be underestimated.[37] Lawyers continue to be responsible for considering their client's claim or defence in its entirety before filing a claim or entering a case as a defendant. This continues to require lawyers to consider from the outset all the factual, evidential and legal eventualities of a case by reference to the full procedural programme provided by the Rules. Even in complex cases most lawyers prefer to set out a full presentation of their case in their initial pleadings. As a result of their preparatory work, even in

32 In these cases the court could finish the proceedings again by early final judgment dismissing the claim or a part of the claim according to Rule 65(2)(a) and (b), or render a positive judgment on preliminary procedural issues or issues on the merits (Rule 66) continuing the proceedings, or go on without a preliminary judgment. In case of a favourable partial judgment (Rule 130(1)(b)) the proceedings will go on (Rule 130(2)).

33 This procedure results again from the interaction of Rules 53(2), 54(2), 53(3) sentence 1, 49(9), 47 with comment 4, 27(1) sentence 1 with comment 3, 55(1), and additionally Rules 49(2) and (4), 61 (particularly in respect of comment 3) in connection with 65(3) and 66(2).

34 See Rule 51, and particularly comments 3 and 4, and Rule 50(2) with comment 2.

35 See Rule 53(6) with comment 12, for the case that the pre-commencement defence mentioned by the claimant contains explicit or tacit admissions of fact asserted by the claimant (Rule 54(3)), especially if the defendant only argues on the basis of affirmative defence (see Rule 54(5) with comment 5).

36 See Rules 57 to 60, and particularly comment 2 to Rule 57.

37 Most continental European codes of civil procedure take the full programme of eventualities as the basis for determining the contents of pleadings; see for further references Rule 53 comment 1.

such cases only issues that they have determined to be of no real likelihood of arising in the dispute tend to be either omitted from their pleadings or only dealt with in a very concise manner.

30. The court must use its management powers on a dialogical basis, i.e., it must hear the parties before issuing case management orders. It must also ensure that it asks the parties to amend any defects in their approach to case management etc., before taking any step to impose a sanction on them for default.[38] The flexibility built into first instance case management, and proceedings generally, must not, however, be abused by lawyers or the court adopting a piecemeal approach designed to prevent concentrated proceedings taking place. As such, neither should take steps to manage proceedings in such a way as to diminish their actual workload through prolonging the course of proceedings.[39]

6. INTEGRATING CONSUMER CASES INTO THE RULES

31. The Rules do not provide for special proceedings with consumers or other parties protected by special rules of mandatory European Union or national law. Due, however, to the flexible application that can be made of the Rules, particularly at first instance, and due to their carefully balanced procedural mechanisms, consumer cases can properly and satisfactorily be integrated into the process they articulate. Procedural protection for consumers should apply in all cases where a party to the dispute was acting on an entrepreneurial basis and the other party was acting in a private capacity, e.g., it should apply to contracts concerning sales, services, insurance, medical treatment etc.[40]

32. In such cases consumers need to be protected against unfair use of provisions concerning jurisdiction. Such consumer protection could be ensured by extending European Union provisions on the regulation of jurisdiction and enforcement to the determination of venue in solely domestic cases. This is provided for in these Rules as they do not develop their own rules concerning venue, which were considered to be superfluous.[41]

33. Another matter of concern may be the existence of applicable mandatory European Union or national laws that ought to be applied by the court *ex officio*, according to case law of the Court of Justice of the European Union.[42] According to the present Rules, the court, and not the parties, should, generally, determine the applicable law, and the parties are not permitted to agree on the non-application of mandatory law.[43] Where a court takes judicial notice of the fact that a

38 For the dialogical character of court management see especially Rules 4 sentence 3, 27(1) sentence 2, 28, 47 comment 4, 49(9), 50, 53(3) sentence 1 with comments 9, 55(1) with comment 5.

39 See Rule 61 comment 3 and Rule 66 comment 4.

40 For this broad definition of 'consumer' see Art. 2 of the Council Directive 93/13/EEC of 5 April 1993 on unfair terms in consumer contracts

41 See below VII. 2.

42 See, for instance, the most recent decisions: Judgment of the Court of 19 December 2019 in the joint cases C-453/18 and C-494/18 Bondora AS v. Carlos V.C. (C-453/18), and XY (C-494/18) (ECLI:EU:C:2019:1118); and Judgment of the Court of 7 November 2019 in Joined Cases C-419/18 and C-483/18: Profi Credit Polska S.A. v Bogumiła Włostowska et al.(C-419/18), and Profi Credit Polska S.A. v OH (C-483/18) (EU:C:2019:930) with further references to preceding decisions. It should be noted, however, that in case of payment order proceedings, which are not the core area of applicability of these Rules (see below VII. 3), the situation differs markedly from the circumstances given in first instance proceedings.

43 See Rule 26(2), sentences 1 and 2 with comments 1 and 2 and Rule 26(3) with comment 5 being of particular relevance to consumer cases and their, partially, mandatory substantive law.

particular mandatory law applies to a case before it, it must ask the party protected by the law, as far as it is necessary to do so, to amend their factual contentions.[44] Looking to a more theoretical case, where a party refuses to take steps to contribute any necessary facts in such a situation, the question may then arise as to whether the court must take evidence *ex officio* in order to protect consumer parties notwithstanding their own unwillingness to help themselves. The Rules leave this latter question to be determined by national judicial practice.[45] Depending on future developments that may be taken by the Court of Justice of the European Union (i.e., if it develops consumer protection into a more fully inquisitorial form of procedure in order to secure the enforcement of mandatory European Union law by European Union Member States' courts), the present Rules may diverge from the approach of the Court of Justice. Such an inquisitorial form of procedure does not fall within the ambit of these Rules.

34. The Rules also impose a duty on the court to ensure that parties enjoy equal treatment. One specific aspect of that duty is the requirement that the court is to suggest to weaker parties possible amendments to cure defects in their statements of case or evidence.[46] The court should not, however, go so far in this regard as to, in effect, become a party's lawyer. Consumers also enjoy specific protection in respect of service of process, as notice must be given in their national language or in wording that is really understandable by the consumer.[47] The Rules also promote consumer protection by providing that waiver of appeal from a judgment by a consumer is admitted in limited circumstances only.[48]

35. In consumer cases, the effects of the general requirement of proportionality[49] are somewhat ambivalent. Depending on the value of the amount in dispute, a remarkable part of cross-border consumer cases may be subject to small claim proceedings under the European Small Claims Regulation[50] or national law. The European Small Claims Regulation and, indirectly, national small claim proceedings result in European Union-wide enforceable judgments.[51] They form a part of the European Union *acquis* and, as discussed below, are therefore not taken account of in these Rules as the European Small Claims Regulation could be used also as a model law for proceedings in domestic cases to be harmonised by national legislation. Nevertheless, the tools used to ensure small claim proceedings remain proportionate deserve attention, as they should be used in a modified form in higher value consumer cases where typically consumers cannot invest the same resources in the litigation as are available to their opponent.

44 See Rule 24(1) sentence 2 with comment 3 on the problems of applicable mandatory law on a more general scale.

45 See, for a similar problem in respect of default proceedings, Rule 138 comment 6.

46 See generally Rule 61(4), however, also Rule 4 comment 3, on setting limits to partisan judicial mangement activities in consumer cases.

47 See Rule 82(1) with comments.

48 See Rule 154(3). According to the broad construction of the term 'consumers' a very large number of parties will be protected by this provision. It is true that there may still be other parties worth of such protection. A clearer definition of those parties protected seems, however, to be preferable. That waivers can be rendered void upon other general reasons arising from a lack of fairness, for instance, is not excluded by this Rule.

49 See Rules 5, 6 and 8.

50 Regulation (EC) No 861/2007 of the European Parliament and of the Council of 11 July 2007 establishing a European Small Claims Procedure. See below, Preamble VII. 3.

51 See Art. 1 first paragraph, second sentence of the European Small Claims Regulation.

36. In addition to any national legislation that requires parties to engage in some form of compulsory means for the promotion of settlement, the court's case management duty also provides the means to promote a cost-effective process for consumer claims. It permits and requires, for instance, as a first step to promote the avoidance of unnecessarily lengthy pleadings,[52] or cost-intensive evidence-taking with several experts or witnesses, reliance on documents that are already in the parties' possession, agreement on the use of a single jointly-instructed court expert, limitations on witness evidence to those witnesses that are likely to have the most substantial amount of probative evidence, and the use of video-conferencing to save costs.[53] As a second step, however, the court must reconsider its management endeavours if parties insist upon their full procedural rights and object to the use of restrictive management measures. The court may, of course, attempt to convince unreasonably disputatious parties by reminding them of the possibility of cost sanctions being imposed as a consequence of the pursuit of pointless procedural activity.[54] Judicial decisions could, however, be challenged if they do not take account of the proper administration of justice when they utilise restrictive management powers.[55]

37. Consumer rights can, particularly, be facilitated through the use of alternative dispute resolution (ADR), and Directive 2013/11/EU on alternative dispute resolution for consumer disputes plays an important role in this respect. The Rules complement these European Union provisions by placing enhanced duties on lawyers and the court to inform parties, and particularly consumer parties, about existing ADR methods and providers.[56] An absolutely necessary element of fair access to justice for consumers is, however, the right to sufficient legal aid, including the cost of legal advice and representation, as well as access to third-party funding and success fee arrangements in appropriate circumstances.[57]

38. That collective proceedings should be considered to be an indispensable part of the way in which a civil justice system helps secure consumer protection in cases of mass harm that, in a significant number of cases, affect consumers should not need explanation.[58] In individual conflicts the ability of parties to litigate on their own behalf and without legal advice or presentation or to be represented by consumer organisations according to provisions of national law[59] may, of course, also encourage and enable consumers to enforce their right in courts.

39. Overall, the Rules considerably strengthen the procedural position of consumers. They take account of the inherent imbalance in resources available to them in litigation, and place particular emphasis on the court's fundamental duty to treat parties equally while not undermining judicial neutrality.

52 See Rule 49(4) and (5), however also Rule 11.

53 See Rule 5 with comment 3, Rule 6 with comment 2, Rule 18(4) with comment 8, Rule 49(6), (10) and (11), Rule 61(1) and (2) especially with comment 2, Rule 62(2)(c).

54 See Rule 8 with comment 2.

55 See Rule 5(2) at the end and Rule 11.

56 See Rules 9(2) with comments 2 and 3 and Rule 10(2) with comment 2.

57 See Rules 244 with comments 3 and Rule 245.

58 See Part XI on collective proceedings.

59 See Rule 14 with comment 1 and Rule 15 with comment 4.

7. SETTLEMENT AS AN INTEGRAL PART OF THE RULES CONCERNING FIRST INSTANCE PROCEEDINGS

40. The development of manifold kinds of ADR, including settlement via out-of-court agreement, has become a common feature of civil justice in all European countries. It has also, arguably, become the dominant procedural policy of the European Union over the last couple of decades. It is a fundamental principle of the Rules that lawyers and courts must encourage parties, on a properly informed basis in appropriate cases, to make use of out-of-court ADR methods.[60] The Rules also provide for in-court-Court-settlements, in respect of which the court's role is not restricted to rendering a decision that gives effect to an agreement reached by the parties,[61] but rather enables the court to actively participate in the process that seeks to assist the parties to reach a consensual resolution of their dispute.[62] This twin track to settlement strikes a compromise between differing historic European traditions concerning the nature of the judicial, i.e., between that of the active or passive judge.

41. An innovative step taken by the Rules, which draws on experience from, for instance, England and France, is the detailed elaboration of a duty placed on parties to take steps to further settlement in the pre-commencement stage of a dispute through the mutual provision of information concerning the dispute,[63] while also encouraging them to try to settle parts of their dispute,[64] even in a form binding the court,[65] if attempts to fully resolve the dispute fail.

42. In drafting Rules on settlement agreements consideration was given to the question whether the court could give effect to a settlement, which was contrary to the law. This was particularly pertinent given European Court of Justice (ECJ) case law, that concerns the question of the court's *ex officio* duty to respect mandatory European Union law.[66] The core of this question is of fundamental character. It affects the principle of party disposition of procedure, and whenever possible, should be resolved consistently in all cases where parties can freely conclude proceedings independently of the legal correctness of the contradicting positions of the parties, e.g., withdrawal and admission of claim, waiver of appeal, judgment in default, settlement etc.

43. In most European legal cultures it appears to be best practice that judgments upon admission, waiver of appeal, judgment in default,[67] and settlements cannot give effect to obligations, declarations or agreements that are otherwise not permitted by law in so far as the text of court orders, declarations or agreements contain provisions contrary to mandatory law.[68] If, however, a reasoned judgment following a contested procedure could not produce the economic consequences contained in an agreed settlement or consequences similar to those, nevertheless it ought to remain open to the parties to dispose of their dispute either by taking relevant

60 See Rule 9 with comments 1 to 3 and Rule 10 with comment 2.

61 See Rule 9(3) with comment 3 and Rule 141(1) with comment 1.

62 See Rule 10(3) with comment 3 and Rule 10(4) with comment 4 addressing the need to avoid a clear conflict of roles.

63 See Rule 51 with comments 1 to 3.

64 See Rule 9(4) with comment 5 and Rule 51(1), (2)(b) and (3)(c) with comment 4.

65 See Rule 57 and following, and particularly the comments to Rule 57.

66 See already above VI.6 with references; and see, for instance, A. Beka, *The Active Role of Courts in Consumer Litigation*, (Intersentia, 2019).

67 See Rule 21 comment 4 for disposition by default.

68 See Rule 141(2) with comment 3.

procedural steps—other than judgment in default against the defendant as the court cannot give effect to a claim that does not meet all necessary legal requirements according to facts as asserted by the applicant—or by way of an agreed settlement.[69]

44. In a free society, citizens are not obliged to enforce mandatory law. As a consequence, freedom of procedural disposition is respected in many legal cultures and courts do not, in principle, exercise any control over parties to civil actions agreeing not to enforce their rights. Different considerations may well, and do, arise in respect of criminal prosecution and justice. The Rules do, however, provide an exception to this general principle where appellate proceedings are concerned, specifically regarding second appeals that engage a public interest, i.e., which raise important questions of law that require clarification, which outweigh the private interests of involved parties.[70]

45. The Rules provide guidelines on limitations that can be imposed on the principle of party disposition. They do so, however, by leaving discretion for national legislative tradition and judicial practice to be taken into account.[71]

8. PARTICULAR FORMS OF PROCEDURE IN SPECIAL PARTS OF THE RULES

46. While a number of special proceedings, such as small claim proceedings, proceedings for payment orders or documentary proceedings were not considered to be either a necessary or beneficial part of these Rules, at the outset of the project agreement was reached that they would include provisional measures. During the project's development it was also agreed that collective redress should be included and then, in its final phase, appeals and means of review were included.

47. The reasons for this choice are manifold. Small claim proceedings and proceedings for payment orders form a central part of the European Union's *acquis communautaire*,[72] and the decided view of the project's promoters was that there was no realistic chance to move beyond the high level of procedural harmonisation that these mechanisms provide. Documentary proceedings were not included as they are utilised in only a small number of European procedural cultures, and they are of limited efficiency due to the need to utilise a final affirmative procedure where evidence-taking is not restricted to documents.

a) Proceedings on Provisional Measures

48. Proceedings on provisional measures were considered to be an essential feature of model rules. In many fields of law their significance, and the variety of different types of such measures, has increased to remarkable degree over the last five decades, e.g. in competition law, intellectual property law, the law of privacy and data protection, through the development of provisional or interim payments in contract law, of freezing orders and preliminary attachments, for the preservation of

69 See Rule 136(2) with comment 1; if the facts asserted by the claimant give a reason to consider applicable mandatory law adverse to a claimant's application to enter a judgment in default, it should be a matter for national court practice to decide whether the claimant could be asked to amend their factual contentions according to the ECJ's case law (see above VI.6 with references, Rule 24 comment 3, and Rule 138 comment 6).

70 See Rule 163(2) with comment 3.

71 See generally Preamble VI. 2 to 4, on the flexible character of the Rules. Also see Rule 138 comment 6.

72 See below VII. 2.

assets and means of evidence etc. In some European countries, however, in contrast to this general pattern of growth, national legislation in this field of civil justice has been no more than very general and not particularly informative. In such countries, it has, in reality, been left to the courts to develop the field through case law. Some countries have, however, reformed their approach to provisional measures both in new national codes and in revisions to established ones.[73] In the European Union it was also felt necessary to develop such measures in order to strengthen cross-border execution in respect of bank accounts through the provision of rights to information for creditors and through the development of an innovative form of preservation order concerning bank accounts.[74] The same innovative approach to the development of means to secure information and to grant protective measures was also taken in the field of intellectual property rights.[75]

49. The need to draw the various strands of development together and systematise them in a Part of the Rules seemed both important and necessary. One particular difficulty that this aspect of the project faced in achieving this systematisation was the hybrid character of this part of civil justice as it combines elements of contentious proceedings and of civil enforcement or execution. In practice, however, proceedings concerning provisional measures in many cases replace contentious proceedings as parties agree to treat decisions rendered as a provisional measure as final decisions obviating the need for there to be main proceedings on the merits.[76] Additionally, many provisional measures are rendered pending proceedings on the merits and are instrumental in securing their success or failure. Such measures can thus be seen to be closely connected with, and necessary for, the conduct of contentious proceedings. Therefore, formal arguments in favour of maintaining the long tradition of a strict separation between contentious court proceedings and civil execution and of considering provisional measures as part of execution could not outweigh arguments in favour of including this important part of civil justice in the Rules.

b) Collective Redress

50. Another field of civil justice which has rapidly increased in importance over the last two decades in Europe is that of collective redress. It forms Part XI of these Rules. Most European States did not initially orient toward the approach taken in the United States of America, which does not generally trust to the willingness and ability of their government, legislation and administration, to protect citizens from harm done by powerful market actors, and develop class actions that enable citizens to claim for compensation and punitive damages, a form of corrective and restorative justice that is achievable independently of administrative or legislative activities. European legal culture, with its paternalistic and social elements, puts greater emphasis on preventive legislative and administrative measures that seek to protect citizens from harm before it occurs. The increasing orientation, particularly of the European Union, towards a more individualistic, competitive society, and the recent inability of European and national legislation and administration to protect citizens efficiently from the excesses of the financial crisis and

73 E.g., France, England, Italy, Spain etc.

74 See Regulation (EU) No. 655/2014 of the European Parliament and of the Council of 15 May 2014 establishing a European Account Preservation Order procedure to facilitate cross-border debt recovery in civil and commercial matters (EAPO Regulation).

75 See Directive 2004/48/EC of the European Parliament and of the Council of 29 April 2004 on the enforcement of intellectual property rights, (IP Enforcement Directive); for more materials see Part X, Introduction, comment 2.

76 See Rule 188 comment 2.

industrial scandals, such as the Diesel fuel scandal, have, however, changed social and political views. These developments have strengthened the position of advocates of class actions, such as the European Commission, of admirers of US economic and legal culture, and of global law firms. This has led to European legislatures, incrementally, developing various forms of mass litigation, which have built on more limited, extant, forms of civil procedure that enable the enforcement of group or public interests. This has led to the development of a diverse range of different forms of collective redress procedure across Europe. It has also led the European Union to develop a number of proposals over the last two decades for degrees of harmonisation of such procedures by Recommendations or Directives.[77] Consequently this area is, at the present time, the most pressing issue for the development of European civil procedure and its future function within the European societies. Given this, the promoters of this project concluded that these Rules would be seriously deficient if they failed to set out harmonisation proposals that could form the basis of future European and national legislation.

c) Proceedings on Appeals

51. Proceedings on appeal and other means of review were not originally intended for inclusion within the project. The ALI/Unidroit Principles only refer to appellate review in Principle 27. That principle struck a compromise between common law countries, where appeals do not generally allow a full rehearing of the case (no *ius novorum* and "closed record") and continental traditions, which originally adopted an approach which mostly provide an appeal by way of a full *de novo* hearing. It is only in more recent times that an increasing number of countries have begun to restrict the *ius novorum*. Part IX of the Rules on Means of Review is the result of remarkable approximation between European procedural systems concerning the approach to be taken to reviewing judicial decisions. The only issue over which serious discussions arose was the requirements concerning the admissibility of first appeals and the *ius novorum* on first appeals. Ultimately a compromise was reached, which resulted in the rules as drafted being widely accepted. It would have been a mistake not to incorporate rules on review and appeals based on, as became apparent during the project, an erroneous belief that because past attempts to harmonise appeals had failed due to, then, seemingly insurmountable obstacles, the present attempt would also fail.

VII. THE *ACQUIS COMMUNAUTAIRE* AND THE RULES

1. GENERAL REMARKS

52. Questions about the relation between the *acquis communautaire* and the Rules do not allow a simple nor even a uniform answer.

53. First, the procedural *acquis communautaire* consists mainly of Directives or Regulations of the European Union, which are designed to regulate the cooperation of, and potential conflicts between, European Union Member States in cross-border cases and at least in part between them and States outside the European Union, i.e., third country States. ELI and Unidroit projects do not exclude non-Member States of the European Union. Whereas the *acquis* is binding law for Member States, it is no more than a form of model law for other countries and particularly for those that seek differing forms of cooperation with the European Union such as the States of the European Economic Area or other States with associative connections to the

77 For references, see Part XI comment 1.

European Union. Countries outside the European Union are becoming increasingly significant as players in the European law-making and are demanding new forms of legislative cooperation, not least following the withdrawal of the United Kingdom from the Union. For European Union Member States that had reserved rights to opt-out of parts of the *acquis*, those parts already have the character of a model law that could be adopted either completely, in part, or in a modified form within their national legislation. That European legal cultures take differing views on the role played by the procedural *acquis* made it clear that a common European project that is not restricted to model rules for EU legislation could not properly exclude the *acquis* from critical reconsideration and proposals of reform. Even where the *acquis* is at present binding law, it is also clear that revisions to it are a normal and necessary phenomenon of a healthy legal and democratic culture, otherwise the *acquis* would freeze in a Procrustean bed of centralised and not always satisfactorily drafted legislation.

54. Secondly, European model rules must address domestic and cross-border cases. If the Rules had been limited to domestic cases, they would not have met legitimate expectations connected with the project arising from the fact that cross-border cases are an inherent part of the daily social and economic reality across the whole of Europe. The interdependence between rules for domestic and for cross-border cases does not permit them to be strictly separated and, therefore, any proposals for revision cannot but take into consideration their potential effect on both types of case.

55. Thirdly, the procedural *acquis* with its Directives and Regulations takes account of this interdependence. Though the *acquis* is designed to facilitate cooperation between European Union Member States, it does not simply contain rules of international civil procedure. In many respects cooperation between different legal systems requires a minimum set of common standards. As a consequence, most Directives or Regulations also set out standards of legal design, which cover areas of law that are traditionally understood to form part of the law applicable to domestic cases, e.g., the Service Regulation[78] or the Regulation on the Taking of Evidence.[79] This interdependence between rules designed to create cooperation and law traditionally applicable to domestic cases meant that the Rules could not adopt a simple approach, which did no more than focus on comparative domestic law while leaving the field of cooperation between States to existing Directives, Regulations or international conventions. Thus parts of the European procedural *acquis communautaire,* while designed to regulate cross-border cases, have, in some cases, tried simultaneously to replace traditional domestic law more or less completely, e.g., Small Claims Regulation or Regulation on Payment Orders.[80] Similarly, some Directives and Regulations that mainly address questions of substantive law also deal with issues of procedural law, particularly the law of evidence, and leave no leeway for additional national domestic law within their scope of applicability.

56. Consideration of the state of procedural legislation in Europe carried out within the project, concluded that the Rules should not try to go beyond the currently extant set of rules and attempt

78 Regulation (EC) No 1393/2007 of the European Parliament and of the Council of 13 November 2007 on the service in the Member States of judicial and extrajudicial documents in civil or commercial matters (service of documents) (the Service Regulation).

79 Council Regulation (EC) No 1206/2001 of 28 May 2001 on cooperation between the courts of the Member States in the taking of evidence in civil or commercial matters (the Evidence Regulation).

80 Regulation (EC) No 1896/2006 of the European Parliament and of the Council of 12 December 2006 creating a European order for payment procedure (EPO Regulation).

to develop a uniform scheme for the coordination of procedural law for domestic cases and cross-border cases. The position taken by the Rules thus required each part of civil procedure to take into account the state of development of European legislation applicable to it and, to then make a pragmatic choice concerning how, and the extent to which, coordination was desirable. For cross-border cases, the Draft Rules of Procedure of the Unified Patent Court, the only European civil procedural code drafted upon agreement between participating European States and the European Union, also adopted this pragmatic approach. In part, they replaced general European provisions for cross-border cases. In other instances, they did no more than refer to them in a general sense, while in others they only referred to them in respect of remaining questions not addressed by special rules.[81]

57. A similar approach to resolving problems arising from the co-existence of model rules and the *acquis communautaire* was adopted by these Rules. In part, the Rules replace existing European sets of rules almost entirely and only leave room for the continuing applicability of some organisational provisions of the procedural *acquis*.[82] In part they articulate a general level of co-existence, while only adding some provisions that are in conflict with, or modify, the *acquis*.[83] In other respects the Rules chose to fully extend European provisions for cross-border cases to domestic cases either by adopting their texts with no more than minor revisions[84] or by tacitly accepting that such an extension is likely to arise in the future.[85]

58. This may sound complicated, but simple solutions would ultimately not have met the expectations associated with a set of model rules that need to be based on an evaluation of existing sources of European and national law and which ought to draw out from them rules of best procedural practice. It must always be noted that the procedural *acquis communautaire* undergoes continuous legislative revision. A set of model rules should not only harmonise and improve national laws but also contribute to the improvement of extant European law.

2. RULES ON JURISDICTION, RECOGNITION AND ENFORCEMENT

59. From the very beginning of the project its promoters unanimously agreed not to draft a special part with rules on jurisdiction and enforcement. The reason for this was straightforward and never seriously disputed. It was the common conviction that the Jurisdiction and Enforcement Regulation, while by no means perfect in every respect, was considered to provide a satisfactory approach to cross-border disputes, not least because of its long history of both substantial and minor revision and the detailed case law concerning its interpretation and operation.

81 See the Draft Rules of Procedure of the Unified Patent Court, e.g., Rule 173 (Taking of Evidence) and Rules 270 and following (Service within the Contracting Member States) as well as Rules 274 and following (Service Outside the Contracting Member States); for the difficulties of approval of the agreement on a Unified Patent Court as a whole, see German Constitutional Court, 13.02.2020, BvR 739/17.

82 See, e.g., Part VI (Service and Due Notice of Proceedings), Introduction, comment 2; another example is Part XI (Collective Proceedings) Introduction comments 1 and following, and Rules 233 and following.

83 See, e.g., Part VII (Access to Information and Evidence), Introduction comment 2, and Rule 128; Rules 202(1), 203 for international jurisdiction for provisional measures.

84 See, e.g., Part VIII, Section 3 (Effects of Pendency and Judgments), Introduction comment 3 and Section 3 A, Introduction comments 1-4.

85 For this group of European legislation to be extended to domestic cases see below VII.2 (Rules on Jurisdiction, Recognition and Enforcment) and 3 (Small Claim Proceedings and Proceedings for Payment Orders).

60. Most of the rules concerning jurisdiction are based on criteria that could equally apply, or apply with a few minor modifications, to the determination of venue. A carefully modified extension of the criteria for cross-border jurisdiction to rules on venue ought to be viewed as the future, royal road for the harmonisation of rules concerning domestic territorial jurisdiction and international jurisdiction. The European-wide acceptance of criteria for jurisdiction, as well as of mechanisms and criteria for recognition and enforcement of the Brussels Regulation, is impressively documented by the 2007 Lugano Convention that to a high degree parallels the solutions of the Brussels Ibis Regulation. Additionally, the Rules do not, in principle at least, make specific provision concerning jurisdiction, recognition and enforcement for third country States. It was thought better to leave such matters to the Brussels Ibis Regulation, which in part, at least, regulates jurisdictional issues regarding cases with connection to third country States,[86] and to the HCCH Conventions on Choice of Court Agreements[87] and on Judgments;[88] the latter two of which are still in a more or less experimental stage. Like the Rules, the Agreement on a Unified Patent Court refers for international jurisdiction to the Brussels Ibis Regulation,[89] questions of venue play a minor role because of the centralised structure of the planned Unified Patent Court with its divisions in only three European cities and its ability to hear cases in every place where this seems to be convenient and feasible.[90] In contrast, recognition and enforcement of judgments are dealt with, to a certain extent, in the Agreement on a Unified Patent Court and its draft Rules of Procedure,[91] albeit without reference to the Brussels Ibis Regulation.[92] The solution taken for the Unified Patent Court was not considered to be an attractive example for the integration of rules on jurisdiction, recognition and enforcement into model rules of a European civil procedure code.

61. The Rules generally avoid touching upon questions of jurisdiction. They do not, for instance, permit rules concerning multiple parties, such as joinder, consolidation, or third-party notice, to be interpreted as rules that regulate multiple party admissibility, while also creating special kinds of territorial or international jurisdiction. Criteria concerning international jurisdiction are left to the Brussels Ibis Regulation,[93] as that has been paralleled in this field by a significant and continuously increasing amount of congruence in numerous European States.[94] The Rules only rarely, and when it is absolutely necessary, either implicitly or explicitly complement or modify the Brussels Ibis Regulation.[95]

86 See, e.g., Arts. 4(2), 25(1) Regulation No. 1215/2012 (Brussels Ibis Regulation).

87 See Convention of 30 June 2005 on Choice of Court Agreements (HCCH Choice of Court Convention).

88 See Convention of 2 July 2019 on the Recognition and Enforcement of Foreign Judgments in Civil or Commercial Matters (HCCH Judgments Convention).

89 See 2013 United Patent Court Agreement, Art. 31.

90 See 2013 United Patent Court Agreement, Arts. 7 and following, 32 and following.

91 See 2013 United Patent Court Agreement, Art. 34 and 2015 Draft Unified Patent Court Rules, Art. 354

92 The Regulation would appear, however, to have been drawn upon as the inspiration.

93 See, e.g., Rule 36(1)(b) with comment 2; Rule 42 comment 3; Rule 146(2), all referring to Art. 8 No. 1 and 2 Brussels Ibis Regulation.

94 See, e.g., for France Art. 333 CCP and generally the comment 3 on Rule 42. In some European countries the rules concerning the admissibility of multi-parties are at least in part interpreted to include the creation of a special venue; see, e.g. § 64 German CCP etc.

95 See, e.g., for pendency Part VIII, Section 3 Introduction, comment 1; Section 3 A, Introduction comment 4 and especially Rule 146 comment 5; for jurisdiction in cases of principal intervention, Rule

3. SMALL CLAIM PROCEEDINGS AND PROCEEDINGS FOR PAYMENT ORDERS

62. The Rules do not cover small claim proceedings and proceedings for payment orders. Both special proceedings are addressed by European Regulations applying to cross-border cases.[96] These Regulations not only regulate cooperation between, and the competences of, European Union Member States in cross-border cases, they also contain a complete and detailed set of rules on on-going proceedings, which only leave Member States with a limited amount of discretion to add to them. The national laws of most Member States, and other European countries, provide for similar simplified proceedings that differ in conception and detail. Small claim proceedings are often consumer cases, although the scope of such claims is often wider and includes claims where the value of disputes exceeds 5,000 euro, which is the present limit for small claim proceedings under the European Regulation. Small claim proceedings and proceedings for payment orders with their simplified rules may be the only procedural means available to many individuals, and particularly those with a low income. They may favour a tendency towards the development of collective proceedings. As such, the quality and social impact of such procedures need to be subject to careful scrutiny. Nevertheless, the promoters of the project decided against developing model rules applicable to these special forms of procedure. One reason for this was that the Regulations already provide a set of model rules for national legislatures to consider in respect of any potential improvements to their existing procedures, and hence the present Rules were unlikely to provide a more innovative approach. Additionally, the prevailing view of the project's reporters and group members was that the exact shape of any future innovation in these areas was likely to be significantly more influenced by the development of artificial intelligence than was likely to be the case for regular proceedings.[97] As a consequence of this, the conclusion was drawn that the time was not yet ripe for model rules or legislative implementation; in the field of small claim proceedings and payment orders the current time is one more suited to rapid development and experimentation rather than model rules. The general principles of civil justice as formulated in Part I of these Rules do, however, set out important parameters concerning the development of what is known as e-justice.

4. *ACQUIS COMMUNAUTAIRE* AND THE CASE LAW OF THE HIGHEST EUROPEAN COURTS

63. The detailed case law of the European Court of Human Rights and that of the Court of Justice of the European Union on, respectively, the European Convention on Human Rights, and the 2000 European Charter of Fundamental Rights, the European Treaties and European secondary law, requires particular mention as it forms an important part of the European Union *acquis communautaire*. The majority of this case law is respected, at least in principle, by the Rules, in so far as it mirrors fundamental values of a common European constitutional tradition.

39 is interpreted as a venue rule in comment 1 in the absence of satisfactory regulation in Art. 8 No. 2 of the Brussels Regulation (recast), for provisional measures these Rules provide for the complementary regulation of jurisdiction, see especially in Rule 202(3) with comment 5, and the same is true in Rules 233 and following for cross-border cases in collective proceedings. For the European Court of Justice's conception of *res judicata*, see below VII. 4.

96 See Regulation No. 861/2007 (EC) of the European Parliament and of the Council establishing a European Small Claims Procedure; Regulation No. 1896/2006 (EC) of the European Parliament and of the Council creating a European order for payment procedure.

97 See Rule 18 comment 9.

But in a free society even these Courts and their decisions cannot stand outside criticism, especially if their decisions derive very detailed results from fundamental and human rights or even secondary European law. For instance, details resulting from the right to public proceedings, as developed by the ECtHR, demanded careful attention by the Rules' drafters. At the same time, however, consideration was given in discussions as to whether and how better approaches might be set out within the Rules.[98] The same is true in respect of the details concerning the procedural transformation of mandatory law[99] or for details concerning the preclusive and positive effects of *res judicata*. Moreover, not all decisions in the field of civil procedure, and this is particularly the case where the European Court of Justice is concerned, are viewed as being particularly well-considered by procedural scholars and judges who have a long and broad expertise in procedure and practice. These Rules are an appropriate instrument to articulate prevailing discomfort with approaches taken in such decisions and to promote a change in approach in the case law of the highest European courts. This position is also reasonable when considered against the background that not all European countries are Member States of the EU and under the jurisdiction of the Court of Justice of the European Union.

VIII. MODERN COMMUNICATION AND RECORDING, ARTIFICIAL INTELLIGENCE AND THE RULES

1. APPROPRIATE USE OF ELECTRONIC COMMUNICATION AND RECORDING

64. A remarkable number of Rules provide for the appropriate use of modern kinds of communication and recording, e.g., electronic communication between court and parties and among parties, video-conferencing or audio transmission in hearings and evidence-taking, disclosure and production of electronic data and documents and their evidential evaluation, video-recording of hearings and evidence-taking, electronic platforms in collective proceedings, etc.[100] The Rules are, however, technology-neutral. They do not go into technical details that may be subject to rapid change and development and may, quite properly, differ between individual countries, although compatibility and interoperability should, at the least, be secured within the European Union. The Rules do not permit the inappropriate use of modern communication or recording methods.[101] While some countries provide detailed measures aimed at regulating the nature and use of such methods,[102] the Rules leave such matters of detail to national regulation and judicial practice[103] Courts do, however, need to ensure that the use of such techniques provides parties with an equal opportunity to present their case, i.e., securing equality of arms and equal treatment.[104]

98 See Rule 17 comment 2 and Rule 18 comments 1 and 2.

99 See above Preface VI. 6 and 7 with references.

100 See Rule 18 and the enumeration of individual provisions in comment 7.

101 See Rule 18(4).

102 See, e.g., France, *Code de l'organisation judiciaire* Art. L 111-12; England, CPR Practice Direction 32, p. 29.1, Annex 3, etc.

103 See Rule 18 comment 8 with examples.

104 See Rule 4 sentence 2.

2. ARTIFICIAL INTELLIGENCE AND THE RULES

65. There were intensive discussions about the need to incorporate rules on the admissibility of the use of artificial intelligence into the Rules.[105] The use of such computer programmes by lawyers to help them prepare their cases, e.g., to provide initial assessments of the merits of their clients' cases, to assist settlement negotiations, or to prepare pleadings, or by third-party litigation funders as a tool to assess whether to invest in litigation, or by insurance companies, is already a reality. It is outside the scope of these Rules to prescribe what forms of technology lawyers practising a liberal profession and other market actors interested in the provision of legal advice or assessment should or should not use. Such matters are best left to the law regulating the conduct of the legal profession, and laws regulating the provision of legal advice generally. Undoubtedly such issues will become increasingly important in so far as regulation is concerned, with the likely increased growth in use of such forms of artificial intelligence and predictive technologies. Artificial intelligence could, however, have been reasonably addressed by these Rules, not least to determine the extent to which its use by courts and judges to help prepare or render decisions (so called e-justice) ought to be permissible. Given developments in, for instance, computerised payment order proceedings, which are already used in some countries, examples of e-arbitration and e-mediation platforms, or the development of artificial intelligence systems to decide court cases, such matters will undoubtedly become increasingly important. The promoters of the project tried to obtain reliable information about the actual performance and capability of existing programs.[106] They concluded that while there had been remarkable progress in development, the prevailing opinion remained that the replacement of human deliberation by judges and fully reasoned human judgments by artificial intelligence decision-making in legal proceedings at first instance may be a possibility for the near future for small claims and similar disputes. For the large majority of civil disputes outside that category, such developments must be viewed with more caution. Moreover, the replacement of human judges with the use of artificial intelligence is not simply an issue of the correctness of and reasoning in legal decisions, but equally and crucially it is a question of mutual human trust between citizens and the State, of democratic scrutiny and accountability of the justice system, and the exercise of State power. It goes to the heart of the relationship between the citizen and the State, and to the nature of society. As such it raises considerations that go far beyond the development of model rules of procedure. Notwithstanding this, the Rules do permit the use of artificial intelligence by judges, to the extent that is consistent with the right to be heard, as any use of such means must be capable of being subject to parties knowing that they are being used and having a fair opportunity to argue about its nature, quality and the conclusions that may be drawn from it.[107]

105 See Rule 18 comment 9.

106 See the particularly insightful studies on the ability of AI systems to predict case outcomes before the European Court of Human Rights and the United States Supreme Court: N. Aletras *et al* 2016: *Predicting judicial decisions of the European Court of Human Rights: a Natural Language Processing Perspective.* Peer J Computer Science 2:e93 https://doi.org/10.7717/peerj-cs.93; C. O'Sullivan & J. Beel, *Predicting the Outcome of Judicial Decisions made by the European Court of Human Rights.* in 27th AIAI Irish Conference on Artificial Intelligence and Cognitive Science, 2019; D.M. Katz *et al* (2017), *A general approach for predicting the behaviour of the Supreme Court of the United States*, PLoS ONE 12(4): e0174698. https://doi.org/10.1371/journal.pone.0174698

107 See Rule 12 comments 1, and 4; Rule 18 comment 9.

MODEL EUROPEAN RULES OF CIVIL PROCEDURE

PART I

GENERAL PROVISIONS

1. This Part sets out a number of general provisions concerning the operation of these Rules. It defines the scope of these Rules, limiting their application to domestic and cross-border civil and commercial disputes. It does so by reference to the definition of such disputes that is commonly accepted throughout Europe (see Rule 1).

2. A number of overarching procedural duties that are imposed upon the court, parties and their lawyers are also articulated (see Rules 2 - 10). The most significant of these duties are the duty of co-operation, which is understood in these Rules to be of fundamental importance to the effective and proper administration of justice, and the general principle of proportionality in dispute resolution, which has itself become an increasingly important procedural principle across Europe since the start of the 21st century. Finally, it articulates and, in some cases, gives concrete effect to a number of fundamental procedural principles that are inherent in the right to fair trial (see Rules 11 - 20)

SECTION 1—SCOPE

Rule 1. Scope

(1) These Rules apply to the resolution of domestic and cross-border disputes in civil and commercial matters whatever the nature of the court.

(2) These Rules do not apply to:

- **(a) the status or legal capacity of natural persons, rights in property arising out of a matrimonial relationship or out of a relationship deemed by the law applicable to such relationship to have comparable effects to marriage;**
- **(b) bankruptcy, proceedings relating to the winding-up of insolvent companies or other legal persons, judicial arrangements, compositions and analogous proceedings;**
- **(c) social security;**
- **(d) arbitration;**
- **(e) maintenance obligations arising from a family relationship, parentage, marriage or affinity;**
- **(f) wills and succession, including maintenance obligations arising by reason of death.**

(3) These Rules may also apply where incidental issues arise which fall within Rule 1(2), if the principal matter in dispute is within the scope of Rule 1(1).

Comments:

1. Rule 1 defines the scope of application of these Rules. It adopts the definition of civil and commercial matters as developed and used in Article 1 of Regulation (EU) No. 1215/2012 on jurisdiction and the recognition and enforcement of judgments in civil and commercial matters (recast) (Brussels Ibis Regulation); and Article 1 of the 2007 Convention on jurisdiction and the recognition and enforcement of judgments in civil and commercial matters, JO L 339/3, 21.12.2007 (Lugano Convention). The ELI/UNIDROIT Model European Rules of Civil Procedure are model rules designed to further the harmonisation of civil

ELI-UNIDROIT Model European Rules of Civil Procedure. ELI & UNIDROIT, Oxford University Press.
 DOI: 10.1093/oso/9780198866589.003.0002

procedure in Europe. They are intended to exemplify potential future procedural legislation by European States, including European Union Member States, as well as by the European Union, the latter of which increasingly legislates on procedural issues that are connected to matters of European Union substantive law. Given this intention and the fact that the definition chosen is common to all or at least the majority of European States, the adoption of this definition of civil and commercial matters as the means to define the scope of these Rules was considered optimal.

2. Rule 1(3) makes it clear that these Rules also apply in cases where the claim for relief is based mainly on law within the scope of Rule 1(1), however, relevant incidental issues that fall under Rule 1(2) are to be determined simultaneously, e.g. whether assets of the defendant were a part of an insolvency estate at the time of the defendant's acquisition.
3. Rule 1(3) is consistent with the European Court of Justice' case law.[1] The question whether the determination of such relevant incidental issues may be *res judicata* is to be considered separately (see Rule 149(2), comment 2).

SECTION 2—PRINCIPLES

A. CO-OPERATION

Rule 2. General

Parties, their lawyers and the court must co-operate to promote the fair, efficient and speedy resolution of the dispute.

Sources:
ALI/UNIDROIT Principles 7.2, 11.1, 11.2. 22.1, 22.2.

Comments:

1. These Rules consider the proper conduct of proceedings to require effective co-operation between the court, parties and their lawyers. The emphasis on co-operation, which has been a feature of some European civil procedural codes since the 19th century and others since the turn of the 21st century, is an important move away from the traditional division between adversarial and inquisitorial conceptions of civil procedure.[2] It is intentionally adopted here, not least, as a means to avoid this historical division that has acted as a barrier to procedural harmonisation. Particular emphasis is placed on the general duty of the court and of parties to co-operate, which is set out in Rule 2, and to give proper effect to specific duties to co-operate with each other in the conduct of proceedings. Specific rules are set out throughout these Rules.
2. The court's role is not limited to its adjudicative function, i.e. to hearing and determining disputes. It is also required to take an active part in the proper administration of justice, noting that this is a continuous process not confined to the proper administration of any individual claim. As such it is required to ensure, whilst maintaining its neutrality as

1 See, for instance Case C-266/01, Judgment of 15 May 2003, Préservatrice Foncière TIARD (C-266/01, ECR 2003 p. I-4867) ECLI:EU:C:2003:282

2 See Council of Europe Recommendation (84)5 on Principles of civil procedure designed to improve the functioning of justice, Principles 2.1 and 2.2.

between parties, that it contributes properly to the fair, efficient and speedy resolution of proceedings.

3. In so far as the speedy resolution of proceedings is concerned, the court must monitor party, and their lawyers', compliance with the various obligations in these Rules to carry out procedural obligations and responsibilities timeously (see, particularly, Rules 4 sentence 3, 47 to 49(2) and (4), 61(2) and (3), 64(4), and 92(1)) and must sanction late factual or evidential contributions in so far as appropriate (see e.g. Rules 27, 54(3) and (4), 63,(2), 64(4), 93, 99).
4. In so far as the efficient prosecution of proceedings is concerned, the court has a number of duties that give effect to its general duty of co-operation, the most important of which require it to suggest amendments to proceedings where parties fail to fulfil their responsibilities correctly and completely (see Rules 4 sentence 3, 24(1), 25(3), 26(2), 33, 49(6) – (11), 53(3), 61(4), 62(2), 64(5), 92(2),and 218) and to respect the parties' right to be heard in order to further and maintain the dialogue between court and parties (see Rules 11, 12(2), 13, 16(1), 24(3), 26(2), 28 sentence 2, 41(1), 50(1), 64(7), 92(2) and (4), 93, 96, 107(2), 186, and 201(3)).
5. The court is under a duty to exercise its management duties fairly. As such it must, for instance, maintain its impartiality and honesty, avoid prejudice, bias, favouritism and self-interest, avoid taking steps to trap parties by contradictory judicial conduct, while ensuring that it treats all parties equally. The absence of such qualities in terms of conduct, may result in judges being disqualified from proceedings albeit this is not addressed in these Rules (although see Rule 179(2)(e)), but which is generally dealt with in a number of European jurisdictions through laws concerning the organisation of the administration of justice. Compliance with these Rules will ordinarily ensure that the court does not treat parties unfairly. There are, however, specific rules dealing with some possible manifestations of unfair conduct by the court, e.g. Rule 4 sentence 2 ensuring equal treatment, Rule 7 concerning the proportionality of sanctions, Rules 11 and 92(4) that require parties be given a fair opportunity to be heard, Rule 27(1), which prohibits the imposition of sanctions for late factual allegations or offers of evidence if the court itself did not comply with its duties to monitor party compliance and, where necessary, raise the possibility of amendments with the parties, or Rules 55 and 96 concerning the right to amend of claims and defences in appropriate cases. A further specific instance of the duty to co-operate concerns the promotion of settlement during the course of proceedings (see Rules 10, 49(1), 62)), and to respect partial settlement (see Rules 9(4), 26(3), 50(2), 51, 57 and following, 107(4), and 120(3)).
6. Rule 2 also imposes the duty to co-operate on parties to conduct litigation in the interest of the proper administration of justice. A party's conduct towards the court, their opponent or other parties or non-parties must further the efficient, speedy, and fair resolution of the dispute, which also includes taking appropriate steps to settle their dispute in the pre-commencement phase and during proceedings. At the same time parties have to manage procedural risks, in their pursuit of success in the proceedings, which are imposed on them by substantive law, the rules concerning the burden of proof and by their dependence on the court's evaluation of the case. Each party runs the risk of not being able to introduce all those facts that are relevant to their case, to adduce enough evidence to convince the court of the truth of facts favourable to their case, and of the veracity of the legal basis of their case.

7. The historic dispute concerning whether parties to litigation should be guided in their approach to litigation by the aim of winning (the sporting theory of justice) or by duties to co-operate (the co-operative procedural working group theory) is not particularly helpful in developing a properly operational conception of civil procedure. Both elements, rules of conduct with corresponding duties and competition between the parties in managing their mutual risks are to be accepted as inescapable and essential elements of procedure. There is competition among parties in managing litigation risk, but competition needs rules and must take place within an effective framework of duties that require co-operation with the court and other parties as emphasised by Rule 2 both in the interest of the parties and the wider public interest in the effective management of the justice system, i.e., in the interest of the proper administration of justice. Whereas the management of litigation risk the aim of which is to secure the desired outcome in the proceedings is guided by natural self-assertion and does not therefore need to be provided for by any specific procedural rule, the necessary framework of duties must be elaborated by careful regulation within rules of procedure and by adequate sanction powers to promote compliance. The legal consequences of any lack of effective management by parties of litigation risks are realised by the ultimate determination of the proceedings by the court, and do not therefore need to be subject to any other evaluation. By way of contrast, sanctions for non-compliance with procedural duties may be ordered by the court. They may, however, only be imposed following an evaluation by the court of the party's ability to fulfil the relevant duty carefully and through incurring reasonable cost. To enable parties to manage both litigation risk and compliance with their procedural duties, they must be afforded the right to be heard by the court in respect of their factual, evidential and legal contentions.
8. The parties' general duty of co-operation set out in Rule 2 is further articulated in a number of specific Rules. In so far as the speedy resolution of proceedings is concerned, parties are under a duty to present their case with all relevant factual, evidential and legal elements as early and completely as appropriate (see Rules 47 and 94) and to do so according to the procedural calendar, time table or relevant court orders (see Rules 49(4), 50(1), and 92(1)). The court may impose sanctions on parties who fail to comply with these duties or who fail to do so in a properly timely fashion (see Rules 27, 63, 64(4) sentence 2, 93, and 99). According to another very important duty of co-operation that strengthens the efficiency of fact finding, parties have to grant access to information and evidence that is under their control to their opponent or other parties, even if disclosure of evidence may be adverse to the disclosing party's interest (see Rules 25(2), 54(3) and (4), 88(3), 93, and 100 and following). A refusal to disclose may result in sanctions being imposed if the court is convinced that information or means of evidence are in the party's custody and disclosure is not unreasonable in the circumstances (Rules 27(3) and (4), and 110).
9. The parties' duty to co-operate fairly includes: the duty to avoid unnecessary disputes and costs by providing pre-commencement information and disclosure (Rule 51 with cost sanctions according to Rule 241(2)); the duty to facilitate future or current case management measures (Rules 3(e), 51(3), 61(3)) with cost sanctions in case of non-compliance (Rule 241(2));the duty to preserve means of evidence before and during proceedings (see Rules 99(b) and 27); the duty to exclude illegally obtained evidence in appropriate cases (Rule 90); the duty to guard against breaches of confidentiality in cases of confidential

information or disclosure (Rules 103 and 104); the duty to ensure that claims do not lack a legitimate interest (Rule 133(e)).The parties' duty to co-operate includes taking reasonable steps to settle the dispute, or at the least to settle parts of it (see Rules 3(a), 9, 51, 57 and following). Unlike in some national European laws and the optional provisions of the European Union's Mediation Directive,[3] this duty is not to be construed strictly as a mandatory requirement that results in claims for relief being inadmissible for non-fulfilment of this requirement. It is, on the contrary, a flexible duty to take such steps to settle disputes to which cost sanctions may only be imposed for non-compliance (see Rule 241(2)).

10. See Rule 3, comment 7 on the duty of co-operation as it applies to parties' lawyers.

Rule 3. Role of the parties and their lawyers

Parties and their lawyers must:

(a) take reasonable and appropriate steps to settle disputes amicably;
(b) contribute to the proper management of the proceedings;
(c) present facts and evidence;
(d) assist the court in the determination of the facts and the applicable law;
(e) act in good faith and avoid procedural abuse when dealing with the court and other parties.

Sources:
ALI/Unidroit Principles 11.1 and 11.5.

Comments:

1. Rule 3 gives a concise statement of the activities that must be carried out by parties in the interest of good administration of justice, and further to their duty to co-operate with the court in the proper conduct of proceedings (see Rule 2). It details the distribution of responsibilities between the court and parties (see Rule 4), without differentiating between duties that are to be fulfilled and risks to be managed (see Rule 2, comment 7). Some activities that are necessary for efficient interaction between court and parties are the duties set out in Rule 3(a) and (e)), while those in Rule 3(b)-(d) may be necessary depending on the particular circumstances of specific proceedings.
2. Rule 3(a) corresponds to Rules 9(1), (3) and (4), 51(1) and (2).
3. Rule 3(b) is further specified by Rules 28, 47, 50(1)-(3), 51(3), 55, 57, 58, 59, 61(2), 65(1), 66(1), 71, 88(3), 92(2), 95(2), 101 and following, 113(1), 117(3), 120(3),126(2), 135, 136(1)(c), 141(1), 146(1) and (3).
4. Rule 3(c) emphasises that aspect of the principle of party disposition, which provides that it is for parties to introduce facts and evidence and, that as a general rule it is not for the court to do so. The court's role is, by contrast, to monitor timeous and complete compliance by the party with its responsibilities and, where necessary, suggest amendments (see Rule 2, comment 4). The parties will, generally, be motivated to comply with this responsibility effectively due to the distribution of risks as determined by substantive law concerning the assertion of facts or provision of evidence (see, for details, Rules 24, 25, 52 and

3 Directive 2008/52/EC of the European Parliament and of the Council of 21 May 2008 on certain aspects of mediation in civil and commercial matters.

following, 92(1), 94, and 95). In some cases, however, they have to fulfil duties to produce evidence in the interest of their opponent or other parties, subject to the possibility that sanctions will be imposed for non-compliance (see Rules 25(2), 53(5), 99, 106(1), 101 and following, and 110).

5. Assistance to the court by the parties in determining the facts and applicable law as provided for by Rule 3(d) is not to be interpreted as a duty imposed on the parties, which is subject to the possibility of sanctions for non-compliance. This is because it is for the court to freely evaluate evidence in order to determine factual matters (Rule 98) and the applicable law (Rule 26(2)). The parties, however, run the risk that the court will reach an adverse evaluation of evidence and an unfavourable determination of applicable law, and have the right to be heard by the court prior to it making any such decision (see Rules 11 and 12, 26(1) and(2), 53(2)(c), 64(7)). Rule 3(d) makes it clear that such party contributions are to be understood as a helpful and welcome dialogue between parties and court to be made and accepted in a cooperative atmosphere even in case of controversial arguments.
6. Rule 3(e) articulates the fair co-operation obligation. It corresponds to those provisions noted at Rule 2, comment 9, above.
7. Rule 3, like Rule 2, extends the parties' procedural responsibilities to their lawyers.[4] In some European jurisdictions, civil procedure codes place procedural responsibilities upon lawyers, whereas other jurisdictions implement a clear separation between the parties' procedural responsibilities and professional conduct rules that are imposed on lawyers. On one level this difference is of no substantive effect, as professional conduct rules require lawyers to act in the best interests of their clients, which results in the same commitment of lawyers to procedural rules as is intended by those procedural codes which impose duties on lawyers. One significant difference, however, is that where such duties are imposed by the procedural code, the court may impose sanctions on non-compliant lawyers, without there being a need for professional misconduct proceedings to be brought before the relevant Bar Association or equivalent body. These Rules are drafted so as to enable the court to take steps directly against non-compliant lawyers. Rule 3 corresponds to Rules 9(2), 51, 99, 104, 110, which enable the court together with Rule 27(3) to sanction lawyer misconduct with fines, *astreinte*, costs, or even damage awards in favour of parties or non-parties. In European jurisdictions where this approach is of longstanding it is apparent that the imposition of such sanctions is rarely necessary or exercised. It is debatable whether and how far national and European codes of professional conduct may set limits to lawyers' procedural activities that are not addressed by procedural rules and are the consequence of a lawyer's obligation to serve the interests of justice as an officer of the law. This question is, however, a matter of serious debate in the law of professional conduct and affects all legal processes where lawyers represent parties and not only civil procedure. Its resolution is, therefore, not within the scope of these Rules.

4 Council of Europe, Recommendation No. R(2000)21 of the Committee of Ministers to Member States on the freedom of exercise of the profession of lawyer; Council of Europe Recommendation R (84)5, Principle 2.3; and the Code of Conduct for European Lawyers of the Council of Bars and Law Societies of Europe (CCBE).

Rule 4. Role of the Court – the General Case Management Duty

The court is responsible for active and effective case management. The court must ensure that parties enjoy equal treatment. Throughout proceedings it shall monitor whether parties and their lawyers comply with their responsibilities under these Rules.

Sources:

ALI/UNIDROIT Principles 3, 7.2, 9.3, 14, and 22.2; Transnational Rules of Civil Procedure (Reporters' Study) Rule 18.

Comments:

1. Rule 4 describes the court's general responsibility for active case management. It does so in the broader context of the duty of co-operation required of the court and parties (see Rule 2). This duty imposed on the court is the most important contribution that the court makes in respect of court-party co-operation (see Rule 2, comments 1 and 2). An important precondition for efficient case management is the requirement that the court ensures that it monitors party compliance with their responsibilities throughout the course of proceedings. The general obligation in Rule 4 is substantiated in numerous ways throughout these Rules (see, further, Rule 2, comments 2 to 5, and Rule 3, comment 3). The traditional scholarly differentiation between formal or procedural court management that comprises organisational measures, and material or substantive case management, which is designed to assist the parties in the responsible pursuit of their cases, is not emphasised in these Rules due to the functional interdependence within them of organisational measures and those aimed at assisting the parties, which in many cases serve both traditional purposes (see Rule 49, comment 3).
2. Rule 4 also imposes an express obligation on the court to secure procedural equality between the parties. Party equality in civil procedure is an aspect of the fundamental right of equality before the law and the general prohibition of discrimination in the enjoyment of any legal right.[5] These Rules grant all parties the same procedural rights without illegitimate discrimination, particularly on the basis of nationality, residence, social status or health impediments. Specific rules are intended to prevent discrimination in specific circumstances (see Rules 20, 82, 113 for interpretation and translation; Rules 54(1), 80(3) for time periods; Rules 18(4), 97(1) and (3) for distance communication technologies; Rules 207 and following, 237, 238 enabling the pursuit of claims for damage awards by economically weaker parties in case of mass litigation; Rules 244, 245 facilitating the pursuit of claims for financially weak parties or in case of high cost risks). The obligation to secure equality treatment protects parties from discrimination by partial court management that favours one party over another, e.g., by prohibiting the court from setting procedural time limits with one party only.
3. While some European jurisdictions take the obligation to secure equal treatment to require the court to take active steps to redress procedural imbalances between the parties, such as ensuring they are on an equal footing where one has legal representation and the other party does not, or where the parties' legal representatives are of different skill or ability, these Rules do not go so far. While the court may properly suggest amendments to

5 Arts. 6(1) and 14 and Art. 1 Protocol No. 12 of the European Convention on Human Rights; and Arts. 20, 21 and 47 of the 2000 European Charter of Fundamental Rights.

parties where there are defects in their statements of case or evidence, they may not do so to such an extent that the court becomes, in effect, the party's lawyer. A judge's inability to strike the right balance between correct case management and partisanship may result in disqualification of the judge (see Rule 2, comments 2 and 5).

B. PROPORTIONALITY

Rule 5. Role of the Court

(1) The court must ensure that the dispute resolution process is proportionate.

(2) In determining whether a process is proportionate the court must take account of the nature, importance and complexity of the particular case and of the need to give effect to its general management duty in all proceedings with due regard for the proper administration of justice.

Sources:

ALI/Unidroit Principles 8(1) sentence 2, 17(2); Transnational Rules of Civil Procedure (Reporters' Study) Rule s 17.1, 28.3.

Comments:

1. Rule 5(1) puts particular emphasis on proportionality as a general principle designed to govern the dispute resolution process as a whole. Whereas in most legal cultures proportionality has been accepted as an important aspect of procedural law in specific circumstances only, e.g. for simplified procedures in small claim proceedings,[6] for evidence-taking to ensure that the least complex and least costly method is used, or in determining the means of evidence-taking, such that the less complicated and costly method is used, proportionality in respect of provisional measures, it has become increasingly significant within European and English law since the start of the 21st century. Examples of approaches to proportionality are: the use of written procedures in place of oral hearings; the allocation of proceedings to generic procedural tracks where the process is tailored to the nature, and predominantly value, of the dispute, limitations on evidence-taking, limitations on the length of hearings etc. Specific examples of this type of approach can be seen in England, France, Germany, Norway, with the English approach via Rule 1 of its Civil Procedure Rules containing the most explicit commitment to procedural proportionality as a general principle. Equally, within the European Union there has been a trend towards proportionality in procedure through, for instance, its attempts to increase the utilisation of mediation as a means to resolve disputes (see Rule 51, comment 2).[7] The intention has again been to save resources and costs by furthering party-agreed civil justice consistently with the aims of the influential North American idea of the multi-door courthouse,[8] replacing, in part, lengthy and costly adjudicative procedure.
2. Rule 5 is committed to the trend towards embedding proportionality as a general procedural principle and does so primarily through general rules rather than ones focused

6 The European Small Claims Regulation (the ESC Regulation).

7 See, further, Judgment of 18 March 2010, Alassini and others (C-317/08 to C-320/08, ECR 2010 p. I-2213) ECLI:EU:C:2010:146

8 F. Sander, Varieties of Dispute Processing, 70 F.R.D. 79, 111 (1976).

on individual cases. This commitment is substantiated, to varying degrees, within the following: Rules 9, 10, 49(1), 51, 53(2)(e), 57 and following, 221 and following, 229 and following, and 241(2), which regulate the promotion of settlement and the use of ADR by courts and parties, even though such processes are not, as such, a part of these Rules.

3. These Rules do not provide for defined procedural case tracks, which provide differing processes for proceedings depending on their value, complexity, and expected cost. Such matching of process to proceeding can be made on a case-by-case basis through effective case management (see Rules 49 and 50). Rule 133(e) may, for instance, permit the court in an appropriate case to refuse cost intensive claims for relief where a claim for relief could be pursued for lower cost if it would provide the claimant with equivalent relief. In evidence-taking, the court may, further to Rule 5, suggest the use of a suitably experienced expert to conduct an Expert Evaluation, limit the number of experts or order evidence to be taken through an expert conference (see Rule 62(2)(c)). Also see Rule 102(2)(c), which permits the court, in exceptional circumstances, to restrict the amount of evidence to be taken where it is under the custody of other parties to proceedings or of non-parties. In so far as provisional measures are concerned, Rules 184(2), 185, 197 emphasise proportionality or, similarly, the suitability or necessity of the particular measure. For the significance of proportionality for party activities, sanctions and costs, see Rules 6-8 and the corresponding commentary.

Rule 6. Role of the parties and their lawyers

Parties and their lawyers must co-operate with the court to promote a proportionate dispute resolution process.

Sources:
See Rule 5, above.

Comments:

1. In so far as party activity could contribute to the promotion of a proportionate dispute resolution process by facilitating settlement and ADR, these Rules provide a number of specific, detailed, provisions that give effect to the general obligation articulated in Rule 6, e.g., Rules 9, 26(3), 51(1) and (2), 57 and following, 221 and following, and 229 and following. The only applicable sanction for a lack of willingness to fulfil these duties concerning settlement are cost sanctions (see Rules 240(1)(a) and (c), and 241(2)).
2. Parties and their lawyers may not always be convinced of the court's proposals to agree on measures that may save costs and personal resources (see Rule 5, comment 3). Refusal may, however, result in cost sanctions (see Rule 241(2)). In serious cases, fines and *astreinte* or claims against lawyers for professional malpractice may, however, be imposed or arise.

Rule 7. Proportionality of sanctions

Sanctions for breach of any of the rules must be proportionate to the seriousness of the matter involved and the harm caused and reflect the extent of participation and the degree to which the conduct was deliberate.

Sources:
ALI/UNIDROIT Principle 17(2); Transnational Rules of Civil Procedure (Reporters' Study) Rule 17.1.

Comments:

1. It is a common principle of all legal cultures based on the rule of law that public power encroaching on liberties has to be exercised in strict accordance with the fundamental principle of proportionality. This is now encapsulated, for instance, in Article 5(4) of the 2012 Treaty on European Union and Article 49(3) of the 2000 European Charter of Fundamental Rights. It is equally implicit in Article 6 of the 1950 European Convention on Human Rights and European national constitutions. As such it cannot but be the case that the principle of proportionality also applies to sanctions ordered by courts. Rule 7 provides a concise enumeration of the most important criteria to be considered when sanctions are to be imposed on parties, lawyers, non-parties etc.
2. In appropriate cases, specific Rules refer to, modify or substantiate this fundamental principle; see, for instance, Rules 27, 28, 63(1) and (2), 64(4), 90, 93, 99, 104, 110, 178, 191, 195(3), 218(1)(a) and (2), 241(2), and 245(4).

Rule 8. Proportionality of costs

Costs of proceedings should, in so far as possible, be reasonable and proportionate to the amount in dispute, the nature and complexity of the particular proceedings, their importance for the parties and the public interest.

Sources:

See Rule 5, above.

Comments:

1. Rule 8 summarises the criteria that define proportionality of costs. It makes it clear that the amount in dispute cannot be the sole, decisive, criterion determinative of the appropriate and desirable level of costs incurred in prosecuting civil proceedings limits. To limit costs by the amount in dispute would result in injustice, as it would preclude citizens with limited financial resources from availing themselves of the regular civil process in cases of major significance for their daily lives. The same can be said for public interest litigation, which may concern a small amount that is in dispute but is of wide public importance. In such cases, those wider factors, amongst others, can properly justify the parties incurring a higher level of costs than an assessment based purely on the dispute's financial value might justify.
2. It is primarily up to the parties and their lawyers to avoid disproportionate costs. They should do so by attempting to settle their disputes in whole or in part (see Rule 5, comment 3 and Rule 6, comment 1). Unreasonable or disproportionate costs are not subject to reimbursement by the losing party (Rule 240(1)(a) and (c)). This limitation on the European (loser-pays) costs rule ought properly to motivate parties so that they, and their lawyers, avoid incurring unnecessary litigation costs. Possible cost sanctions, fines or *astreinte* as well as potential claims for damages may also operate to motivate lawyers to comply with their professional duties. The benefit of such a deterrent effect should not, however, be overestimated (see Rule 3, comment 7, Rule 6, comment 2 and Rule 27(3) and (4)). The court must itself take an active role in assisting the parties in their efforts to keep litigation costs proportionate. It may do so, for instance, by making appropriate proposals for the effective management of the claim by the parties and their lawyers (see Rule 5, comment 3).

C. SETTLEMENT

Rule 9. Role of the parties and their lawyers

(1) Parties must co-operate in seeking to resolve their dispute consensually, both before and after proceedings begin.

(2) Lawyers must inform the parties about the availability of consensual dispute resolution methods, assist them in selecting the most suitable method, and, where appropriate, encourage its use. They must ensure that they use any mandatory method.

(3) Parties may ask the court to render a settlement agreement enforceable.

(4) When a consensual settlement as a whole cannot be reached, parties must take all reasonable opportunities to reduce the number of contested issues prior to adjudication.

Sources:

ALI/UNIDROIT Principles 7.2, 24.3.

Comments:

1. Rule 9(1) states the general duty of parties to co-operate with each other in order to resolve their dispute consensually. This duty has developed into a common European standard over the last two decades (see Rule 5, comments 1 and 2, Rule 51, comment 2), and can be traced to the duty not to mis-use procedure identified by Council of Europe Recommendation R(84)5, principle 2(2-3). The duty to seek to resolve disputes, either in whole or in part, consensually during the pre-commencement phase is further articulated in Rule 51. In the event that settlement is not possible, the parties are encouraged to, at least, attempt to reduce the issues in dispute prior to adjudication (see Rules 26(3) and 57 and following).
2. Rule 9(2) describes the professional duty placed on lawyers, which requires them to inform parties about available alternative dispute resolution methods and to assist them in choosing the method most appropriate to their dispute. Within the European Union, this can be facilitated for consumer disputes through the application of the ADR Directive as implemented by national legislation, as it requires the mandatory provision of ADR procedures and promotes the creation of ADR providers.[9] Consequently, information on ADR is readily available to both parties and lawyers. Whether or not pre-commencement ADR is mandatory, and hence a question of the admissibility of proceedings, is a matter for national legislation in European jurisdictions (see Rule 133(f)).[10] An increasing number of European jurisdictions have, however, made some form of pre-commencement ADR, usually mediation, mandatory, e.g., Italy. Other jurisdictions have promoted its use pre-commencement through the use of cost sanctions where a party has unreasonably refused to engage in ADR, e.g., England (see Rule 241(2)). In other European jurisdictions, which take a more liberal understanding of the position of future parties to litigation, participation in ADR proceedings remains clearly voluntary. Whichever approach is taken at a national level, it ought always to be made clear to parties that notwithstanding the degree of compulsion to take part in ADR, except where they have voluntarily agreed to resolve their dispute via arbitration, whether or not they settle their dispute via ADR is entirely a

9 See Art. 5 and following and 13 and following of the ADR Directive.

10 As recognised within the European Union by Art. 5(2) of the Mediation Directive.

matter of choice. Mandatory ADR must not be misunderstood to mean mandatory settlement.[11] Costs sanctions should not be conceived as, nor are they intended to operate as, a means to reduce this commitment to voluntariness in reaching settlement. National courts ought therefore to be careful to avoid considering the use of costs sanctions as a fetter on the right of access to justice.

3. The professional obligation of lawyers to encourage parties to use ADR (Rule 9(2)) only concerns cases where its use is appropriate. ADR's use should not therefore be encouraged where it would clearly result in unnecessary time and expense, or in cases where ADR would not be appropriate, e.g., where the dispute concerns a novel legal question, where criminality is alleged as part of the civil proceedings. In those European jurisdictions where the use of ADR is mandatory, the party's lawyer must ensure they are given robust advice concerning their participation to ensure that they use the process properly (Rule 9(2)). In appearing their client is free, however, to explain why they may not be willing or able to resolve the dispute via the ADR method.
4. Rule 9(3) is intended to facilitate the enforcement of settlements. Rule 141 supplements Rule 9(3).
5. Rule 9(4) encourages parties to reach agreement on individual issues in dispute if attempts to resolve the dispute fully are unsuccessful. Rules 26(3), 51, and 57 and following give concrete effect to Rule 9(4). Additionally, they detail the approach to take to party-agreed court proceedings, which are based on the settlement of individual issues.

Rule 10. Role of the Court

(1) The court must facilitate settlement at any stage of the proceedings. Particularly, it must ensure that the parties consider settlement in the preparatory stage of proceedings and at case management conferences. If necessary for furthering the settlement process, it may order the parties to appear before it in person.

(2) The court must inform the parties about the availability of different types of settlement methods. It may suggest or recommend the use of specific consensual dispute resolution methods.

(3) The court may participate in settlement attempts and assist the parties in reaching a consensual resolution. It may also assist in drafting settlement agreements.

(4) Where a judge mediates during a settlement process and receives information in the absence of one of the parties, that judge must not decide the case.

Sources:

ALI/UNIDROIT Principles 24.1 and 24.2.

Comments:

1. Rule 10(1) emphasises the need for parties to maintain their efforts to settle their dispute with the court's assistance throughout the course of proceedings. It is evident the possibility of settlement may increase during proceedings, as much as it may decrease, depending on the particular circumstances. It may increase, for instance, through the court providing an Early Neutral Evaluation during the preparatory phase of the case management hearing (see Rule 61). It could, equally, increase following the parties' evaluating their respective claims upon early disclosure and evidence-taking (see Rules 49(1), (8),

11 *Ibid.*

(9), (11), and 62). Rule 10(1) properly specifies the court's power to summon the party in person to appear before it in order to facilitate settlement (see Rules 16(2), and 49(10)).

2. Rule 10(2) substantiates the court's duty to provide the parties with information concerning available ADR methods.[12] This duty complements that imposed upon lawyers' obligation (Rule 9, comment 2). Suggestions by the court may, sometimes, conflict with those made by the parties' lawyers. In such a case the judge should be careful not to come between party and lawyer, so as to avoid giving the perception of bias such as to result in their being disqualified from continued involvement in the proceedings. Judicial pressure to settle must be avoided, and Rule 10(2) must be read accordingly. The court must at all times be mindful of the fact that it is a parties' right to settle their dispute and never an obligation to settle. Parties should not, therefore, be prevented from exercising their right of access to the judicial system.[13]
3. Rule 10(3) permits judges to participate actively in settlement endeavours. Some European jurisdictions have traditionally not permitted judges to take such a role. This has particularly been the case in those jurisdictions where the traditional legal culture has been one that has favoured the concept of the passive judge, and continue to favour the use of out-of-court ADR providers so as to maintain judicial neutrality by not providing judges with a dual adjudicative and non-adjudicative role. Other European jurisdictions, those with a tradition of a more active judiciary, are however more accustomed to such a dialogical interaction between judges and parties as well as to the open exchange of argument concerning settlement. This latter approach may consider a rights-based settlement proposal a logical result on the road to justice. Where this is the case, applications to disqualify judges on the basis of a lack of neutrality are rare where the judge does not diverge from a fair discussion of arguments to come to a rights-based solution by judgment or settlement. It should be noted, of course that rights-based settlement is not the only form of settlement that may be reached, and that settlement is often interest-based. Within these Rules, Rule 10(3) seeks to strengthen the trend towards judicial involvement in settlement endeavours, while providing discretion as to how best to achieve this to the particular circumstances such that both traditional models can be incorporated. As such the trend towards approximation furthered by the procedural practice of international arbitral tribunals with arbitrators from differing cultures and with differing experiences is accommodated within the Rules.[14]
4. Rule 10(4) sets necessary and clear limits to judicial mediation. It does so where it becomes evident that there is a conflict between the judicial, adjudicative, function and that of facilitating mediation. As such it forbids judges who take part in private caucusing during judicial mediation from continuing involvement with the proceedings should the mediation not result in a settlement. Such private caucusing is incompatible with the right to be heard (see Rules 11 to 13), which does not permit parties to engage in private communication with judges. Such a restriction is commonly accepted and accords with both national European practice concerning ADR, such as that of England concerning judge-led Early Neutral Evaluation, and that of the European Union, as provided for in Article 3(a) and 7(1) of the Mediation Directive.

12 Also see Art. 5(1) of the Mediation Directive.

13 Also see Art. 5(2) of the Mediation Directive.

14 Also Art. 3(a) of the Mediation Directive.

D. RIGHT TO BE HEARD

Rule 11. Fair opportunity to present claim and defence

The court must manage proceedings to ensure that parties have a fair opportunity to present their case and evidence, to respond to their respective claims and defences and to any court orders or matters raised by the court.

Sources:
ALI/Unidroit Principles 5 and 22.

Comments:

1. The right to be heard articulated in Rule 11 is a very old or even ancient procedural principle (*audiatur et altera pars, audi alteram partem*). It is a constitutive element of procedural justice. Its fundamental importance has become indisputable, both as a matter of historic and modern practice. It is recognised as an essential part of fair proceedings as guaranteed by international conventions, especially Article 6(1) of the European Convention on Human Rights and the second paragraph of Article 47 of the European Charter of Fundamental Rights. Rule 11 summarises the most valuable manifestations of this fundamental right as it applies to civil proceedings. Moreover, it makes clear that the right to be heard is not only a right of the parties to be exercised upon their own initiative but is also something that must be facilitated ("ensured") by active court management carried out in the interests of justice. Parties to litigation must be given a fair opportunity to take notice of all aspects of court process concerning their proceedings, whether that concerns procedural steps taken by other parties, of witnesses, experts and relevant non-parties. The court must ensure that parties have sufficient opportunity to make submissions concerning such matters.
2. Rule 11 is complemented by numerous other Rules that give effect to the right to be heard in specific situations, while ensuring that its importance cannot be overlooked by the court: see Rules 24(3), 26(2), 28, 41(1), 50(1), 64(7), 92(2) and (4), 93, 96, 107(2), 186, and 201(3).
3. Rule 11 is complemented by special rules that articulate the court's duty to ensure compliance with the right to be heard. Rule 12 substantiates the right to be heard by the court before it makes decisions in proceedings. Rule 13 articulates the prohibition on private communications between the court and parties, and makes provision to cure breaches of that prohibition. Rule 20 makes the court responsible for interpretation and translation in those cases where a party, witness or non-party either does not understand the language of the proceedings or needs assistance due to, for instance, a hearing or speech impediment, to participate in the proceedings effectively. In respect of pleadings, Rules 52 and following, and service of process and information between parties, Rules 68 and following contain the core elements of the right to be heard, concerning which the court is either directly responsible or is under a duty to monitor party compliance (see Rules 4(3), 48, and 71).
4. Rule 11 should be interpreted and applied consistently with the court's general duty of co-operation (see Rule 2, comment 2), as furthering the dialogue between court and parties is a necessary precondition for effective co-operation.
5. The right to be heard in person rather than via legal representation in Rule 16 is a specific manifestation of the right to be heard.

Rule 12. Basis of Court Decisions

(1) **In reaching any decision in proceedings the court must consider all factual, evidential, and legal issues advanced by the parties. Court decisions must specifically set out their reasoning concerning substantial issues.**
(2) **The court must not base its decisions on issues that parties have not had an opportunity to address.**

Sources:
ALI/Unidroit Principles 5.6, 16.6, 22.1 and 23.2; Transnational Rules of Civil Procedure (Reporters' Study) Rules 28.2 and 31.2.

Comments:

1. Rule 12(1) makes it clear that providing the parties with a fair opportunity to present their cases completely, does not exhaust the scope and content of the right to be heard, which in Europe is accepted as being an essential part of the fundamental right to fair trial (see Rule 11, comment 1). A fair trial process also requires the court to genuinely take account of the parties' arguments and contentions in formulating its decision. Judicial consideration of pleadings, facts, evidence and legal argument underpins the formation of a judge's internal conviction concerning factual findings (see Rule 98 regarding evaluation of evidence) and legal conclusions, and that they are in accordance with the law, and that they are just and fair. As this is an internal mental process, it is not possible to fully control or document a judge's legal reasoning. However, judges are under an obligation to explain the reasoning in their judgments. This process not only provides an explanation to the parties why they either succeeded or failed in their claims or defences, but it also acts as a means to minimise the possibility that judges may determine cases in an arbitrary or unjustified manner. It also forms the means by which appeals can be founded, while it generally provides a means by which the operation of the justice system can be properly scrutinised by the public. This is the purpose of Rule 12(1).
2. According to the second sentence in Rule 12(1) judicial decisions must address the parties' factual, evidential and legal contentions. In so far as possible, parties must be able to control whether the court properly considered their arguments to be satisfied that none of their relevant factual allegations and means of evidence were overlooked or otherwise not taken account of by the court. Not all arguments put forward by parties may be substantial enough to warrant detailed or serious consideration by the court. This is particularly the case where parties, in long and detailed pleadings, set out arguments and issues that are of minor or no real significance to the determination of the dispute. To avoid any unnecessary discussions of points or issues that evidently lack relevance, this Rule limits the court's duty to give reasons (also known as motivation) for its decisions to those substantial issues that are reasonably in dispute. This limitation is consistent with the general principle of proportionality of the dispute resolution process (see Rule 5). The European Court of Justice has stressed the importance of giving reasons for decisions as being a part of the fundamental right enshrined in Article 47(2) of the European Charter of Fundamental Rights and Article 6(1) of the European Convention on Human Rights (also see Rule 11, comment 1).[15] Rule 12(1) provides leeway for national jurisdictions to develop and/or

15 ECJ, Judgment of 6 September 2012, Trade Agency, C-619/10, ECLI:EU:C:2012:531, para 52; for the European Convention on Human Rights see ECJ, Judgment of 14 December 2006, ASML (C-283/05, ECR 2006 p. I-12041) ECLI:EU:C:2006:787, para 28.

maintain differing domestic practices concerning the giving of reasons for decisions. In some jurisdictions the decision is first given, frequently orally, with written reasons given later and in writing. In other European jurisdictions, the court's decision and explanation are given together. Ordinarily reasons for decisions should be given in written form in order to enable a party that wishes to appeal from the decision to do so effectively. *Lex fori* may provide that the parties can waive their right to receive a reasoned judgment, although care should be taken to ensure that the public's right to open justice is not improperly compromised by such a waive. Where such waiver can be effected it may be explicit or by conduct (see, e.g., Rule 154, agreement of all parties not to appeal).

3. The practice in many jurisdictions is that important interim decisions, e.g., the grant of an important interim injunction concerning the substance of the case, should also involve evidential and legal reasoning. The requirement contained in Rule 12(1) should equally apply to situations where the court's determination of ultimate issues may be split and dealt with separately, e.g., liability and quantum (see Rules 66, and 130(1)(d)). From a different point of view, some jurisdictions do not require certain specific judgments to be reasoned. This may be the case with default judgments, although that is not to say, as the European Court of Justice held in the Trade Agency case, that some assessment of the overall proceedings in such cases may be justified. As it put it, "*(. . .) the courts of the Member State in which enforcement is sought may refuse to enforce a judgment given in default of appearance which disposes of the substance of the dispute but which does not contain an assessment of the subject-matter or the basis of the action and which lacks any argument of its merits, only if it appears to the court, after an overall assessment of the proceedings and in the light of all the relevant circumstances, that that judgment is a manifest and disproportionate breach of the defendant's right to a fair trial referred to in the second paragraph of Article 47 of the Charter, on account of the impossibility of bringing an appropriate and effective appeal against it*"[16].
4. Rule 12(2) concerns an important core element of the right to be heard. It substantiates Rule 11 in so far as that rule requires parties to be provided a fair opportunity to respond to "matters raised by the court". Rule 12(2) typically concerns the introduction of new facts, evidence, or legal arguments by the court without any prior notice to them or opportunity to be heard. In practice this may occur if the court takes contested facts as being notorious (taking judicial notice of publicly well-known matters, see Rule 88(1)(c)) without giving prior notice to the parties that it intends to do so, if the court takes a document from parallel proceedings as a basis of evidence concerning contested facts without the parties being able to comment previously, or if the court takes the most recent judgment of a higher court as the legal basis for its decision without the parties being afforded an opportunity to make submissions. Another group of cases is more difficult to be determined if, in making its decision, the court goes back to factual, evidential or legal contentions contained or mentioned in the pleadings but which were not addressed in the hearings by the parties or the court. In this or similar situations the parties had an opportunity to make submissions, but the question may be whether there was a fair opportunity for them do so (see Rule 11). Rule 12(2) should be interpreted in the light of Rules 2, 4 sentence 1, and 11. A consequence of not providing the parties with an opportunity to make submissions on such issues before the court reaches its decision, may result in the parties seeking to reopen

16 *Ibid.*

the proceedings. Parties should therefore, at the least, be given an opportunity to make submissions, even if they are only made in written form, before a decision is reached.

5. It must be emphasised that the fundamental importance of the right to receive a properly reasoned decision is not just a matter of private interest for parties to litigation. Transparency in the delivery of open justice, through the public promulgation of reasoned judgments is an essential underpinning for the public acceptance of judicial decisions, public confidence in the justice system and the rule of law.

Rule 13. Communications with the Court

(1) The court must not communicate with a party in the absence of other parties. This prohibition does not apply to without-notice proceedings or to routine procedural administration.

(2) All communications by parties with the court must be provided to all other parties at the time when they are made to the court.

(3) When the court becomes aware of a failure to comply with the requirement in Rule 13(2), it must promptly provide the parties with the content of the communication.

Sources:

ALI/UNIDROIT Principles 1.4, 8.2; Transnational Rules of Civil Procedure (Reporters' Study) Rules 7.3, 10.4, and 17.2.

Comments:

1. Rule 13(1) prohibits parties' communication with the court privately, i.e., in the absence of other parties. This prohibition is not only a consequence of the right to be heard, which includes the right of parties to attend oral court hearings, hearings for evidence-taking as well as telephone- and video-conferences that replace oral hearings in the judge's presence in a court room. It equally follows from the requirement that courts are impartial and are seen to be impartial (see Article 6(1) of the European Convention on Human Rights, and Article 47(2) of the European Charter of Fundamental Rights). Where a party is able to communicate in private or in confidence with the court, to the exclusion of other parties, it may tend to undermine the appearance of impartiality, just as it undermines the other party's ability to exercise their right to be heard. Where such private communications occur, it may result in a judge's disqualification for bias. The prohibition requires emphasis at a time when private communications (caucusing) between parties and, for instance, mediators is commonplace. While such conduct may be perfectly permissible in such means to further settlement, Rule 13(1) makes it clear that such caucusing is not permitted for judges in the course of civil proceedings. Moreover, Rule 10(4) prohibits judges who engage in such caucusing where they receive information from the parties in private and in confidence whilst the conduct settlement processes results in the disqualification from further conduct of any civil proceedings concerning those parties if the dispute does not settle (see Rule 10, comment 4).
2. Rule 13(1) makes it clear that the prohibition concerning without-notice (*ex parte*) proceedings does not apply to such proceedings that are regulated by Rules concerning provisional measures, where urgency is required and notice would undermine the proper administration of justice. In such cases the absence of notice is rectified by the possibility of a late on-notice (*inter partes*) hearing (see Rule 186). Another exception to the general rule, concerns routine procedural administration, e.g. communication by phone or spontaneous oral communication in the court building concerning the organisation and timing

of hearings or evidence taking. This exception should be construed narrowly. Care must be taken to ensure that such administrative communications are not permitted to stray into matters of substance concerning the dispute.

3. Rule 13(2) establishes the parties' duty to provide any information provided to the court to all other parties at the same time as it is given to the court. This can be achieved directly by sending the communication to the court and other parties simultaneously, or indirectly by sending a copy following direction by the court (see Rule 71, comments 1 and 2 on responsibility for service).
4. Rule 13(3) emphasises the court's responsibility to correct defects in compliance with Rules 13(1) and (2). It corresponds to Rules 4 sentence 3 and 48, which establish the court's duty to monitor the parties' timely compliance with these Rules and to seek any necessary amendment (see Rules 4 sentence 1, 47, 49(9), 13(2)).

E. REPRESENTATION AND ASSISTANCE

Rule 14. Self-representation and mandatory representation

Except when legal representation is required by law, parties have a right to represent themselves in proceeding.

Sources:
ALI/UNIDROIT Principle 4.

Comments:

1. Rule 14 articulates the right to self-representation as a general rule, with mandatory legal representation the exception. This approach is taken due to the varying practice across European jurisdictions, while leaving it to national law to determine the question whether the right of parties to represent themselves ought properly to be circumscribed in the interests of the administration of justice. This approach will enable those European jurisdictions where compulsory legal representation is long established either at first instance or in appellate jurisdictions, to maintain that approach. It will also enable those countries, such as common law jurisdictions, that place specific weight on the right of self-representation as a fundamental aspect of party autonomy to maintain such a commitment. These Rules generally do not interfere with national traditions of representation in courts that at least in part, have deeply rooted differing understandings of the position of citizens and their relationship to State authority.
2. According to these Rules, in first appeal courts the court determines whether legal representation is necessary in the light of the party's ability to argue their appeal effectively taking account of the legal issues and difficulty of the case (see Rule 164(1)). In principle, however, representation is not considered to be mandatory in either first instance or first appeal courts. It is only in second appeal courts that these Rules require mandatory legal representation (see Rule 164(2)). In practice, parties frequently prefer to engage lawyers to represent them, even where there is no legal requirement to that effect. Representation may, of course, depend upon available financial resources, and in some cases may be a question of the quality of legal aid or other kinds of funding, which varies across Europe (see Rules 244 and 245). The question of whether or not representation should be mandatory should not be given greater weight than the more fundamental question of ensuring

that effective means of litigation funding should be available to enable parties to finance meritorious claims, including financing legal representation.

3. Self-representation requires a natural person's capacity to exercise rights in civil proceedings (see Rule 30). Legal persons must be represented by such natural persons who are entitled to represent them according to the applicable substantive law (see Rule 31). Whether in-house lawyers are permitted to represent their employers, where they are legal persons, depends upon the applicable legal professional rules of conduct.

Rule 15. Representation and assistance in Court

(1) Parties may engage a lawyer of their own choice. They may do so both when they choose to be, and when they are required by law to be, represented by a lawyer. This right includes the right to representation by a lawyer admitted to practice in the forum and to receive active assistance before the court from a lawyer admitted to practice elsewhere.

(2) Parties may, where the law permits it, be represented or assisted in court by an individual or organisation other than a lawyer.

(3) When representing or assisting a party the court must respect a lawyer's professional independence. This includes ensuring that lawyers are able to fulfil their duty of loyalty to their client and maintain client confidentiality.

Sources:

ALI/UNIDROIT Principle 4.

Comments:

1. Rule 15(1) states the parties' right to engage a lawyer of their own choice. This right is protected by European national constitutions, Article 6(1) and 6(3) of the European Convention on Human Rights, the latter of which refers to its existence in respect of criminal proceedings without any prejudice to it being part of the general fair trial guarantee. It is also recognised in Article 47(2) of the European Charter of Fundamental Rights. It is additionally affirmed by Article 15(1) of the European Charter of Fundamental Rights, which protects the freedom to exercise a profession, including a lawyer's freedom to conclude contracts with clients which would be illusionary without the corresponding right of parties to engage a lawyer of their own choice.
2. Rule 15(1) also clarifies that a party's right to engage a lawyer of their own choice applies where legal representation is optional and when it is mandatory. If a party is unable to find a lawyer of their own choice where representation is mandatory either generally or in a specific circumstance (see Rule 164(1) and (2)), it is a matter for national professional conduct rules to make provision for the court, following party consultation, to determine which lawyer is to represent the party. Where a party lacks resources sufficient to enable them to be represented by a lawyer, legal aid should be available (see Rule 14, comment 2).
3. Finally, Rule 15(1) specifies that party choice of legal representation is limited to those lawyers who are admitted to practice in the forum. Within the European Union, choice of lawyer may extend to lawyers from one Member State registered to practice in another Member State further to Articles 2–9 of Directive 98/5/EC and national legislation and profession rules implementing free movement of lawyers within the Union.[17] Rule 15(1)

17 Directive 98/5/EC of the European Parliament and of the Council of 16 February 1998 to facilitate practice of the profession of lawyer on a permanent basis in a Member State other than that in which the qualification was obtained.

also provides for the possibility that lawyers admitted to practice in a foreign jurisdiction may actively assist in proceedings. Such assistance may be permitted further to European Union law[18] or in accordance with national provisions, such as those in common law jurisdictions where the court may authorise such assistance on a case-by-case basis. Active assistance means that the assisting lawyer is permitted to argue before the court in conjunction with a lawyer practising in the jurisdiction. Such assistance is, where necessary, subject to control by the court, i.e., it may be limited or revoked in the event of abusive conduct by the lawyer. Where active assistance is permitted, responsibility for presenting the case remains with the lawyer admitted to practice in the jurisdiction. This is particularly important where the two lawyers have differing opinions on how to prosecute the proceedings. Such divergence is, however, rare in practice.

4. Rule 15(2) takes into account differing approaches across European jurisdictions as to the extent to which the provision of legal representation is restricted to lawyers. While the European Union recognises that the provision of a monopoly in respect of representation before courts by lawyers is justified by the public interest in the administration of justice,[19] European jurisdictions take differing approaches to the extent to which such a monopoly should apply. Some European jurisdictions provide generous exceptions to such a monopoly to licenced associations, officers of public bodies, or in-house lawyers. It should be noted that in part such exceptions differ little, in practice, from the power to permit legal persons to be self-represented (see Rule 14, comment 3). Rule 15(2) takes a very liberal approach to this issue. It maintains the approach taken by national European traditions.
5. Rule 15(3) addresses possible conflicts between a lawyer's duties to co-operate with the court and other parties and their lawyers, and the professional duties they owe to their clients, e.g., their duty of loyalty to their client and their duty to maintain confidentiality. The Rule deliberately emphasises the requirement that courts are to respect lawyers' professional independence, with particular reference to the duty of loyalty and confidentiality. In this way it emphasises their importance where any conflict may arise with the duty of co-operation. Such conflicts may, particularly, arise where the duty to co-operate is inconsistent with the client's interests, e.g., where there is a conflict between the party's desire to limit the time and expense of pursuing their claim and the court's promotion of settlement, which may result in an increase in the delay in the court's determination of the claim. Such conflicts between procedural duties to co-operate (see Rules 5 and following, 9 and following, 51, and 57 and following) and the professional duties of loyalty and confidentiality may require lawyers to determine the priority to be given to the respective duties. This may result in precedence being given the professional duties in order to promote the best interests of their client, even where that may result in the duty to co-operate being breached with the possibility of sanctions being imposed in respect of the breach. While it would be advisable for national codes of professional conduct to address such conflicts, generally they do not. An example of a well-developed approach is that set out in the US Model

18 See Art. 5(2) of Council Directive 77/249/EEC of 22 March 1977 to facilitate the effective exercise by lawyers of freedom to provide services, and Art. 5(3) of Directive 98/5/EC.

19 See Art. 56 of the 2012 Treaty on the Functioning of the European Union, Directives 98/5/EC and 77/249/EC.

Rules of Professional Conduct,[20] which require lawyers to try to serve their client's interests in priority to procedural best practice, subject to clear limits concerning participation in criminal or otherwise clearly illegal activities. As noted above, courts are well-aware of the potential for such conflicts to arise and the difficult position in which they place lawyers. As such their resort to the use of sanctions for breaches of procedural rules in such circumstances is minimal (see Rule 3, comment 7). These Rules do not determine details of professional conduct, although comment on the limit to duty of co-operation of lawyers in respect of lawyers' professional duties is necessary.

Rule 16. Hearing Parties

(1) Parties have the right to be heard in person by the court.

(2) The court may always hear parties in person.

Comments:

1. The right of parties to be heard by the court in person is extant in the majority of European jurisdictions. The right to be heard in person embraces the right to argue in court as well as the right to give evidence in person. Both kinds of contributions need to be considered separately regarding purpose, contents, and form.
2. The right to give evidence in person is the means through which a party is able to give testamentary factual evidence according to their own perception (see Rules 118 and 114(3)). In some jurisdictions parties can be called as witnesses and rules on taking witness evidence apply. Other jurisdictions permit party examination or the old–fashioned party oath on specified facts only upon the application of the opposing party. Rule 118 permits party examination upon the application of any party and rules on taking witness evidence apply, albeit the power to sanction a party for refusing to give evidence is limited to drawing relevant inferences, which are generally adverse to a party's case (see Rule 118 and comments).
3. A party's right to argue in person is self-evident in so far as self-representation is permitted (see Rule 14, comment 1) because the two rights coincide. Where legal representation is mandatory a conflict may, however, arise between the activities of the lawyer and the party in person. Regular procedural applications cannot be made by a party in person, as that would be inconsistent with the aim of mandatory representation, i.e., the aim of reducing the prospect of procedural error or misconduct. Where there is any divergence between matters put before the court by a party and their lawyer, the court must seek clarification from them. The court must also seek clarification in cases where there is a gap in information provided to it or any misunderstanding that may arise during the preparatory stage of proceedings (see Rule 49(9)). If the party doubts the correctness and skill of their lawyer's procedural applications or their legal contentions the court may, in so far as reasonable, ask the lawyer to reconsider their approach. The court must, however, accept the lawyer's decision on the contents of procedural applications as final, and should avoid taking any steps that might damage the relationship of trust and confidence between a party and their lawyer. Some procedural systems developed special rules for diverging factual contentions. These Rules leave it to the courts' practice to resolve such details as well as the consequences of any such divergence in cases of non-mandatory representation. The court

20 Rule 1(2)(a) of the Model Rules of Professional Conduct <https://www.americanbar.org/groups/professional_responsibility/publications/model_rules_of_professional_conduct/rule_1_2_scope_of_representation_allocation_of_authority_between_client_lawyer/>.

should, however, always take steps to clarify whether factual contentions based on a party's own perception are designed to give evidence by party examination or only to contribute to factual contentions (see Rule 49(11)).The court should not accord evidential effect to factual contentions made outside proceedings regulated by Rule 118. The right to argue in person includes the right to attend in person hearings intended to promote settlement as well as the right to contribute in person to settlement discussions.

4. The right of a party to be heard by the court in person contrasts with the tradition of continental learned procedure and procedure which it influenced, which did not permit parties to have such personal access to judges who were to decide their claims in order to avoid personal influence of the parties on judges and their decision-making. As a consequence of the enlightenment and reforms following the French Revolution, an individual's right of personal access to the court developed as the predominate approach to the delivery of civil justice. This right of personal access is now recognised as an aspect of the right to fair trial guaranteed by Article 6(1) and (3) of the European Convention on Human Rights and Article 47(2) of the European Charter of Fundamental Rights. This does not mean, however, that personal access must be granted in each instance of civil proceedings, as with the right to an oral hearing it does not apply to the entirety of proceedings. Wherever there is a right to an oral hearing the right to be heard in person applies.
5. The right of a party to be heard in person (Rule 16(1)) corresponds to the court's power to hear a party in person and to require a party's appearance in person (see Rules 16(2) and 49(10)). Like the right to be heard in person, hearing a party upon a court order may be designed to facilitate their arguments or contentions to be heard by the court or to facilitate evidence-taking via a party-examination (see Rule 118). Parties are also often ordered to appear in person in order to facilitate settlement endeavours (see Rule 49(1) and (10)).

F. ORAL, WRITTEN AND PUBLIC PROCEEDINGS

Rule 17. Public proceedings

(1) Hearings and court decisions, including their reasoning, must, as a general rule, be public.

(2) The court may order the proceedings, or parts thereof, especially oral hearings and the taking of evidence, to be in private (in camera) for reasons of public policy, including national security, privacy, or professional secrets, including business confidentiality, or in the interests of the administration of justice. Where necessary the court may make suitable protective orders to maintain the privacy or confidentiality of hearings held or evidence taken in private.

(3) Judgments and their reasoning shall be accessible to the public to the extent that proceedings are open to the public. When hearings have been in private, publicity of the judgment may be limited to its operative part.

(4) Court files and records shall be publicly accessible at least to persons with a legal interest in them and to those making a legitimate inquiry.

(5) The identity of parties, witnesses and other natural persons mentioned in the judgment may be private where strictly necessary.

Sources:

ALI/UNIDROIT Principles 20.1, 20.3 and 22.3; Transnational Rules of Civil Procedure (Reporters' Study) Rules 24.1, 24.2, 24.3., 24.5, 24.6, 24.7, and 30.2.

Comments:

1. Rule 17(1) formalises the principle of publicity, or open justice. That civil proceedings, including hearings and judgments, are held in public is a fundamental principle recognised and practiced in all developed procedural cultures. It is a constitutive element of democracy that citizens should be able to exercise a minimum of control over all aspects of State power, legislation, public administration, and administration of justice by the judiciary. Public justice is the means by which democratic accountability of the civil justice system is maintained. It ensures that the public, the media and Parliaments are provided with sufficient information to enable them to engage in a fair, informed and competent discussion of court proceedings. Such transparency is required in order to secure the stability and effective functioning of democracies, and particularly to secure the rule of law. The principle of publicity is thus guaranteed by both Articles 6(1) and 8 of the European Convention on Human Rights, and by Article 47(2) of the European Charter of Fundamental Rights, as well as European national constitutional commitments to the rule of law. In the main, publicity is realised via media access and scrutiny of the courts, evidence-taking and judicial decisions. Increasing digitisation of proceedings may contribute to the direct provision of publicity to the public via increasing use of video-conferencing, distance communication technology or live-broadcasting of proceedings, although such matters may be limited in order to secure the privacy of parties and witnesses (see below comment 3; also see Storme Report, Article 6; Article 8(1) of the IBA Rules on the Taking of Evidence in International Arbitration (2010)).
2. It should be noted that the principle of publicity or of open justice is not simply a right of parties. It is a public right. Restrictions upon it ought not, therefore, to be permitted by party consent, except in so far as the public interest conditions provided for in Rule 17(2) are satisfied (also see Rules 26(3), 57 and following, particularly Rule 58). In this, civil proceedings differ from arbitral proceedings, which are generally held in private. While there may be a concern to increase the attractiveness of civil proceedings for multi-national and similarly large enterprises by rendering the publicity principle subject to the principle of party disposition, this ought to be resisted in so far as it will tend to undermine the public's right to publicity and to freedom of expression concerning civil proceedings. Rule 17(1) maintains the right to publicity as a general rule. It does not permit the principle of party disposition to take precedence over it, although see Rule 17(2) for permissible derogations from the right. This approach is consistent with that taken by the European Court of Human Rights (also see Rule 18, comment 1).
3. Rule 17(2) permits proceedings to be held in private in order to protect public interests like national security, privacy, professional secrets or the due administration of justice (also see Article 6(1) of the European Convention on Human Rights). This Rule must be read together with Rules 91(2)(c) to (2)(e) that grant privileges and immunities for parties or non-parties, which partially protect the same or similar interests. Holding proceedings in private may facilitate effective evidence-taking and disclosure where interests are adverse to holding the proceeding in public, and may further justify a refusal to apply such privileges or immunities. This is especially true of trade and business secrets or public interest issues. It should be noted that parties and non-parties might not always be subject to the same balancing test, as the need to protect non-parties from disclosure may be greater than that applicable to parties. The proper administration of justice may be affected if public hearings and evidence-taking could diminish the likelihood that the court could ascertain

the truth due to a febrile or hostile public atmosphere or due to public threats to the parties or witnesses, which may inhibit parties or witnesses coming forward to give evidence or, in the case of the parties to proceedings, inhibit their willingness to put all their cards on the table. Publicity should be restricted to no more than is necessary to protect the relevant interest identified in this Rule.

4. Rule 17(2) provides the basis for the court to ensure that where derogations from open justice are in place protective orders can be made to give effect to the restriction on public justice. Hearings or evidence-taking in private may not suffice to protect the privacy or confidentiality of trade, business or other professional secrets. This may, particularly, be the case where other parties, experts or witnesses are present during the hearing or evidence-taking. In order to further protect such matters, the court may order all those persons present in the court to maintain secrecy. It may do so under threat of punishment according to the court's contempt power and/or according to any special provisions of national criminal law and/or under threat of liability for damages in favour of the party affected. The court may also order that the full disclosure or production of any of the means of evidence may only be granted to an expert who is to provide a report at a private hearing, or to restrict access to specific sources of evidence to the parties' lawyers or experts subject to a specific duty of confidentiality. Restricting party access to their opponent's or other parties' evidence is a limit on the fundamental right to be heard. It must therefore be justified by strong reasons, applying a test that balances the parties' right to be heard with their opponent's and other parties' right to secure and efficient and fair trial, i.e., their right to a public hearing and to evidence being taken in public. In the particular case of access to evidence that is in the custody of a party's opponent or of other parties, Rules 103 and 104 provide potential measures that can be applied to restrict access to evidence, as well as sanctions that may be applied for breaches of confidentiality. Courts may properly apply these rules in cases where the party that is providing evidence applies to the court for its secrets or privacy to be protected. It is a matter for individual judicial discretion on a case-by-case basis to determine the most protective measure. The court should, however, seek to ensure that it uses the measure that imposes the least restriction on the principle of publicity. Any such measure must also be proportionate (see Rule 7, comment 1).
5. Rule 17(3) provides a special kind of publicity for judgments that were issued in public proceedings. As already noted (see Rule 12, comment 2), European practice concerning the extent to which judgments are public differs. Judgments, including their reasoning and operative parts, may be pronounced orally in open court. In some European jurisdictions it is only the operative part that is pronounced orally with the reasoning set out in writing. Other jurisdictions prefer to deliver the whole judgment in writing. Other jurisdictions provide the court with a discretion concerning how the judgment is delivered or permit it to be delivered according to the parties' wishes. Public accessibility of judgments, as required by Rule 17(3), means that however the judgment may initially be delivered, it must be made accessible in written form to the public. How public access is secured is a matter for national regulation. In many European jurisdictions this is achieved through publication on the court's website either via open access or via a paywall, i.e., either free or paid access. In other jurisdictions judgments are available via written application to the court. Superior or higher court judgments are regularly published in official editions, while in other jurisdictions judgments are published, either in paper or electronic form, in law journals. While access fees concerning reproduction costs of such judgments may be permissible, judgments ought not to be accessible for a fee. Judges ought not to be permitted

to assert copyright over judgments, and hence be able to demand reproduction fees. Rule 17(3) also provides for public access to be restricted in the rare case that proceedings took place in private (in camera).

6. Rule 17(4) addresses the public accessibility of court files and records. In many European jurisdictions court records are accessible to the public, subject to general restrictions concerning publicity (see comments 3 and 4, above). Other European jurisdictions place more emphasis on privacy and permit access to records only in case of plausible legal interest, e.g., lawyers in parallel proceedings or researching case law, or where there is a legitimate reason justifying access that outweighs any countervailing interest, such as the public interest in national security, in the proper administration of justice or party interest in privacy or confidentiality of business secrets, e.g., scholarly inquiry, journalistic investigation, or the interest of non-parties in obtaining information that could be found in other proceedings.

7. Rule 17(5) restricts the right to privacy of parties, witnesses, and other natural persons in so far as the protection of anonymity is affected. It is protected where strictly necessary. In some European jurisdictions it is best practice because it is understood to be an essential aspect of the principle of publicity to publish the full name of natural persons in judgments. In other European jurisdictions party-anonymisation before publication of judgments is the rule. In others, party-anonymisation is a standard, particularly where national legislation may not have provided for exemptions under Article 23 of the European Union's General Data Protection Regulation[21] to court proceedings and judgments where that applies. According to Rule 17(5), the court may protect a natural person's identity by requiring proceedings to be anonymised where that is strictly necessary to protect, for instance, their privacy, the rights of children, or the proper administration of justice. While this approach may place more weight on publicity than is afforded in those European jurisdictions that adopt a more restrictive approach, it may not produce a significant change in practice as substantive law can and often does control the media's ability to report proceedings, i.e., through statutory reporting restrictions. The identity of legal persons, firms or enterprises is not subject to the protection afforded by this Rule. This is a beneficial development as there are no convincing reasons why such entities should be granted anonymity. In so far as the public interest is concerned, publicity should prevail over the interest of such firms to be able to litigate anonymously.

8. The fundamental importance of oral proceedings cannot be underestimated. Public access to such proceedings provides a much clearer and immediate impression of the nature and character of the legal dispute, and the socio-economic interests that underpin it and the court's judgment. While it is the case, contrary to some suggestions, that written proceedings are accessible to the public, they are not as immediate or readily accessible to observers, particularly in respect of the dialogue between the court and parties. In the absence of, or following a substantive reduction in, oral hearings, publicity of proceedings may abate. Video-conferencing and similar communication technologies may contribute to reduce the trend towards written proceedings, although the virtual reproduction of the real world may not fully replicate the immediacy of oral proceedings. Such developments are, however, preferable to any further move towards written process.

21 Regulation (EU) 2016/679 of the European Parliament and of the Council of 27 April 2016 on the protection of natural persons with regard to the processing of personal data and on the free movement of such data, and repealing Directive 95/46/EC (General Data Protection Regulation).

Rule 18. Oral and Written Proceedings

(1) Pleadings and applications must be presented initially in writing.

(2) The court may order parties to present oral argument and carry out the oral examination of witnesses or experts. Where a party requests it, the court must permit oral argument, and may permit oral examination.

(3) The court may order witnesses and experts to submit written statements.

(4) In so far as appropriate, proceedings may be conducted using any available means of information and communication technology.

Sources:

ALI/UNIDROIT Principle 19.

Comments:

1. The right to an oral hearing of a party's case is a part of the right to fair trial guaranteed by Article 6(1) of the European Convention on Human Rights and Article 47(2) of the European Charter of Fundamental Rights. This fundamental right may, however, be subject to exceptions, as provided for in the case law of the European Court of Human Rights. Such exceptions include: first, that oral hearings may, in principle, only take place upon a party's application. They need not therefore be generally mandatory, although a court is competent to order an oral hearing on its own motion (*ex officio*); and secondly, an oral hearing is not mandatory in all instances, i.e., they may not be mandatory for some forms of interim hearing or for some forms of appellate hearing such as those that do not determine factual or evidential issues. Oral hearings in appellate proceedings that are of significant importance to the parties may, however, be mandatory (also see Rule 17, comment 2).
2. Rule 18 is consistent with the framework of Article 6(1) of the European Convention on Human Rights and the corresponding case law of the European Court of Human Rights (see comment 1 above). The current approach taken by European legislatures, based on a firm understanding of the advantage it provides to the speedy and cost-effective administration of justice, is to avoid a specific emphasis on either oral or written forms of procedure, i.e., a balanced approach has properly been recognised as the optimum approach to take. Only in specific forms or stages of proceedings is a clear preference for either oral or written proceedings now found, i.e., written proceedings in small claims cases or in proceedings concerning appeals on points of law. As different European jurisdictions strike the balance between written and oral proceedings differently, Rule 18 and its corresponding Rules adopt a middle course by combining the advantages of different approaches.
3. Rule 18(1) articulates the clear preference for written pleadings in the first phase of proceedings. Written factual, evidential and legal contentions ensure that the correct documentation concerning the parties' case is submitted to the court and other parties, thus contributing to the achievement of substantive accuracy as well as the timely and cost-effective prosecution of the proceedings. The question remains how far later changes and modifications in oral hearings or oral final conclusions may complement a parties' presentation of their case. In some jurisdictions the contents of written pleadings determine a party's factual and evidential contentions, the exact wording of their claim for relief or of other applications, and permissible amendments or modifications should thus be made in written form. Other jurisdictions permit oral modifications to such matters to be made during hearings, including conclusions submitted by the parties during a final hearing, to be documented in the court's protocol or records. Rule 55 regulates party-amendments

during the pleading stage to be served in written form on other parties (Rule 55(3) and comment 1 and 4). Rule 55(3) also applies to amendments made in the light of suggestions made by the court during the pleading stage (see Rules 53(3) and 55, comment 5). During the preparatory phase (see Rules 61 and following) amendments upon a party's application or motion are permissible if they are not sought late (see Rule 27(1)). The court may also suggest amendments (see Rule 61(4)), which should be served on the other parties in written form or with the court's protocol (see Rule 55(3), comment 5). Further amendments are permitted later in the proceedings where they are suggested by the court or, in particular circumstances, upon a party's application or motion (see Rules 63(1) and (2) and Rule 64(4)).They may be made in written form or orally and documented in the protocol to be served on the other parties with the court's protocol. The court should grant sufficient time for a written or oral response, with the time being as short as is reasonable in the circumstances of the case. Rule 18(1) requires pleadings to be in writing only in the initial stage of proceedings. In all other stages the court may permit pleadings to be set out orally and documented in its protocol or records. The parties may assist the court to determine the applicable law or to evaluate evidence through making oral submissions or argument at oral hearings during the preparatory stage and in the final hearing and especially in hearings where the court will make its final conclusions in the proceedings. Judicial practice should be flexible in its approach so as to avoid negative consequences arising from a rigid adherence to the use of written process.

4. According to Rule 18(2), in general it is up to the court's discretion to order oral hearings where parties could present oral argument. This discretion must, however, be exercised in accordance with Rules corresponding to Rule 18(2), e.g., Rules 49(2), 61 (case management hearings); Rules 64, 65(3) and 66(2) (final hearings); and, within the framework of the European Court of Human Rights' case law (see comment 1 above). In the preparatory stage of proceedings it is for the court to decide whether to hold hearings or to require the exchange of written information and arguments. There ought, however, to be at least one early case management hearing. While the court must permit oral argument where a party makes such a request, it may, however, reasonably limit the number of oral hearings. Rule 64 provides for there to be a mandatory final hearing. Only in specific cases may a judgment be rendered without there being a preceding hearing, and the parties do not request otherwise (see Rules 65(3) and 66(2)). The Rules on oral proceedings are designed to permit flexibility, to avoid an arid formalist approach, while fulfilling the requirements of fundamental rights.
5. Rules 18(2) and 18(3) address witness and expert oral and written evidence-taking. The court may, in its discretion, permit evidence to be given by witness statement, order expert reports to be submitted in written form, require evidence to be given orally, or a combination thereof according to the circumstances of the case (see Rules 117 and 124). Parties have, however, a right to request evidence to be taken orally (see Rules 18(3), 117(3), and 124(2)). Such flexibility in the choice of oral or written forms of evidence is emphasised, given the clear tendency in the development of civil procedure in the majority of European jurisdictions since the turn of the 21st century that has sought to reduce litigation cost and time while ensuring that procedure is proportionate to the nature of the proceedings (see Rules 5 and following).
6. These Rules do not explicitly address whether and how far appellate proceedings must be oral and public proceedings. In most European jurisdictions, it is within the court's discretion to determine whether appeals that only raise issues of law should be carried out

through a public hearing or whether they are to be determined without a hearing solely on the basis of written pleadings. The discretion is exercised depending on the substance of the appeal and the importance to the public of the issues raised. Some apex appellate courts place specific emphasis on the importance of oral submissions from, and dialogue with, the parties' lawyers in appellate proceedings. This is particularly the case in those countries where, in order to improve the quality of pleadings and appeals brought before the apex appellate court, only those members of the legal profession who have been specifically admitted to do so may appear before the apex court. In other jurisdictions oral hearings before such courts are extremely rare. In countries where first appeals on facts and law are permissible, be it on a large or a restricted scale, oral hearings may be mandatory unless the appeal lacks real merit. In the latter case, the appeal may be decided without an oral hearing. These Rules broadly leave it to the appellate court's discretion to determine whether an oral hearing is necessary, within the framework developed by the European Court of Human Rights (see comments 1 and 2 above). As a general rule however, first appellate courts must hold an oral hearing and take oral evidence in cases where the effect of their judgment would be to overrule the first instance decision on either factual or evidential grounds without referring the proceedings back to the first instance court for decision (see Rule 170). Where new facts or evidence are raised on a first appeal, the Rules on oral hearings applicable to first instance proceedings apply (see Rule 168).

7. In so far as appropriate, Rule 18(4) supports the use of information and communication technologies. Various other Rules complement and expand upon this general rule, see: Rule 17(3) in connection with Rule 18(4) on electronic publication of judgments (see Rule 17, comment 5); Rule 61(2) on the use of electronic means of communication for case management hearings (e.g., video or audio transmission); Rule 74(1)(b) and (1)(c) on service by electronic means that guarantees receipt; Rule 79 on the mandatory provision of an electronic address for service by lawyers; Rule 97(2) on mandatory video recording of hearings where evidence is taken; Rule 97(3) on evidence-taking by video-conferencing or similar distance communication technologies; Rule 111(2) on electronic documents and data of all types and kinds of storage; Rule 111(3) on the production of electronic documents or data in electronic form; Rule 112(2) on the probative force of electronically recorded authentic instruments; Rule 115(2) on the oral examination of witnesses by video-conferencing or similar technology; and, Rule 220 on the use of a secure electronic platform ensuring efficient management for collective proceedings. All these rules address the use of information technologies. They do not prescribe specific technological requirements, as they are intended to be technology-neutral so as not to inhibit the application of the Rules to future technological developments. European jurisdictions and/or the European Union may, however, make specific provision for technical standards, compatibility and inter-operability of present and future information and electronic communication technology. These Rules are intended to be compatible with such standards or requirements.
8. Rule 18(4), however, only supports use of electronic communication in so far as its use is appropriate. Appropriateness is determined by manifold factors that must be considered by a court if it is to properly order the use of such forms of communication. Use of video-conferencing or audio-transmission in hearings may not always be appropriate in cases where only one party is not present in the courtroom and their opponent and other parties attend the hearing in person. In such a situation the parties may not stand on an equal footing in respect of their ability to maintain an overview of all that occurs in the

courtroom, and particularly of the spontaneous reactions and responses of parties and witnesses. To secure equal treatment (see Rule 4 sentence 2), the court may not decide to hold a hearing that would finally determine the outcome of the proceedings by video-conference if only one party can attend by that method unless that party gives their fully informed consent to such a hearing. If a party objects to taking part by video-conference the court may only set aside such an objection where the hearing concerns matters of routine organisation or case management. Similar problems may arise when oral testimony is to be taken by video-conference due to a witness living a long distance from the court, and the witness objects to such a process, because they are unaccustomed to such a process, and applies for a new hearing date in order to enable them to travel to the court. Mandatory video recording of hearings where evidence is taken may promote the correct evaluation of oral proof at first instance as well as on any appeal. Care should, however, be taken to such evidence due to the known possibility that individuals are liable to change their behaviour, gestures, responses, and language when they are aware that they are being recorded via a permanent and reproducible medium through which their evidence is to be evaluated. The Rules on use of electronic communication were drafted following a discussion of such factors. The prevailing view was that the judiciary should have at its disposal appropriate modern means of electronic communication, and that they should be given the discretion to determine their appropriate use without the need for specific technical rules to be formulated.

9. These Rules do not address questions of the use of artificial intelligence or e-justice. At present, computer programmes based on the evaluation of a multitude of similar cases or on a system of legal rules may provide an early prediction of the possible outcome of a dispute. Such programmes are already in use in the private sector, i.e., by law firms and other businesses. Evidence has shown that in some circumstances they may be highly accurate. Undoubtedly future development will improve the operation and reliability of such programmes. These Rules do not make provision for the use of such programmes within the civil justice system. In so far as they may be applied in future, their use should be determined by the judiciary as an aid to decision-making and not as a substitute for it. For instance, judges may properly use such programmes as a means to test their preliminary conclusions or to control for simple mistakes. The extent to which they use them must be made available to the parties, consistently with the right to be heard, so that they may make comment upon what the programme suggests. Questions concerning the control and availability of such products in the private sector, particularly in so far as their use may have an impact upon any legal monopoly over the provision of legal advice, is outside the scope of these Rules and is a matter for national regulation. The fundamental issue for the future will be the extent to which the use of such programmes, without any judicial control, will be permitted or prohibited to finally determine proceedings. In some European jurisdictions, such as Estonia, initial steps towards the use of AI programmes to finally determine low value claims are already being developed. In other jurisdictions similar initial steps are being taken to computer decision-making in respect of payment orders that create executable titles based on the allegation of facts and specific forms of documentary evidence. The most significant potential area of such e-justice developments, however, lie in small claims. In such cases, cost and time could be saved by an AI-generated first instance decision, with the possibility of a human judge deciding any appeal from that decision. There are two reasons why these Rules do not address this important issue for the future development of civil justice. First, specific small claim procedures or order

for payment procedures are not within the scope of these rules, and it is this part of civil justice where the development of e-justice may arise and could be reasonably successful. Secondly, the replacement of human judges by computers in regular civil disputes would be a fundamental decision for human society with serious consequences for the relationship between citizens and State and for the modern conception of democracy and the rule of law that is based on mutual trust between citizens and the human representatives of State power. The prevailing opinion within the groups responsible for drafting these Rules did not feel the need to address the possibility of any such radical change, as it was not viewed as a realistic prospect. In any event, should the introduction of AI decision-making in regular proceedings without there being any responsible and final human control take place, such a development could not be influenced by or prohibited by model procedural rules to any real extent.

G. LANGUAGES, INTERPRETATION AND TRANSLATION

Rule 19. Language of the Court

Proceedings, including documents and oral communications, must as a general rule be in a language of the court. The court may permit all or part of the proceedings to be conducted in other languages where doing that would not prejudice the parties or the right to a public hearing.

Sources:
ALI/UNIDROIT Principle 6.

Comments:

1. Rule 19 sentence 1 contains the approach to the language in which proceedings should be conducted that is accepted and practiced throughout the world. Generally, the court's language will be that of the official language or languages of the forum in which the court is located. Parties, judges, and lawyers will, usually, be fluent in at least one of the official languages.
2. Rule 19 sentence 2 permits exceptions to the general rule. It does so, taking account of the fact that in modern Europe the exchange of goods and services and the corresponding increase in mobility of people has resulted in an increasingly diverse populous. If the court and the lawyers representing the parties have sufficient competence in a common foreign language, which will generally but not exclusively be the English language, Rule 19 sentence 2 permits the court to conduct the proceeding in that language. That possibility is, however, always subject to the condition that the parties themselves are able to follow the course of proceedings, possibly with the help of their lawyers or an interpreter, and that the language chosen is so widespread and well-understood that the right to a public oral hearing and the right to be heard do not become illusionary; again, these points suggest the use of English may be the most likely alternative language capable of properly being chosen. This Rule also facilitates the pragmatic use of a foreign language in specific parts of the proceedings, e.g., for the examination of foreign witnesses (also see Rule 116(2)).
3. English must be considered the language of the court in the sense of Rule 19, if individual European countries establish special courts for international commercial or business

disputes, which proceed on the basis that the parties have consented to the use of the English language in the proceedings (also see Rule 20, comment 5).

Rule 20. Interpretation and translation

(1) Interpretation or translation must be provided by the court to parties who are not sufficiently competent in the language used in the proceedings. The right to interpretation includes the right of parties with hearing or speech impediments to receive appropriate assistance. Such interpretation and translation shall ensure the proceedings are fair by enabling the parties to participate in them effectively.

(2) Where documents are translated, the parties may agree, or the court may order, that such translation be limited to such parts of the documents as necessary to ensure the proceedings are fair and that the parties are able to participate effectively in them.

Sources:
ALI/UNIDROIT Principle 6.3; Transnational Rules of Civil Procedure (Reporters' Study) Rule 8.3.

Comments:

1. Rule 20(1) defines the parties' right to translation if they are not sufficiently competent in the language of the court or a language that is, exceptionally, being used by the court (see Rule 19 with comments). It is a particular manifestation of the parties' right to be heard (see Rule 11) because it is designed to ensure that parties can fully understand all matters raised by the court, their opponent, other parties, witnesses, non-parties and all other individuals who are participating in the proceedings. It thus also enables them to respond adequately to such matters. The right to translation may primarily be used where parties represent themselves in person, as it can be expected that lawyers admitted to practice in the forum are familiar with, or at the least competent in, the court's language (see Rule 19, comment 1). In those exceptional cases where the court permits the use of a foreign language it may be that a party's lawyer is not competent in it. In such a case translation will be necessary in order to enable the lawyer to provide effective and efficient representation. The court may, however, only use a foreign language generally during proceedings if it has ascertained that its use will not prejudice a party (see Rule 19). It is likely therefore that it will be rare for a lawyer to require translation during the proceedings, and then only generally if the choice of a foreign language concerns only a part of proceedings.
2. Rule 20(1) does not explicitly address the case where a party is not sufficiently competent in the language of the proceedings, and they either attend court without their lawyer or they attend with their lawyer and in neither circumstance is the party heard in person (see Rules 16(1) and (2)). In such circumstances, it is for the court to determine, according to national practice, whether the appointment of an interpreter or translator is necessary to facilitate the party's right to address the court in person, or whether information provided by the party's lawyer is sufficient to give effect to the right to be heard. The same approach applies in those cases where an additional second lawyer, who is not admitted to practice in the forum, assists a party (see Rule 15(1)). An interpreter or translator should be appointed by the court if communication between the affected party and the court or other parties is to be translated. Parties are always permitted to bring their own translator or interpreter to a hearing to facilitate internal party communication. Reasonable and necessary interpretation or translation costs may be reimbursed according to Rule 240(1)(b).

3. Rule 20(1) emphasises that the right to interpretation applies to parties with hearing and speech impediments. In such cases the court must appoint an interpreter where such a party is present in person before the court in order to enable them to participate effectively in the proceedings. It cannot properly be expected that the party's lawyer will be able to carry out the interpretative function.
4. Rule 20(2) concerns the translation of relevant documents into the language used by the court. Translation is mandatory if documents do not use the language of the court and the court does not permit the use of another language according to Rule 19 sentence 2. Such permission may, particularly, be given in commercial cases where the court is competent in English and the relevant documents as well as the parties' correspondence in respect of the transaction in dispute was also in English. The reasonable restriction, especially where documents are lengthy, of any such translation to parts relevant and necessary for the fair and efficient proceedings is of particular importance in commercial cases with voluminous records and business papers.
5. Where European countries have established specialist international commercial courts and parties litigate before them based on consent to the jurisdiction (see Rule 19, comment 3), English is the language of the court by way of party consent. It is a matter for the parties to appoint lawyers who are competent in English. Translations may be necessary for parties attending such hearings in person if they are not sufficiently competent in English in order to ensure that they can contribute orally to the proceedings. Such translations should be provided for, either upon the court's or the parties' own motion.
6. For translation that is necessary in respect of witness evidence that is given in a foreign language, see Rule 116(1) and (2) as well as Rule 19, comment 2.

SECTION 3—PROCEEDINGS

A. COMMENCEMENT, TERMINATION, CONCENTRATION AND SCOPE

Rule 21. Commencement and termination

(1) Proceedings may only be instituted by a party. The court cannot institute proceedings on its own motion.

(2) Parties may terminate proceedings in whole or in part by withdrawal, admission of the claim or settlement.

Sources:

ALI/UNIDROIT Principle 10.1.

Comments:

1. All modern procedural systems recognise the principle of party initiative in civil matters, which is rooted in the overarching principle of party autonomy over private rights. It is for the holders of property rights and other private rights to decide whether to defend and enforce them. In many European jurisdictions this form of freedom of disposition (the dispositive principle) over private rights is guaranteed by their national constitution. It is also guaranteed on a European level by Article 17(1) and the second paragraph of Article 47 of the European Charter of Fundamental Rights, and Article 6(1) of the European Convention on Human Rights.

2. In respect of collective proceedings, the principle of party initiative in civil matters is subject to modifications necessary in the interest of all holders of the same private rights (see collective interest injunctions, Rules 204 to 206) or in the interest of groups of private rights holders who have been affected by mass harms (see collective proceedings, Rule 207 and following). At the same time, the public interest of the society as a whole, justifies the existence of a form of process that facilitates the protection of the rights of all citizens or of groups of citizens. Additionally, the public interest in a well-functioning court system requires a special procedural mechanism suitable to protect collective interests efficiently and in accordance with individual fundamental rights. Collective proceedings in Part XI do not, however, break completely with the principle of party initiative. They permit forms of representation by specially qualified claimants and, in so far as necessary, they protect individual rights holders by opt-in or opt-out mechanisms. Also see Rules 29 and following; Rules 52 and following; and Rule 68 and following.
3. Rule 21(2) describes the most important modes of party disposition in respect of the termination of civil proceedings common to all European legal cultures. It can properly be considered to be the counterpart of Rule 21(1). Also see Rules 3, 9 and following; Rules 51, 56, 141, 163, and 241(2).
4. It should be conceded that there are other means by which parties may terminate proceedings, which are not explicitly mentioned in these Rules, e.g., an agreed stay or party passivity for a period of time with the consequence that the proceedings are not listed for hearing by the court. Rules concerning such matters are, however, technical and ought properly to be left to national legislation. A party's intentional failure to appear, which results in a default judgment (see Rule 135) can also be considered to be a form of voluntary termination in some legal cultures. This is not wrong, but it should be noted that such an approach involves a form of contempt for other parties to proceedings, for other individuals involved in the proceedings, and ultimately of the court itself. It is as if the party that fails to appear could have admitted the claim in time and given notice to the court and the opponent and thereby save the time and resources of all involved. Such conduct thus would breach the duty owed by parties to the court and to other litigants (see Rules 2, 3 and 6). Discussion concerning the question whether default judgments are to some degree a means to sanction improper or disloyal behaviour is best left to procedural theory and historical scholarship, although the requirements for setting aside default judgments may indicate that forms of disapproval of the defaulting party's behaviour may be the prevailing attitude within European legal cultures (see Rule 139).

Rule 22. Concentration of Legal and Factual Issues

(1) Parties must bring all the legal and factual elements in support of, or in objection to, a claim for relief that arise out of the same cause of action in one single proceeding.

(2) Non-compliance with Rule 22(1) renders proceedings on the same claim for relief arising out of the same cause of action inadmissible. This preclusion does not apply if

(a) subsequent to the earlier proceeding, there has been a change in relevant facts on which judgment in those proceedings was based, or

(b) the non-compliant party has obtained or acquired a new right since judgment was given in the earlier proceeding.

Comments:

1. Rule 22 describes the consequences of the preclusive, "negative" effects of judgments becoming *res judicata*, which force parties to litigation to bring all legal and factual elements that support or are adverse to a claim for relief in one single first proceeding before the court seised. In some legal systems these consequences are traditionally discussed together with the preconditions, requirements and positive consequences of *res judicata* that are set out here in Rules 147 and following. Other legal cultures put much more emphasis on the need to ensure that all legal and factual arguments are contained in the first proceeding on the relief claimed, so as to then ensure that preclusion does not arise later in unexpected or surprising ways. This point of view is the one adopted in these Rules.
2. The concentration principle articulated in Rule 22(1) only applies to factual and legal grounds, which can be invoked to sustain or challenge the claim for relief brought before the court. It does not require that the parties concentrate all claims for relief[22] arising out of the same facts in a single proceeding. It is not therefore similar to the English case law on claim preclusion based on Henderson v Henderson [1843–1860] All ER Rep 378, which precludes a new claim if the party had a previous opportunity to raise a claim in connection with the previous litigation.[23] It is also not similar to the European Court of Justice's broad construction of the "same cause of action" in determining the scope of *lis pendens* (see Rule 142 comment 2 with references). Rule 22 strikes a compromise between the very broad common law conception of claim preclusion and the more restricted conception of some countries of Romance tradition, which limits claim preclusion to supporting legal and factual elements actually subject to dispute in the first proceeding. Both solutions aim at preventing abuse of process and at concentrating litigation, although they differ in scope and measure. Rule 22 does not exclude a partial claim. However, only explicit partial claims[24] should be admissible. It should be stressed that in this respect, there are important differences in the procedural cultures of the European Union member States and, more broadly, European jurisdictions. Some do take a more liberal approach to admitting partial claims placing significant weight on the effect that the value at stake in the proceedings has on the costs to be paid by parties.
3. Rule 22(1) corresponds to Rule 26(2). According to this Rule it is the court's responsibility to determine the correct legal basis of a party's claim for relief. It requires the court to consider and to apply, of its own motion (*ex officio*) all legal provisions relevant for a party's case. Under this provision, cases where a court's decision takes into consideration only a part of the relevant law and of related relevant facts, may be very rare because the parties are also required to contribute to the correct application of all relevant law (see Rules 3(d), 11, 12, 26(1) and 26(2)). In legal systems where, until now, it was traditionally the parties' responsibility to find the correct legal basis of their case and to convince the court of its correctness, these Rules taken as a whole may facilitate the proper presentation of their cases without weakening their position. If parties agree on the legal basis of a claim or agree to limit the scope of the court's decision-making to specific issues the

22 E.g., "*demandes*", "*prétentions*", "*Klaganträge*", "*domanda*", "*demanda*" etc.

23 See further, Johnson v Gore Wood & Co [2002] 2 AC 1, 32-3, 59.

24 Or "*offene Teilklage*".

concentration principle as set out in Rule 22(1) does not apply (see Rules 26(3), 57 and following).

4. Rule 22(1) does not include any statement as to whether parties are under duty to present at first instance all the contentions of law on which the claim for relief can be based. This issue only has a very limited significance under these Rules because the court is responsible for determining the correct legal basis of a claim for relief. Any error or failure on the part of the court of first instance in this regard could form basis of an appeal if the requirements set out in Rule 166 are fulfilled. As an incorrect determination of the applicable law is not a procedural error on the part of the court in the sense articulated in Rule 178, there is no requirement to challenge it immediately in order to avoid waiver. If new legal contentions are necessarily combined with new factual contentions they should, in principle, be permitted in appellate proceedings, albeit subject to restrictive requirements set out in Rules 157(2)(d), 166, and 168(1).
5. In specific circumstances, the principle of concentration, which if disregarded would normally lead to a substantial preclusion, should be set aside and the claimant should be permitted to pursue a second, identical, claim for relief in subsequent proceedings. This should be the case where new facts have arisen subsequent to the earlier proceeding, e.g., where a management agent is initially given no authorisation to sue on behalf of the co-owners of property, but is later authorised to do so, or where a zoning map, which formed the basis of the first proceedings, was subsequently declared to be void by an administrative court subsequent to those proceedings, or where the fulfilment of a claim for relief following judgment had taken place and the debtor seeks negative declaratory relief because the creditor continues to maintain that their right has not been satisfied. A subsequent change in the law should not, however, be considered to be a new fact that would justify permitting a party to commence fresh litigation concerning the same claim for relief; whether this may be different in case of injunctions with far reaching future effects or in other similar constellations is a matter that ought properly be left to judicial practice and case law. A new claim for relief in a second proceeding should also be admissible where the litigant has obtained or acquired a new right since the judgment in the first proceeding. This is the case, for instance, when the first proceeding was dismissed, on the basis that the claimant was not the creditor of the claim sued for or otherwise lacked litigation capacity (see Rule 30 and following), and subsequently the same claimant acquired the debt, i.e., became the creditor, and sued upon assignment. Special rules apply in case of judgments requiring periodical performance (see Rule 150).
6. The expression "subsequent to the earlier proceeding" in Rule 22(2) sentence 2(a) means the period of time following the stage during which parties are permitted to advance additional factual contentions and contentions of law derived from any such additional facts in the pending proceedings (see Rules 63 and 64(4)). It should be noted that factual contentions, which happened after the closing of pleadings or before the conclusion of a final hearing will regularly be admitted by courts in order to avoid subsequent proceedings because they fulfil the requirements of Rules 63(2) and 64(4). It will, as a consequence, often be the case that the conclusion of the final hearing may be the final opportunity for parties to secure the admission of factual and/or legal contentions. Furthermore, first appeals may be based on new facts and appellate courts may take evidence of contested new facts (see, Rules 168(1)(a), 168(2)(c), 169, and 170). Alternatively, they may refer such matters back

to a first instance court, the consequence of which will be a new hearing and evidence-taking at first instance. The question will be whether it is the free choice of affected parties to initiate a second claim or to bring an appeal in cases where new facts would be the only reason under pinning an appeal. The existence of a choice of possible remedies, as in this instance, is evident in all legal cultures. Such choice is often left to practice, which generally prefers the choice that is, in reality, the cheaper and simpler remedy (also see Rule 133(e) and 153).

Rule 23. Scope

(1) The scope of the dispute is determined by the claims and defences of the parties in the pleadings, including amendments.

(2) The court must decide on, and only on, the relief claimed.

Source:

ALI/UNIDROIT Principle 10.3.

Comments:

1. Rule 23 is an aspect of the principle of party disposition over essential elements of civil procedure (see Rule 21). The definition of the scope of the dispute in Rule 23(1) is necessary in order to develop criteria for the obligatory contents of a court's decision. The court's decision on the claim for relief is based on the facts as asserted in the pleadings by the claimant and defendant. The court has to differentiate between relevant and not relevant facts, contested and uncontested facts, relevant and irrelevant evidence, proven and not proven contested facts, it has to evaluate the results of evidence-taking, and to take into consideration the evidential and legal contentions of the parties. This is not only true for facts and means of evidence in the complaint but also for facts and means of evidence in the defendant's affirmative defence (see Rule 12(1)). It is important to note that the court's reasoning in its judgment has to address all substantial issues raised in the dispute that are within its specified scope (see Rule 12(1) and (2)). A dispute's scope, as defined by Rule 23(1), not only describes the scope of the right to be heard (see Rules 11 and 12) but it also determines the decisive criteria for evidential relevance (see Rules 88, 89, 93 – 95) and the scope of the judgment in the proceeding's *res judicata* (see Rule 149).
2. Rule 23(2) makes it clear that the court has to decide on the claim for relief as formulated by the claimant. The court is not permitted to change the formulation of the claim for relief of its own motion (*ex officio*). The court may grant a part of the party's claim for relief, but it may not grant something other than that which was claimed. The court is also not authorised to grant more than sued for, even if this could be done in accordance with the substantive law applicable to the case.
3. When providing the parties a reasonable opportunity to present their arguments on the law applicable to the case according to the court's perspective (see Rule 26(1) and (2)), the court may give an indication that the relief sought does not harmonise with the law applicable as chosen and construed by the court. The court could, however, be challenged if it explicitly or conclusively recommended a formulation that exceeds the claim for relief as originally presented by the claimant. The requirements for amendments of claims must be satisfied in case of later changes (see Rule 55).

B. FACTS, EVIDENCE AND APPLICABLE LAW

Rule 24. Facts

(1) The parties must put forward such facts as support their claim or defence. The court may invite the parties to clarify or supplement these facts.

(2) The court must not consider facts not introduced by the parties.

(3) The court may consider such facts not specifically addressed by a party but that are necessarily implied by matters of fact put forward by the parties or which are contained within the case file. It may only do so if they are relevant to a party's claim or defence and the parties have been given a reasonable opportunity to respond.

Sources:

ALI/UNIDROIT Principles 11(3) and 11(2).

Comments:

1. In nearly all European jurisdictions and legal cultures the court is not responsible for finding or searching for facts. It is for the parties to introduce facts; courts are not, in principle, permitted to introduce facts of their own motion (*ex officio*). This approach is adopted in these Rules (see Rules 24(1) and 24(2)). In socialist European countries there were and are still some legal systems, where the court had and has to investigate the factual basis of a legal dispute of its own motion (*ex officio*). Party disposition over facts is not a necessary consequence of the adoption of the principle of party disposition over rights or of private autonomy. A commitment to party disposition over facts is, however, more consistent with the equivalent commitment to party disposition over rights, than is a commitment to the court being required to carry out factual inquiries of its own motion (*ex officio*). This is the case because a broad understanding of the principle of party autonomy encompasses the right of parties to agree to resolve their disputes based on mutually agreed facts, which would thus avoid raising factual matters before the courts for their determination. For a court to be required to conduct its own factual inquiries, it would need to be provided with sufficient inquisitorial procedures, powers and administrative staff. Such an apparatus, in order to be efficient, would necessarily be a very expensive form of dispute resolution process. As such it has never been realised in practice in Europe. It has generally been the case that party motivation to ensure that their claim or defence succeeds, i.e., that they are the winner in the litigation, has resulted in sufficient factual evidence being adduced in proceedings. In those European jurisdictions where the court has a broader responsibility for clarifying factual matters, its inquisitorial or investigative powers are used rarely. This is due to the parties tending to ensure that any necessary clarifications are made.
2. Rule 24(1) allocates responsibility for introducing facts between the parties consistently with the allocation of the burden of proof, as that is set out in the governing substantive law. It must therefore be read consistently with Rule 25. In general, the burden of proof and the burden to introduce all relevant facts to be proven in case of dispute coincide. This is expressed by the requirement in Rule 24(1) that the parties must "put forward such facts as support their claim and defence". This distribution of risk between the parties goes back to Roman procedure and has survived in both common law and civil law tradition today. The idea is to divide legal norms into claims, defences (*exceptions*), replies (*répliques*) as a response to defences, and so on. Terminology and details of the concrete

distribution differ between legal cultures, but the idea is common to all developed procedural systems. Given this, it is the basis of the procedural model in these Rules. This does not mean, however, that the burden imposed on parties to introduce relevant facts is without limit. Rules on pleadings (see Rules 52-55) provide for the framework for parties to set out their factual allegations in detail. They also permit parties to set out less detailed factual contentions if they can show good cause for being unable to provide details and can also demonstrate that there is plausible dispute on the merits (Rule 53(3)). Consequently, the party's opponent has to respond in as detailed a manner as possible, and the party may use all means of evidence that are reasonably specified (see Rule 25, comment 4) in order to provide further clarification. If a party has to assert negative facts, e.g., the lack of a legal ground for the acquisition of property, some legal cultures shift the burden of giving particulars to that party's opponent who is then required to identify possible legal grounds for the acquisition. This results in the party, who was originally placed under the burden of giving particulars of the non-existence of all possible legal grounds for the property acquisition, must only provide particulars of the lack of legal grounds as asserted by the opponent. These Rules leave details concerning such shifting burdens to national practice and case law.

3. Rules 24(1) and (2) are a concrete instance of the principle of co-operation between court and parties (Rules 2, 3(c) and (d), and 4 sentence 3). They are also an important practical aspect of the court's responsibility for active and effective case management (see Rules 4 sentence 1, 47-49, 53(3) and 61(3)). Some continental European legal traditions draw a distinction between organisational or procedural case management (*generelle Prozessleitungspflicht*) and material or substantive case management (*materielle Prozessleitungspflicht*), the latter of which relates to the court's role in actively monitoring and where necessary guiding parties' proper presentation of their respective cases. The common law tradition only acknowledges procedural case management. Both the first and second sentences of Rule 24(1) properly construed are an essential element of material or substantive case management. It is of note that both sub-rules are, notwithstanding the common law's general approach to case management, commonplace in European common law jurisdictions. If the court that is monitoring party compliance with their responsibilities becomes aware of a lack of relevant facts it may invite the party affected to clarify and supplement its factual contentions. In some European countries within the Germanic procedural tradition, the court must give an indication to the parties that further or specific facts may need to be provided by the parties. In most countries within the Romance tradition and within the common law countries, no such strict obligation to assist the parties is placed upon the court, although courts in such jurisdictions may, as part of their inherent or overriding discretion provide neutral assistance to the parties or should remain passive in such circumstances. Again, both sentences of Rule 24(1) provide the basis for courts to exercise a degree of judicial discretion in this regard. As it must be read and construed against the background of the Rules on co-operation between the court and parties there should be no room for the court to provide assistance to parties in an arbitrary or less than even-handed fashion. As such under the present Rules, only in exceptional circumstances should a court not provide a responsible amount of judicial assistance to the parties to better enable them to articulate their respective cases. If, for instance, a party's factual allegations provide a clear indication to the court of the applicability of mandatory European or national law it should invite the party who has the benefit of that law to clarify and, where necessary, supplement its factual assertions to better enable the court to determine the proceedings on the basis of

the applicable mandatory law. Notwithstanding this, these Rules do not provide the basis for the development of a strongly inquisitorial or investigative approach by courts. They are intended to do no more than provide a basis for effective judicial stimulation of party activity.

4. Rule 24(3) modifies Rule 24(2) and its strict rule against the introduction of facts by the court. It permits the introduction of facts that are necessarily implied by the factual contentions of a party and by any facts contained within the court file. The court may also, further to the second sentence of Rule 24(1), invite the parties to supplement their factual assertions in the light of any facts implied by the parties' factual contentions or contained within the court file. Whether the court chooses to permit facts to be introduced, following it giving an indication to the parties of what facts may beneficially be introduced, or to invite the parties to supplement their prior factual assertions may depend upon the circumstances of the case.
5. In some cases it may be advantageous for the claimant or defendant, of their own motion, to introduce facts that are potentially favourable to their opponent in their first pleading. This may be particularly important if such facts had come to light during the pre-action phase of proceedings (Rule 9(1)). In such a circumstance, the claimant or defendant may take the opportunity to respond by admitting, denying their relevance, contesting, or claiming an affirmative defence. Such anticipation of an opponent's pleadings, though contributing in this way to a more concentrated form of process, is not a general obligation imposed on parties to proceedings. It is a matter of discretion (see Rule 53(6)).These Rules do not establish as a procedural principle a general obligation upon parties to provide the court from the start of proceedings with a full account of the information about all the facts known by that party and which are possibly relevant to the case. Only in cases where fraud is threatened, where a party is clearly acting in bad faith (see Rule 3(e)) or if the proceedings are without-notice (*ex parte*) does such an obligation exist (see Rule 186 (3)). Generally, however, in on-notice (*inter partes*) proceedings, there is no need or justification for imposing such an obligation. The general approach based on the distribution of the burden of proof and the understanding that each party can be trusted to promote their own claim in the proceedings is sufficient. As such there seems no good reason to propose any alteration of prevailing practice of most European jurisdictions in favour of holistic and unarticulated pleadings, and these Rules have no such intention.

Rule 25. Evidence

(1) Each party is required to prove all the relevant facts supporting its case. Parties must offer evidence supporting their factual contentions. Substantive law determines the burden of proof.

(2) Each party has, in principle, a right to access all forms of relevant, non-privileged and reasonably identified evidence. In so far as appropriate, parties and non-parties must contribute to disclosure and production of evidence. It is not a basis of objection to such disclosure by a party that disclosure may favour the opponent or other parties.

(3) In so far as appropriate the court may invite the parties to supplement their offers of evidence. Exceptionally, it may take evidence on its own motion.

Source:

ALI/Unidroit Principles 3.1, 5.4, 16.1, 16.2, 21.1; Transnational Rules of Civil Procedure (Reporters' Study) Rule 28.1.

Comments:

1. Rule 25 articulates the distribution of roles between the court and parties and amongst parties in respect of evidence-taking. It must be read together with Rule 24, which specifies the court's and parties' respective roles concerning the introduction of facts, and with Part VII of these Rules on Access to Information and Evidence.
2. The burden of proof in sentence 1 of Rule 25(1) distributes the risk that evidential support for the existence of facts favourable to a party's case fails because their non-existence becomes clear or their existence remains unclear (on the standard of proof, see Rule 87). Such a distribution of risk between claimants and defendants is common to all developed legal systems (see Rule 24, comment 2). It is a fundamental requirement of justice. In most cases the enforcement of private rights becomes more or less impossible if one party only bears the risk of establishing all legal requirements relevant to their dispute. Substantive law determines the facts underpinning the respective rights and defences and, thus, it is consequently for substantive law to determine the criteria applicable to determine the distribution of the burden of proof amongst the parties to proceedings. This approach is also taken in European private international law.[25] Situations in which the burden of proof may be reversed are primarily matters of substantive law. In some European jurisdictions, judges are, however, entitled to shift the burden of proof from claimant to defendant or vice versa, particularly where there have been infringements of the duty to co-operate (see Rules 2-4, 25(2)), e.g., lack of co-operation through a failure to respond in detail to factual assertions (Rule 54(3) and (4)) or a failure to provide documents required by the party upon whom the burden of proof is ordinarily placed (Rule 100). It should be noted, however, that it is arguable whether such instances can properly be characterised as involving a genuine reversal of the burden of proof or whether they are simply an application of rules on admission of facts or on drawing adverse inferences (see Rules 27(3), 54(3), and 110). Nothing in these Rules should be taken as limiting a judge's discretion to apply such criteria, when appropriate (on the contrary, see Rules 7 and 103).
3. The burden of proof should be clearly distinguished from the burden to adduce or give evidence, which is dealt with in sentence 2 of Rule 25(1). The burden to adduce evidence describes the risk of not being able to persuade the court of an evidential result favourable to a party's case. Generally, the burden to adduce evidence lies upon the party that bears the burden of proof. In contrast to the burden of proof, which does not generally change in the course of the proceedings, the burden to adduce evidence may often shift between the parties, particularly where there is a risk that the party that bears the burden of proof may adduce enough evidence to persuade the court and that, consequently, there is a case to answer on the issue, which justifies a shift in the burden to the other party ("shifting of the burden after discharge of the burden" or "*need to respond to the opponent's case*", "*empêcher la conviction du juge de se former en faveur de son adversaire*", "*Gegenbeweisführungslast*", "*necesidad de la contraprueba*", "*prova contraria diretta o indiretta*" etc.). The burden to adduce evidence is a correlate of the right to give evidence, and hence is an essential aspect of the right to be heard (see Rules 11 and 12). As such it enables a party to manage the risk of being unable to convince the court on issues in its case.

25 See, for instance, Art. 18 of Regulation (EC) No 593/2008 of the European Parliament and of the Council of 17 June 2008 on the law applicable to contractual obligations (Rome I) and Art. 22 Regulation (EC) No 864/2007 of the European Parliament and of the Council of 11 July 2007 on the law applicable to non-contractual obligations (Rome II).

4. Rule 25(2) articulates each party's right of access to relevant evidence that is not subject to any evidential privilege and under the control and custody of their opponent or non-parties (see Rules 89, 91 and 100-110). By requiring reasonable identification of specific forms of evidence, this Rule corresponds to the requirement that facts are set out in reasonable detail, as well as the application of a reasonableness standard elsewhere in these Rules (see Rule 53(2)(a), Rule 24, comment 2, and Rules 53(2)(b) and (3), and 102(1), (2)(c) and 103(2)). By applying reasonableness as the criterion here, these Rules provide a significant guideline to differentiate between impermissible evidential fishing-expeditions and permissible, plausible general factual allegations and the permissible specification of categories of documents or objects that may, in part, be subject to private and confidential inspection, particularly in cases of access to electronically stored evidence (on electronic evidence see Rule 111(2)).
5. The third sentence of Rule 25(2) makes it clear that the longstanding principle that a party to litigation is not required to put weapons into the hands of their opponent (*nemo contra se edere tenetur*) and to contribute to the success of their opponent's case ought not to be of any significance in developed procedural systems. It should, however, be stressed that this rule has not been applied in a strict sense in any developed procedural system for a significant period of history. On the contrary, procedural systems have adopted differing approaches to the requirements, scope and frequency of application of obligations upon parties to disclose and produce evidence. Such differences have, over recent decades diminished across European jurisdictions. Any fear that an obligation to produce and disclose evidence could be subject to abuse, and hence resisted, ought properly to be set aside now, particularly when, as in these Rules, such obligations are limited in scope by the test of reasonableness and must be applied consistently with the general duty of co-operation and the overarching principle of proportionality (see Rules 2, 3, and 5-8).
6. The first sentence in Rule 25(3), in a similar manner to the second sentence in Rule 24(1), provides the court with the power to carry out substantive case management by inviting the parties to supplement their offers of evidence. Rule 25(3) particularly corresponds to the general rule on court management in sentences 1 and 3 of Rule 4 and with the specific rules on substantive case management set out at Rules 49(9) and (11), Rule, 53(2) and (5), 55, 62(2)(a) and (e), 64(5)(c) and (6) sentence 1, and, Rule 92(2).
7. The second sentence of Rule 25(3) differs from the first sentence of Rule 24 (3) in that it provides a power, to be exercised exceptionally, for the court to take evidence on its own motion (*ex officio*). In this it provides a wider power than that set out in the first sentence of Rule 24(3), which permits the court to take account of facts that are conclusively implied by the parties' allegations and by facts that are already within the case file, e.g., in the report of the police on the traffic accident that is the factual basis of the proceedings at stake. This small difference between the two rules concerning active judicial fact-finding is well-founded as judicial intervention in party disposition over a dispute's factual basis would appear to be much more intensive if judges were permitted to introduce new facts than if they can only adduce additional evidence on facts already introduced by the parties. In practice, however, both forms of judicial intervention are likely to be of little effect as courts are not, generally, provided with sufficient resources to conduct their own investigations of factual and evidential matters. In reality, notwithstanding such powers, courts are likely to continue to be limited to such materials as are introduced by parties' pleadings, with the court doing no more than making suggestions to the parties, under its substantive case management powers, of what supplementary evidence may be necessary (see the

first sentence of Rule 25(3) and Rule 92 especially with comment 4). As such the use of the power in the second sentence of Rule 25(3) is likely to be used only exceptionally.

8. In many European jurisdictions, there appears to be an increasing practice for parties to agree upon the allocation of the burden of proof or on the admission or exclusion of certain forms of evidence. The validity of such agreements is a matter of substantive law. In civil law and in civil proceedings party autonomy remains a basic principle, however, it should be clear that such agreements should not be held to be binding where they are contrary to public policy, i.e., where they lead to manifest injustice such as can arise where there is a significant imbalance in economic power and/or in experience between the parties; see, for instance, the approach in Council Directive 93/13/EEC of 5 April 1993 on unfair terms in consumer contracts, among the terms of which may be considered unfair, the Annex includes those which have the object or effect of imposing on the consumer a burden of proof which, according to the applicable law, should lie with another party to the contract (Annex 1(q)).

Rule 26. Applicable law

(1) While taking account of any applicable special provisions, the parties may present legal arguments supporting their claim or defence.

(2) The court must determine the correct legal basis for its decision. This includes matters determined on the basis of foreign law. It may only do so having provided the parties a reasonable opportunity to present their arguments on the applicable law.

(3) Where parties are free to dispose of their rights, they may agree on the legal basis of the claim or on specific issues in the claim. Such an agreement must be explicit and must, even if it was made before commencement of the proceedings, be set out in the pleadings. The agreement binds the court.

Sources:

ALI/Unidroit Principles 5.5, 11, 19.1, 22.1-3.

Comments:

1. In all European jurisdictions, it is for the court to determine the correct legal basis upon which it will determine claims for relief, whether that is domestic or foreign law (see the first sentence of Rule 26(2)). Different jurisdictions and European legal traditions adopt different approaches to how this is achieved. Some European countries stand in the tradition of the early Italian and canon law procedure, which developed rules concerning *iura novit curia* and *da mihi facta, dabo tibi ius*. Such rules remain of central importance in the law and legal practice in jurisdictions within the Latin legal tradition, and to a certain extent in those jurisdictions within the Germanic legal tradition. In common law jurisdictions, however, the general approach by the courts has been to base their decisions upon the law as pleaded by the parties, although there has been a readiness over recent years for common law courts to supplement the pleaded law with their own legal research. A further approach is notable in some European jurisdictions within the French legal tradition, where the court will ordinarily base its decision on the parties' legal contentions, but may also determine the applicable law independently of the parties and of its own initiative (*ex officio*). Rule 26(2) is intended to establish a clear rule specifying that the court is responsible for determining the law, while in no way restricting its decision to what is submitted by the parties. This approach does not affect the fundamental right of the parties to

contribute to the decision-making process (see Rules 11 and 12), not least so that they may seek to persuade the court that their contentions on the correct legal basis are correct (see Rule 3(d); for taking account of applicable special provisions see, e.g., Rules 26(3), 53(2)(c), 54(2), (5) and (6), 57 and following).

2. Rule 26 emphasises the parties' right to contribute to the determination of the correct legal basis of their dispute. It thus makes clear that the parties' right is taken seriously as an essential element of the right to be heard (see Rules 11 and 12). Parties ought therefore to set out their views on the correct law in their pleadings (see Rule 53(2)(c)), and also in the presentation of their arguments before the court. Rule 26 does not contain an explicit duty requiring the court to hear the parties on the question of the correct legal basis of their dispute, as this may have been too strong an obligation to be imposed on courts for European jurisdictions that have long-established contrary traditions. However, due to the general principle of co-operation between court and party (see Rules 2-4), and the court's duty not to surprise the parties (see Rules 26(2) sentence 3), even in the absence of an explicit duty under this Rule, the court will still need to ensure that it works with the parties, i.e., that it, at the least, affords them an opportunity to be heard on the issue. It should furthermore do so consistently with the obligation placed upon it to conduct both procedural and substantive case management (see Rules 2 and 4). Effective and efficient case management can only be achieved where the law governing the issues in dispute is clear. Court and party co-operation in case management requires both to know and accept the court's understanding of legal issues (see in particular Rules 3(b), 4 sentences 1 and 3, 47 – 50, 61 – 62, 64(5), and 92). It is not without good reason that effective case management has been much more difficult in procedural systems where parties present their full case, i.e., all their legal arguments, factual contentions and evidence, for the first time at trial, and where different judges are responsible for pre-trial case management and for the trial itself. The fundamental underpinning of the present Rules is intended to move beyond such an approach, and to promote the development of a more dialogical form of procedure within European jurisdictions.

3. Rule 26(2) articulates the court's responsibility to determine the law, including any foreign law, applicable to the dispute. This is consistent with both ALI/UNIDROIT Principle 22.1 and the approach taken in conflict of laws. First, it should be noted that the law relating to conflict of laws, which determines the applicability of foreign law, is considered to be substantive domestic law even if it is European law common to all European Union Member States or forms part of international contracts. As with all domestic law it is governed by the first sentence of Rule 26(2) and not by the second sentence in that sub-rule. The final determination of the contents of applicable foreign law has, strictly speaking, always been the responsibility of the courts of all legal cultures. This is not new and not the sense in which Rule 26(2)'s reference to foreign law should be interpreted. It may, however, be somewhat novel to treat domestic and foreign law more or less equally concerning the manner in which a court will determine their content as applicable to proceedings before it. Such equal treatment is a consequence of the balance struck between court and party activity concerning the determination of the correct substantive law, which these Rules have developed. The intention underpinning this balance is to overcome opposing European traditions, some of which emphasise the role of the court, others which emphasise the role of parties, in this regard. Such different approaches generally fail to place proper weight on the fact that the optimum practice adopted by most courts is one that requires extensive co-operation between court and parties (see Rule 3, comment 5), and that this produces

the best results concerning the determination of the content of substantive law and particularly substantive foreign law.

In domestic cases, under Rule 26(2) it is for the court to take judicial notice of any statutory, codified or case law, and apply the law to the specific facts of the claims for relief arising in each proceeding. To achieve this, judges should have such law and relevant commentary available to them. In rare cases, where a part of domestic law is particularly specialised or obscure, the court may appoint an expert to help clarify its understanding of the law (see Rule 120(1)). Additionally, where the law is uncertain or unclear, parties may submit evidence from party-appointed experts (see Rule 119). The same approach can be taken in respect of foreign law, although there the issue may be complicated due to the law being in a foreign language with which the court may not be familiar. In some cases, however, a judge or judges of a court may be familiar with either the language or the law of the other jurisdiction, particularly where, for instance, it is that of a neighbouring European State or where the court is one that employs specific judicial bodies for transnational cases or has a specific transnational jurisdiction. Where, however, the court either lacks the linguistic skills or legal knowledge, it may appoint an expert witness, or invite the parties to do so, in order to provide it with the necessary information (see Rules 119 and 120). Additionally, although it may not always suffice, the European Convention on Information on Foreign Law (of 7 June, 1968, Council of Europe, European Treaty Series-No. 62) facilitates information about foreign law within Europe. In considering the correct applicable law, the court should provide parties with an opportunity to be heard on the issue before it decides the issue (see the third sentence in Rule 26(2)).

In some European legal cultures courts have developed special rules in cases where the contents of foreign law remained open to interpretation. Rather than develop their own construction of the foreign law or develop their own case law on the subject, they have applied rules from neighbouring legal cultures or rules common to the foreign law's legal family. In some cases where such approaches do not yield satisfactory results, some jurisdictions have chosen to deal with such issues on the basis of the law of the forum, albeit some only do this with party consent. Consent may also determine the applicability of another foreign law suitable for the parties' case (see para. 4, below). Such rules are part of the substantive law of conflicts and are, therefore, not affected by a court's competence to determine the contents of applicable foreign law according to Rule 26(2) and must therefore be taken into consideration by the court in determining the applicability of foreign law.

The relative difference between techniques for determining domestic and foreign law was the main reason for the present Rules modifying, in so far as they do, the approach taken in the ALI/Unidroit Principles to the question of the court's responsibility for determining the correct legal basis of claims for relief in proceedings.

4. Because of the need for expert evidence to be adduced in order to enable courts to determine the content of any applicable foreign law, nearly all legal cultures consider the determination of such questions to be ones of fact. Therefore, the law of evidence will apply, although it is generally accepted that the contents of foreign law are likely to be special types of facts, with specific features and procedural peculiarities unique to the subject matter. Consequently, in any appeal from findings concerning the content of foreign law, the appellate court must apply the Rules applicable to fact-finding in appeals (see Rules 168, 169 and 172(1)(b) and (2)). The veracity of any application of foreign law as such is not a reason for appeals on law in most procedural systems. Appellants, as is the case in legal systems across the world generally, ought to challenge procedural errors in respect of

fact-finding concerning the content of foreign law. In practice categorising foreign law as a factual issue plays a limited role in the determination of an appeal. This is due to appellate courts approaching such questions by considering whether the result of the application of the foreign law is convincing. If it does not appear so, then that will be on issues concerning the genesis of the expert evidence and its evaluation by the court. In such circumstances it is likely to allow any such appeal on procedural grounds. Upon any second appeal, i.e., on issues of law, the likely result of a successful appeal will be for the proceedings to be referred back to the first or second instance court for new expert evidence to be obtained in the light of the second appeal court's guidance on the issue of law. This particular treatment of any findings concerning the content of foreign law in an appellate review arises from the principle that appeal courts should not generally be required to engage in evidence-taking, not least because in some cases they will not have sufficient expertise in handling expert witnesses. While it may be open to debate whether and how decisions concerning foreign law should be approached via appellate review, however, these Rules are intended to emphasise the need for effective co-operation and interaction between the court and parties at first or second instance, while they are not intended to interfere with longstanding approaches to appeal on points of law.

5. In so far as appropriate, Rule 26(3) extends the application of the dispositive principle to the determination of applicable law. Some European legal systems, which apply the rule *iura novit curia* in a very strict manner, adopt a very narrow or restrictive approach to permitting parties to apply the dispositive principle to applicable law. That being said, even in such systems the extent to which party disposition over applicable law is disputed, and courts regularly accept assertions of 'legal facts', which contain conclusions as to the law which are implicitly contained within pleadings, that have been agreed by the parties, e.g., where a "sales agreement" is said to be the legal basis of the dispute by both parties, and neither raises questions concerning how the agreement was concluded. Other European legal cultures that take a more pragmatic approach to *iura novit curia* or which, at least originally, adopted a more party-dominated approach to procedure are more open to the concept of party disposition over law. These Rules adopt a liberal approach to respecting the parties' right to dispose of their private rights. Consequently, parties are also considered to be capable of agreeing on the law that governs their rights. The one exception to this is that they cannot agree on issues concerning legal provisions that are of mandatory application in the public interest or which are mandatory in order to further the interests of justice, i.e., mandatory protection for consumers and similarly situated parties that are afforded specific procedural protection in proceedings against more powerful parties. This kind of choice of law can be limited to specific issues of the dispute, albeit that any such choices made by the parties must be in reasonable accord with the remaining law to be applied by the court according to general Rules. It is imperative that the parties inform the court of their binding agreement at the commencement of proceedings, in order to ensure that the court does not waste time and resources conducting unnecessary work in ignorance of the agreement. Parties may, if they have not done so before the commencement of the proceedings, bind the Court by determining the legal basis of their dispute or the specific issues in the dispute to which they intend to limit the proceedings.

6. Rule 26(3) also applies to the law of conflicts in so far as the rules of the law of conflicts allow for a choice of foreign law applicable to the dispute.[26] Any applicable foreign law will

26 See, for instance, Arts. 3, 6(2), 7(3) and 8 of Rome I Regulation; and Art. 14 of Rome II Regulation.

determine requirements of and extent to which parties can dispose of their rights under this Rule.

7. Rule 26(3) articulates the right that parties have to narrow the scope of proceedings by agreeing to its legal basis or agreeing to limit it to specific issues. Such agreements must be explicit and will bind the court. This is an aspect of the dispositive principle. Also see Rules 57-60, concerning the basis on which procedural rules are subject to the dispositive principle.

C. SANCTIONS FOR NON-COMPLIANCE AND RELIEF FROM SANCTIONS

Rule 27. Sanctions for Non-Compliance with Rules and court Orders

(1) The court shall disregard factual allegations, modifications of claims and defences, and offers of evidence that are introduced later than permitted by these rules or by court orders, including those concerning amendment. Preclusion does not apply if the court could have taken notice of the party's failure or mistake and itself failed to raise with the parties whether they wished to seek an amendment or relief from sanction.

(2) As a general rule, the court may continue the proceedings and decide on the merits based on the facts and evidence available to it.

(3) The court may draw negative factual inferences, order a party or their lawyer to bear the costs of non-compliance, or in serious cases of non-compliance render an *astreinte*, an order for payment of a fine, administrative sanction as provided by national law, or hold the non-compliant party in contempt.

(4) In assessing the nature of any compensation or fine under this rule, the court may require payment on the following bases: a lump sum; an amount per period of breach; or, an amount per offence. In the latter two cases the amount may be subject to a maximum as determined by the court.

Sources:

ALI/Unidroit Principle 17.

Comments:

1. Rule 27 prescribes various possible sanctions against parties and, in appropriate cases, against their lawyers. The list of sanctions is neither exhaustive nor mandatory. It contains, however, the kinds of sanctions traditionally applied in European jurisdictions. Implementation of sanctions is linked to national sovereignty and national legal traditions; national law may therefore play a significant role here. Rule 27 is complemented by other Rules that provide for the imposition of sanctions against non-compliant parties according to the differing necessities of various procedural stages (see, for instance, Rules 54(3) and (4), 63(1) and (2), and 64(4)). Rule 27 does not address the imposition of sanctions against non-parties. Rules 99, 104, 110, and 122(4) modify Rule 27 as is necessary and appropriate where evidence-taking and access to evidence is concerned in order to apply sanctions to non-parties. Rules 156, 157(3), 159(3), 168, and 178 modify sanctions in respect of non-compliance where appellate process is concerned. Rules 190, 191, and 195 modify the approach to sanctions in respect of provisional measures. Rules 213(2) and 218(1)(a) modify the approach to sanctions in respect of collective proceedings.

2. Sanctions must be proportionate (see Rule 7). Rule 27 provides guidance on the application of proportionality to the adverse consequences, sanctions that can be imposed on parties for procedural non-compliance. The most common form of non-compliance is late compliance with an obligation (see Rule 27(1)). Late compliance may arise where a party either fails to conduct proceedings consistently with the general obligation to conduct proceedings in a speedy and careful manner (see Rules 2 and 47) or fails to comply with a requirement to carry out a procedural act by a specified time (see Rules 49(4) and 50). An effective albeit often excessive sanction for non-compliance is for the court to refuse to permit such a party to rely upon facts or evidence submitted late or to refuse to permit a late amendment to be made. In such circumstances the court will go on to decide the proceedings on the merits based on such facts and evidence that were submitted in time (see Rule 27(2)). For instance, if a party's affirmative defence is too late, the court may determine the claim for relief on its merits without considering that defence. In some cases such an approach may be too severe, in others the nature of the non-compliance would justify such a sanction. It is thus of central importance for a court imposing a sanction to ensure that it is proportionate to the nature and consequences of non-compliance. Such a sanction may be proportionate where its adverse effect is unlikely to have a significant adverse impact on the court's ability to determine the merits. Equally, it may be proportionate where the extent of the non-compliance is significant, and has had an adverse impact on the other party's right to receive a fair trial or on the court's ability to properly manage the proceedings taking account of the non-compliance on its own resources and the need to secure the effective administration of justice generally. The proportionality of any sanction will necessarily depend on the circumstances of the individual case and its consequences for the parties and the court. In an appropriate case, the court may permit late compliance and impose a cost sanction on the non-compliant party (see Rules 27(3) and 55).
3. Imposing a sanction on a party that excludes facts, evidence or proposed amendments to their claim or defence where they complied with a procedural obligation but did so outside the time for compliance, i.e., late or belated compliance, may be too severe a consequence for non-compliance where it was not done deliberately or where the non-compliant party was unaware of their failure to comply. This is particularly the case where the court was aware of the party's error and itself failed to inform the party in order to facilitate effective compliance. Consequently, Rule 27(1) excludes such preclusion arising from a party's belated compliance where there was a failure on the court's part to monitor procedural compliance effectively (see Rule 4, sentence 3). This rule is an aspect of the principle of co-operation between parties and court (see Rules 3(b) and (c), and Rule 4 sentences 1 and 3) and of the principle of proportionality of sanctions (see Rule 7). At the same time it avoids undue pressure being placed on parties to present factual or evidential contentions that may only be relevant to the parties' case in certain circumstances ("*eventualiter*") and should, therefore, only be pleaded, following the making of a relevant case management order by the court. Formerly, and especially in continental European jurisdictions, parties were under an obligation, the "*Eventualmaxime*", to do all that was possibly necessary to the proceedings at a specific point in the proceedings. This, however, led to lengthy and, at least in part, unnecessary pleadings, which in turn created unnecessary costs to the parties and the court, while undermining the court's ability to deliver justice efficiently and speedily. That approach is not supported in these Rules given the need to secure the efficient, speedy and proportionate conduct of proceedings, and the need to ensure that public resources provided to the courts are managed effectively.

4. The possibility of drawing adverse inferences is addressed by Rule 27(3). This form of sanction may be of particular relevance where there is non-compliance with the obligation imposed on parties to contribute to fact-finding in the interest of their opponent (see Rules 25(2), 54 (3) and (4), 99, and 110). Drawing adverse inferences may also imply taking facts as having been established and this, in turn, could lead to claims, defences, or allegations being dismissed in whole or in part. European jurisdictions and legal cultures practice this common form of adverse consequence concerning the scope of adverse inferences differently. Common law jurisdictions, for instance, exercise a broad overriding discretion to draw such inferences, whereas continental European jurisdictions tend to adopt a more restrictive approach to drawing broad adverse inferences, i.e., they adopt a more limited approach such that they take as established only those facts directly affected by the misconduct. It is worth recalling that in Marco Gambazzi (C-394/07, 2 April 2009) the European Court of Justice, in a case involving the public policy clause as ground to refuse recognition and enforcement, had to deal with a sanction imposed by an English court, consisting in the exclusion of the defendant from the proceedings due to non-compliance with an earlier obligation requiring the disclosure of assets imposed by a preceding freezing order. The ECJ did not determine, but left it to the requested State judicial authority (in this case to the Italian courts) to determine if, "following a comprehensive assessment of the proceedings and in the light of all the circumstances, it appears to it that that exclusion measure constituted a manifest and disproportionate infringement of the defendant's right to be heard." Subsequent to this guidance, the Italian courts held that in fact the relevant sanctions deployed by the English court was not disproportionate. This decision, rendered on a question of recognition of foreign judgments, can be taken as supportive of a tolerant approach across European jurisdictions to an understanding of what sanctions may be proportionate. Where, however, sanctions concerning adverse inferences are concerned the present Rules take the more restrictive approach, limiting the sanction to the direct consequences of misconduct and its compensation.
5. Whereas adverse inferences as well as compensatory cost decisions (see Rule 241(2)) are sanctions against parties common to all European jurisdictions, other kinds of sanctions like *astreinte*, fines, administrative sanctions or committal for contempt (Rule 27(3) and (4)) are only used in some jurisdictions for non-compliance with civil enforcement of final judgments, whereas in others they are used to enforce procedural obligations in pending civil proceedings. Other European jurisdictions only permit some sanctions to be imposed on parties to proceedings, i.e., they are not capable of being applied to non-parties, and even then, are only imposed rarely and in exceptional circumstances. The differential approach to sanctions is a consequence of differing ideas concerning the purpose of civil procedure across European jurisdictions. If the enforcement of private rights is considered to be civil procedure's dominant purpose, the disadvantage that non-compliance creates for the defaulting party, i.e., losing the case, may be viewed as a sufficient adverse consequence, i.e., sanction. If a party's right to secure the truth from their opponent and the public interest in ensuring that proceedings are conducted fairly by both parties are equally important elements of the procedure's purpose within a specific legal culture, in some cases, at least, the application of direct sanctions for procedural misconduct may be considered to be necessary. In practice it will rarely be the case that adverse inferences or compensatory cost decisions fail to protect a party that is

adversely affected by their opponent's procedural non-compliance sufficiently. Examples of such rare cases are where a party is unable to formulate their own claim for relief effectively without having knowledge of factual matters that are within their opponent's knowledge and control.

6. These Rules leave the details of sanctions to national law. They provide no more than general guidelines for giving proper effect to such sanctions (see Rule 27(4)). It is for national law to determine the exact nature of pecuniary sanctions that may be imposed on non-compliant parties, and not least to determine whether fines or *astreintes* should be an available sanction bearing in mind that the former are paid to the State and the latter to the non-compliant party's opponent. In assessing which form of available sanction to impose, a court should consider, amongst other things, the seriousness of the matter and the harm caused, the extent to which the non-compliant party participated in the breach of rules, and the degree to which the conduct was deliberate. Consistent with this, severe or aggravated misconduct by parties, such as submitting perjured evidence or violent or threatening behaviour, may lead to more serious sanctions and criminal liability. It is important to stress that a sanction may be appropriate even where the non-compliant conduct was not deliberate.
7. Within these Rules, provisional or protective measures are understood to be a special form of court proceedings that promote the proper administration of justice. They are not a form of preventive execution, as understood in some European jurisdictions (see Rules 184 and following). As such, non-compliance with such measures are dealt as sanctions (see Rules 27(3) and (4) and 191). As is generally the case with sanctions for non-compliance, it is a matter for the court to consider the appropriate sanction to apply from the various means available. Interim payments are excluded from this Rule as such an order is enforceable upon a respondent's assets.
8. A fine or compensation paid under Rule 27(3) and (4) should either be paid to the State or the applicant. Additionally, a respondent that fails to comply with a sanction may be subject to committal for contempt of court or to administrative sanctions. Rule 195 extends the court's power to sanction non-compliance to non-parties who were made subject to asset preservation orders.

Rule 28. Relief from the consequences of procedural non-compliance

Where a sanction for non-compliance with a rule or court order has been imposed, the subject of the sanction may apply for relief from that sanction. In considering whether, on application by a party, to exercise its discretion to grant relief the court must take account of the need for proceedings to be conducted consistently with the principles of co-operation and proportionality.

Comments:

1. Rule 28 makes clear that the adverse consequences, sanctions, for procedural non-compliance by parties to proceedings can be varied or revoked by the court on the application of the party affected. The reconsideration of such sanctions is consistent with the principles of co-operation (see Rules 2 - 4) and proportionality (see Rules 5 – 8). Also see Rule 50(3), which permits the court to reconsider, vary or revoke case management orders.

2. The court is not permitted to sanction misconduct or to vary and revoke sanctions on its own motion (*ex officio*) without first giving the parties a fair opportunity to be heard (see Rule 11).
3. Parties affected by procedural errors on the part of the court should challenge them immediately in order to avoid any possible consequences of conclusive waiver (see Rule 178). Non-parties affected by procedural rulings or sanctions have a right to appeal (see Rule 180). Parties affected by sanctions only have a right to appeal in special cases (see Rules 179(1) and (2)(d)).

PART II

PARTIES

SECTION 1—GENERAL PART

INTRODUCTION

This part of the Rules aims to ensure that the court is properly accessible to all persons who have a legitimate interest in bringing or defending proceedings, i.e., in vindicating or enforcing rights. Parties to litigation can be persons who are able to hold rights under substantive law (Rule 29). Parties' litigation capacity presupposes that they have the capacity to exercise such rights under substantive law. Lacking litigation capacity, parties have to be represented according to applicable law (Rule 30). Where a party, such as a legal person, lacks litigation capacity they must be represented by such natural persons as are entitled by substantive law to represent them (Rule 31). Those who have litigation capacity must bring proceedings in their own name unless otherwise permitted by special provisions (Rule 34). Multi-party litigation can take the form of a collective proceedings in which the group members are not regular parties (see Part XI). An authorised person may, in the public interest, act as a main party or intervene in proceedings (Rule 35).

In appropriate cases, proceedings may be brought by several claimants or against several defendants as parties joined to the litigation (Rule 36). The court may order the consolidation of separate proceedings for the purpose of properly managing them (Rule 37). A proceeding shall be brought by or against parties jointly when it is necessary that the court's judgment bind all of them in the same terms (Rule 38). Anyone not a party who claims a right in the subject matter of that proceeding may file a claim directly against one or more of the parties with the court (Rule 39). Anyone who has a legitimate interest in a proceeding between parties may intervene in support of a party to those proceedings (Rule 40). A party may notify a non-party of the dispute if the party might have a claim against or be subject to a claim by the non-party depending on the outcome of the proceedings (Rule 42). With the court's consent, submissions concerning important issues in the action may be received from natural or legal persons or other entities with the consent of the court (Rule 43). At any time after the commencement of proceedings substitution or succession of a party by another person is possible if required by law or if it is necessary in the interest of good administration of justice (Rule 44).

Rule 29. The Parties to Proceedings

(1) Parties to civil proceedings are all the persons by and against whom the proceedings are brought.

(2) Anyone who has the capacity to hold a right under substantive law may be a party to civil proceedings.

Comments:

1. A number of European jurisdictions provide basic rules on the question of who can be a party to civil proceedings. It is a widespread European concept to take a formal approach

ELI-Unidroit Model European Rules of Civil Procedure. ELI & Unidroit, Oxford University Press.
 DOI: 10.1093/oso/9780198866589.003.0003

with respect to the definition of "parties". Irrespective of who is (under substantive law) the creditor or debtor, a party is anybody who has brought proceedings or against whom proceedings have been brought and who has the capacity to hold rights under substantive law.

2. The capacity to sue or be sued is to be clearly distinguished from the capacity to act during proceedings ("litigation capacity", see Rule 30). Both questions are almost always closely linked to substantive law and reflect the idea that the capacity to sue or be sued corresponds to the general ability under substantive law to be the holder of rights or obligations. All natural and legal persons have that ability, but it may be extended for example to unborn children and entities that are not legal persons, such as trade unions, trusts, etc.
3. For cross-border situations there is a special conflict-of-laws rule (see Rules 45 and 46).

Rule 30. Litigation Capacity of Natural Persons

(1) Litigation capacity is the capacity to exercise rights in civil proceedings.

(2) Anyone who has the capacity to exercise rights or obligations in their own name under the substantive law shall be deemed to have litigation capacity.

(3) Anyone not within the scope of Rule 30(2) must be represented in proceedings by a representative according to the rules of the applicable law.

Comments:

1. The terminology for litigation capacity varies amongst European jurisdictions, e.g., legal standing, litigation capacity, capacity to proceed, capacity to conduct proceedings or procedural legal capacity. All the different expressions, however, describe the same phenomenon (see Rule 29, comments). Rule 30(2) adopts the concept that is used in numerous European jurisdictions, which simply refers to the decisions made in substantive law with respect to the ability to act on one's own account.
2. The term "capacity to exercise rights" is generally taken to refer to the capacity to enter into contracts. Some European jurisdictions do, however, have different rules concerning capacity to enter into contracts and for liability in tort law depending on the age of the persons and their ability to consider the legal consequences of their acts. Rule 30(2) thus adopts a general form of words, emphasising that capacity is determined by the applicable substantive law of the jurisdiction.
3. Persons who do not have full capacity under the applicable substantive law, even if they are a party to the proceedings, cannot conduct the proceedings on their own. They must be represented during the proceedings by their legal representative (see Rule 31), which should not be confused with the lawyer that is acting in the litigation based on a power of attorney or retainer.
4. The "applicable law" in the sense of Rule 30(3) can be either substantive or procedural law, but it does not mean applicable law in the sense of conflict of laws rules. Rules for cross-border situations are set out at Rule 45 and following.

Rule 31. Representation of Legal Persons and other entities

Legal persons and other entities that are parties must exercise their rights through natural persons who are entitled to represent them according to the substantive law.

Comments:

1. According to Rule 29(2) the capacity to sue or be sued includes natural and legal persons as well as other entities, if under the applicable substantive law such an entity has the capacity to hold a right. Consequently, Rule 31 provides a rule on representation, which includes "other entities", e.g., trusts, partnerships or unincorporated associations.
2. Rule 31 could, in future, also include technical entities, e.g., robots or artificial intelligence, as "other entities" if they have legal capacity under substantive law.

Rule 32. Proof of Representation

The court may, at any time in the proceedings, order the representative to prove the existence or scope of their power to act.

Comments:

1. Where the court doubts a representative's authority to represent a party or the scope of such representation, or where one of the parties challenges the existence or extent of such authority, the court may ask for proof. Rule 32 complements the general principle provided for in Rule 33, but it only applies to representation as provided by Rule 31. As such it does not apply to representation by a lawyer.
2. The scope of authority to represent a party is not defined in these Rules, as that will be determined by substantive law.

Rule 33. Court Review of its own motion (ex officio *review)*

The Court shall at all times ensure compliance with Rules 29 to 31 and make any appropriate order.

Comments:

1. European jurisdictions have different concepts for reviewing the requirements that must be met for proceedings to be admissible (see Rule 133 on admissibility). In all cases, the requirements set out in Rules 29 to 31 are of such importance, particularly in respect of the protection of parties that lack litigation capacity, that courts should, of their own motion (*ex officio*) ensure that they are monitoring compliance with the requirements of these rules (also see Rule 4 sentence 3). While some European jurisdictions, such as Belgium, explicitly prohibit such a form of review, it is an approach that broadly prevails across Europe, and to a certain extent therefore can properly modify the general principle of party disposition.
2. Rule 33 also provides courts with a broad discretion to take such steps as are necessary to protect, for example, a party who lacks litigation capacity and has no representative (Rule 30(3)). In such a situation the court may appoint a representative or take other steps to ensure representation. It may stay the proceedings until a representative has been appointed.

Rule 34. Persons Entitled to Bring Proceedings

Persons with litigation capacity must bring proceedings in their own name and on the basis of their own substantive rights unless either these Rules or substantive law otherwise permit.

Comments:

1. The rule that claimants can only bring proceedings based on their own substantive rights is a basic principle in many European civil procedure codes although often without there being an explicit rule to that effect. In specific circumstances, procedural or substantive law may exceptionally permit an individual to bring proceedings in their own name, even though it is based on another person's claim. In these Rules the provisions on collective proceedings provide an exception to the principle set out in this Rule (see Rules 205-206, on collective interest injunctions, and Rule 207 and following, collective proceedings). Additionally, for example, insurance law, trust law or rules under substantive law permitting derivative actions or subrogation can provide similar exceptions.
2. Where proceedings are brought by someone other than the right-holder upon agreement, the requirements of admissibility vary between European jurisdictions. Some require that the claimant has either a legal interest or at least a substantial economic interest to bring an action in the interest of the other person. While such matters can be left to substantive law, there is a general need to ensure that safeguards are in place to prevent misuse by the original "owner" of the claim authorising proceedings to be brought by another person who does not have sufficient financial resources to meet any potential adverse cost order. Rules 3(e) and 133(e) may apply to prevent such abuse. Moreover, the Rules concerning the denial of legal aid (Rule 244(1)) or sanctions against lawyers involved (Rule 27(3) and (4)) may also be relevant in this regard.

Rule 35. Public Interest

A person who is authorised by law to act in the public interest, may act as a party or intervene in any proceedings.

Sources:

ALI/UNIDROIT Principle 13.

Comments:

1. Some European jurisdictions have the tradition that public prosecutors or public regulators may intervene in civil proceedings in order to protect a relevant public interest. This will often apply in family proceedings, which are beyond the scope of these Rules, but may also become necessary in civil proceedings, e.g., in claims for damages arising from alleged anti-trust law infringements. It is, also, very often the case that the legal issues raised in appellate proceedings are often of general public interest. In such circumstances, it may become necessary for a representative of the public interest to be joined as a party to the proceedings, and thereby ensure that the appellate court can issue a final judgment. This is particularly important where the actual parties to the proceedings abandon the appeal.
2. More generally, intervention may be permitted in order to enable issues of public interest to be properly raised in the proceedings. The extent to which this form of intervention can be used will depend on European Union law and the law of the forum (see also for appeals Rule 153, comment 2).

SECTION 2—SPECIAL PART

A. MULTIPLE PARTIES

1. Joinder of parties

Rule 36. Voluntary Joinder of Parties

(1) Multiple parties may bring or defend claims in a single proceeding. They may do so if
(a) their claims are closely connected, and
(b) the court has jurisdiction with respect to all parties.
(2) The court may, where it is necessary for the purpose of properly managing the proceedings, order the claims to continue as separate proceedings.
(3) Each of the joined parties acts on their own account. Their actions or omissions in the proceedings shall not prejudice the other joined parties.

Sources:
ALI/UNIDROIT Principle 12.1; Transnational Rules of Civil Procedure (Reporters' Study) Rule 5.1.

Comments:
1. Joinder of parties is a widespread concept in Europe albeit with numerous differences in terminology and in the requirements that must be met to give effect to it. Rule 36 provides a broad concept. The term "voluntary", which may also be called "permissive", joinder, which only requires there to be a close connection between claims, is used in order to distinguish it from "mandatory" joinder (Rule 38), where joinder is necessary for a specific reason. Parties may join their claims in a single action where the claims are legally or factually related ("closely connected") or where they are asserting a single joint legal right, e.g., they are joint owners of a property. Where a single claimant has claims against multiple defendants they may only be asserted in a single proceeding where the commonality requirement is satisfied, e.g., where a landlord can sue several tenants on the same ground.
2. Any rule on joinder of parties is closely related to the jurisdiction of the court. Rule 36(1)(b) emphasises that joinder is only possible if the court has jurisdiction with respect to all claims and parties. It does not create a jurisdictional rule of its own.[1]
3. The main difference between voluntary and necessary joinder of parties lies in the procedural consequences. In the case of voluntary joinder, the claims remain separate and are only formally bundled together for a joint hearing or the taking of evidence. Each party therefore acts on their own account without any procedural effects on the other joint parties. The court must also treat joined parties as individuals and, for example, summon them individually to hearings. Such joinder necessarily promotes effective management of proceedings and promotes proportionality (see Rules 5, 6, 37, 49 and 50)
4. Rule 36(1) deals with the situation where claimants have already commenced proceedings together or where one or several claimants have commenced proceedings against several defendants. Even if the requirements of Rule 36(2) are fulfilled, the court must be able to deal with those proceedings flexibly. It therefore provides the court with discretion to separate the joined claims and defences into separate proceedings. For consolidation of

1 In cross-border settings Art. 8(1) of the Brussels Ibis Regulation) provides a broad basis for the joinder of parties domiciled in another European Union Member State.

separately filed actions see Rule 37. In the case of genuine mass claims, where there are hundreds or thousands of claimants or numerous defendants, a simple joinder of parties may not be an efficient way to handle the litigation and numerous technical problems may arise, e.g., with respect to service, or provisional enforcement. Given this such claims are dealt with in Part XI.

Rule 37. Consolidation of Separate Proceedings

The court may order the consolidation of separate proceedings pending before it to enable them to be managed properly in a single proceeding.

Sources:
ALI/UNIDROIT Principle 12.5.

Comments:

1. If the parties do not bring a single proceeding jointly from the outset or do not sue several defendants jointly, the court should have the power to consolidate them into a single proceeding.
2. The requirements of Rule 36(1) must be fulfilled to effect consolidation under Rule 37, and any such consolidation must be necessary to facilitate effective case management.
3. The consolidation of proceedings that are pending before different courts must not disregard rules on jurisdiction (see Rule 146(2), comment 4).

Rule 38. Necessary Joinder of Parties

(1) A proceeding must be brought by or against parties jointly where either the joint nature of the legal right or the substantive law requires a judgment to bind all of the joined parties in the same terms.

(2) A procedural act carried out by one or more of the joined parties shall affect all such parties.

(3) In the case of settlement, waiver of claim, or an admission, all the joined parties must consent to be bound by the act.

Comments:

1. Necessary joinder is a procedural concept which follows the classifications and specifications of substantive law. Where the claims or obligations of several persons are so closely connected that they cannot be adjudicated upon differently, or where individuals jointly hold a right and the court can only therefore decide the case on a unitary basis i.e., its decision cannot but bind all the claimants or defendants, joinder of such parties is "necessary". Examples of such situations are, for instance, where claimants can only act jointly under substantive law or where defendants can only be subject to a collective liability. If joinder of parties is in fact necessary, the proceedings must be brought jointly by claimants or against defendants. If the parties fail to do so, the proceedings will be dismissed.
2. In some European jurisdictions, a significant consequence of necessary joinder is that if one of the parties does not appear they are taken to be represented by the other joint party or parties and, hence, they cannot be subject to any judgment by default.[2] Rule

2 See, for instance, Austria CCP § 14; Bulgaria CCP Sec. 216(2); Germany CCP § 62; Greece CCP Art. 76(4).

38(2) and (3) adopt a broader concept,[3] according to which any procedural act by one of the joint parties operates to the advantage of all of them, with the exceptions provided in Rule 38(3).

3. The situations described in Rule 38(3) are exceptional because settlements, waivers of claims or admission by defendant that acknowledge the validity of the claim, rather than merely of particular facts, will either completely or partially terminate the proceedings and no decision on the merits will be necessary. Therefore all joint parties must be part of the settlement or consent to the waiver or admission.

2. Intervention and Third Parties

Rule 39. Principal Intervention

Anyone not a party to proceedings who claims a right in its subject matter, may bring a claim directly against one or more of the parties in the court, in which the dispute is pending at first instance or, if the Court so permits, on appeal.

Sources:
ALI/Unidroit Principle 12.2

Comments:

1. Principal (or main) intervention is a widely accepted concept. The requirements for intervention necessarily differ across Europe. In essence, Rule 39 is a venue rule, and should therefore have a limited scope of application. It permits a non-party to intervene on their own initiative in those cases where they have a claim to be entitled to the claim or right which is the subject matter of a pending action between other parties. In terms of jurisdiction the non-party may benefit from the fact that proceedings are already pending and that they may sue both parties who are already before the court where proceedings are pending. Rule 39, for example, authorises a non-party to pending proceedings to intervene where they claim to be the owner of real estate property that the claimant and the defendant also claim to own.
2. Rule 39 is based on the assumption that the intervenor has a right to intervene and that the intervention is not subject to admission or discretion by the court.[4] If the requirements for such intervention are not met, any application or proceeding brought by the intervenor will be dismissed on general procedural grounds.
3. European jurisdictions differ with respect to the possibility and time frame for pursuing a main or principal intervention depending on their appellate process. Rule 39 follows the widely accepted approach that principal intervention, at first instance, is permitted at any time. If intervention were permitted until a final and binding judgment was handed down, the intervenor might be restricted in their ability to present new facts and evidence depending on the respective appellate system. Therefore Rule 39 requires court permission for any principal intervention at the appellate level and the court in exercising its

3 See, for instance, Greece CCP Art. 76(3); Sweden CJP, Ch. 14 § 8(2); Switzerland Federal CCP Art. 70(2).

4 See, for instance, Belgium CCP Sec. 813; Bulgaria CCP Sec. 225; Hungary CCP Sec. 55, 56; Sweden CJP Sec. 10.

discretion will have to take into consideration the benefits of such intervention in the light of the scope of the applicable appellate (see Rules 169 and 174).

4. As the intervenor becomes a party to the proceedings, Rules 29-33 apply automatically upon intervention taking place.

Rule 40. Voluntary Intervention in Support of a Party

(1) Anyone who has a legitimate interest in one or more parties succeeding in proceedings may intervene in support of their claim or defence. They may intervene at any time before the final hearing is concluded.

(2) The intervenor in support of a party may not object to any procedural step already taken in the proceeding. Intervenors may, however, take any procedural step that the party they support may take if this is not in conflict with any procedural step taken by that party.

Comments:

1. Intervention in support, or accessory intervention, can be found in numerous European jurisdictions. It can be either the voluntary intervention by a non-party or mandatory intervention based on notice being given by one of the parties (see Rule 42). Under the most common form, accessory intervention permits a person who was not originally party to the proceedings to intervene in support of one of the parties whose success or not in the pending proceedings affects the interests or the legal position of the intervenor.
2. The consequences of such intervention differ considerably across Europe. In France and European jurisdictions that have adopted the French system[5] the intervenor becomes a party to the proceedings and the judgment binds them. However, since the intervention in support is accessory to the main claim, the intervenor may participate in any appeal procedure or second appeal procedure only if the supported party brings such an appeal or second appeal. Nevertheless the intervenor may bring an appeal in their own right if the respondent to the appeal does not contest it and the appeal court will have no power to dismiss such an appeal in those circumstances on that ground. In other European jurisdictions the court will not decide on the alleged claim of the supported party against the intervenor.[6] The intervenor does not become a party to the litigation, but can act in the interest of the supported party or even take over the presentation of their case. Nevertheless, a final judgment will have a binding effect on the intervenor, where they are subject to a non-party notice (Rule 42). This effect will apply in such circumstances irrespective of whether the non-party becomes an intervenor or refuses to join the proceedings. This effect, however, becomes relevant only in any subsequent litigation between the supported party and the intervenor. In order to avoid complex rules on the binding effect of a judgment between the parties upon the intervenor, Rule 42 assumes that the intervenor in support becomes a party to the litigation.

5 See, for instance, Arts. 331-333 of the French CCP and Sec. 223 of the Bulgarian CCP.

6 See, for instance, such as Austria, OGH verst Senat, 8.4.1997, 1 Ob 2123/96d (OLG Linz 29.2.1996, 11 R 33/95); LG Wels 12.4. 1995, 1 Cg 291/92), in JBl. 1997, 368; Germany CCP § 72-74, 68; Hungary CCP Sec. 58-60; Italy CCP Arts. 106, 167(2), 272; Sweden CJP Ch. 14 § 12; Switzerland CCP Arts. 80. 77.

3. Some European jurisdictions, such as Belgium, France or Germany, permit intervention in support at any time until the end of the trial and the intervenor takes the case as they find it. This has been adopted as a general principle in Rule 40(1). As the court has to decide on the application to intervene (Rule 41), the court may balance the pros and cons of an intervention in appellate proceedings.
4. It is also common ground that an intervenor needs not only accept the procedural situation as it is at the time of their intervention. They are not allowed to contradict the position already taken by the supported party. They can thus only support a party. Therefore the intervenor is not allowed to take procedural actions that are inconsistent with or contradict those taken by the supported party.[7]

Rule 41. Notice by Voluntary Intervenors

(1) Anyone seeking to participate in proceedings as an intervenor under the preceding Rules must make an application to the court. The application must state the basis on which intervention is sought. Notice of the application shall be given to the parties.

(2) The parties shall be heard concerning the proposed intervention. The court may order the applicant and the parties to attend an oral hearing.

(3) An application to intervene does not suspend the proceedings unless the court orders otherwise.

Comments:

1. Rule 41 applies to Rule 39 only in so far as permission is necessary for principal intervention in the appellate instance. It does not apply to principal intervention in proceedings pending at first instance.
2. It is a widely accepted that intervention in support of one of the parties requires court permission. Therefore a formal application is necessary and the parties must be notified. Notice within the meaning of Rule 41(1) means formal service on the parties. The court should hear the parties before it rules on the intervenor's application (Rule 41(2)). If the requirements of Rule 40(1) are not met, the court should refuse to permit intervention to take place. If there is a dispute over admissibility of the intervention, the proceedings should not be delayed and the court may continue with the proceedings in order to avoid the process being used abusively (Rule 41(3)).
3. Rules 40 and 41 adopt a system according to which the non-party becomes a regular party to the proceedings and can be subject to a *res judicata* decision with respect to the claim against them. Therefore a non-party notice (Rule 42) must fulfil the requirements of a document instituting the proceedings and formal service is thus necessary.

Rule 42. Third-Party Notice

(1) A party may give any person notice of the dispute if, in the event of that party's claim or defence being unsuccessful, they might have a claim against or be subject to a claim by that person.

(2) A person given notice under Rule 42(1) becomes a party to the proceedings unless the court, upon application, orders otherwise.

7 See, for instance, Germany CCP § 67; Greece CCP Art. 82; Switzerland Federal CCP Art. 76 [2].

(3) **The third-party notice must state the matter at issue and the reason why they have been given such notice.**

Comments:

1. Rule 42(1) sets out the requirements of third-party notice. It is necessary that a party demonstrates that they have a claim against a third-party or that they will be subject to a claim by them, if they lose the claim in the pending proceeding. For instance, in a dispute between the seller and buyer of an allegedly defective car, the seller, if held liable in the litigation with the buyer, may have a claim for recourse against the car manufacturer. The seller may therefore serve a third-party notice on the manufacturer. Unsuccessful within Rule 42(1) means either partially or totally unsuccessful.
2. Rule 42 adopts a system according to which the third-party becomes a regular party to the proceedings and can be subject to a *res judicata* decision with respect to the claim against them. Therefore any third-party notice must fulfil the requirements of a document instituting the proceedings and formal service is thus necessary.
3. Rule 42 may result in existing rules on jurisdiction, which are not part of these rules, to be modified. If the third-party becomes a party, generally as a defendant, to the pending proceeding regardless of whether the court seised has jurisdiction for an action against the non-party according to any applicable rules on jurisdiction, third-party notices would have far-reaching consequences not covered by Rule 42 without an additional clarifying rule on jurisdiction such as that set out in Article 8(2) of the Brussels Ibis Regulation. In contrast, in the French system, solely upon service of notice the third-party cannot contest the court's jurisdiction and cannot even invoke an agreement on jurisdiction with the party having initiated the third-party notice.[8] Lacking any rule on jurisdiction that covers jurisdiction over the third-party, the court must deny the admissibility of the third-party notice (see Rule 42(2)).
4. Rule 42 does not allow the court to invite the parties to serve a third-party notice or to issue such a notice of its own motion (*ex officio*).
5. See Rule 54 on the application of this Rule to defendants.

Rule 43. ***Amicus Curiae***

(1) **Any natural or legal person, or other entity, may provide the court with submissions concerning important issues in proceedings with the consent of the court. The court may also invite such submissions.**

(2) **Before giving its consent, or inviting submissions, under Rule 43(1) the court must consult the parties.**

Sources:

ALI/UNIDROIT Principle 13.

Comments:

1. Rule 43 permits "entities" to act as *amicus curiae*. This includes unincorporated public or private organisations, NGOs and other interest groups, public regulators, and Ombudsman.

8 See Art 333 of the French CPC.

B. SUBSTITUTION AND SUCCESSION OF PARTIES

Rule 44. Substitution and Succession

(1) At any time after proceedings are commenced the court must permit the substitution or the succession of a party by another person where the law requires it.

(2) At any time after proceedings are commenced the court may permit the substitution or the succession of a party by another person if that is appropriate in the interest of the good administration of justice.

(3) Unless the court orders otherwise, the proceedings continue upon substitution or succession of a party from the position they had reached at the time substitution or succession was effected.

Sources:
ALI/Unidroit Principles 12.3.

Comments:

1. Rule 44 covers two situations. Primarily it deals with voluntary substitution, e.g., where a claimant discovers that they have sued the wrong defendant or where a claimant is not the proper party because, for instance, a company's legal representative brings proceedings in their name rather than the company's name. In many European jurisdictions, such as France or Belgium, it is not possible to substitute a person who is not a proper party before the final judgment. In such cases the final judgment will usually decide that the proceedings were brought against the wrong defendant. In other European jurisdictions, such as Germany or the United Kingdom, it is possible to effect the substitution of a party for the proper party as soon as such a mistake is known. Such an approach may be subject to party consent or court approval. This approach, adopted here, reduces delay, and promotes proportionality in proceedings.
2. Rule 44(1) also deals with party succession arising from the assignment of claims for relief, the transfer of debts, the death of a party, loss of capacity to litigate, or insolvency.
3. Where substantive law or other procedural rules, such as arising from insolvency law, require party substitution the court may not normally refuse to order substitution to take effect (Rule 44(1)). In all other cases the court must order substitution to take place in accordance with Rule 44(2). As a general rule, proceedings are not suspended when substitution takes effect, however it may be necessary for the court to make provision for the party succeeding or substituting for the original party to be given time to prepare their case properly. The court may thus grant an adjournment of the proceedings.
4. The court's decision on costs (Rule 239) must particularly take account of the substituted party's costs and their possible reimbursement according to the specific circumstances of the proceedings (see generally Rule 241).

SECTION 3—CROSS BORDER ISSUES

Rule 45. Capacity of foreign nationals to be a party

The capacity of foreign nationals or legal persons incorporated outside the forum State shall be assessed for foreign nationals according to the law of the country of their habitual

residence or their citizenship, and for legal persons according to the law of the State of their incorporation.

Comments:

1. It is a generally accepted rule that the capacity of foreign persons to be a party to proceedings is to be assessed according to the law of the country of their nationality. Where an individual has capacity under the law of the country of their nationality, they will have the capacity to be a party to proceedings.
2. Notwithstanding the generally accepted approach, Rule 45 adopts the approach to determining capacity that is broadly found in European conflict of laws, i.e., that in the absence of party choice, applicable law is determined by the habitual residence of affected persons rather than nationality.[9]

   It is also settled case law of the European Court of Justice that companies incorporated in a European Union Member State may transfer their centre of administration or seat without losing the capacity to hold rights, and hence their capacity to be a party in civil litigation, acquired in the place where they were incorporated. Rule 45 extends this approach to persons who have their habitual residence outside, or are incorporated outside, the European Union.

Rule 46. Litigation capacity

(1) A non-resident's litigation capacity shall be assessed according to the law of their habitual residence or their citizenship.

(2) A non-resident who lacks capacity to conduct litigation under the law of their habitual residence or citizenship but has such capacity under the law of the forum State may take procedural steps in proceedings on their own behalf.

(3) A legal person, incorporated outside the forum State, shall have its litigation capacity assessed according to the law of the place of incorporation.

Comments:

1. It is a common and generally accepted rule that, in principle, litigation capacity is governed by the same law that determines capacity to be a party. Nevertheless, non-residents who lack litigation capacity under the law of the country of their habitual residence may still act on their behalf if they have litigation capacity in the forum State (see Rule 30 on litigation capacity).
2. A foreign association should have the same right to bring an action in the forum State as an association registered in that State. This should be the case except where specific administrative authorisation is required (see Rules 204 – 205, and 208 and following).

9 See, for instance, Rome I and II Regulations and Regulation (EU) No 650/2012 of the European Parliament and of the Council of 4 July 2012 on jurisdiction, applicable law, recognition and enforcement of decisions and acceptance and enforcement of authentic instruments in matters of succession and on the creation of a European Certificate of Succession. Also see the European Court of Justice's case law on the transfer of the seat of companies within the European Union (Judgments of 5 November 2002, Überseering (C-208/00, ECR 2002 p. I-9919) ECLI:EU:C:2002:632; of 9 March 1999, Centros (C-212/97, ECR 1999 p. I-1459) ECLI:EU:C:1999:126; and of 30 September 2003, Inspire Art (C-167/01, ECR 2003 p. I-10155) ECLI:EU:C:2003:512).

PART III

CASE MANAGEMENT

Rule 47. Careful Conduct of litigation by the Parties

Parties must present their claims, defences, factual allegations and offers of evidence as early and completely as possible and as appropriate to the careful conduct of litigation in order to secure procedural expedition.

Sources:
ALI/Unidroit Principles 7, 11 and 22.

Comments:

1. In general, responsibility for the efficient and speedy resolution of disputes is shared between the court and parties (see Rule 2). The court will not be able to fulfil its general case management duty (see Rule 4) without party co-operation (see Rules 3(b) and (e)). Rule 47 articulates the mandatory duty placed on parties requiring their co-operation with the court and its content.
2. Some European codes of civil procedure set short time limits for individual procedural steps to be taken by the parties consistently with their duty to conduct proceedings in a responsible manner consistent with the aims of securing expedition and efficiency. Moreover, they provide courts with the power to extend time limits in appropriate circumstances, such as where a party has been unable to comply with the initial time limit for reasons outside their control. Other European procedural codes set out a more liberal approach, avoiding short time limits and providing flexible time limits, which can be adapted to the needs of individual cases depending on the circumstances of the proceedings, for the completion of procedural obligations. In such codes the procedural calendar is, in principle, considered an essential part of the court's responsibility for active case management (see Rules 2, 4, and 49(4)), with specific time limits being the exception rather than the rule (see, for instance, Rules 54(1), 156, 159, 165, 179(3), and 183).
3. The efficiency of flexible judicial timetables depends on the parties providing the court with all necessary and relevant information concerning their approach to the proceedings. To carry out its management responsibility effectively, the court must have the parties' co-operation. Hence the need for the present obligation on the parties to provide the court with relevant information in a timely fashion. In so far as appropriate, the pre-commencement duty placed on parties to provide each other with information concerning the core elements of their dispute, and potential management timetable for proceedings, facilitates the later provision of adequate information to the court (see Rule 51).
4. Court and party co-operation concerning the effective management of proceedings does not, however, mean that parties are required to provide the court with all relevant matters concerning their respective cases, e.g., facts and evidence, from the start of proceedings. Effective co-operation with the court and effective management requires the court and parties to ensure that such material is presented at an appropriate time, in the circumstances of the case, so that the court can properly manage its overall caseload effectively (see Rule 27, comment 3). Consequently, and consistent with the principle of proportionality (see Rules 5-7), it would generally be sufficient for parties to provide the court at the initial stage of proceedings with factual assertions and information on relevant means of

ELI-Unidroit Model European Rules of Civil Procedure. ELI & Unidroit, Oxford University Press.
 DOI: 10.1093/oso/9780198866589.003.0004

evidence-taking, to the extent that their relevance to the proceedings is, at that stage, reasonably clear and foreseeable. Party co-operation requires them to take reasonable steps; it is not an absolute or strict obligation. To ensure that parties fulfil their duty to co-operate properly, the court ought to monitor their conduct throughout the proceedings. It ought to require the parties to take such steps as it considers necessary to fulfil the obligation when it considers that such steps are necessary for the proper management of proceedings (see Rules 4 sentence 3, 24(1) and (2), 25(3), 26(2) and 48).

Rule 48. Court control of proceedings

At all stages of the proceedings the court must monitor whether parties and their lawyers comply with Rule 47 and any order made under Rule 49.

Sources:
ALI/UNIDROIT Principles 7.1, 14, 22.1 and 2.

Comments:

1. Rule 48 should be read together with the general rules on co-operation between parties and court (see Rules 2-4). Those Rules also address the court's continuing duty to monitor parties' compliance with their responsibilities (see Rule 4(3)). Rule 48 specifically refers to the parties' duty to conduct the litigation carefully with a view to securing procedural expedition (see Rule 47) and to the parties' duty to pay due attention to, i.e., comply with, the court's case management orders (see Rules 49 and 50).
2. The court is required to monitor all of the parties' procedural responsibilities. On the one hand it must monitor how the parties manage their own procedural risks, such as the burden to introduce all facts relevant to their case (see Rule 24(1)), to offer sufficient means of evidence (see Rules 25(1) and 94) and cogent legal contentions (see Rule 26(1)) to convince the court of their case. On the other hand it is required to monitor how the parties fulfil their duties properly and in a timely fashion, breach of which may result in the imposition of sanctions or other adverse consequences arising from the non-compliance such as, for instance, preclusion (see Rules 27, 47, and 93), the drawing of adverse inferences (see Rules 27(3), 54(3), 88(1)(b) and (3), 99(a) and 110), or costs, fines, or *astreintes*, or proceedings for contempt of court (see Rules 27(3) and (4) and Rule 99(b)).
3. The court may not preclude or otherwise sanction a party if it did not carry out its monitoring role effectively, and as a consequence the parties fail to comply with these Rules and thus are required to seek an amendment or other relief (see Rule 27(1)).
4. See further Rule 33, which establishes the court's duty to ensure compliance with Rules 29-31 and provides the means to take remedial action in respect of non-compliance.

Rule 49. Means of Case management

Where necessary for the proper management of proceedings, the court shall, in particular:

(1) encourage parties to take active steps to settle their dispute or parts of their dispute and, where appropriate, to use alternative dispute resolution methods;
(2) schedule case management conferences;
(3) determine the type and the form of the procedure;
(4) set a timetable or procedural calendar with deadlines for procedural steps to be taken by parties and/or their lawyers;
(5) limit the number and length of future submissions;

(6) determine the order in which issues should be tried and whether proceedings should be consolidated or separated;

(7) determine the separation of questions concerning jurisdiction, provisional measures and statutes of limitation for early decision upon special hearings;

(8) consider necessary amendments regarding the parties' proper representation, the consequences of changes related to the parties to litigation and the participation of third parties, intervenors, or other persons;

(9) consider amendments to the pleadings or offers of evidence in the light of the parties' contentions;

(10) require a party's appearance in person or require a party's representative, who should be fully informed of all matters relevant to the proceedings, to be present at a court hearing;

(11) address the availability, admissibility, form, disclosure and exchange of evidence and, if adequate to the state of proceedings,

(a) determine the admissibility of evidence;

(b) order the taking of evidence.

Sources:

ALI/UNIDROIT Principles 7, 22.2, and 14; Transnational Rules of Civil Procedure (Reporters' Study) Rule 18.

Comments:

1. Rule 49 sets out the court's general duty of active case management (Rule 4(1)), which is part of the principle of co-operation (Rules 2-4). Some European jurisdiction's national procedural codes do not specify or enumerate the possible means by which a court can manage cases; they simply articulate the power in a general rule. At the present time there is, however, a strong legislative tendency towards listing the court's various possible means of case management because comparative and historical procedural empiricism may demonstrate that reminding judges of their various powers, competences, and duties is beneficial and that it properly stimulates their organisational endeavours by ensuring that they maintain a sufficient degree of oversight of individual proceedings and take proper steps to guide the parties in the proper conduct of litigation.[1]
2. Traditionally continental procedural scholarship differentiates between organisation of procedural and material or substantive court management (see Rule 24). The former includes managing the time schedule and necessary organisational steps in proceedings whereas the latter involves judicial control of the relevance of facts and the means of evidence for the parties' cases, including the provision of judicial feedback aimed at protecting the parties from failing to properly develop their respective cases. Today, organisational or procedural judicial case management is common standard of all European procedural cultures be they traditionally oriented to more judge-dominated or more party-dominated

1 See, e.g., for France CCP, particularly Arts. 760 and following, 763 to 771, which enumerates the possible means of case managment available to the president of the responsible judicial body and of the instructing judge; for Spain, CCP Arts. 415 to 429, which list nearly all available means of case management applicable to an early management hearing; for Germany, CCP, particularly § 273; for England, see CPR, Part 3, particularly Rule 3.1 and 3.1 A, for complex cases Part 29 with PD 29 and for the commercial court Part 58 with PD 58; for Italy, CCP Art. 185; for Austria, CCP §§ 180 (2), 182, 183, 257, 258; for Switzerland, CCP Arts. 56, 124 to 127; for the Draft Unified Patent Court Rules, Rule 9 and Rules 331 and following, and specifically the lists in Rules 332 and 334; for the Netherlands, see

procedural models. Differences do, however, still exist in respect of material or substantive case management. In some European jurisdictions it is practised as a strict duty, whereas in others it is viewed as a judicial competence that is to be exercised flexibly by the court as an aspect of its overriding discretion. A further approach is seen in other European jurisdictions which adopt a mixed approach with both strict duties and discretionary measures. Others again, such as the common law jurisdictions do not recognise material or substantive case management. These Rule adopt the third, mixed, solution with some case management powers being subject to a strict duty, and hence must be carried out, with others being discretionary, and hence may be carried out by the court.

3. While a strict differentiation between the two types of case management may be discerned in scholarly works, in practice such a sharp differentiation is neither possible nor particularly helpful. There is a strong interdependence between organisational and substantive case management, and some management methods may in reality have both an organisational and substantive character. The simple reason for this interdependence is the fact that beneficial organisational case management is only possible on the basis of an understanding of the decisive issues of the dispute by the court in the light of communication with the parties. Rule 49, therefore, does not list possible means of case management according to whether they can be categorised as organisational or substantive forms of case management. On the contrary, it sets out the means of case management in the sequence in which they would be expected to be utilised in the timely progression of proceedings, and in respect of how they would be considered during the various procedural stages. It is apparent, however, that the order suggested here is debatable.
4. All of the means of judicial case management correspond with other Rules that detail the subject of a possible court order. The following list of comments is designed to give a survey of the most important corresponding Rules for each of the listed means of case management.
   i. Settlement endeavours: Rules 3(a), 9, 10, 26(3), 51, 57 and following, 141, 241(2), 221 and following, and 229 and following.
   ii. Case management conferences: Rules 61, 65(3), 66(2), and 178(2).
   iii. Type and form of the procedure: Some national civil procedure codes provide for different procedural tracks adapted to the degree of complexity of the case. The European Small Claims Regulation in transnational cases contains special procedural rules for simplified proceedings, and national forms of small claim procedures are still in force for domestic cases in most European Union Member States, as well as in other European jurisdictions. In some countries small claims are subject to rules concerning special jurisdiction and, consequently, determination of the type of procedure and of subject-matter jurisdiction (Rule 49(7)) may coincide. These Rules propose model rules for ordinary civil proceedings and leave, in principle, the constitution of special kinds of procedure, for instance of document-based procedure or of procedures in billing matters, to national design. Such design may also be facilitated through the flexible use of the general case management powers in these Rules. These Rules do, however, provide for special sets of provisions that could be considered a special type or form of procedure. They do so rarely though, e.g., joint applications for

especially Rule 7.6 of the Rules for the International Chambers of the Amsterdam District Court and Court of Appeal (NCC).

party-agreed-proceedings (Rules 57 – 60 in connection with Rule 26(3)), proceedings that terminate with early final judgments (Rule 65) or proceedings on preliminary issues (Rule 66) that modify the generally applicable Rules, proceedings using digitised forms of communication and video-conferences (Rules 18(4), 97(3)), or collective proceedings (Rules 204 and following) which provide for special rules on case management (Rules 213, 215, 218(1)(e)).

iv. Timetable with deadlines: Rules 61(3), 92(1), 213(2), 215(3), 223(2)(b), and 232(b).
v. Limitation of the number and length of submissions: Rule 5 (proportionality) and Rule 11 (fair opportunity for the presentation of a parties' case).
vi. Order of issues to be tried: Rules 64(5)(a) and 92(1). Rules 36 – 38, 146 on consolidation and separation;
vii. Separation of determination on jurisdiction, provisional measures and limitation: Rules 51(3)(c), 65(2)(a), 66(1)(a), 67, 184 and following.
viii. Amendments regarding party representation: Rules 14, 15, 29-32, 33, 164 on changes related to the parties, and Rules 39-44 on the participation of non-parties.
ix. Amendments to pleadings or offers of evidence: Rules 23(1), 27(1), 55, 59, 63(2), 64(4), 96.
x. Party appearance and representation: Rules 16(2), 49(10), 64(5)(b), 65(3), 66(2).
xi. Availability, admissibility, form, disclosure, exchange and taking of evidence: Rules 3(c), 25, 51(2)(c), 53(2)(b) and (4), 55(1), 57(3), 62(2), 63, 64(5)(c), (6) and (7), 88(3), 89-96, 97, 100 and following, and 111 and following.

Rule 50. Case Management Orders

(1) The court may make any case management order on its own motion or on application of a party. When orders or decisions are made without prior consultation with the parties or on a without-notice (*ex parte*) basis, parties not previously heard may apply for the order or decision to be reconsidered at a hearing or on the basis of written submissions.

(2) If the parties agree on a case management measure the court shall not determine differently without good reason.

(3) The court may vary or revoke any case management order upon a party's or its own motion.

Sources:

ALI/UNIDROIT Principles 7.2 and 14; Transnational Rules of Civil Procedure (Reporters' Study) Rules 18.3, 20, 22.1 and 22.2, 22.4, and 23.

Comments:

1. All European jurisdictions' procedural codes employ court orders or court directions as a means of communication between the court and parties in order to facilitate effective case management as provided in Rules 48 and 49. In most systems, however, there is no generally effective mechanism to generate court orders, to revoke or modify them. Some procedural codes place specific weight, and provide rules accordingly, on the right to be heard before the court is able to render, modify or revoke court orders. Others lack any real regulation, which can lead judges into poor managerial practice such that they render orders etc., without having communicated with the parties in the manner of a corporate executive or an official administering a command economy. Rule 50 is intended to ensure that management under these Rules is carried out effectively and with sufficient respect for

the parties' right to be heard. It ought to be carried out so as to ensure that the management process is not too complicated, time-consuming or expensive. (see Rule 11).

2. The process of rendering court orders under Rule 50 is intended to be characterised by flexibility in so far as court orders can be made on the court's own initiative or upon the application or motion of a party. Prior consultation with the parties is a matter of discretion. The same applies to modification or revocation of court orders (see Rule 50(1)).To give appropriate effect to the right to be heard, upon a party's application for an order made without it being heard previously to be reconsidered, it must be reconsidered in the light of the parties' submissions (see Rule 50(1) and Rule 11 establishing a right to respond to any court order). Flexibility prevails again in authorising the court to determine whether such submissions should be in oral or written form according to its overriding discretion when deciding how to deal with a party's application for a rehearing. The significance of the parties' right to be heard is made clear by Rule 50(2), which requires the court to articulate a good reason for refusing to approve a party-agreed case management order.
3. Numerous Rules correspond with Rule 50: Rules 48 and 27, 28 on monitoring compliance with court orders and on sanctions for non-compliance; Rules 92(1) and (3), 99, 102(2), 104, 105(2), 106(2), 107, 110, 120(3), 121(3), 122(3), 126(2) and (4) on court orders regarding evidence-taking; Rule 178 on immediate challenges to procedural errors by the court and conclusive waiver by the parties; and Rules 213(2) and (4), 215(3) and (4), 218(2), 219(2), 229, and 232(b) on specific modifications concerning collective proceeding orders.
4. A serious problem for European jurisdictions' national procedural codes has been the availability of separate appeals concerning procedural errors in lower courts. On the one hand, it may increase the duration of proceedings if serious mistakes are only subject to appellate review of final decisions on the whole dispute. On the other hand, the ready and generous availability of an appellate process can be a significant source of unnecessary litigation delay and duration. These Rules, in principle, do not permit separate appeals against rulings on challenges of procedural errors. This general rule is subject to a very limited number of exceptions (see Rule 179). In appropriate cases, Rule 66 and Rule 130(1)(d) permit a judgment on a preliminary procedural issue, which could be *res judicata* (see Rule 148(1)) to be subject to an appeal (see Rule 153). It is, however, within the court's overriding discretion, which must itself be exercised consistently with its general duties (see Rules 4 and 5), whether to render a separate judgment on preliminary procedural issues. In exercising that discretion, the court may take into consideration the possibility of appellate proceedings because, in the absence of the possibility of an appeal, its judgment may in the circumstances be unreasonable. Given this possibility to render such a judgment and the nature of the applicable discretion, the general lack of access to appeal for procedural errors is not subject to any serious prospect of abuse.
5. Rule 50 does not regulate the procedural rights of third parties or non-parties who are affected by court orders directly. Special rules apply, in some cases with reference to Rule 50. Non-parties are, for instance, subject to sanctions if they fail to comply with duties to contribute to evidence-taking (see Rule 99). Also see Rules 27 and 28, concerning applications for relief. Orders requiring access to evidence to be given by parties and non-parties (see Rules 107 and 101) are to be rendered by the court according to Rule 50, such that applications by any non-party affected by the order may be made seeking its reconsideration, revocation or modification (see Rule 107(4)); orders granting access to evidence made

without-notice are allowed in exceptional cases only and orders made before proceedings have commenced and without the court having heard affected parties or non-parties are ordinarily not permitted (see Rule 107(2) and (3)). Non-parties have, in contrast to parties, a general right of appeal having challenged procedural errors in time (see Rules 178, 180).

6. See Rule 27 on sanctions for non-compliance and Rule 48 on monitoring.

PART IV

COMMENCEMENT OF PROCEEDINGS

SECTION 1—PRE-COMMENCEMENT PROCEDURAL DUTIES

Rule 51. Duty to promote consensual resolution and effective management

(1) Before proceedings are issued, parties shall co-operate with each other in order to avoid unnecessary disputes and costs, to facilitate the early consensual resolution of their dispute and, where such a resolution is not possible, the proportionate management of future proceedings according to Rules 2-11 and 47-50.

(2) In order to further the general duty set out in Rule 51(1) parties may:

(a) provide each other with concise details of their potential claims or defences;

(b) clarify and, wherever possible, narrow the legal and factual issues in dispute; and

(c) identify relevant evidence so as to facilitate effective and early assessment of the merits of their positions.

(3) Parties may also:

(a) consider a possible timetable for proceedings;

(b) estimate the potential cost of proceedings;

(c) consider issues of limitation, jurisdiction, provisional measures, and of any other procedural matter.

Sources:
ALI/UNIDROIT Principles 24.3 and 25.2.

Comments:

1. Rule 51 implements the general principles on co-operation and settlement set out in Rules 2, 3 and 9. Rules 3(a) and 9, which describe the obligation placed on parties to contribute to settlement endeavours, are particular instances of the general principle of co-operation in respect of the duty to promote the fair, efficient and speedy resolution of the dispute (see Rule 2).
2. The Mediation Directive does not provide for mandatory mediation as a pre-condition to commencing proceedings. It neither does so implicitly through, for instance the threat of cost sanctions in cases where a party unreasonably refuses to co-operate in pre-action settlement attempts, nor does it do so explicitly. It does, however, emphasise that European Union Member States may adopt such measures to mandate pre-action mediation.[1] Some Member States have done so. Other European jurisdictions have adopted the use of cost sanctions to encourage parties to engage in pre-action settlement endeavours. The most intensive kind of at least indirectly mandatory pre-action settlement endeavours are contained in the English Pre-Action Protocols, which set out detailed best practice guidance to parties to potential proceedings. That guidance expects parties to provide each other with sufficient information to facilitate settlement attempts during the pre-action phase of proceedings, which even if unsuccessful can promote more effective post-commencement

1 Art. 5(2) of the Mediation Directive.

ELI-UNIDROIT Model European Rules of Civil Procedure. ELI & UNIDROIT, Oxford University Press.
 DOI: 10.1093/oso/9780198866589.003.0005

case management. Rule 51 is intended to strike a fair balance between mandatory pre-action settlement attempts and those systems that do not provide for such encouragement of settlement. It does so by requiring the parties to potential litigation to take steps to clarify the essential elements of the dispute at the earliest possible stage (Rule 51(1)).

3. The extent to which settlement attempts will succeed during the pre-action phase will, to a significant degree, depend upon the parties' willingness to provide each other with sufficient information concerning their view of the dispute. Rule 51(2) details the nature of information that ought to be provided by parties to each other during the pre-action phase; the approach taken is already best practice amongst lawyers across Europe. Such information is designed to clarify the legal and factual issues and the evidential aspects of the potential proceedings and to enable parties to calculate their litigation risk, i.e., the risk that they will succeed or not in proceedings if they were to be determined by the court, and to consider the advantages that may arise from an effective compromise of their dispute. Infringement of such best practice may result in cost sanctions or the imposition of an obligation on the party that failed to act consistently with this Rule to pay compensation to the other party (see 5, below)
4. Where parties attempt to resolve their disputes during the pre-action phase it is not unusual that, even where they do not settle the dispute, they will resolve an, or several, contentious issues (see Rule 9(4)). That may promote more efficient case management following commencement. As a consequence, during the pre-action phase, parties could also consider together issues concerning the proper management of proceedings (see Rule 51(3)). They ought also do so where they fail to settle any issue during the pre-action phase. Parties should also consider considering with each other the potential costs of proceedings during this phase, as it may enable them to consider the nature and extent of evidence, e.g., whether expert evidence is necessary and if so who might be instructed. Again, this may help promote the efficient and proportionate management of proceedings should the parties not settle their dispute. It may also help them reach agreement on issues that are, in the light of such considerations, not seriously disputed. In so far as Rule 51(3) is concerned, it should be read against the background of Rule 26(3), which permits the parties to agree upon issues of non-mandatory law, and Rules 57-60, which permit the parties to agree to limit the court's competence to determine specific, individual, issues in dispute as well as to vary by mutual agreement those procedural rules that are subject to the principal of party disposition.
5. Costs sanctions may be imposed by the court on parties who through being unreasonably disputatious failed to co-operate with each other during the pre-action phase and who, consequently, raised or maintained issues in proceedings unnecessarily, unreasonably refused to settle their dispute or issues in it (see Rule 241(2)).Where a party's lawyers fail to act consistently with their pre-action duties (see Rule 9(2)) they may be liable to pay the party instructing them compensation in respect of any cost sanctions imposed upon them, i.e., imposed upon the party instructing them.
6. Parties should ensure that any attempts they make to settle their dispute during the pre-action phase are proportionate to the nature of their dispute (see Rules 3(a), (b), (e), and 8).The amount in dispute, the nature and complexity of the dispute, the importance of the dispute to the parties, and the public interest in its correct resolution should be taken into account when parties and their lawyers try to come to a pre-action agreement to settle their dispute either in whole or in part. Pre-action attempts to resolve disputes ought not

to engender significant costs, particularly in low value disputes. They should also be concluded in a reasonable time and terminated when it becomes clear that one party is not willing to participate reasonably in the process. Where parties are not represented by lawyers, the question whether they have taken reasonable steps to settle their dispute should be assessed by reference to what is reasonable for laymen rather than what would be reasonable for a party in receipt of legal advice.

7. These Rules do not address the relationship between settlement attempts under Rule 51 and a mediation process. No hard rule can be given in this respect. In some circumstances mediation could precede the pre-action phase of proceedings under Rule 51, in other cases it may come after the provision of information required by Rule 51(2). Rule 51 is, however, primarily focused upon the promotion of negotiation between the parties, rather than a more formal mediation process that relies upon the instruction of a neutral third party to facilitate either a rights-based or interest-based resolution of the dispute. Parties and their lawyers must ensure that they do not duplicate ADR methods during the pre-action phase.
8. Consistently with the approach that is taken by extant provisions in European or national law that suspend prescription during the course of settlement negotiations, legislative measures should make similar provision applicable, either fully or in part, to any pre-commencement settlement endeavours according to Rule 51.

SECTION 2—COMMENCEMENT AND PLEADINGS

A. STATEMENT OF CLAIM

Rule 52. Submission of the Statement of Claim

To commence proceedings the claimant must submit a statement of claim to the court, as provided in Rule 53. Notice shall be given as provided in Part VI.

Sources:

ALI/UNIDROIT Principle 5.1 and 10.1; Transnational Rules of Civil Procedure (Reporters' Study) Rule 11 in connection with Rules 7.1 and 7.2.1, 7.2.3

Comments:

1. Rule 52 sentence 1 implements the principle of party disposition from the outset of proceedings (see Rule 21(1)). A claimant may exercise their right of disposition at the earliest stage of proceedings by withdrawal of the claim, while a defendant may do so by admission of the claim upon notice being given (see Rule 56). The requirement of due notice (Rule 52 sentence 2 is an essential element of the right to be heard and a foundation of the court's jurisdiction over the parties (see Rule 11). It is a fundamental principle of justice.
2. Rule 52 refers to Rule 53, as that specifies the necessary content of a statement of claim, as well as to Rules 68 and following for the requirements of due notice and correct service. The rules on service also contain provisions about the information that must be given to a defendant concerning the procedural steps necessary to contest the claim (see Rule 69), as well as the consequences of a failure to enter an appearance (see Rule 70). Such a distribution of provisions concerning such information among differing sections of procedural

codes follows the order preferred by European jurisdictions as well as by European Union legislation[2] as well as by international conventions in cross-border disputes.[3]

Rule 53. Contents of the Statement of Claim

(1) The statement of claim must state, as a minimum, the designation of the specific court and of the parties, the relief sought and the grounds therefore.

(2) The statement of claim should:

(a) state the relevant facts on which the claim is based in reasonable detail as to time, place, participants and events;

(b) describe with sufficient specification the available means of evidence to be offered in support of factual allegations;

(c) refer to the legal grounds that support the claim, including foreign law, in a way that is sufficient to permit the court to determine the claim's legal validity;

(d) state the detailed remedy requested, including the monetary amount or the specified terms of any other remedy sought;

(e) allege compliance with any applicable condition precedent, according to applicable national law, to bringing the claim, such as parties having to engage in pre-commencement conciliation or mediation, or having to issue a formal demand concerning the subject matter of the dispute.

(3) If a claimant does not fully comply with the requirements of Rule 53(2), the court must invite the claimant to amend the statement of claim. If a claimant shows good cause why it is not possible to provide details of relevant facts or specify the means of evidence in their statement of claim but the statement of claim nevertheless demonstrates that there is plausible dispute on the merits, the court should give due regard to the possibility that relevant detailed facts will develop later in the course of the taking of evidence.

(4) Whenever possible, means of evidence on which a claimant relies, must be attached to the statement of claim, if feasible with a copy for the defendant and other parties.

(5) A claimant may apply, in their statement of claim, for access to evidence under the custody or control of a defendant or non-party and which are to be offered in support of the claimant's allegations.

(6) The claimant may respond in a statement of claim to the defendant's defence as known from any exchange of arguments before commencement of proceedings. In this case Rule 54 applies to this part of their statement of claim.

(7) If the claimant makes a third-party claim or cross-claim seeking relief from a third party or a co-claimant Rule 53 applies correspondingly.

Sources:

ALI/UNIDROIT Principles 5.1 – 5.4, 9.2, 11.3, 19.1; Transnational Rules of Civil Procedure (Reporters' Study) Rule 11 and 12.

2 See, for instance, Art. 19 of Regulation (EC) No 1393/2007 on service of documents and repealing Council Regulation (EC) No 1348/2000 on the service in the Member States of judicial and extrajudicial documents in civil or commercial matters (the ESR); Art. 17 of Regulation (EC) No 805/2004 of the European Parliament and of the Council of 21 April 2004 creating a European Enforcement Order for uncontested claims (the EEO Regulation); and, Art. 12 of the EPO Regulation.

3 See, for instance, Arts. 15 and 16 of the Convention of 15 November 1965 on the Service Abroad of Judicial and Extrajudicial Documents in Civil or Commercial Matters (HCCH 1965 Service Convention)

Comments:

1. The Rules on pleadings are, in principle, a common heritage of all European procedural systems. They developed in the tradition of the continental learned procedure and the corresponding procedure in the English equity courts and then common law procedure generally following their merger in the 1870s. While differences remain across Europe, the common origin of pleading techniques underpinned the development of these Rules,[4] which are designed to give concrete effect to the principles governing court and party contribution to correct fact finding and legal determination (see Rules 2 – 8, 11, 18, and 21 – 28).
2. Rule 53(1) sets out the minimum necessary contents of a statement of claim: designation of the court seised; party identity; the relief sought, and its factual grounds. In some European jurisdictions, courts will dismiss claims that fail to satisfy such mandatory minimum standards. In other jurisdictions the court must first invite the non-compliant party to amend the claim form, following which the claim may be dismissed if the claim is not brought into compliance. These Rules leave the approach to this issue to national practice.
3. Rule 53(2) specifies additional requirements concerning the contents of statements of claim that should be fulfilled. In some European jurisdictions all the requirements of Rules 53(1) and (2) are mandatory. In other jurisdictions the statement of claim must only contain the criteria set out Rule 53(1), and the additional requirements contained in Rule 53(2) are to be set out in a second statement. These Rules strike the compromise between both alternatives. They leave the choice to the claimant, subject to the court's case management power to order inclusion of the matters set out in Rule 53(2) (see Rule 53(3)). The differences between both alternatives are, in practice, not generally significant.
4. Rule 53(2)(a) gives concrete effect to Rule 24(1). The requirement to provide reasonably particularised factual contentions is a common prerequisite of correct pleading in all European jurisdictions. It is good practice to bind parties to a specific account, and thus to avoid general assertions that could be pleaded without the parties giving any real or sufficient consideration of their possible truth. In specific circumstances, the parties may be permitted by the court to provide less detailed factual contentions where they can demonstrate a good reason for so doing (see Rule 53(3)).
5. Rule 53(2)(b) corresponds to Rule 25(1) and, parallel with Rule 53(2)(a), emphasises the need to specify means of evidence offered with sufficient specification. Rules 53(2)(a) and (b) are both designed to avoid fishing expeditions, which would enable parties to make enquiries of their opponent or of non-parties without their factual contentions having

4 For the prevailing common features of pleading techniques in Europe see, e.g., for France, CCP Art. 53 and following, particularly Art. 56 and additionally Arts. 753, 765 together with Arts. 4, 6, 8, 9, 11 and following; for Italy, particularly CCP Arts. 163, 167; for Spain, CCP Art. 399 and following, Art 405 ff. and following; for Germany, CCP §§ 253, 130; for Austria, CCP §§ 226 and following, §§ 230, 239 and following; for Switzerland, CCP Art. 221 and following; for the Draft Unified Patent Court Rules, Rules 12 and following, Rule 23 and following; for England, CPR Part 16 and PD 16; however, differing from continental codes mutual disclosure of evidence may take place in the pre-commencement stage according to the pre-action protocols or in the disclosure stage after pleadings though production and designation of means of evidence in the pleadings is in special circumstances mandatory (see, e.g., Practice Direction (PD) 16 Claim form 4.3 for medical reports or 7.3 for written agreements); for modifictions in complex cases or proceedings of the commercial court see Parts 29 and 58 with their PDs; for the ESC Regulation see Art. 4 with claim form (Annex I) and Art. 5 with answer form (Annex III).

a sufficient degree of plausibility. Assertions of very general facts and offers of evidence without any detailed specification of individual means of evidence frequently coincide. Again, in such circumstances, the court may allow exceptions from regular standards of sufficient specification where there is good reason to do so (see Rule 53(3)). (Also see also Rules 24, comment 2, and 102.)

6. Rule 53(2)(c) refers to the parties' right to present legal arguments supporting their case as generally addressed in Rule 26(1). This could, and should, be done in the pleadings in a timely manner in order to enable the court to determine the applicable law effectively. It could, however, be done at a later point in the proceedings on the parties' own initiative or following prompting by the court (see Rule 26, comment 2). The description of the quality of presenting legal arguments is a recommendation, and as noted above not a mandatory requirement of correct pleadings. Ultimately, the court is responsible for determining the correct application of the law, but a claimant will run the risk of failing to convince the court of a legal conception favourable to its case.
7. Rule 53(2)(d) requires claimants to provide a detailed specification of the relief sought. Articulating the claim for relief clearly and with certainty is a necessary feature of good pleading practice, as the claim for relief binds the court and the terms of any executable order in the court's judgment (see Rules 23(2), and 131(e)). If the claim for relief is unclear, the proceedings may be dismissed on procedural grounds, following a failure to rectify the defect upon the court prompting the claimant to do so by way of amendment (See Rules 55(1) and 56(1)). In certain circumstances, the court may permit the claim for relief to lack a degree of specificity, e.g., where a claimant is unable to determine from the outset of the claim the exact amount of financial compensation claimed or where compensation is a matter of judicial discretion. Details on this are left to national judicial practice.
8. Rule 53(2)(e) requires information on pre-conditions applicable to the commencement of proceedings to be specified in the statements of claim. Such pre-conditions may arise under national law, such as mandatory pre-commencement mediation which has become increasingly common in European jurisdictions since 2010, or the mandatory giving of a formal demand prior to commencement.
9. Rule 53(3) permits exceptions from strict fact pleading in those cases where claimants can show good cause for their inability to serve more and better particulars or their inability exactly to specify particular means of evidence, especially when facts occurred in the knowledge or control of other parties or non-parties (see Rule 24, comment 2 and Rule 53(2)(b), comments 4 and 5). Given that the wide distribution of knowledge and evidence is a commonplace feature of modern life such a strict approach would be particularly problematic as it would undermine the courts' ability to do justice. In resolving the tension between strictness in pleading and party knowledge, this Rule has adopted the prevailing tendency amongst the highest European national courts. That tendency is to permit general facts to be asserted if a party demonstrates the plausibility of the merits relevant to the case, while setting out specific grounds for the assumptions underpinning the assertion. The probability demanded here is much lower than that adopted in respect of *prima facie* evidence in continental European procedures, or in the case of *res ipsa loquitur* in common law jurisdictions. It is not a kind of evidence but only a first step towards giving some evidence. The absence of clarity and certainty in this requirement, which leaves the decision whether to open the door to fact-finding proceedings

to the court's overriding discretion has often been criticised as a form of leaving the delivery of justice to judicial arbitrariness. Ultimately, no better solution can be discerned. English courts with their long tradition of differentiating between impermissible fishing expeditions and permissible, broad disclosure measures demonstrates that no hard and fast rule can be laid down to determine the extent to which particulars should precede disclosure or disclosure should precede particulars, and that each case will depend on its own circumstances. These Rules can do no better. They open the door to fact-finding upon the demonstration of the plausibility of the merits of evidence-taking in the flexible preparatory stage and in the final hearing (for the receding significance of the differentiation between evidence-taking and disclosure see Rule 62, comments). In such cases, the court may, consequently, also permit applications for the production of categories of documents or electronic data instead of individually specified documents or electronic data being set out in the statement of claim (see Rules 53(5) and Rule 102).

10. Rule 53(4) is designed to further the timely provision of information to the court and the parties by exchange of documents, electronic data and other mobile means of evidence. As such it is a form of automatic disclosure. It corresponds to Rule 25(1), 92, 93 sentence 1, 111(3), and 117(1).
11. Rule 53(5) permits applications for access to evidence that is under the control or custody of another party, i.e., the defendant, or non-parties to be set out in the statement of claim and further pleadings. It does so in the interest of speedy expedition of the case. Also see Rules 25(2), 101 and following.
12. Rule 53(6) makes it clear that a claimant may respond to any defence made in the pre-commencement phase of proceedings in so far as they believe to be reasonable. A duty to respond to matters raised prior to the statement of claim only exists in special circumstances (see Rule 24, comment 5).
13. Rule 53(7) corresponds to Rule 42 concerning third-party notice. It does not, however, create a special kind of venue or personal jurisdiction, which is not already granted by special provisions set out in European Union or national law; see, for instance, Article 8(2) Brussels Ibis Regulation. Rules on jurisdiction are outside the scope of these Rules (also see Rule 42, comments).

Rule 54. Statement of Defence and Counterclaims

(1) A defendant must, within 30 consecutive days from the date of service of notice, respond to the claimant's statement of claim. In appropriate cases, the court may properly extend the time for answer by court order.

(2) Rule 53 concerning the details of statements of claims applies to the defendant's response.

(3) Any failure by a defendant, whether explicit or tacit to deny an allegation contained in the claimant's statement of claim may be considered an admission for the purpose of the proceeding and obviates proof thereof.

(4) A defendant must set out in their response to the claimant's statement of claim which allegations are admitted or contested. A contested allegation is one that is either denied, neither admitted nor denied, or for which an alternative statement of facts is alleged. Where the defendant can neither admit nor deny reasons must be given in the defence why that is the case.

(5) If a defendant relies on an affirmative defence, their response to the claimant's statement of claim must allege all facts sufficient to permit the court to determine the legal

validity of the defence, and offer means of evidence in support of the factual allegations. Rules 53(2)(a)-(c), (3) and (4) apply. The claimant may answer affirmative defences.

(6) The defendant may state a counterclaim seeking relief from a claimant. The defendant may also state a claim against a co-defendant or a third party. Rule 53 applies. The parties so addressed must answer these claims as provided in the previous provisions.

Sources:

ALI/UNIDROIT Principles 5.1, 5.4, 5.5, and 11.3-11.5; Transnational Rules of Civil Procedure (Reporters' Study) Rules 5.1 and 5.2, 7. 1, 7.2.1 and 7.2.3, 13.

Comments:

1. Rule 54(1) sets the time limit for the defendant to respond to a claimant's statement of claim. That time limit may, in an appropriate case, be varied by the court (also see Rule 47, comment 2).
2. Rule 54(2) ensures that parties enjoy equal treatment by the court (see Rule 4(2)). It does so by providing a common, generally applicable standard for the content of pleadings (see Rules 53(2)(a), (b) and (3)).
3. Rule 54(3) specifies the consequence that follows from a defendant's failure to deny an allegation asserted by the claimant. In principle, it provides that the absence of a denial is to be taken as an admission, and thus the claimant need not prove the allegation (also see Rules 88(1)(a) and (b) and 93). This Rule promotes procedural proportionality and reduces the cost and time of proceedings, as it enables defendants to limit the scope of the dispute by choosing not to contest specific matters set out in the pleadings. Some European jurisdiction's procedural codes construe this effect as a necessary consequence of the defendant choosing not to contest the specific allegation. Other European jurisdictions provide the court with a discretion concerning the effect to be given to a defendant's failure to contest an allegation. Rule 54(3) indicates that these Rules have not adopted the former, strict, approach. The discretion it affords the court is, however, one that should only be exercised in exceptional circumstances. If a factual allegation is clearly uncontested, the strict approach should apply (see Rules 88(1)(a) and (b)). If, however, the uncontested allegation is underpinned by mandatory legal provisions, or if it is uncontested because the defendant has failed to submit their defence in time, the court ought to raise the matter with the parties and require them to clarify whether they do, in fact, intend to leave the allegation uncontested (see Rule 24, comment 3 and Rule 93). Only after having raised the matter with the defendant, and the defendant has not sought to rectify the matter either through an amendment to their pleadings or by late submission of their defence, should the court consider the allegation as being uncontested.
4. Rule 54(4) sets out how a defendant should contest the claimant's allegations. Where allegations are contested, they can either be denied (a bare denial) or denied with a response that sets out an alternative statement of facts. If a defendant denies any knowledge of the allegation and is thus unable to either admit or deny it, they must set out convincing reasons explaining their lack of knowledge, so as to avoid negative conclusions being drawn. In some European jurisdictions a defendant is only permitted to deny an allegation through claiming to lack knowledge of it, where a defendant first demonstrates that they have endeavoured to obtain information concerning the allegation. Such details should be left to national judicial practice.
5. Rule 54(5) sets out how a defendant may respond to a claimant's allegations by setting out an affirmative defence, that leaves the claimant's allegations uncontested, but which

sets out a positive case that prevents the formation of the claimant's claim for relief, or renders it invalid or ineffective. Common forms of affirmative defence are: that the claim has already been satisfied; set-off; contractual incapacity on the part of the defendant; that a contract is ineffective due to fraud; that the claim settled before the proceedings were commenced, etc. A defendant's affirmative defence must comply with the requirements applicable to a statement of claim (Rule 54(5)). If a claimant submits a reply to a defendant's affirmative defence (Rule 54(5)), Rule 54 applies accordingly.

6. Rule 54(6) provides the basis for defendants to bring counterclaims against claimants. It does not, however, provide any special rules concerning venue if such is not granted by other special provisions, such as Article 8(3) of the Brussels Ibis Regulation or by similar provisions contained in national law. A defendant may issue a third-party claim, as provided for claimants in Rule 53(7) according to Rule 42 (see Rule 53, comment 7).

Rule 55. Amendments to Pleadings

(1) A party, upon showing good cause to the court and upon notice to other parties, has a right to amend its claims or defences when the amendment does not unreasonably delay the proceeding or otherwise result in injustice. In particular, amendments may be justified to take account of events occurring after those alleged in earlier pleadings, newly discovered facts or evidence that could not previously have been obtained through reasonable diligence, or new evidence obtained from the exchange of evidence.

(2) Permission to amend must be granted on such terms as are just, including, where necessary, adjournment or continuance, or compensation by an award of costs to another party.

(3) The amendment must be served on the opposing party who has 30 consecutive days in which to respond, or such time as the court may order.

(4) Any party may apply to the court for an order requiring another party to provide by amendment a more specific statement of that party's pleading on the ground that the challenged statement does not comply with the requirements of these Rules. Such a request temporarily suspends the duty to answer.

Sources:

ALI/UNIDROIT Principles 10.4, 22.2.1, 28.1 and 2; Transnational Rules of Civil Procedure (Reporters' Study) Rules 14 and 18.3.

Comments:

1. These Rules provide three different procedures for amendment: amendment consequent to the court's suggestion, which is not addressed explicitly in Rule 55; amendment upon the application of the party affected by the matter to which the amendment relates, e.g., an amendment to the claim for relief sought by a claimant (Rules 55(1)-(3)); and, one sought by a party to the proceedings, which seeks an amendment to another party's pleadings (Rule 55(4)).
2. Amendments to pleadings are an essential aspect of the court's case management role (see Rule 4 sentence 1). The court must monitor party compliance with their responsibilities (see Rules 4 sentence 3, and 48). Parties must also, in properly managing their claims, ensure that they introduce all relevant facts (see Rule 24(1)), adduce sufficient evidence to convince the court of the existence of all facts favourable to their respective cases (see Rules 25(1) and (2)), and take sufficient steps to convince the court of the validity of their contentions concerning the law applicable to their case (see Rule 26). Parties must also

fulfil their duty to contribute to the speedy resolution of the dispute (see Rules 2 and 48), to provide their opponent with proper access to information and evidence (see Rules 25(2) and 100 and following) and to act fairly and in good faith (Rule 3(e)). In all these cases, where the parties fail to properly carry out their duties, the court may suggest appropriate amendments to enable the parties to rectify any such defect and thus to pursue their claim or defence to trial (see Rules 24, 25 (3), 26(2), 27(1), 33, 49(8) and (9), 53(3), and 96).

3. Rule 55(1) does not apply to amendments that are suggested by the court. It only applies to those amendments sought by the parties.
4. Rule 55(4) enables parties to apply for a court order that will require another party to amend otherwise incomplete or incorrect pleadings. Such an application will only address a particular form of procedural non-compliance, i.e., a failure to provide sufficiently detailed pleadings, and is only designed to cure that defect, the court's competence to grant amendments is much broader and includes all kinds of orders that are necessary to facilitate proper case management (see Rules 47 - 50). Consequently, a court that issues an order for amendment is not limited to the restricted scope of Rule 55(4) in any order it makes under that Rule.
5. Mistakes and errors in formulating pleadings are frequent, particularly in complex case. As a consequence, all European jurisdictions provide parties with the ability to apply to amend their claims. Such amendments should not be unreasonable in scope or nature, nor should they result in disproportionate cost or delay (Rule 55(1)). That Rule provides some examples where an amendment should generally be permitted, as the source of the amendment was not the result of any mistake or culpability (oversight, slight slip from general compliance with Rule 47, or negligence etc.) by the party seeking the amendment. Where the court noted a failure to comply with Rule 47 and failed to bring it to the party's attention at the time, that party cannot be sanctioned by preclusion (Rule 27(1)).
6. Rules 55(2) and (3) apply to all types of procedures, where an amendment is sought. They are intended to protect other parties to proceedings from any negative consequences that may arise from permitting an amendment to be made. This type of approach is both fair and reasonable.

Rule 56. Withdrawal and admission of the claim

(1) With the defendant or defendants' consent, the claimant may terminate the proceeding or any part of it by complete or partial withdrawal of the claim without prejudice save as to costs. Unilateral withdrawal without prejudice is only permitted if made before the first hearing of the court. In any case the claimant shall bear the reasonable and adequate costs of other parties.

(2) A defendant may terminate the proceeding or any part of it by admission of the whole claim or a part of the claim. The claimant may thereafter file a request to obtain judgment.

Sources:

ALI/UNIDROIT Principle 10.5.

Comments:

1. Rule 56 expands upon Rule 21(2) in respect of the withdrawal or admission of claims (see Rule 21, comments 1 and 4). All European jurisdictions' procedural codes contain similar rules on the withdrawal or admission of claims.

2. The difference between withdrawal by consent and where it is made without consent, as well as between withdrawal before and after the first hearing and any corresponding consequences arising in respect of prejudice and costs is common to most European jurisdictions. It helps to avoid the possibility that claimant and defendants are treated unequally. After the commencement of proceedings, a defendant has a legitimate interest in the proceedings being finally determined so that they are not troubled with further and later attempts to initiate the same claim anew. Equally, the public interest in the proper administration of justice justifies procedures that conserve judicial resources and which help to avoid future attempts to litigate the same claim, at the least where proceedings have progressed to a first hearing before withdrawal. In cases where a claimant withdraws the proceedings, they are generally required to bear the cost of court fees and to reimburse costs incurred by other parties. The court may vary such a cost decision where a defendant failed to provide sufficient information during the pre-commencement phase or was otherwise uncooperative, (see Rules 51, comment 5, and 241(2)), or upon settlement by the parties.
3. When a defendant admits a claim either in whole or in part that terminates the dispute accordingly. A claimant may apply for a judgment based upon such an admission to obtain an executable title, particularly where a defendant failed to voluntarily fulfil any obligations arising upon the admission, or if the parties did not agree on an enforceable settlement upon the admission. In principle, a defendant will have to bear the costs arising in respect of the admission if the court does not decide otherwise according to Rule 241(2). This may particularly be the case where an admission was made at a late stage based on information following the late provision of information that ought to have been provided by the defendant during the pre-commencement phase (see Rule 51, comment 5).

B. JOINT APPLICATION FOR PARTY-AGREED-PROCEEDINGS

Rule 57. Contents of the joint application

(1) A joint application is a statement of claim in which parties jointly may submit to the court their agreement according to Rule 26, their respective claims and defences, the issues on which they disagree and which are to be determined by the court, and their respective arguments on those disputed issues.

(2) In order to be admissible, the joint application must contain:

(a) the designation of the parties;

(b) the designation of the court before which the proceedings are brought;

(c) the relief sought, including the monetary amount or the specified terms of any other remedy sought; and

(d) the relevant facts and the legal grounds, on which the action is based.

(3) A joint application must describe the available means of evidence to be offered in support of factual allegations. Whenever possible, such evidence must be attached to the application.

(4) It must be signed and dated by the parties.

Comments:

1. Rules 57 – 60 are the consequence of the general approach taken in these Rules that is aimed at promoting party initiative, so that they take an active approach to seeking to settle their disputes and also, where that is not possible, to settle some of the individual issues

that form the basis of their dispute. In this way the Rules generally, and these particular rules, seek to promote proportionality in dispute resolution by promoting party conduct that could reduce the court's decision-making function to only those issues that could not be resolved by party agreement (see Rules 3(a) and (e), 9(1) and (4), 26(3), and Rule 51). In this way they seek to save human resources and costs, as well as court resources (see Rules 2, 6 and 8).

2. In many European jurisdictions their civil procedural codes rely upon the imposition of cost sanctions to deter uncooperative behaviour and practices by parties during the pre-commencement phase of proceedings. In some jurisdictions, such as England or France, detailed rules describe the parties' responsibilities to effect the early resolution of issues that would otherwise be decided by the court. The need to encourage parties to resolve specific issues in dispute by agreement, and also to increase the attraction of this procedural development by binding the court to such agreements, has been increasingly promoted in the practice of arbitral tribunals over the last few decades. This is particularly the case in, for instance, France, where the French Code of Civil Procedure in its "*requête conjointe*" explicitly permits a form of party-agreed proceedings that restricts the court's competence to determine only those issues that are contested, while at the same time binding the court to the agreement reached by the parties.[5] A characteristic feature of this form of party-agreed-proceeding is the combination of increasing party, including their lawyers, autonomy and responsibility. These Rules, through Rules 57-60, propose a closed conception of party contribution to determine the focus of proceedings, such that it is limited to only the truly serious issues in dispute. As such it seeks to avoid the development of an approach whereby the parties could use the Rules tactically.
3. Rule 57(1) provides a concise definition of: the purpose and material contents of a joint application; the law applicable upon agreement according to Rule 26(3); claims and defences; the issues in dispute that are to be determined by the court; and, the parties' arguments.
4. Rules 57(2)-(4) enumerates such details as are necessary for the joint application. These requirements are broadly congruent with those of Rules 52-54, albeit that they are adapted to the circumstances of a joint application.

Rule 58. Related agreements

In so far as procedural rules are subject to party disposition, parties may agree on any procedural matter, such as the jurisdiction of the court, provisional measures, and publicity of hearings (see Rule 26(3)).

Comments:

1. Rule 58 makes it clear that party agreement may encompass questions of procedural law that are subject to party disposition. It does not provide a strict rule on how the court is to determine the applicability of party disposition. A similar issue arises when the admissibility of a waiver of procedural rules by the parties is in dispute and is to be considered by the court. Ultimately most procedural systems leave the decision on the availability of party disposition to judicial practice. As such it is only in special cases, such as where parties agree questions of jurisdiction, that party disposition may be subject to detailed or explicit regulation. This is the approach adopted in these Rules.

5 Art. 57 and following of the French CCP.

Rule 59. Amendment

(1) Parties have a right to amend their joint application when the amendment does not unreasonably delay management of the proceedings. In particular, amendments may be justified in order to take account of events occurring after those alleged in earlier pleadings, or newly discovered facts or evidence that could not previously have been obtained through reasonable diligence.

(2) Amendments are only admissible upon agreement of the parties.

Comments:

1. Rule 59 adapts the application for amendment, and of the right to amend, to requirements of joint applications. The requirements as such are the same as those in Rule 55(1).
2. The rules on amendment following a suggestion by the court or upon application by another party or parties are the same as those set out in Rule 55, comments 2, 3 and 5.

Rule 60. Termination of party-agreed-proceedings

Before party-agreed-proceedings are determined by the court, parties may terminate them or any part of them by complete or partial joint withdrawal.

Comment:

Rule 60 makes it clear that only the joint withdrawal of proceedings by parties that had made a joint application for party-agreed-proceedings may terminate them either in whole or in part. (See Rule 56(1).)

PART V

PROCEEDINGS PREPARATORY TO A FINAL HEARING

Rule 61. Case management hearings to prepare for the final hearing and determination

(1) To prepare for a final hearing, the court may hold an early case management hearing and if necessary further ones as the case progresses.

(2) Case management hearings may be held in person. If appropriate the court may proceed in written form or use any available electronic means of communication.

(3) In or immediately after a case management hearing, the court should, upon consultation with the parties: set a timetable or procedural calendar with deadlines for parties to complete their procedural obligations; set the timetable for a final hearing; and, the possible date by which judgment will be given.

(4) Whenever appropriate, the court may provide parties with advice relevant to their preparation for the final hearing and judgment. Such advice should, in so far as possible, be given in the early case management hearing. Case management orders should be made in or immediately after the early case management hearing.

Sources:
ALI/Unidroit Principles 7.2, 9.1, 9.3.1, 9.3.2, and 14; Transnational Rules of Civil Procedure (Reporters' Study) Rule 18.2.

Comments:

1. The procedural model underlying these Rules consists of three phases: the written pleading phase, which is regulated by Rules 52 – 60, the interim phase designed to prepare the case for final determination, which is regulated by Rules 61 – 63, and the final phase, which is regulated by Rule 64 and ordinarily takes the form of a concentrated final hearing where the parties present evidence on such issue as remain to be determined by the court and make their concluding arguments. This structure is sufficiently flexible to meet the varying requirements of individual cases, and their specific procedural requirements. In many cases proceedings may conclude with an early final judgment without there being any need for an elaborate concentrated final hearing (see Rule 65). In some cases judgments that determine preliminary procedural issues, or legal issues, on the merits may precede a final judgment (see Rule 66), and in urgent cases the court may make an order for provisional measures before it gives a decision at a concentrated final hearing (see Rule 67). In complex cases, it must be expected that one early case management hearing may not be sufficient to discharge the court's duty to actively manage cases (see Rules 4 and 61(1)).
2. An early case management hearing (see Rule 61(1)) forms part of civil proceedings in the majority of European jurisdictions. Judicial responsibility for active and effective case management (see Rules 2 and 4), has been accepted in all European procedural cultures since the 1980s. It includes reasonable judicial planning and scheduling, when carried out in consultation with the parties, from the start of proceedings. As a rule, a case

ELI-Unidroit Model European Rules of Civil Procedure. ELI & Unidroit, Oxford University Press.
 DOI: 10.1093/oso/9780198866589.003.0006

management hearing should be held after the exchange of the parties' statements of case. If necessary, where it is apparent to the court that the parties' pleadings are incomplete, the court may, by written case management order issued before the early case management hearing, suggest possible amendments to the pleadings (see Rules 50 and 53(3)). That being said, in complex or otherwise difficult cases, it would be preferable to make such an order at an early oral hearing. Early case management hearings are not, however, mandatory. In simple or low value cases, such a hearing may be disproportionate in terms of cost and time to the parties and the court. In such cases, the court ought to make a written case management order to enable the parties to properly prepare for the final hearing (see Rules 50 and 61(2)). Ordinarily, however, such hearings ought to take place in person or, at least, via any available electronic means of communication.

3. The structure of the procedural model that underpins these Rules represents a clear rejection of discontinuous or of piecemeal proceedings, which involve a lengthy sequence of hearings, which result in unnecessary cost and delay. As a consequence, the fact that these Rules provide a discretion for the court to hold more than one case management hearing (see Rule 61(1)) should not be understood as an invitation to adopt a discontinuous, piecemeal approach to proceedings. The discretion to hold more than one case management hearing should only be exercised in appropriate circumstances, such as complex cases or where there has been an unexpected change in the parties' original positions during the course of the proceedings. In such cases further case management hearings may be necessary to properly manage the proceedings.
4. Rule 61(3) describes the most effective approach to scheduling proceedings in that it requires the court, in co-operation with the parties, to determine at the earliest point in the proceedings, the timetable for the proceedings and its key milestones, e.g., trial and judgment. Party co-operation, which ought properly to have been in place since the pre-commencement phase of proceedings (see Rule 51) is required to ensure the efficacy of this Rule. That party co-operation ought to have been in place since the pre-commencement phase ought to result in this Rule being properly carried into effect. Notwithstanding the importance of early case management, it will often neither be feasible nor helpful in some cases. Equally, in some cases a management timetable may need to be revised during the course of proceedings. This Rule should not, therefore, be interpreted as restricting or otherwise limiting the court's power to revise or amend the timetable either of its own motion (*ex officio*) or on the application of a party.
5. Rule 61(4) corresponds to all the other rules on court management: Rules 4, 24(1), 25(3), 26(2), 27(1), 48 – 50, and 53(3). Rule 61(4) emphasises how important it is for the proper management of proceedings for the court to provide advice to the parties and to issue case management orders as early as possible.
6. Case management by the court carried out in consultation and co-operation with the parties (see Rule 61(3)) is significantly more important where parties jointly apply to bring party-agreed-proceedings (see Rules 57 – 60). In such a case, the court should ensure that it has a detailed understanding of the parties' real intentions, the extent to which it can rely on party consent to the procedure, and the strength of the parties' willingness to base their future relationship on a legal process that combines agreed elements with those that will be subject to an adversarial process and judgment.

Rule 62. Means of Case Management during the pre-final hearing phase

(1) The court may use all the means of case management set out in Rules 49(1), (3)-(6).

(2) **Appropriate measures for the disclosure of evidence and the taking of evidence before a final hearing are, particularly,**
  (a) **the production and mutual exchange of documents;**
  (b) **requests for written witness statements and their exchange;**
  (c) **the appointment of a court expert and expert conferences between a court-appointed expert and experts appointed by the parties, or between court-appointed experts;**
  (d) **requests for information from third parties, including public authorities;**
  (e) **personal inspection of evidence by the court.**

Sources:
ALI/UNIDROIT Principles 7.2, 9.3.3 – 9.3.6; Transnational Rules of Civil Procedure (Reporters' Study) Rules 18.3.1, 18.3.4 and 18.3.5.

Comments:

1. Rule 62(1) in connection with Rules 49(1) and (3) – (6) addresses means of case management that are to be employed in or after the early management hearing. They are designed to ensure that the court takes such organisational measures as are necessary to facilitate the effective conduct of preparatory proceedings, including settlement endeavours, determination of the type and form of on-going proceedings, the procedural calendar or timetable, any limitation in terms of the number and/or length of submissions, the consolidation or separation of proceedings, or the order in which issues are to be tried.
2. Rule 62(2) refers to the means of case management specified in Rules 49(9) – (11). It does so in order to specifically direct the court and parties to those issues that are of most immediate relevance for the effective planning of a final hearing, e.g., disclosure orders and other orders pertinent to evidence-taking. Rule 62 does not address the other means of case management enumerated in Rules 49(7) and (8), which may be relevant for the preparation of early final judgments according to Rule 65, judgments on preliminary procedural issues or on legal issues on the merits according to Rule 66, or orders for provisional measures according to Rule 67 (also see Rule 61, comment 1).
3. Rule 62(2) does not specifically differentiate between disclosure and the taking of evidence during the pre-final hearing phase. Traditionally, disclosure or discovery denoted a procedural mechanism designed to inform parties of facts and available evidence prior to a trial where they had to convince the court by giving such evidence in respect of contested facts. The purpose of disclosure or discovery was not to provide the court with information. It was to provide the parties with information, which they could then choose to adduce as evidence. Evidence-taking was on the contrary designed to convince the court during trial. The procedural model underlying these Rules abandons the strict differentiation between disclosure or discovery on the one hand and evidence-taking on the other. The interim phase as a preparatory procedural stage serves not only to inform the parties and to enable them to prepare for a final hearing, it is now also designed to inform the court or the judge and to anticipate or replace in part evidence-taking in the final hearing. Rule 62(2) in particular enumerates the means of information-gathering suitable for this dual purpose: production of documents to an opponent, to other parties, and to the court that is capable, in principle, of rendering facts uncontested or, at the least, limiting the dispute to issues of interpretation; witness statements that result in a party not having to call a witness to give oral evidence, or as a means to remove or limit the need to examine the witness at an oral hearing in whole or in part; expert reports

including expert conferences to inform parties and court of such evidence, to again render the issues it deals with uncontested or, at the least to limit the need to conduct an oral examination of experts at the final hearing; requests for information from parties and court that may make evidence-taking unnecessary or may limit its scope; inspection by the court to replace the need for the examination of witnesses or experts etc. The adoption of this model in these Rules has been facilitated by converging developments in this area of civil procedure in the common law jurisdictions and in some continental European jurisdictions (also see Rule 97, comment 1).

Rule 63. The Closing of Preparatory Proceedings

(1) As soon as the court is satisfied that both parties have had a reasonable opportunity to present their case during the preparatory proceedings and that it has had an opportunity to clarify issues and take any relevant evidence before the final hearing in accordance with Rule 62(2), it will close the proceedings and refer the case to the final hearing. Once the pre-final hearing phase of proceedings is closed, no further submissions, arguments or evidence are allowed, except as provided by Rule 63(2) and Rule 64(4).

(2) Only under very exceptional circumstances may the court, on its own motion (*ex officio*) or upon a party's well-founded application, permit further statements and submissions.

Comments:

1. Rule 63(1) requires the preparatory phase of proceedings to be formally closed. This is subject to the court's overriding discretion to ensure that it and the parties have had an appropriate amount of time and opportunity to clarify factual allegations and to take notice of available evidence in so far as is reasonable in order to prepare for the final hearing. In applying this discretion, the court should take account of any serious issues that are decisive to the proper determination of the proceedings, which could be tried before it gives its final judgment.
2. Formal closing of the preparatory phase and subsequent referral of proceedings to a final hearing has been a long-standing, common tradition in all well-developed European procedural systems and cultures. Formally closing the instruction or preparation of proceedings so that it may move to a final hearing has generally been the responsibility of an instructing, preparatory or procedural judge. Referral is to the judicial body or judge competent to deal with final hearing and render a final decision.
3. In modern times, some procedural systems still maintain this traditional structure. In other systems it is increasingly the case that the same judge sitting alone at first instance will be responsible for the preparatory and final hearings and for rendering the final judgment. Referral to another judge or judicial body is thus no longer necessary. Therefore, in these Rules the significance of closing is diminished, as it is accepted that in all likelihood it will always be the same judge who decides issues concerning the preclusion of late factual or evidential contentions on the basis of general rules that govern the careful conduct of proceedings (see Rules 2, 3(b), 27(1), 28, and 47) without there being a real need for the preparatory phase to be subject to a formal closing. Nevertheless, these Rules maintain the tradition of formal closing. They do so because of the fact that there remain judicial structures that justify its continuance, while it also provides a benefit to the parties, and the court, by providing a final warning to the parties to take

care of any possible preclusion, i.e., it helps to promote the effective and proportionate management of proceedings.

4. Once the preparatory phase is formally closed, there is a strict rule that parties may no longer make any further submissions (Rule 63(1)). That strict rule is, however, subject to some limited exceptions justified by reference to the fundamental right to be heard (see Rule 11). Therefore, Rule 63(2) permits exceptions in very limited circumstances, ones that are more severe than the generally applicable requirements of Rules 27(1) and 47. The exceptions must be grounded on exceptional reasons. Even after closing, Rule 27(1) applies and does not permit preclusion in those situations where there has been an absence of effective, of careful, court management.

Rule 64. The Final Hearing

(1) In so far as practicable, the final hearing should be concentrated. A concentrated final hearing may be adapted to the use of electronic communication techniques.

(2) The final hearing must be before the judge or judges who are to give the final judgment.

(3) Ordinarily, the court should take oral evidence and evidence on those issues that are still matters of serious dispute between the parties.

(4) All relevant evidence not received by the court in the preparatory proceedings may be taken in the final hearing. New evidence not offered in the pleadings or upon amendment in the preparatory stage may be admitted only if a party shows strong and overwhelming reasons for not having produced it earlier.

(5) The court must properly manage the final hearing according to Rules 48-49. In particular, it must

(a) determine the order in which issues shall be tried;

(b) require a party's appearance in person or require a party's representative, who should be fully-informed of all matters relevant to the proceedings, to be present at the hearing;

(c) order the taking of evidence.

(6) Documentary or other tangible evidence must have been disclosed to all other parties prior to the final hearing. Oral evidence may be taken only if notice has been given to all parties of the identity of the person to be examined and the substance of their intended evidence.

(7) Parties must have an opportunity to submit their final conclusions including statements on the results of evidence-taking.

Sources:

ALI/UNIDROIT Principles 9.4 and 22.3; Transnational Rules of Civil Procedure (Reporters' Study) Rules 29.1 – 29.3 and 31.1.

Comments:

1. Rule 64(1) establishes that a concentrated final hearing is the general rule. The structure of proceedings under these Rules does not permit piecemeal proceedings with a sequence of numerous hearings, which ultimately result in unnecessary delay (see Rule 61, comment 3). The Rules do not in the absence of good reasons, therefore, tolerate the division of a final hearing into a series of hearings. An exception may, for instance, be justified if the court properly gives a judgment on the merits on liability (see Rule 66(1)(b)), and then goes on to hear and determine issues of quantum. In such cases the final hearing may quite properly be divided into, at least, two parts, not least to promote proportionality as

the parties may be able to reach a settlement on quantum following judgment on liability. According to Rule 64(1) the court may use electronic communication techniques. This may, for instance, be applicable where parties are in different time zones. In such cases, any necessary intermissions in the proceedings ought not to be considered an infringement of the concentration rule.

2. Rule 64(2) addresses the principle of immediacy, according to which only those judges who adjudicate in the final hearing are competent to give the final judgment. This principle has a long common tradition across all of European civil procedure. It has been, however, of limited significance in continental European jurisdictions. According to the prevailing continental European understanding, it does not apply to those hearings that precede the final hearing where aspects or, in some jurisdictions, where all of the evidence may be taken and considered by the court. In such cases this limited approach to the principle of immediacy has only prevented judges from rendering judgments without them having conducted the hearing where the parties make their final submissions on the evidence and where any preceding oral consultations between court and parties may take place. Rule 64(2) combined with Rule 64(3) extends, in part, the scope of immediacy to mandatory evidence-taking within the final hearing (also see Rule 97(1), comment 2). At the same time, it strengthens the significance of oral proceedings (see Rule 18). The use of communication technology (Rule 64(1)) and especially of video-conferencing creates new forms of immediacy and orality of proceedings, albeit of a lesser effect than when parties and witnesses are physically before the court (also see Rule 97(3)). These Rules, however, consider such a development arising from communication technology to be more efficient and citizen-oriented than written proceedings. The immediacy principle is the main one to facilitate the best evaluation of evidence which is, in principle, not bound to specific rules (see Rule 98).
3. Rule 64(3) makes clear that the main emphasis of evidence-taking should take place in the final hearing and not in the preparatory phase of proceedings. This applies to oral evidence, as much as it does to evidence-taking regarding those disputed issues which are central to the proceedings. These Rules do not adopt any tendency towards wholly written proceedings, whether in traditional, paper-form, or via modern, digital, technology. They maintain a preference for parties being able to present their case before the court in person either via direct personal appearance in court or by an appearance in court facilitated by means of modern communication techniques. These Rules do not support any further move away from oral to written process.
4. Rule 64(4) extends evidence-taking in final hearings to all evidence that has not already been taken in the preparatory phase of proceedings. It provides the court and parties with some leeway to adduce late evidence, however it only does so if the strict requirements of the Rule are met. The aim underpinning this Rule is to increase, on a step by step basis, the strict application of preclusion from a relatively generous level during the pleading phase and preparatory proceedings (see Rules 27(1), 47, 54(3), 55, 93, 96, with comments) to the period after closing (see Rule 63(2)) and the final hearing (see Rule 64(2)). It is necessary here to instantiate a well-balanced compromise between a strict approach and flexibility (also see Rule 22, comment 6). Where, however, a party has to respond to new factual or evidential contentions that arise as a consequence of the court's failure to manage proceedings effectively, Rule 27(1) applies.
5. Rule 64(5) addresses those means of case management that are particularly important for the proper preparation of a final hearing. Corresponding rules are for Rule 64(5)(a): Rules

49(6), 92(1) and (2); for Rule 64(5)(b): Rules 16(2), 49(10), and 118; and, for Rule 64(5)(c): Rules 49(11)(b), 92(1), and 107.

6. Rule 64(6) is intended to protect the court and parties from surprise at a final hearing, while at the same time preventing a concentrated final hearing from being unnecessarily disrupted leading to unnecessary cost and delay in the proceedings. Rules that correspond to the disclosure requirement in Rule 64(6) are Rules 2, 3(b), 11, 27(1), 47, 49(11), 53(2)(b) and (4), 54(2), 88(3), 92(1), 94, 95(1), 115(1). Rules that correspond to the taking of oral evidence in Rule 64(6) are: Rules 2, 3(b), 11, 27(1), 47, 53(2)(b), 54(2), 94, 95(2), 124(1) and (2).
7. Rule 64(7) is a specific instance of the right to be heard in a final hearing (see Rule 11). It places specific emphasis on the parties' right to address the results of evidence-taking.

Rule 65. Early Final Judgments

(1) The court, on its own motion or on the application of a party, may give an early final judgment upon simplified proceedings.

(2) In an early final judgment the court may

(a) determine that it lacks jurisdiction or competence to adjudicate the dispute or whether the claim is inadmissible due to a failure to comply with other procedural requirements; or

(b) give a final judgment or a judgment on part of the claim for relief by only deciding questions of law based on non-contested facts, or on the basis that there has been a failure by the parties to assert necessary and relevant facts timeously, or there has been a failure to proffer necessary means of evidence timeously; or

(c) give a judgment upon the withdrawal of a claim, whether that was permitted or consented to, or upon an admission by the defendant.

(3) Rules 61–64 and Part VIII of these Rules apply, as appropriate to an early final judgment.

Sources:

ALI/UNIDROIT Principles 9.3.3 and 9.3.5; Transnational Rules of Civil Procedure (Reporters' Study) Rule 19.

Comments:

1. Rules 61 – 64 describe the approach to be taken in proceedings where all the procedural requirements for adjudication are met, and where after the pleading phase (Rules 52 – 60) the court has to take evidence on contested facts (Rules 87 and following) in order to then render a final judgment on the merits following a final, concentrated, hearing. There are, however, many cases that are ripe for decision without any need to go through all possible stages of proceedings. Such cases are, for instance, those where procedural requirements that are necessary for adjudication are not met, where the parties have failed to produce relevant or contested facts, or they have failed to submit factual or evidential contentions timeously. Consequently, in such circumstances proceedings ought to be simplified, and may conclude earlier than would ordinarily be the case. In continental European civil procedure, judges have, and have for many centuries, decided cases according to their development, and there has been, therefore, no good reason, to categorise judgments according to their timely conduct or, even, their expense. In contrast, in common law jurisdictions, in common law courts (albeit not in equity courts), the tribunal of fact was originally the jury. As a consequence, in order to avoid the necessity of time consuming and complex

organisational measures related to fact-finding it became usual to differentiate between decisions that terminated proceedings prior to a jury trial and verdict. Where a judge could render a final decision without a jury, the decision was referred to as a summary judgment because its basis was a simplified form of procedure. Reference to summary judgment in common law jurisdictions survived the disappearance of the civil jury. This term is not used in these Rules, which try to avoid terminology that comes from specific national or cultural procedural institutions or techniques. The terminology used here is intended to focus on the functionality of the procedure, which in this instance concerns a simplified procedure that will result in the termination of proceedings earlier than a final hearing. Rule 65 covers, in so far as possible, all those cases that conclude earlier than a final hearing in both continental and common law European traditions. Early final judgments terminate proceedings at first instance in the same way that a final judgment terminates proceedings (see Rule 130(1)(a) – (c)). They may be subject to an appeal if they meet the conditions applicable to appeals.

2. Rule 65(2)(a) addresses early final judgments on procedural grounds. In all European procedural systems, however, they may differ in the details, courts may render judgments on the merits only if they are satisfied that certain procedural requirements, such as jurisdiction, competence to adjudicate or other procedural requirements as enumerated or referred to in Rule 133 are met. Failure to comply with such requirements results in the mandatory dismissal of a claim if, upon the court monitoring the proceedings, a claimant is unable to cure any such defect timeously (see Rules 4 sentence 3, 33, 47, 48, 49(8), 55). All of these defects are in common law jurisdictions considered to be reasons to render a summary judgment. In these Rules, they come within the scope of the early final judgment; this is also true for frivolous or abusive claims or claims that are commenced where there is no legitimate interest in the claimant so doing (see Rule 65(2)(a) in connection with Rule 133(a)-(e), with comments).
3. Rule 65(2)(b) specifies those cases where the court is able to render a judgment without any evidence-taking because: non-contested facts do not justify upholding the claim for relief or any affirmative defence pleaded; the claimant or defendant failed to, or failed to timeously, assert all necessary facts relevant, or evidence necessary, for the claim or any affirmative defence. Such judgments may dismiss a claim or defence in such circumstances, although this should only be carried out after the court has offered the party or parties suggestions concerning how they may seek to amend their case. These various circumstances may result in what common law jurisdictions characterise as summary judgments. In part, they fulfil the requirements of what was historically referred to as a demurrer. Additionally, early final judgments may also be rendered if there is clear documentary evidence for contested facts, and the party's opponent or other parties fail, or fail timeously, to offer evidence for an adverse interpretation of those factual contentions, or supportive of an affirmative defence.
4. Rule 65(2)(c) corresponds to Rule 56, as it permits the making of an early final judgment upon the withdrawal of claim or upon a party's admission.
5. Rule 65(3) determines the application of Rules 61 – 64 in so far as appropriate. This means that, ordinarily, a final hearing should take place where the parties could be heard, legal issues could be tried, and the parties can submit their final arguments. Regularly, the court will decide without taking evidence. There are, however, exceptions. Where, for instance, there are doubts concerning compliance with procedural requirements (Rule 65(2)(a)), by

taking evidence through the production of documents or witness evidence, or, somewhat debatably, in cases concerning the applicability of foreign law by the production of expert evidence (see Rule 26, comment 3). In such cases Rules 61 – 64 may apply accordingly. In simple cases the court may make a management order to inform the parties of its intention and decide the dispute upon written arguments submitted by the parties without holding an oral hearing.

Rule 66. Judgments on Preliminary Procedural Issues or on Legal Issues on the Merits

(1) The court on its own motion or on the application of a party may give a judgment

(a) deciding a preliminary procedural issue, or

(b) deciding a legal issue on the merits

(2) Rules 61–64 and Part VIII of these Rules apply, as appropriate to the issue to be determined under this Rule. Judgments on preliminary procedural requirements according to Rule 133 are subject to independent appeal.

Sources:

ALI/UNIDROIT Principles 9.3.3, 9.3.5; Transnational Rules of Civil Procedure (Reporters' Study) Rules 19.1.3, 19.2.

Comments:

1. According to Rule 66(1)(a) the court may give binding judgments that determine preliminary procedural issues. This precludes further consideration of such issues and thereby contributes to concentrated proceedings (see Rules 2, 4 sentence 1).
2. Preliminary procedural issues include, amongst other things, disputes about procedural requirements that must be met during the preparatory phase and for a judgment on the merits to be given by the court (see Rule 133). If the court concludes that procedural requirements have not been met, it must dismiss the proceedings by giving an early final judgment (see Rule 65(2)(a)). If the court finds that such a requirement has been met, it may go on to proceed to determine the proceedings on the merits. In appropriate cases, however, it may make sense to render a judgment on a procedural requirement, which can then be appealed (see Rule 66(2)), and then to continue the proceedings if the judgment was not appealed from or was confirmed on appeal. In doing so, the court may save time and costs that the judiciary and the parties may incur if the proceedings continue and the judgment on the merits is later overturned on appeal on the basis that a procedural requirement was not complied with prior to the judgment. On the other hand, there may be cases where the court finds it advantageous, in the interest of securing the early termination of the proceedings as a whole, to have the decision of a higher court on the preliminary procedural question at stake, while at the same time continuing to proceed to determine the proceedings on the merits. In such a case it will thus run the risk of unnecessarily increasing its workload and party costs (see Rule 130(2)).
3. In addition to questions concerning procedural requirements, preliminary procedural issues which could be decided by judgment in the sense of this Rule are, amongst other things: disputes concerning a party or non-party's duty to produce documents or concerning the authenticity of documents; disputes concerning the admissibility of a proposed amendment; or, the court's assessment that the proceedings have not been terminated by a valid agreement of the parties.

4. Appeals against judgments that determine preliminary procedural issues are permitted according to the general rules on appeals. They should, however, be rare in order to avoid the costs and delay that can result from too much satellite litigation. These Rules permit judgments to be made on preliminary procedural issues with the expectation that courts and judges will only do so when such a step is necessary. The discretion should not be exercised abusively in order to facilitate a temporary reduction in judicial workload. Judgments on procedural preliminary issues are *res judicata* in so far as a rehearing could only be permitted upon a change of the factual basis of incidental procedural issues (see Rule 21, comment 5).
5. In the large majority of cases the court should decide preliminary procedural issues by simple court order according to its overriding discretion (see Rule 50). Appeals on the review of court orders are generally excluded independently of the contents of the ruling (see Rule 179(1)), however further objections remain admissible against simple court orders (see Rule 178). Rule 179(2) allows for miscellaneous appeals only in special circumstances, although it always does so where a non-party is affected independently of the nature of the court's ruling (see Rule 180).
6. Rule 66(1)(b) enables the court to give judgments deciding specific legal issues pertaining to the merits of the case and, which have been raised by the parties. It does not permit such judgments to be made in respect of factual issues. Such judgments may further the speedy resolution of proceedings, as judgments on such issues can become *res judicata*, either directly or after an appellate procedure (see Rules 130(1)(d) and (2), 147, 153 and following).
7. A judgment on a specific legal issue on the merits makes most sense where the parties disagree on both the legal ground and the amount of the claim. In such cases, it may be most efficient to first decide on the ground of the claim before proceeding to the complicated and time-consuming determination of the quantum to be paid by a defendant. The most important examples in this respect are judgments that reject contentions that a claim is time-barred, and judgments that determine defendant liability. For example, in a personal injury case in which both liability and the quantum of damages are disputed, the court may give a judgment on liability, leaving quantum to be determined at a later date. The judgment may be combined with a court order requiring evidence to be taken concerning quantum, in case the liability judgment is not subject to an appeal or if it is appealed, it is confirmed.
8. A judgment on a specific legal issue on the merits, e.g., the judgment confirming the existence of the legal ground of a claim for damages or denying that the claim is time-barred, is a regular judgment with respect to appeals and *res judicata*. However, as such a judgment is limited to the specific legal issue, this judgment does not finally determine the whole matter. Therefore, it must be supplemented by a subsequent judgment. In our example, that would be a judgment that determines the exact amount of damages and orders the defendant to pay. In the proceedings that take place between the judgment on the specific issue and the subsequent judgment, the specific issue that has already been determined must be taken as the basis upon which the further proceedings take place; it may not be litigated anew.
9. Whether the court enters a judgment on a specific issue on the merits is a matter of discretion. The court will take into account its obligation to promote the fair, efficient and speedy resolution of the dispute, as set out in Rule 2. In special cases, it may be preferable to render

a judgment on a specific legal issue and at the same time to proceed to deal with the full claim for relief (see comment 2 above, and Rule 139(2)).

Rule 67. Provisional Measures and Interim Payment Orders

The court may make any order for provisional measures according to Part X or for an interim payment as provided by Part X, Rules 199 and following.

Sources:

ALI/UNIDROIT Principles 5.8 and 9.3.3; Transnational Rules of Civil Procedure (Reporters' Study) Rules 4.5.

Comments:

1. Rule 67 makes clear that the phase between pleadings and final hearing provides a good opportunity to consider, and order, a well-founded provisional measure based on the parties' more fully-developed knowledge of the case as a whole (also see Rule 49(7)). As such it highlights to the court and the parties the possibility of such measures, which may, if ordered, promote the proper administration of justice, effective case management and proportionality.
2. According to Rule 51(3)(c) parties may consider during the pre-commencement phase the necessity and contents of provisional measures thereby facilitating the court's later decision-making by proposals that they consent to being made.

PART VI

SERVICE AND DUE NOTICE OF PROCEEDINGS

INTRODUCTION

1. This Part contains rules on the service of judicial documents for domestic and cross-border cases. Sections 1 and 2 provide rules which are generally applicable, no matter whether the addressee is domiciled or residing in the forum State or abroad. Section 3 sets out special rules for cross-border cases and distinguishes between cases in which documents must be served on an addressee domiciled within the European Union and cases in which they reside outside the European Union.

2. While the ALI/UNIDROIT Principles are the starting point for this Part, they do not provide detailed provisions for the service of documents. They were also designed for cross-border litigation (see ALI/UNIDROIT Principle 5). To devise European rules consideration was given to the European Union *acquis*, particularly the ESR Regulation, specific provisions relating to service of documents in the EEO Regulation, the ESC Regulation, the EPO Regulation and the Draft Unified Patent Court Rules, as well as rules on service in use in European jurisdictions, as well as the relevant case law of the European Court of Justice.

3. This Part applies to both domestic and cross-border cases. With respect to service of documents in a cross-border setting it provides some rules that deviate from the ESR Regulation (see Rules 82 to 84 and comments). Nevertheless, the ESR Regulation is intended to apply to the extent that this part does not provide rules of its own, particularly regarding its provisions on communication and organisational matters. The aim has been to provide a functioning and modern model for service rules.

SECTION 1 – GENERAL PART—SERVICE, DUE NOTICE AND THE RIGHT TO BE HEARD

Rule 68. Service of documents and minimum content

(1) Statements of claim and any other procedural documents amending the relief sought or seeking new relief under Rule 55 should be served in accordance with Rules 74-78 and 80-81.

(2) The statement of claim or documents seeking to amend proceedings must comply with the requirements of Rules 53 and 55.

Sources:

ALI/UNIDROIT Principle 5.1.

Comments:

1. Section 1 deals with service of documents that institute proceedings (Rule 68); an issue that needs to be addressed separately due to the importance of establishing the court's jurisdiction over the parties and guaranteeing the defendant's right to be heard. Rules 68

ELI-UNIDROIT Model European Rules of Civil Procedure. ELI & UNIDROIT, Oxford University Press.
 DOI: 10.1093/oso/9780198866589.003.0007

and 69 set the minimum standard of information that must be given to defendants to enable them to prepare their defence and avoid entry of a default judgment. Rule 72 sets the scope of application of the general rules on service and defers to other parts of these Rules whether formal service of documents is required in particular situations. There are no uniform standards in Europe for which types of documents, and under which circumstances, formal service is required. The same may apply to various documents during the proceedings. These Rules provide situation and context-specific rules concerning the service of particular documents (see Rules 39, 42, 44, 53(3) and (7), 54(6), 55(3), 69, 134).

2. Compliance with a party's right to be heard is not only essential for defendants in respect of the documents instituting proceedings. When proceedings are pending, their subject-matter may be extended due to a counterclaim, an interpleader, or a third-party notice. Consequently, this Rule extends the service requirements to other procedural documents which amend the relief sought or extend the proceedings to persons other than the original claimant and defendant. As a consequence, "parties" in this Rule also includes third parties (see Rules 39 and following).
3. Document(s) that institute proceedings must identify the parties to proceedings. This will normally include at least their names and addresses and, if applicable, the name and address of their representatives (also see Article 7(2) of the EPO Regulation). Further specification is unnecessary and, if given, could be misunderstood to enumerate all forms of necessary information.
4. There is no explicit requirement for the service of annexes to a claim. While there is a widespread consensus that, as a basic principle, annexes if used, must be served on defendants, where they are not necessary to enable the defendant to understand the claim's subject-matter exceptions can be made.
5. European jurisdictions' national procedural codes vary considerably with respect to the question whether claimants must set out the legal grounds relied on in the claim filed. Again, as Rule 68 provides only a minimum standard as to necessary information, further specification is unnecessary.

Rule 69. Information about the procedural steps necessary to contest the claim

The statement of claim must clearly state the following:

(a) the procedural requirements for contesting the claim, including where applicable: the time limit for contesting the claim; the time of any scheduled court hearing; the name and address of the court or other institution to which a response to the claim should be sent or before which to appear, and whether representation by a lawyer is mandatory; and

(b) the consequences of a failure to respond or to appear in court, in particular, where applicable, the possibility that a judgment may be entered against the defendant in default of responding to the claim and the liability for costs related to the court proceedings.

Sources:

ALI/UNIDROIT Principle 5.1.

Comments:

1. Rule 69 is in principle based on Article 17 of the EEO Regulation as ALI/UNIDROIT Principle 5.1 seemed to be too broad. The information specified in Rule 69 must be

provided to the defendant in order to fulfil the obligation of a fair hearing and to reduce the possibility that a default judgment will be entered.

2. The rules for service of the statement of claim also apply to amendments made under Rules 53(3) and 55(1) and in respect of notice to the parties requiring their attendance at any hearing (see Rule 68, comment 1).

Rule 70. Where the defendant fails to enter an appearance

Where the defendant has not responded to the statement of claim or not appeared in court, default judgment shall only be given according to Rule 138(3).

Comment:

The Rules on entry of default judgment are set out at Rule 135 and following. Rule 70 incorporates reference to those Rules by way of cross-reference to the criteria for entry of default judgment, and particularly those relating to service, articulated in Rule 138 (see Rule 138, comment 3).

SECTION 2—RESPONSIBILITY FOR AND METHODS OF SERVICE

A. GENERAL PROVISIONS

Rule 71. Responsibility for service

(1) Responsibility for service of documents lies with the court/parties.
(2) If responsibility lies with the court, upon application the court may entrust a party with service of documents if appropriate.
(3) Where responsibility lies with the parties the court retains supervisory control which may include the power to set aside service.

Comments:

1. There is no consensus amongst European jurisdictions concerning responsibility for service of process. In a number of jurisdictions responsibility lies with the court, e.g., Austria, England, Estonia, Finland, Germany, Greece, Italy, Lithuania, Romania, Spain, Sweden, and Switzerland. Other jurisdictions place responsibility in the hands of the parties either generally or in respect of specific documents, such as judgments, see, Slovakia. In a small number of European jurisdictions, such as France, Belgium, Netherlands and Luxembourg, where proceedings do not start by filing a claim with the court, but when the claimant first sends the documents to the defendant, responsibility normally does not lie with the court but with the claimant or a bailiff. Given this plurality of approaches, this Rule leaves it to the jurisdiction to determine the choice to be taken. It does so as harmonisation does not seem to be necessary, and may well depend on matters outside the scope of procedural rules such as court organisation and/or the organisation of the legal and or bailiffs' professions in any particular European jurisdiction. The essential point is to choose the means that is most effective.
2. If a European jurisdiction places responsibility for service generally on the court, there might, nevertheless, be good reasons to entrust the claimant with responsibility for serving specific documents, particularly those instituting proceedings. Rule 71 provides for such an exception to be incorporated. If, on the contrary, a European jurisdiction decides to

leave responsibility for the service of the documents with the parties, the court should in any case be able to exercise a supervisory control and to set aside service if appropriate.

3. In a cross-border situation within the European Union, access to national service providers and designated national electronic platforms may be difficult, particularly if the parties and not the court are responsible for service. All European Union Member States should be obliged to grant access to service providers and their platforms. For technical reasons it may be necessary for access only to be provided indirectly via those institutions of the State that operate such platforms.

Rule 72. Applicability of rules

The following rules on service methods apply to the documents referred to in Rule 68 and to any other documents required to be served including court decisions.

Comments:

1. In principle the same rules on service should apply to all kinds of documents to be served during civil proceedings. However, service of the documents instituting proceedings is particularly important as it establishes the court's jurisdiction over the parties and is an essential means of giving proper effect to the defendant's right to be heard. Consequently, Rules 68-69 provide a minimum standard for the content of such documents and, thus, protect against entry of a default judgment.
2. Rules concerning the service of any documents outside the scope of this Rule and Rule 68 are either provided for separately in these Rules or are outside their scope (see Rule 68, comment 1).

Rule 73. Priority of methods guaranteeing receipt

Documents shall be served using a method that guarantees receipt (Rules 74-76). If such service is not possible, alternative service methods apply, as specified in Rule 78. Where the address for service is unknown or other methods of service have failed, methods of last resort, specified in Rule 80, may be used to effect service.

Sources:

ALI/Unidroit Principle 5.1.

Comments:

1. ALI/Unidroit Principle 5.1 can be interpreted to mean that personal service on the defendant is not required in all cases. In the European context, principles or rules are not restricted to commercial cases, rules should therefore ensure that they are able to properly protect consumers and natural persons adequately. To that end a considerable number of European jurisdictions, e.g., Austria, Belgium, France, Germany, Italy, Lithuania, Luxembourg, Netherlands, Poland and Romania, have put in place a hierarchy of service methods, which prioritise personal service or methods which require some form of confirmation of receipt. In other jurisdictions, such as England and Switzerland, there is no hierarchy. Other jurisdictions, such as Sweden and Finland, have adopted flexible rules.
2. In order to provide the best possible protection of the defendant's right to be heard, it is particularly important to guarantee that the documents instituting proceedings reach them. The rules therefore put the focus on a method of service which guarantees that the court receives a receipt signed by the addressee or their (legal) representative. This

corresponds to Article 13 of the ESC Regulation, which gives priority to postal service attested by an acknowledgement of receipt. Once proceedings are pending, according to Rule 79, service can be effected from lawyer-to-lawyer if the parties are represented by lawyers.

B. METHODS OF SERVICE

Rule 74. Service guaranteeing receipt

(1) Service guaranteeing receipt includes

(a) service by physical delivery attested to by an acknowledgement of receipt signed by the addressee or by a document signed by a court officer, bailiff, post officer or other competent person who effected the service stating that the addressee has accepted the document, and the date of the service;

(b) service via a designated electronic information system using appropriately high technical standards attested to by an acknowledgement of receipt that the system generates automatically where the addressee has a legal obligation to register with that system. Such an obligation shall be imposed on legal persons and on natural persons engaging in independent professional activities for disputes relating to their trade or profession;

(c) service by other electronic means if the addressee has previously and explicitly agreed to use this service method or is under a legal obligation to register an e-mail address for the purpose of service. Such service must be attested to by the addressee's acknowledgement of receipt, which must include the date of receipt, and which is returned by the addressee;

(d) postal service attested to by an acknowledgement of receipt, which must include the date of receipt, and which is signed and returned by the addressee.

(2) Where an acknowledgment of receipt, under Rule 74(1)(c) or (d), is not received within a designated time, service according to Rule 74(1)(a) or (b), if available, should be attempted before alternative service methods can be used.

Comments:

1. This Rule lists all methods of service which generate proof of receipt by the addressee or the person effecting service. It is intended to be an exhaustive list of methods. Whereas the EEO and EPO Regulations are based on the concept of receipt of an acknowledgment of service, the Draft Unified Patent Court Rules, particularly Rule 271, do not require any receipt as proof of service. Service of judicial documents without receipt is, however, not a common standard in European jurisdictions for regular civil litigation.
2. Service via a designated electronic information system with an automatically generated proof of receipt requires the addressee's prior registration. Rule 74(1)(b) indirectly imposes such obligation on all legal and natural persons when they are carrying out professional activities. As a consequence, this speedy method of service should become the standard method for such entities.
3. Electronic service, Rule 74(1)(c), or regular postal service, Rule 74(1)(d), are also speedy methods of service by which documents are sent directly to the addressee, but an acknowledgement of receipt can only be obtained if it is sent back by the addressee voluntarily.

Therefore this method is only appropriate if there is a good chance of obtaining a receipt. If the addressee, however, does not return a receipt, there is no valid service of the documents and service according to Rule 74(1)(a) or (b) must be attempted.

Service by court officers or other person designated under national law

4 Rule 74(1)(a) refers to service effected by court officers or employees, bailiffs or any person who is competent to do so under national law. This type of service is widely accepted in Europe, e.g., in Austria, Belgium, England, Germany, Greece, France, Luxembourg, Netherlands, Romania, Spain, and Switzerland.

5. In order to provide a flexible approach, it is not necessary to specify the time or place where documents may be served on the addressee. Rule 74(1)(a) allows service wherever the addressee is lawfully encountered although in some European jurisdictions there are specifications such as residence, workplace, place of business.

Service by electronic means

6. Electronic service is available in many European jurisdictions, albeit subject to a variety of different safeguards, e.g., Austria, Belgium, England, Estonia, France, Germany, Greece, Italy, Lithuania, Luxembourg, Romania, Spain, and Switzerland. Some European jurisdictions exclude electronic service from the service of the documents instituting proceedings because the defendant's explicit prior consent is necessary for this method to be used. As such it is often unavailable before proceedings have started, as is the case in Germany, Finland and Sweden.

7. Some specific features of electronic service must be taken into account when implementing such service rules: (1) normal e-mail service cannot always be considered a safe technical method for the delivery of judicial documents, (2) the sender of the documents must be clearly identified, and (3) the holder of one or several e-mail accounts can be expected to check them regularly only if they are aware that judicial documents can also be served by using an electronic address.

8. Electronic service should therefore only be allowed if appropriately high technical standards are used which guarantee the identity of the sender, safe transmission, and a strong possibility that the addressee will receive notice of the documents. These are also the requirements set out in Rule 271 of the Draft Unified Patent Court Rules, which provides an Annex with a list of secure identification and transmission standards which are applicable for the Unified Patent Court. For the Rule here, it is not necessary or helpful to provide a uniform technical standard although it might be desirable for cross-border service of documents in the future. For the present there are many different methods of electronic service in European jurisdictions and therefore it seems neither possible nor advisable to identify specific electronic means for the purpose of this Rule. Article 13 of the EEO Regulation provides, for example, fax or e-mail, but there are also some European Union jurisdictions that require the use of special electronic platforms or officially approved transmitting agencies, e.g., Austria, Estonia, Switzerland. As a consequence it is sufficient to emphasise the necessity of high technical standards in Rule 74(1)(b).

9. Rule 271(1) of the Draft Unified Patent Court Rules permits service to an "electronic address which the defendant has provided for the purpose of service in the proceedings". It thus requires the defendant's consent. Article 13 of the EEO Regulation does not mention the requirement of the addressee's formal consent to this type of service, but it seems

necessary to distinguish between legal entities such as companies or persons engaging in independent professional activities on the one hand and natural persons on the other hand. Private companies, public authorities, and lawyers can be expected to check their accounts on a daily or at least regular basis. Rule 74 gives effect to such a legal obligation and as a consequence permits the use of the registered e-mail addresses, electronic account or registration on a specific electronic platform or system for the service of judicial documents. In these cases a receipt automatically generated by the system is sufficient.

10. For persons not mentioned in Rule 74(1)(b), especially consumers, a different approach is necessary (Rule 74(1)(c)). The majority of European jurisdictions do not currently impose any obligation on them to make an electronic address available for official purposes. In the absence of such a legal obligation the addressee's prior consent to use an electronic address seems necessary to protect their right to be heard with respect to documents instituting proceedings and in order to prevent the court from using an e-mail address or electronic mailbox which is no longer used and not regularly checked by the defendant.

Postal service

11. Postal service is allowed in a number of European jurisdictions, e.g., Austria, Germany, England, Estonia, Finland, Greece, Poland, Spain, Sweden, albeit not in France where it is only permitted in certain situations. Also see Article 14 of the ESR Regulation. In fact the term "registered mail" depends to a large extent on domestic postal regulations which use different types of receipts and differ with respect to the group of people to whom documents may be handed over if the addressee is not encountered personally. Rule 74(1)(d) requires an acknowledgement of receipt signed and returned by the addressee within a specified period of time. Once it has expired, the court may proceed under Rule 74(2) and make a second attempt at service. Normal post service where letters are simply deposited in a letter box without the return of a receipt is not sufficient for Rule 74(1)(d) but if a postal officer delivers the documents to the addressee personally, Rule 74(1)(a) will apply.

Acknowledgment of receipt

12. This Rule does not explicitly stipulate that a particular standard form must be used as acknowledgement of receipt and that the documents sent by post or electronic mail must include such a standard form to be filled in and sent back by the addressee. However, such a standard form will help in effecting service and the use of such is strongly recommended.

Rule 75. Service on legal persons by physical delivery

If Rule 74(1)(a) or (d) applies, service on a statutory representative of a legal person can be effected at the business premises. Business premises include the principal place of business, the place of the legal person's statutory seat, the central administration, or a branch, agency or establishment if the dispute arises out of the activity of that branch, agency or establishment.

Comments:

1. According to Rule 74(1)(b) service on legal persons will normally be effected via a designated electronic information system once the legal entity has registered for the system. Service by physical delivery or postal service will therefore be an exception. Both methods,

however, require specifications with respect to legal entities. Documents can be delivered to a legal representative, but the place of service must be specified.

2. While some European jurisdictions, e.g., Italy, Finland or Sweden, permit service to be effected on a lawyer at their private dwelling or residence, it seems more appropriate to require service to be effected at their business premises. Such an approach draws a clear distinction between the lawyer as the addressee of the documents as their client's representative and the lawyer as a private individual. Rule 271(5) of the Draft Unified Patent Court Rules takes a similar approach. It, however, permits service at any permanent or temporary place of business. As such it permits service on companies at branch offices or agencies. This solution might be acceptable for patent litigation. For normal civil proceedings it seems more appropriate for service of documents at a branch, agency or other such establishment to be permissible only where it is closely connected to the dispute. This is especially the case in contractual disputes where a company may not expect service of judicial documents at a branch which had nothing to do with the contract that forms the basis of the dispute.

Rule 76. Service on representatives

(1) If a minor or a party that lacks legal capacity has a legal custodian or guardian, service on them is equivalent to service on the addressee.

(2) Service on a person nominated to receive service by the addressee is equivalent to service on the addressee.

Comments:

1. Rule 76 covers two different situations. Rule 76(1) deals with service of documents on those parties to litigation who lack litigation capacity. Rule 76(2) provides a general rule that enables parties to nominate any other adult to receive documents to accept service on their behalf. If documents are served upon an individual who has a power of attorney to accept them on behalf of the addressee that is equivalent to service on the addressee.
2. Rule 76(1) recognises that in general minors or parties who lack full legal capacity under substantive law are not allowed to conduct civil proceedings on their own behalf (see Rules 30 and following). Such situations are generally dealt with throughout European jurisdictions by permitting service to be effected on individuals who are not formally parties to proceedings. This Rule is thus based on the concept that minors and other such parties that lack legal capacity must be represented for the purposes of service according to substantive or otherwise applicable law.
3. Rule 76(2) is based on Article 15 of the EEO Regulation. Its equivalent is also contained in some European jurisdiction's procedural codes, e.g., Estonia and Germany. There is no limit as to whom may be nominated, i.e., nomination is not restricted to lawyers.

Rule 77. Refusal to accept service

Service according to Rule 74(1)(a) also includes service attested to by a document signed by the competent person who effected the service and stating that the addressee refused to receive the document. The document must be deposited at a specified place for a certain period of time for the purpose of collection by the addressee who has been informed where and when to collect the document.

Comments:

1. Service rules should provide a solution for situations where an addressee deliberately refuses to accept the documents to be served. It is a widespread concept in Europe that an addressee's refusal to accept service should not prevent the legal effects of service from taking effect. Rules, however, differ with respect to whether the refusal must be with good reason or not. Typical examples given for a good reason to refuse service are cases of a mistaken identity. In European Union cross-border settings, Article 8 of the ESR Regulation has adopted the concept that the addressee may refuse to accept service of documents at the time of service or by returning the documents to the receiving agency within one week if they do not comply with the language requirements set out in Article 8 of the ESR Regulation.
2. The approach taken here differs from the established European and European Union approaches. First, it should be noted that if the person who refuses to accept service is not the addressee of the documents, service will be invalid: see Rule 74. Secondly, if the language requirements of Rule 82 are not met it is neither necessary to refuse to accept service nor will such a refusal be equivalent to service. In this case service of documents will be ineffective and Rule 83 emphasises the fact that Rule 81 concerning curing defective service does not apply.
3. Another important question is whether where a person refuses to accept service, the person attempting to effect service should take back the documents to be served or leave them. The domestic rules of some European jurisdictions, e.g., Estonia, Germany, Greece and Romania, provide that where an addressee refuses to accept the documents, they must either be left with the addressee or must be deposited for collection. This is the optimum approach. If the refusal to accept the documents has the same consequences as a delivery of the documents, the addressee should at least be in the position to find out about the contents of the documents. Therefore, Rule 77 corresponds to Article 13(1)(b) of the EEO Regulation but goes beyond it as it makes provision for the addressee to be given the opportunity to collect the documents.

Rule 78. Alternative service methods

(1) If the addressee is not available for service according to Rule 74, the following alternative service methods effected by a court officer, bailiff, postal officer or other competent person are available

(a) service at the addressee's home address on persons who are living in the same household as the addressee or are employed by the addressee, and who are able and willing to accept the document;

(b) in the case of a self-employed addressee or a legal person, service at the addressee's business premises on persons who are employed by the addressee, and who are able and willing to accept the document;

(c) depositing the document at a post office or with competent public authorities and placing written notification of that deposit in the addressee's mailbox. In such a case the notification must clearly identify the document as a court document, the date by which it must be collected, the place where it can be collected and the contact details of the relevant person effecting service. Service is only effected when the document is collected.

(2) Service according to Rule 78(1)(a) and(b) shall be attested to by:

(a) a document signed by the competent person who effected service, indicating:

(i) the method of service used;

(ii) the date of service; and

(iii) the name of that person and their relationship to the addressee,

or

(b) an acknowledgement of receipt by the person served.

(3) Service according to Rule 78(1)(a) and (b) is not allowed if the recipient is the party opposing the addressee in the proceedings.

(4) Service according to Rule 78(1)(c) shall be attested to by:

(a) a document signed by the competent person who effected service, indicating:

(i) the method of service used; and

(ii) the date of collection,

or

(b) an acknowledgement of receipt by the person served.

Comments:

1. The text is based on Article 14(1)(a)-(d), and (3) of the EEO Regulation with some modifications.
2. In order to promote effective service, it seems appropriate to only permit alternative service to be effected on persons who are willing to accept the documents and who are willing to agree to deliver them to the addressee. Rule 78 does not, however, imply that a person in the addressee's household or an employee is obliged to accept service of documents. Such an obligation might have far-reaching consequences, such as a liability for damages if the documents are not delivered to the addressee or are given to them too late to prevent entry of a default judgment. It is a matter of substantive law to determine if such an obligation should be imposed and, if so, its consequences.
3. Rule 78 permits alternative service if personal service is not possible. It does not require a second attempt to achieve personal service to be made. Rule 74(2) must, however, be taken into consideration.
4. Alternative service is in many European jurisdictions restricted to family members. As it may be difficult to determine who is a family member, as this depends on national substantive law, it is preferable to permit alternative service on all persons living in the same household. This type of approach is taken in a number of European jurisdictions, e.g. Finland, France, Greece, and Poland. It requires there to be a sufficiently close relationship to the addressee to assume that the documents will be forwarded to them.
5. Alternative service on children is less reliable. In some European jurisdictions there are clear rules governing the minimum age children must have attained to be legally responsible, such that they could accept service, e.g., Belgium (16 yrs), Finland (15 yrs), France (12 yrs), Italy (14 yrs), Luxembourg (15 yrs), Spain (14 yrs), Switzerland (16 yrs). Other jurisdictions use more general wording and leave it to the courts to decide the question of responsibility on an individual basis, e.g., Germany, Greece, and Romania. For the sake of legal certainty, a clear threshold could be defined, but a more flexible approach seemed to be appropriate for this Rule, which therefore requires the ability to accept the documents. In any case, considering their age the person must give the impression that they can reasonably be expected to forward the documents. A case-by-case decision by the person effecting service will thus be necessary.
6. Alternative service on employees of legal persons that are a party to the proceedings is a common European standard. An employee must hold a position according to which

they can reasonably be relied on to forward the documents to the addressee, e.g., a valid labour or employment contract is not necessary if the individual in fact works for the addressee. Consequently, there is a general reference to the employee's ability in Rules 78(1)(a) and (b). Handing over documents to cleaning personnel should, for example, not be sufficient to accept service in a large company, in a small company or private household it may be different. Thus, a case-by-case decision by the person effecting service will be necessary.

7. Depositing the documents in a mailbox or a safe mailbox is permitted in a number of European jurisdictions, albeit only as a subsidiary method of service. Depositing documents to be served for the collection by the addressee at a local post office or a bailiff's office is, however, preferable, as it can prevent the documents being lost. Such an approach is widely adopted in Europe, e.g., in Austria, Belgium, France, Greece, Italy, Luxembourg, Netherlands and Slovakia. For the addressee's information a written notification should be placed in their mailbox. If no mailbox is available, the person effecting service may use other suitable means of informing the addressee, e.g., pinning the notification to the addressee's door. These rules avoid fictitious service as an alternative method and therefore Rule 78(1)(c) states that in this case service is only completed if the addressee actually collects the documents. If they do not collect them, service can be effected according to Rule 80.
8. Rule 78(3) articulates a widespread European approach, see for instance Austria, Germany, Lithuania, and Switzerland, although it is not always articulated explicitly within procedural codes. If the recipient is the party opposing the addressee in the proceedings, they may be in a situation of a conflict of interest and be tempted not to forward the document to the addressee.

Rule 79. Service of documents during proceedings

(1) During proceedings, if a party is represented by a lawyer, service of documents may normally be effected on the lawyer or from lawyer-to-lawyer without Court intervention. Lawyers must provide an electronic address that can be used for service of documents.

(2) During proceedings, if a party is represented by a lawyer, they must notify the Court and any lawyer who represents other parties or intervenors of any change of postal or electronic address.

(3) During proceedings, parties must notify the court of any change of residence, of place of business or of their postal or electronic address.

Comments:

1. A number of European jurisdictions permit lawyer-to-lawyer service once proceedings have commenced and the parties are legally represented, e.g., Belgium, England, Estonia, France, Germany, Greece, Italy, Lithuania, Luxembourg, the Netherlands, Poland, Romania, and Spain. Such a rule should therefore be adopted for reasons of efficiency. Lawyer-to-lawyer service avoids the risk that a party does not forward documents to their lawyer timeously and prevents or minimises the risk that lawyers lose time to respond to the documents. As some countries allow individuals other than registered members of the local bar association to appear in court, this Rule encompasses all established forms of legal representative.

2. Some European jurisdictions require lawyers to provide a registered electronic address for the purpose of service of legal documents, e.g., Estonia and Germany. This is adopted here as a general rule given the increasing use of electronic communication methods. It includes registration on a designated electronic information system according to Rule 74(1)(b). For the sake of clarity 'during proceedings' means the relevant civil proceedings, not any subsequent enforcement proceedings, but where a court decision or judgment is to be served, Rule 79 applies.
3. Rule 79(2) imposes an obligation on the parties to notify the court of any change of address etc., in order to facilitate service of documents. Service from lawyer-to-lawyer will not apply for the service of all documents. Orders requiring attendance at hearings need to be served on the party in person (see Rules 16(2), 49(10), 64(5), 65(3), 66(2), and 118).

Rule 80. Service methods of last resort

(1) If service by methods that guarantee receipt (Rules 74-77) or alternative service (Rule 78) is not possible because the addressee's address is unknown or service has otherwise failed, service of documents may be effected as follows:
(a) by publication of a notice to the addressee in a form provided for by law of the forum State, including publication in electronic registers accessible to the public, and
(b) by sending a notice to the addressee's last known address or e-mail address, if applicable.
(c) For the purpose of subparagraphs (a) and (b), notice means information which clearly states the character of the document to be served as a court document, the legal effect of the notification as effecting service, information as to where the addressee can collect the documents or copies thereof, and the date by which they have to be collected.

(2) The address is unknown if the Court or the party responsible for service has made every reasonable effort to discover the addressee's present address. Efforts to find the present address must be documented in the Court files.

(3) Service shall be deemed to be effected within two weeks after publication of the notice and after having sent the notice to the last known address or e-mail address, as applicable. If there is no last known address or e-mail address service shall be deemed to be effected within two weeks after publication of the notice.

Comments:

1. Rule 80 applies where the address for service is unknown. It also applies where other service methods have failed. At present, in a cross-border setting neither the European Service Regulation nor the Convention of 15 November 1965 on the Service Abroad of Judicial and Extrajudicial Documents in Civil of Commercial Matters (the HCCH 1965 Service Convention) are applicable if the addressee's address is unknown (see, Article 1(2) of the ESR Regulation; Article 1 paragraph 2 of the HCCH 1965 Service Convention). For domestic cases national rules often provide a type of fictitious service. This particularly applies to documents instituting proceedings in order to guarantee the claimant's right to access to justice when they are unable to locate the defendant. Failure of service in the sense of Rule 80 includes cases where service according to Rule 74 has failed, and furthermore neither the addressee nor any other person to whom the documents could be delivered for the purposes of Rule 78 have been encountered, nor did the addressee collect the document deposited according to Rule 78(1)(c).

2. In order to protect the defendant's right to be heard, reasonable efforts to find the defendant by those responsible for effecting service must be required and should be documented where the address is unknown (see also Rule 138(3)).
3. Service by publication of a notification on the court door, in official journals or a publicly accessible electronic register is available in many European jurisdictions. In those jurisdictions that have adopted the system of "*remise au parquet*" a public notice is not always necessary, but this form of fictional service has not been accepted by the HCCH 1965 Service Convention or the ESR Regulation. Rules in European jurisdictions vary as to the place where public service is allowed, e.g., the place where the court seised is located, the place of the addressee's last residence. It does not seem to be necessary to harmonise the rules in this respect as a publication in a publicly accessible electronic register is likely to become the default approach in future. The wording of the Rule is broad enough to cover giving notice via text message, "Facebook", WhatsApp, or other social media although it is not publication in the narrow sense.
4. Service at the last known residence or place of business is possible in England, France, and Luxembourg. In Belgium and the Netherlands, documents are left with the royal prosecutor. In 2011, the European Court of Justice also accepted service at the last known address, if the defendant had a contractual obligation to notify the claimant of any change of his residence or domicile.[1] Not only should there be an obligation to publish a notice under Rule 80(1)(a) but the notice should also be sent to the last known address in order to provide a realistic chance for the addressee to collect the documents where service according to Rules 74 or 78 has failed.
5. Time limits for service are well-established. Different European jurisdictions adopt different time limits, e.g., Austria (14 days), Romania (15 days), Italy (20 days), Switzerland (7 days for downloading electronically served documents). 14 days is adopted here in Rule 80(3) as the most appropriate reasonable time limit balancing the interests of claimants, defendants and the efficient prosecution of proceedings. Rule 84 provides an exception for cross-border cases.

Rule 81. Cure for defective service

If service of documents does not meet the requirements of Rules 74-79, such non-compliance will be cured if the addressee's conduct proves that they received the document to be served personally and in sufficient time for them to arrange their defence or in any other way respond as required by the nature of the document.

Comments:

1. Whereas the European Service Regulation does not provide rules for curing defective service,[2] such a power is commonplace in European jurisdiction's national procedural codes,

1 Judgment of 17 November 2011, Hypoteční banka (C-327/10, ECR 2011 p. I-11543) ECLI:EU:C:2011:745; and, Judgment of 15 March 2012, G v Cornelius de Visser (C-292/10) ECLI:EU:C:2012:142)

2 Art. 8(3) of the ESR Regulation is not exactly a device to cure a defect in service because service of documents which does not comply with the language requirements of Art. 8(1) does not constitute a violation of the ESR Regulation and does not make the procedure invalid (Order of the Court of 4 May 2016 Monster Energy Company v European Union Intellectual Property Office (C-603/15 P) ECLI:EU:C:2016:332)

e.g., in Austria, England, Estonia, Germany, Greece, Poland, Romania, and Switzerland.[3] In this respect it is generally understood that where an addressee actually receives documents then any formal defect in service falls away as irrelevant. This is an appropriate result as the primary function of service of documents, i.e., to ensure the addressee has proper access to the information in the documents, – is fulfilled by actual receipt. Rule 81, accordingly, takes the same approach.

2. If the service of a document fixes the date on which a deadline starts to run, the addressee may not have sufficient time to respond. Therefore, non-compliance with the service rules will be cured only if the addressee has also had sufficient time to arrange for their defence or respond in any other appropriate way as required by the document served. Such cases are also dealt with in the context of default judgment (Rules 70, 138 and following) or they can be addressed in the general context of restitution *in integrum* which is not generally dealt with in these Rules
3. The text of this Rule was based on Article 18 of the EEO Regulation. It is, however, broader in its application than that Article, as Rule 81 applies not only to service of documents that institute proceedings, but also applies to those documents that summon parties to court hearings.

SECTION 3—CROSS BORDER ISSUES

A. IN THE EUROPEAN UNION

Rule 82. Language requirements

(1) In the case of natural persons not engaging in independent professional activities the documents referred to in Rule 68 and the information referred to in Rule 69 must be in a language of the proceedings and, unless it is evident that the addressee understands the language of the forum, also in a language of the European Union Member State of the individual's habitual residence.

(2) In the case of legal persons the documents referred to in Rule 68 and the information referred to in Rule 69 must be in a language of the proceedings, and also the language of the legal person's principal place of business, its statutory seat or of the principal documents in the transaction.

Sources:

ALI/Unidroit Principle 5.2.

Comments:

1. Rules 82(1) and (2) are based on the understanding that consumers or natural persons need better protection than corporations, which is an established principle in European national law and European Union law. This Rule, however, differs from European Union law. It takes a better law approach because, at the least, the protection of consumers should not be sacrificed for the sake of costs of translation. In respect of B2B litigation, the exception in Rule 82(2) helps in reducing translation costs, if the language of the forum and the language of the transaction correspond, e.g., should negotiations and a business transaction have been made in English, but the court seised is for example in France, a translation

3 This approach is not however taken in Belgium, France or the Netherlands.

from French to English would still be necessary unless the French courts permit the proceedings to be conducted in English.

2. Although the language and translation required do not guarantee, in all cases, that the addressee understands the documents properly, they constitute an acceptable presumption. The place of habitual residence and the place of the principal place of business refer to a factual link between the addressee and the place of service.
3. The ESR Regulation adopts the position that it is up to the defendant to respond if they are unable to understand the documents served. Rule 82 reverses the approach taken in the Regulation. It reverts to an objective approach, and as such the court should not simply rely on the claimant's allegations as to the defendant's language skills. Rule 82 refrains from providing a list of criteria for language skills. The Rule must, however, clearly express that an exception from the translation requirement is only acceptable in rare cases, e.g., if a claimant can produce a document written by the defendant in the respective language or has evidence proving that the defendant's profession involves such language skills, e.g., they are a language teacher or interpreter, or that the defendant formerly lived in the forum State for some time and that it can therefore be presumed that they know the language. The same can apply if the defendant is a national of the forum State but is presently living elsewhere.
4. By contrast to the ESR Regulation, it is not necessary to provide defendants with a formal right to refuse acceptance or reject documents, if service does not comply with the language requirements of Rule 82. Such a right would need further specifications with respect to time, place and form of the refusal and can be a potential source of procedural error. If the documents do not comply with Rule 82, service is ineffective and cannot be cured based on Rule 81. The defendant can invoke the ineffectiveness of the service in the courts of the forum.

Rule 83. Non-application of Rule 81

If service of documents does not comply with the language requirements of Rule 82, Rule 81 does not apply.

Comments:

1. Rule 83 provides that a failure to comply with the language requirements of Rule 82 will render service ineffective.
2. Rule 82 does not, however, provide the addressee of documents with a formal right to refuse service, as is provided, for instance, by Article 8 of the ESR Regulation. Such a formal right to refuse service is not necessary as long as the addressee can object to the service of documents in the pending proceedings. In order to preserve that possibility, where the addressee actually receives the documents albeit in a language which is not consistent with the requirements of Rule 82, the defect should not be cured.

Rule 84. Modification of time periods

If the addressee is domiciled in a European Union Member State different from the forum State then the time periods provided in Rule 80(3) are four weeks instead of two weeks.

Comments:

1. Rule 80 provides rules of service of last resort, which apply where all other methods of service provided in Rules 74-78 have failed.

2. The time limits specified to be applicable to the service methods specified in Rule 80(3) are modified by Rule 84. While the two week period for service specified in Rule 80(3) appears to be appropriate for domestic cases as it offers the addressee a reasonable opportunity to receive the notice and obtain the documents, this does not seem appropriate for cross-border service. In cross-border situations a longer time period appears reasonable to ensure that the addressee has a fair opportunity to receive notice and to obtain the documents from their last known address, or to obtain notice of the publication in the forum State.

B. OUTSIDE THE EUROPEAN UNION

Rule 85. General Rule

The preceding rules also apply when the addressee has no domicile or habitual residence within the European Union, subject to Rule 86.

Comments:

1. All the Rules within this Part are applicable for the service of documents if the addressee does not have a domicile or habitual residence within the European Union. Where a European Union Member State is also a Contracting State of the HCCH 1965 Service Convention, see Rule 86.
2. In respect of the possible use of electronic service as it will often include a cross-border element, this Rule avoids the ambiguous wording "service abroad" set out in Article 1 of the HCCH 1965 Service Convention. It replaces it with the requirement that the addressee has no "domicile or habitual residence" within the European Union.

*Rule 86. **Relationship to the HCCH 1965 Service Convention***

Where there is occasion to transmit a judicial or extra-judicial document for service outside the European Union, the application of the preceding rules is without prejudice to the application of the HCCH 1965 Service Convention.

Comments:

1. In respect of European Union Member States, either as the forum State or the State where the addressee of the documents has a domicile or habitual residence, which are also Contracting States of the HCCH 1965 Service Convention, that Convention shall prevail.

PART VII

ACCESS TO INFORMATION AND EVIDENCE

INTRODUCTION

1. The provision and testing of evidence is central to civil procedure. Effective access to information and evidence are basic tools that ensure access to justice is a real rather than a merely theoretical right (Article 6.1 of the European Convention on Human Rights; Article 47 of the European Charter of Fundamental Rights).

2. There is a great deal of variety across European jurisdictions in respect of the approach taken to evidence-taking, and particularly to access to relevant information. This is a consequence of a variety of factors: the distinction between the civil law/common law; legal history; and procedural culture, and particularly the distribution of roles between the court, judiciary and parties. Comparative research demonstrates that there is a strong divergence regarding many fundamental issues of the law of evidence, for example: differing degrees of formalism in evidence-taking; differing approaches to the principle of immediacy; and, differing approaches to the ease with which information or evidence in the control of opposing parties or non-parties can be obtained. Inevitably different jurisdictions demonstrate different levels of satisfaction with their rules of evidence, e.g., evidentiary value depends on how evidence was taken, and this, in turn, influences how effective access to justice may be in practical terms where factual matters may only be proved by witness evidence, e.g., in many tort cases. Additionally, the ease, or otherwise, with which access to information and evidence can be secured will have an impact upon the likelihood of claims being pursued in proceedings.

3. Divergence in approaches to evidence may be the source of difficulties in cross-border litigation. The Evidence Regulation and the HCCH 1970 Evidence Convention[1] are not aimed at harmonising the rules on evidence at an international level and, therefore, they cannot mitigate the potential for such divergent approaches to evidentiary matters, such as access to information and the production of evidence held by opponents and third parties, hampering cooperation.

4. The present Part attempts to identify the best approach to access to information and evidence. It does so through identifying the common core of the law of evidence and the best, or more convenient, rules, including those related to the management of evidence, in use in European jurisdictions. To do so it has particularly account of the ALI/UNIDROIT Principles, the IBA Rules of Evidence and of legal instruments addressing the issue of evidence and access to information within the European Union (Directives on: IP rights;[2] competition damages claims;[3] the ESC Regulation; and the Draft Unified Patent Court Rules).

1 Convention of 18 March 1970 on the Taking of Evidence Abroad in Civil or Commercial Matters (HCCH 1970 Evidence Convention).

2 Directive 2004/48/EC of the European Parliament and of the Council of 29 April 2004 on the enforcement of intellectual property rights (the IP Enforcement Directive).

3 Directive 2014/104/EU of the European Parliament and of the Council of 26 November 2014 on certain rules governing actions for damages under national law for infringements of the competition law provisions of the Member States and of the European Union (the Competition Damages Directive).

ELI-UNIDROIT Model European Rules of Civil Procedure. ELI & UNIDROIT, Oxford University Press.
 DOI: 10.1093/oso/9780198866589.003.0008

SECTION 1—GENERAL PART

A. GENERAL PROVISIONS ON EVIDENCE

Rule 87. Standard of Proof

A contested issue of fact is proven when the court is reasonably convinced of its truth.

Source:
ALI/UNIDROIT Principle 21.2; Transnational Rules of Civil Procedure (Reporters' Study) Rule 28.2.

Comments:

1. Setting the standard of proof in civil proceedings is of paramount importance. It plays a profound role in determining both the parties' litigation strategy, but equally the approach the court takes to fact-finding. In legal theory it is common to refer to different possible standards of proof, each of which require the judge to reach different degrees of conviction. The minimum acceptable standard, and degree of conviction, is that the judge is satisfied on the balance of probabilities, i.e., the judge is convinced that the existence of a fact is more probable than not. Rule 87 is intended to establish a qualified high standard of proof in civil proceedings. It requires the court to be 'reasonably convinced' of the existence of a fact. This should be understood to mean 'as close to being fully convinced as possible', accepting that being fully convinced is an ideal that cannot generally be realised in practice.
2. "Truth" in this context must be read free from any philosophical connotation. It is merely intended to describe the level or degree of confidence sufficient for the court to pronounce a decision on the facts. "Convinced" must also be treated with caution. It should be understood to be a synonym for "satisfied". It is, therefore, necessary to assume, consistently with the aim of establishing a high standard, that there is a certain degree of flexibility and a need to adapt to the individual circumstances of each set of proceedings in the approach to the standard of truth for a court to be "reasonably convinced".
3. A court may only consider itself to be convinced or satisfied of the truth of a factual allegation, when it has taken account of all relevant evidence, or other valid methods of proof such as those described in Rule 88. A court may never base its decision on issues of fact upon its own private knowledge.

Rule 88. Matters Not Requiring Positive Evidence

(1) The following do not require positive evidence:
  (a) admitted facts;
  (b) uncontested facts;
  (c) facts which are notorious to the court.

(2) The existence of facts can be presumed on the basis of other proven facts.

(3) When a party has possession or control of evidence concerning a relevant fact and that party, without justification, fails to produce it, the court may consider that relevant fact to be proven.

Source:
ALI/UNIDROIT Principle 21.3.

Comments:

1. Rule 88(1) reflects the approach taken to matters that most European jurisdictions accept do not need positive proof.

2. In Rule 88(1) "admitted facts" should be understood in the sense of having been "actively" or "expressly" admitted. "Uncontested facts" are related to the principle of party autonomy, i.e., it is a matter for the parties if they wish to contest a fact put forward by their opponent. In some jurisdictions, uncontested facts bind the court, whereas in others the court is simply allowed to consider such uncontested facts as having been proven or true. The question of evaluation of such uncontested facts, under these Rules, is a matter of free evaluation by the court (Rule 98). For fact to be "notorious", it must be notorious to the court, i.e., they are well-established matters of common knowledge to the community and in the context where the court is located. Examples are: the public underground system in the capital city is crowded during rush-hours; tigers are not an indigenous species of Western European States. The court may inform the parties that it considers a fact to be notorious. Where it does do so it may release the party adducing such evidence from having to prove it positively. The court must not, however, take account of matters that are within the judge's private knowledge of the relevant facts in a case, i.e., knowledge gathered through means different from those established in these Rules.
3. The use of presumptions, as those set out in Rule 88(2), is a system to determine the truth of facts known to all legal systems. Unless otherwise established by the law, presumptions are always rebuttable.
4. Rule 88(3), consistently with the preceding parts of Rule 88, provides a specific means of establishing the truth of a contested fact. If a party fails to present evidence where it could do so, the court may infer that the evidence would be harmful to the party's case and may deem the fact to have been proven. This Rule is related to Rule 99 on sanctions, where a party disobeys a court order to produce evidence. What is a "relevant fact" should be interpreted consistently with Rules 24, 89 and 92.

Rule 89. Relevance

(1) Relevant evidence is admissible.

(2) The court, whether of its own motion or on application by a party, shall exclude evidence that is irrelevant. Relevance is determined by the court by reference to the matters alleged in the parties' pleadings.

Sources:

Transnational Rules of Civil Procedure (Reporters' Study) Rules 25.1, 28.3.2, and 25.2.

Comments:

1. Rule 89 must be interpreted in the light of Rules 23 and 25, which concern the scope of the pleadings and the obligation placed on parties to prove relevant facts by offering such evidence as supports their factual contentions.
2. Rule 89(2) is intended to clarify the nature of the court's duties and powers where evidence submitted by a party is irrelevant. It is for the court to determine evidentiary relevance. Where evidence is disclosed spontaneously by a party or as a consequence of an order to secure access to evidence, the court in its discretion may exclude it where it is redundant, unnecessarily burdensome, creates too great a cost or delay, or gives rise to unfair prejudice. The court must assess these issues as part of the process by which it manages evidence-taking (see Rules 49(11), 62(2), 64 (4)-(6) and 92). These issues are not, and should not be considered to be, an aspect of the question whether evidence is relevant. When considering evidentiary relevance, the court must consider the nature and scope of any proposed

evidence, its connection to facts or issues in dispute in the proceedings, and whether it is likely to be probative.

Rule 90. Illegally Obtained Evidence

(1) **Except where Rule 90(2) applies, illegally obtained evidence must be excluded from the proceedings.**

(2) **Exceptionally, the court may admit illegally obtained evidence if it is the only way to establish the facts. In exercising its discretion to admit such evidence the court must take into account the behaviour of the other party or of non-parties and the gravity of the infringement.**

Sources:
Transnational Rules of Civil Procedure (Reporters' Study) Rule 25.1.

Comments:

1. The issue of illegally obtained evidence is not treated in a comparable way in all European jurisdictions. The approach set out as the general rule in Rule 90(1) is that taken by some jurisdictions. The exception set out in Rule 90(2) reflects the approach that has been accepted on a number of occasions by the European Court of Human Rights under an exception it has established and which is said to arise from the right to evidence. For example, it has accepted that where illegally obtained evidence is the only way to establish facts and thus meet the burden of proof, it should be admissible.[4]
2. The general rule under Rule 90(1) is, however, that illegally obtained evidence is inadmissible and should be excluded. This is particularly important where the illegality arises from an infringement of a party's or a non-party's fundamental rights. Exclusion should be understood in the sense that the evidence must not be relied upon by the court in any decision in the proceedings.
3. Exceptions to the general rule, under Rule 90(2), should be rare. They should only be permitted by the court carrying out a careful balancing exercise, which considers all relevant interests, including the right of access to evidence, fundamental rights' protection, especially, those connected to privacy, good faith and fair play.
4. Standards applied to define illegality vary from one jurisdiction to another. Different approaches to the application of this Rule may then be taken depending on the substantive law of the jurisdiction. Different approaches may, for instance, be taken to evidence obtained by, for instance: opening a letter addressed to somebody without their consent; recording a conversation without the speaker's knowledge; an employer accessing personal files of an employee's computer; or utilising images recorded by a dash cam located in the front of a car. Evidence obtained by torture must always be excluded.
5. It must be stressed that permitting the possibility of exceptions to the general rule should not be taken to promote illegality in evidence-gathering. The general rule in Rule 90(1) is, on the contrary, intended to deter illegality. This is in particular the case given that the Rules in this Part are intended to provide parties with fair, reasonable and appropriate means to secure evidence.

4 See ECtHR L.L. v. France (Application no. 7508/02) Second Section Judgment of 10 October 2006, concerning Art. 41; N.N. and T.A. v. Belgium, (Application no. 65097/01), Judgment of 9 February 2006.

Rule 91. Evidentiary Privileges and Immunities

(1) Effect should be given to privileges, immunities, and similar protections for all persons who are heard in order to provide information in a case or concerning the production of evidence or other information.

(2) In particular, evidence may not be elicited in violation of:

(a) the right of a spouse, partner equal to a spouse or close relative of a party to refuse testimony;

(b) the right of a person not to incriminate themselves;

(c) legal professional privilege, any other professional privilege, confidence, trade secrets and other similar interests as provided by law;

(d) confidentiality of communications in settlement negotiations unless the negotiations have occurred in a public hearing or overriding public interests so require;

(e) national security interests, State secrets or other equivalent public interest issues.

(3) The court should consider whether these protections justify a party's failure to disclose evidence or other information when deciding whether to draw adverse inferences or to impose sanctions.

(4) The court should recognise these protections when imposing sanctions on a party or non-party in order to compel disclosure of evidence or other information.

(5) A claim of privilege, immunity or other similar protection made with respect to a document shall describe it in sufficient detail to enable another party to challenge the claim.

Sources:

ALI/Unidroit Principles 18.1, 18.2 and 18.3.

Comments:

1. The reason behind the privileges is the need to protect some interests despite the importance of locating the best evidence to ascertain the truth. For instance, family relations, confidentiality in professional relations and the privilege against self-incrimination (*nemo tenetur se ipsum accusare*) are such protected interests. Therefore, nobody shall be obliged to sign a written witness statement or to give evidence at an oral hearing if they are a spouse, partner equal to a spouse under applicable national law, descendant, sibling or the parent of a party. A witness may also refuse to answer questions if answering them would violate an applicable professional privilege or other duty of confidentiality imposed by national law.
2. The court is under a duty to protect privileges under Rule 91 of its own motion (*ex officio*). A court may not, however, be aware of relevant privileges. The Rule thus depends upon the parties co-operating with the court to draw attention to any such privileges (see Rule 6). Absolute privileges must be protected in all cases. Privileges can also be relative, in which case where the protected person consents to set aside the privilege, it will be forfeit. Such privileges may also be set aside where, in specific cases, there is a paramount duty imposed on the court, under substantive law, to find the truth. (See Draft Unified Patent Court Rules, Rule 179.3.)
3. Some privileges are based on the right to keep silent, e.g., close relatives have this right, whereas professional privileges do not depend upon the individual who could give the evidence, e.g., legal professional privilege is the client's privilege and not that of the lawyer

and thus can only be waived by the client. In other cases relevant public interests are at stake and only the State can waive the privilege. Whenever it is a right of a person to give evidence or keep silent, and they have chosen to waive the privilege, e.g., by being sworn to give witness evidence during the trial, they cannot then change their mind. Once a privilege has been waived it cannot be re-asserted.

4. It is possible that a privilege may be waived inadvertently. Where this is the case, the court should consider whether the protection afforded by Rule 91(1) has been lost or whether it should be maintained. In determining that question it should take account of the principle underlying the privilege.
5. This Rule must be read together with the Rules on Access to Evidence Orders, which are restricted to non-privileged evidence (see Rule 100(a) and following). (See Storme Report, Article 4.1.3.).
6. In so far as Rule 91(1) is concerned, *in personam* privileges cover all persons, irrespective of their procedural status, who are heard in order to get information in the case. Temporally, the protection covers the whole proceedings, including hearings and gathering of information at a pre-trial stage.
7. Rule 91(2)(a) articulates the protection afforded to family relationships. The definition of the circle of persons covered by the privilege is strictly linked to family law and should therefore be done by national law. Rule 91(2)(b) protects the privilege against self-incrimination as it is established in national law.
8. Rule 91(2)(c) covers all situations where privileges are based on some protected interest, i.e., one that is given greater weight than the interest in securing the best evidence and truth-finding. Its scope is to be defined by national law. Typically, those interests are based on professional confidentiality, e.g., lawyers, the clergy, health professionals, journalists. Other interests may also be protected, such as for instance, trade secrets (see Article 9 of the of the Trade Secrets Directive.[5]). Reference to "similar interests as provided by law" ought to be interpreted in an open and flexible manner. It could, therefore, refer to the private international law of the forum. In most cases, the relevant private international law rule will refer to the law of the forum as the applicable law to determine the extent of the privilege or equivalent situation. In some cases, however, it might be the law applicable to the legal relationship covered by the privilege, e.g., lawyer-client privilege.
9. Rule 91(2)(d) acknowledges mediation privilege, i.e., the protection afforded to the content of settlement discussions between parties. It reflects the protection recognised in Article 7 of the Mediation Directive. According to the Directive, mediators or those involved in the mediation process are not, as a general rule, obliged to give evidence in judicial proceedings regarding information obtained during that process. Exceptions to this are, however, where the evidence is: (a) necessary for overriding considerations of public policy, particularly to protect an individual's physical integrity; or (b) disclosure of the

5 Directive (EU) 2016/943 of the European Parliament and of the Council of 8 June 2016 on the protection of undisclosed know-how and business information (trade secrets) against their unlawful acquisition, use and disclosure (the Trade Secrets Directive).

content of the agreement is necessary to enable its terms to be implemented or enforced. The latter can be understood to be a matter of fact.

10. Rule 91(2)(e) reflects the fact that most legal orders accept that there are certain public interests, such as national security, which override any interest in access to evidence.
11. Rule 91(2) should not be read as an exhaustive list of all possible heads of privilege, immunity or similar protection that could be claimed successfully. National legislation must be left a margin of appreciation to extend the scope of such privileges and immunities.
12. In the field of cross-border litigation, Article 14.1 of the Evidence Regulation must be considered in so far as it provides a basis upon which an individual can refuse to give evidence.
13. Rule 91(3) places a limit upon the court's ability to draw adverse inferences or imposes sanctions when an individual asserts a privilege. Its application means that the court may not draw such inferences or impose sanctions unless it concludes that the asserted privilege does not justify, i.e., provide a valid reason for, the failure to provide evidence or information.
14. Rule 91(4) requires the court to take proper account of the various privileges when considering the imposition of sanctions. It should ensure that they are not imposed where a privilege is asserted validly. Both courts and other public authorities ought to guarantee the effective application of evidentiary privileges.
15. Rule 91(5) is intended to ensure that privileges are not abused or mis-used. In order to ensure that they may not be used to hide information and pieces of evidence, this Rule provides that where an individual asserts a privilege in respect of a specific piece of information or document, they must identify it precisely. This is intended to ensure that a party who wishes to challenge the assertion may do so effectively. The Rule must, however, be interpreted cautiously to avoid a party relying on it to challenge an assertion of privilege from using it to embark on an attempt to obtain details concerning the protected information and, thereby, undermine the privilege's efficacy.

B. MANAGEMENT OF EVIDENCE

Rule 92. Management and Presentation of Evidence

(1) Whenever necessary and appropriate, the court must order the taking of relevant evidence offered by a party. Where the court makes such an order it may make case management orders concerning the sequence and timing of the production of evidence. The court may also make orders, where appropriate, concerning the form in which evidence will be produced. Rules 49(9) and (11), 50, 62, 64(3)-(6) and 107 apply.

(2) The court, while affording the parties an opportunity to respond, may suggest evidence not previously proposed by a party, which it considers may be relevant to an issue in dispute. If a party accepts such a suggestion, the court will order the taking of that evidence so that it may be offered in support of that party's contentions of fact and law.

(3) Exceptionally, the court may, while affording the parties an opportunity to respond, order the taking of evidence not previously proposed by a party.

(4) The court shall provide each party with a fair opportunity and adequate time to respond to evidence presented by another party or taken by the court.

Sources:

ALI/UNIDROIT Principles 5.4-5.5, 9.3, 14.1-3, and 22.2.2; Transnational Rules of Civil Procedure (Reporters' Study) Rules 18.3.4 and 28.3.1.

Comments:

1. In some jurisdictions there is a fundamental right to evidence enshrined in national constitutions. Such a right has also been held to be an aspect of the right to fair trial under Article 6(1) of the European Convention on Human Rights. Rule 92(1) implements those rights and emphasises the paramount importance of the right to evidence within the general framework of the right of access to justice. This Rule must be applied consistently with the right to be heard and the right of defence, such that when the court considers whether it is necessary or appropriate to order evidence to be taken it must afford the parties an opportunity to make submissions on those issues (see Rules 11 and 16(1), 49(11), 50(1) sentence 2,50(2), 55(1) sentence 2, 61(2) to (4)).
2. Rule 92(1) reflects the modern emphasis upon case management (see Rules 49(9) and (11), and 50). Orders made concerning the taking of relevant evidence must be proportionate (see Rules 5, 6, 89). Reference to "necessary" is not intended to indicate that the court has a general power to order evidence to be taken of its own motion (*ex officio*). A limited power in that respect is set out in Rule 92(3) read together with Rule 25(3). Reference to necessity in Rule 92(1) is intended to clarify that the court will have to take such steps as are required to enable admissible evidence to be taken, e.g., to make provision to enable witnesses to be heard. Reference to the "form in which evidence will be produced" includes, where appropriate, the new technologies such as information technology, electronic and other forms of communication technology and media (also see Rules 97(3), 111(2), 112(2), and 124(2)).
3. Rule 92(1) encompasses the most important decisions that the court will make concerning evidence. There might, therefore, be good reason for a party to challenge them. Such a challenge may arise in two possible ways. First, the party whose evidence was refused may try to have it admitted. Secondly, the party may also challenge the admission of evidence requested by its opponent, if it deems it to be inadmissible. Rule 92 does not define a specific means to challenge the court's decision. Part IX provides for immediate review and reconsideration upon a challenge concerning procedural error (see Rules 178, 50(3)) and, additionally, in special cases concerning miscellaneous appeal (see Rule 179(2)).The outcome of a later appeal against a final judgment, which is based on the court's refusal to admit relevant evidence depends on the party having properly and previously, and hence unsuccessfully, challenged the decision at the time it was made (for remedies of non parties, see comment 6).
4. Rules 92(2) and (3) together with the general Rule 25(3) concern a controversial issue, for which European jurisdictions do not adopt a common approach. The approach set out is intended to encapsulate a compromise, which properly applied ought to provide an optimum approach for the future. Both Rules have a common starting point. They first require the court to assess the case and the evidence proposed by the parties. It then must consider what, if any, additional evidence would assist it in carrying out its fact-finding role, i.e., what additional evidence is necessary or useful in that respect. The two Rules provide the court with discretionary powers to deal with the situation where it considers

further evidence would be beneficial. First, Rule 92(2) provides the court with a limited power to suggest to the parties what additional evidence could be adduced by the parties themselves. Where a party agrees with the court's indication, it may then go on to order that evidence to be taken. This discretionary power is intended to be consistent with the principle of party disposition and does not provide a basis upon which the court can order evidence to be taken on its own motion (*ex officio*). Secondly, Rule 92(3) provides the court with a limited power to order evidence to be taken on its own motion (*ex officio*). This power should only be exercised in exceptional circumstances, as the general rule should be for the court to rely upon the parties to elicit and present evidence to support their claims and defences. This Rule is without prejudice to Rule 120, concerning the appointment of court-appointed experts. The exceptional power in Rule 92(3) could, for instance, be exercised by the court where it apprehends that a transaction or dealings between the parties was illegal, or that a contractual term is null and void, such as may be required under European Union consumer protection law (see Preamble VI.6 and Rules 24 comment 3, 26 comments 1, 2 and 5). It might also be necessary for the court to take an active role under Rule 92(3) if one, or even both, parties are not legally represented and are thus unable to identify relevant evidence. Additionally, the powers under Rules 92(2) and (3) are considered to be more acceptable in proceedings where the principle of party autonomy does not apply in full (e.g. proceedings regarding damages caused by infringement of European antitrust law where courts could be bound to the results of inquiries of public authorities). That being said, they must both be exercised cautiously. Before exercising its powers under these Rules the court must consider the cost of the measure and choose the less, or least, expensive option, i.e., an order under Rule 92(2) or (3), where the results would otherwise be expected to be equally satisfactory (see Rule 89). If the court orders evidence to be taken under either of these Rules, it must afford the parties an opportunity to make submissions before finalising such an order (Rule 92(4)).

5. The court may not introduce new facts through exercising its powers under Rule 92(2) or (3) (see Rules 23 and 24(2)).
6. The provisions in this Rule are not intended to suggest that orders made are not subject to an affected non-party's right of appeal (see Part IX, Rules 178, 180).
7. See Rule 11 on presenting claims and defences generally.

Rule 93. Admission by a Failure to Challenge Evidence

The court may take a party's unjustified failure to make a timely response to an opposing party's contention as a sufficient basis for considering that contention to be admitted or accepted. Before doing so the court must inform the party that it is considering drawing such a conclusion concerning the evidence and provide them with an opportunity to respond.

Source:

ALI/UNIDROIT Principle 11.4.

Comments:

1. Rule 93 corresponds to Rules 27 and 47, 48, in respect of late factual contentions, and Rule 88(1)(b), regarding uncontested facts. It is related to the principle of party autonomy. It does not mandate the court to take any particular action. On the contrary it provides the court with a discretion concerning the effect that party failure to challenge evidence is to have in proceedings.

2. The Rule also establishes a specific requirement, which must be complied with by the court before it draws any adverse inference from a party failure to challenge evidence. It requires the court to inform the party that has failed to challenge evidence that it is considering drawing such adverse inferences. Such information should be provided in the most appropriate manner so as to enable that party to take any appropriate steps to challenge the evidence, if they so wish, e.g., at a hearing where the court is considering drawing adverse inferences or at a preliminary, evidentiary, hearing or a case management hearing. The Rule thus serves to ensure that a party is not taken to have conceded an issue of fact inadvertently.
3. A timely response may consist of a mere denial of the alleged fact. It may also, if the court permits it, be a response given at a stage in the proceedings where further contentions of fact are being made by the parties.

Rule 94. Early Party Identification of Evidence

Parties must identify evidence which they intend to produce to support the factual allegations set out in their pleadings.

Sources:

ALI/UNIDROIT Principles 9.2 and 11.3; Transnational Rules of Civil Procedure (Reporters' Study) Rule 12.1.

Comments:

1. Rule 2 requires the parties to co-operate to promote the fair, efficient and speedy resolution of proceedings. Rule 94 sets out a specific instance of that general principle as it requires parties to identify evidence at an early stage of proceedings, usually in its initial phase, i.e., within their pleadings (also see Rule 25, 53).
2. The manner in which parties are required to identify evidence may depend on the circumstances of specific proceedings. It may, for instance, be sufficient to name and list the evidence, e.g., witness names; the nature of physical evidence, its location, and who has control over it; or, if it is a document a copy may need to be attached to the initial pleadings (see Rule 53(4)).

Rule 95. Notification of Evidence

(1) Parties must make documentary or tangible evidence available to other parties.

(2) Parties may only propose witness evidence if notice is given to all other parties of the relevant witnesses' identity and the subject-matter of their proposed evidence.

(3) The court may direct that parties keep evidence of which they have been notified confidential.

Sources:

Transnational Rules of Civil Procedure (Reporters' Study) Rule 29.3.

Comments:

1. The duty of notification set out in Rule 95 is necessary in order to render proceedings fair, since it enables the other party, in due course, to challenge evidence (see also Rules 25(2), 49(11), 51(2)(c), 54(4), 64(6)). Where, therefore, lack of prior notification should entail preclusive effects, any affected evidence should not be admissible. (See Storme Report, Rules 4.1 and 4.2.1.)

2. In some jurisdictions, evidence must be made available to the other party before being presented in court. In other legal systems evidence may or must be made available both to the other party and to the court at the same time, i.e., when it is presented using electronic communication procedures. In some jurisdictions, the court itself will ensure that evidence already produced to it is duly notified to all parties. In any case, the notification requirement is a fundamental issue in the preparation of evidence, particularly as notice prevents parties from presenting evidence abusively or in bad faith. Given this, notification must be done in such a manner and within a time framework that enables the opposing party to duly analyse the evidence and, as the case may be, challenge its admissibility.
3. Documentary evidence in Rule 95(1) covers any sort of information which can be recorded or stored, including that which is recorded or stored electronically. This Rule must be read in conjunction with Rule 111. Tangible evidence concerns any non-documentary evidence which can be presented physically to the court.
4. Witness identification under Rule 95(2) applies to witnesses of fact and expert witnesses (see Rule 119). Exceptions may be made to this Rule, where there is a clear need to protect a witness's identity, e.g., whistle-blowers in competition damages claims (see Rule 17(5)).
5. The notion of the "subject-matter of their proposed evidence" in Rule 95(2) is directly linked with relevance addressed by Rule 89. Depending on the nature of the subject matter, evidence may be more or less relevant to facts in issue, e.g., it may be relevant to the main facts in issue or it may only be relevant to specific issues on which a witness has given statements in other proceedings or before public authorities. Some jurisdictions adopt the approach that notice of the subject-matter of the evidence requires advance notice of the witnesses' oral evidence, or advance notice of documents that will in due course become evidence and be subject to further examination.
6. Evidence must, where ordered, be kept confidential by the parties under Rule 95(3), which must itself be interpreted in conformity with Rules 103 and 104.

Rule 96. Additional Evidence after Amendment

The court may, while affording the parties an opportunity to respond, permit or invite a party to clarify or amend their factual contentions and to offer additional evidence accordingly.

Source:

ALI/Unidroit Principle 22.2.1.

Comments:

1. Rule 96 is primarily concerned with case management of evidence. It is particularly related to Rules 11, 49(11), 53(2)(a) and 92(4).
2. Effective case management is of particular importance in the field of evidence. Reference to clarification and amendment in this Rule should be interpreted in a reasonably restrictive manner. This approach is intended to safeguard good faith and ensure Rules on preclusion and the timely identification of facts and evidence are not disregarded (see, for instance, Rules 27, 47, 48, 63(2), 64(4) and 94).

C. PRESENTATION AND EVALUATION OF EVIDENCE

Rule 97. Conduct of Hearings where evidence is to be adduced

(1) **Whenever appropriate, the court will hear and receive evidence directly at a hearing before the parties unless, exceptionally, it has authorised evidence to be taken by an individual authorised to act on its behalf or at another location.**

(2) **Any hearing where evidence is taken shall be video recorded, provided that the necessary technical equipment is available. The video recording must be kept under the court's direction.**

(3) **The taking of evidence, in hearings or in camera, can involve, where appropriate, the use of technology, such as videoconferencing or similar distance communication technologies.**

Sources:

ALI/UNIDROIT Principles 20.1, 20.3 and 22.3; Transnational Rules of Civil Procedure (Reporters' Study) Rules 24.1, 24.2, 24.3, 24.5, 24.6, 24.7, and 30.2.

Comments:

1. The presence of the court when receiving evidence (Rule 97(1)) is a basic procedural safeguard and an aspect of the principle of immediacy (see Rule 64(2)). During the preparatory stage of proceedings (see Rule 62) it may not always be appropriate for evidence to be taken at a hearing. Nevertheless, this could happen where, for instance, the court attends evidence-taking upon entry to land together with an expert in the presence of the parties for clarification of facts in issue in the proceedings. In general, however, a court-appointed expert would inspect land and property without the court or the parties being present. If both parties are satisfied by a report prepared by an expert in such circumstances, then its report and its results will become uncontested facts and the expert's work will be considered to be a form of disclosure (see Rules 88(1)(b) and 124). If one party attacks the report with the aid of its own party-appointed expert, the court-appointed expert should prepare a second report to the satisfaction of the court or be examined orally at a final hearing, and the inspection of the property should be considered to be an initial form of evidence-taking by the court. Similarly witness statements may lead to facts being uncontested or becoming a part of evidence-taking when that witness is examined orally on the basis of a written statement. Documents provided to the parties and the court in the preparatory stage of proceedings may also result in facts being uncontested. They may also be the basis of an oral hearing the aim of which is to ascertain the correct meaning of the document. The flexibility of this preparatory stage stimulates clarificatory activities outside hearings, which may later develop into a means by which evidence can be taken at a final hearing. Ultimately, the modern flexible structure of civil proceedings underlying these Rules often results in no clear borderline being capable of being drawn between traditional disclosure and evidence-taking (see especially Rules 62 comment 3, 64).

   In certain circumstances, the court may authorise an individual to take evidence on its behalf, i.e., for reasons of efficiency, cost or proportionality (Rule 97(1)). Examples of such cases are where, for instance, evidence has to be taken in a foreign jurisdiction and the court authorises a lawyer to take such evidence in that jurisdiction (see for instance the position under the Evidence Regulation). This should, however, happen only in exceptional circumstances where the court cannot access the evidence directly, due to the importance of immediacy, e.g. because a witness is in a remote country and cannot be summoned to the jurisdiction. Therefore, to circumvent those obstacles new technologies should preferably be envisaged. In some jurisdictions, children, at least in certain sorts of cases, are not heard directly by the court, but rather by an official appointed by the court. This Rule should not be an obstacle to such practice, as long as the prevailing interest of the children so require it.

2. The main purpose of Rule 97 is to ensure that individuals are questioned directly in the immediate proceedings. If this is not possible or reasonable but the value of the evidence can still be assessed in a trustworthy way, modern technology, such as video-conferencing may be used. In cross-border situations, State sovereignty may cause problems because a domestic court cannot hear persons abroad. Therefore, in cases of legal assistance and judicial co-operation, the court may authorise a suitable individual to act on its behalf to take and preserve evidence for it to consider at a final hearing. In such situations, where the evidence is not taken in the presence of the parties at a final hearing supplementary questioning by the parties and their ability to challenge the evidence has, however, to be respected in order to secure procedural justice.
3. This Rule also addresses the issue of the location. In exceptional circumstances, an evidentiary hearing may take place at a place different from the courtroom, e.g., in a private residence, in a hospital, in prison etc. Distance communication technologies may also be a viable alternative in such situations.
4. National practices, in respect of Rule 97(2) may vary. The main requirement is that the hearing must be recorded and verified afterwards, provided that the necessary technical equipment is available. States should provide their courts with such equipment. A summary record of the hearings must be kept under the court's direction. If a party wants to receive a copy of the record, it is a matter for national law whether a fee, and if so the amount, should be charged.
5. The use of technology, in respect of Rule 97(3), for evidentiary purposes may consist, for instance, in displaying electronic programmes in front of the court in order to permit it to know the contents of non-documentary electronically stored information, in activating audio or video software, or in using electronic devices and systems such as video-conferences to secure direct communication with an individual, such as a witness or an expert who is located at a different place. This Rule is based on the assumption that oral evidence is more credible if a witness or expert is physically present in the courtroom.
6. A general preference for the use of distance communication technologies is noted in respect of small claims, as that is consistent with the proportionality principle.[6] However, as travel costs will mostly be higher than the costs of a video-conference, the generalisation of such a practice for all claims might be expected. This in turn may, however, lead to the possibility of the elimination of direct oral hearings before the court. Such a result would itself be disproportionate and inappropriate. It would also raise serious questions concerning the publicity principle.

6 See the ESC Regulation.

Recourse to the use of communications technology at the performance of the taking of evidence in cross-border cases is also foreseen by Article 10(4) of the European Evidence Regulation 1206/2001 (EC), unless this is incompatible with the law of the Member State of the requested court or by reason of major practical difficulties such as the lack of access to the technical means.

Rule 98. Evaluation of Evidence

The court will freely evaluate evidence.

Source:
ALI/UNIDROIT Principles 16.6, 22.1 and 23.2; Transnational Rules of Civil Procedure (Reporters' Study) Rules 28.2 and 31.2.

Comments:
1. Rule 98 addresses how a judge deals with evidence when reaching a final decision on the merits.
2. The general rule is the evidence should be subject to free evaluation by the court. In some European jurisdictions, the law attributes binding or enhanced value to certain types of evidence, e.g. public or authentic documents.
3. The free evaluation of evidence means that the court has the power to interpret evidence in a manner different from that proposed by the parties. It does not, however, relieve the court from its fundamental duty to give reasons for its final decision (see Rule 12(1) and Rule 131).

Rule 99. Sanctions concerning Evidence

The court, whether on its own motion or on application by a party, may impose sanctions under Rule 27 when:
(a) a person has unjustifiably failed to attend to give evidence or to answer proper questions, or to produce a document or other item of evidence;
(b) a person has otherwise obstructed the fair application of the rules concerning evidence.

Sources:
ALI/UNIDROIT Principles 17.1, 17.2, 17.3, and 17.4; Transnational Rules of Civil Procedure (Reporters' Study) Rule 28.3.3.

Comments:
1. Rule 99(a) describes certain types of non-compliance with orders concerning evidence, which justify the imposition of sanctions.
2. Rule 99(b) provides for the court with a broader discretion to impose sanctions for conduct that obstructs the efficacy of evidence orders, e.g., through threating witnesses, destroying evidence, or providing an opponent with an such a large amount of evidence that it imposes an unjustifiable cost or time burden upon them.

SECTION 2—ACCESS TO EVIDENCE ORDERS

Rule 100. General Framework

When making orders under the Rules in this Part the court will give effect to the following principles:

(a) as a general rule, each party should have access to all forms of relevant and non-privileged evidence;

(b) in response to a party's application, under Rule 101, seeking access to evidence, the court will, if the application is granted, direct the production of relevant, non-privileged, and sufficiently identified evidence held or controlled by another party or, if necessary, by a non-party, even if such production might be adverse to that person's interests.

Sources:

ALI/UNIDROIT Principles 16.1 and 16.2.

Comments:

1. Rule 100 is intended to provide a general framework within which access to evidence orders considered or made under this Part should be approached[7] (also see Rule 25(2)). The Rules in this Part are intended to set out European best practice. They are particularly intended to ensure that access to evidence is secured in a manner that is very different from US-style discovery.
2. Evidence, under Rule 100(a), includes all forms of evidence listed in Section 3 of this Part of the Rules and includes, therefore, witness evidence, parties' statements, expert evidence, documents (including electronically stored information), and evidence derived from the inspection of things, entry upon land, or, under appropriate circumstances, from the physical or mental examination of an individual.
3. In Rule 100(b), "if necessary" is concerned with the notion of subsidiarity, i.e., non-parties should only be involved when there are no other available means to access evidence. "Person" is meant to cover parties and non-parties. The requirement of a "reasonable" identification of evidence has to be interpreted as a balance between a too restrictive and a too broad approach and is further developed by Rule 103(1). The term "evidence" has to be understood in a very broad sense. It encompasses information and data that can later be transformed into real or documentary evidence. In that sense, the scope of access could be more properly described as "sources of evidence", i.e., documents in a wide sense, objects, and information which the requesting party could later formally adduce as evidence. Evidence is also considered to be "held" or "controlled" by another person when it is electronically stored information or where the information remains in their mind. In the latter situation the only possible measure to access evidence would be by way of an interrogatory or a written statement.

Rule 101. Application for Access to Evidence

(1) Subject to the considerations and procedure contained in these Rules, any claimant or defendant, or any prospective claimant who intends to commence proceedings, can apply to the court for an order securing access to relevant and non-privileged evidence held or controlled by other parties or non-parties.

7 Also see Storme Report, Arts. 4.3, 4.4. and 4.5; Arts. 6 to 8 IP Enforcement Directive.

(2) An application for an order securing access to evidence may include an application for the imposition of measures to protect or preserve evidence, including an application for provisional or protective measures under Part X.

(3) Material or information supplied under this rule only becomes evidence when it is formally introduced as such into the proceedings by a party or exceptionally by the court according to Rules 25(3), 92(2) and (3) and 107(2).

Source:
ALI/UNIDROIT Principles 16.1 and 16.2.

Comments:

1. Rule 101 sets out the process through which an application to secure evidence is to be made. It provides the core of the system for making orders under this Part. It has to be read in the light of the following Rules, where strict requirements are established in order to prevent an interpretation of them that could lead to the introduction of US-style discovery.[8]
2. Parties and prospective parties can apply for orders under this Rule. Such orders may be obtained to prepare a claim or, prior, to enable a prospective claimant to determine if they will initiate proceedings or not, and if so against whom.
3. An order under Rule 101(1) may apply to traditional documents but also to all other forms of relevant information, i.e., electronic documents and all other means of storing or accessing information or data, including sound and images. Orders may also be applied for in respect of expert reports, witnesses, objects or places to be inspected by the court. An order providing access to evidence can be accompanied, where appropriate, by an evidence preservation order under Rule 198.
4. In so far as Rule 101(3) is concerned, it is for an applicant to determine what evidence to submit from documents or information obtained. It is not for the court to consider or place evidentiary value upon information secured by the parties via its orders. Similarly, it is for parties to determine whether to rely on a potential witness's evidence.
5. See Part X – Provisional and Protective Measures in respect of such measures concerning evidence.

Rule 102. Relevant Criteria where an application for access to evidence is made

(1) A party or prospective party applying for an order for access to evidence must

(a) identify, as accurately as possible in the light of the circumstances of the case, the specific sources of evidence to which access is sought, or alternatively

(b) identify closely defined categories of evidence by reference to their nature, content, or date.

(2) An application must satisfy the court of the plausibility of the merits of the applicant's claim or defence by demonstrating that

(a) the requested evidence is necessary for the proof or proposed proof of issues in dispute in proceedings or in contemplated proceedings;

(b) the applicant cannot otherwise gain access to this evidence without the court's assistance; and

8 See Storme Report, Arts. 4.3- 4.5; Arts. 6 to 8 IP Enforcement Directive; and, Recital 18 and Art. 5 of the Competition Damages Directive.

(c) **the nature and amount of evidence subject to the application is reasonable and proportionate. For this purpose the court will take into account the legitimate interests of all parties and all interested non-parties.**

(3) If an application for access to evidence is made prior to the commencement of proceedings, the applicant must indicate with sufficient precision all elements necessary to enable the court to identify the claim for relief which the applicant intends to make.

(4) The court may not grant any application under this Rule which involves a vague, speculative, or unjustifiably wide-ranging search for information.

Comments:

1. The requirements set out in this Rule are important to ensure that the court only makes an order that is both necessary and adequately supported. The requirements specified in it are intended to prevent potential applicants from using it as means to carry out fishing expeditions, i.e., when applications are too premature or speculative, and to ensure that the system, as a whole, is fair and just. If an applicant requires more information than is necessary, the danger is that implementing the order would impose a disproportionate burden on the opponent.[9]
2. To enable the court to assess whether the application is premature or unnecessarily broad, in cases where proceedings have not yet been initiated, the Rule makes it clear that the applicant must support it with adequate details of the contemplated proceedings.
3. In certain circumstances an order may be necessary to enable the applicant to identify the defendant or the nature of the claim for relief in contemplated proceedings. This would be the case, for instance, where an insurance company denies that it is bound by an insurance policy on the basis that it was entered into by an individual who at the time the contract was entered into had ceased to be its employee but refuses to provide proof of that fact. In such a case, depending on the content of the information gathered two different claims might be envisaged, e.g., a contract claim against the insurance company or a tort claim against the person who purported to act as its representative.
4. Courts may make orders under this Rule only where substance of the application is sufficiently specific, proportionate, and reasonable (Rules 102(2) and (3); see also Rule 6).

Rule 103. Confidential Information

(1) The court shall consider whether an application under Rule 101 for access to evidence concerns or includes confidential information, especially in relation to non-parties. In so doing, the court must have regard to all relevant rules concerning the protection of confidential information.

(2) Where necessary, in the light of the circumstances of the case, the court, amongst other things, may make an order for access to evidence containing confidential information adjusted in one or more of the following ways in order to protect the relevant interest in maintaining confidentiality

(a) **redacting relevant sensitive passages in documents;**

(b) **conducting hearings *in camera*;**

9 See for instance, Arts. 6 and 8 of the IP Enforcement Directive; Arts. 5 and 6(4) and 6(10) of the Competition Damages Directive.

(c) **restricting the persons allowed to gain access to or inspect the proposed evidence;**
(d) **instructing experts to produce a summary of the information in an aggregated or otherwise non-confidential form;**
(e) **writing a non-confidential version of a judicial decision in which passages containing confidential data are deleted;**
(f) **limiting access to certain sources of evidence to the representatives and lawyers of the parties and to experts who are subject to a duty of confidentiality.**

Comments:

1. Rule 103 should be read with Rule 17(2), as it strikes a balance between the need to grant orders even where the material is commercially sensitive or otherwise confidential and the information-holder's interest, including any legal obligation, is to maintain confidentiality.[10]
2. Rule 103(2) provides the court with a flexible range of measures that can be ordered to protect confidential information, while properly balancing the competing interests of accessibility and confidentiality in a practical and effective manner. The list of measures is not, however, intended to be exhaustive. In exceptional occasions, for instance, confidential information, e.g., concerning particularly important trade secrets, may only be shown to the court, but not to an applicant seeking access, in order to, at the least enable the court to decide if the information should be made available to the applicant.[11]

Rule 104. Sanctions for Breach of Confidentiality

(1) **If a person breaches any duty of confidentiality the aggrieved party may apply to the court for an order imposing one or more of the following sanctions**
  (a) **wholly or partially dismissing a party in breach's claim or defence, where the substantive proceedings are still pending;**
  (b) **declaring the party or other person in breach liable for damages and ordering payment of such compensation;**
  (c) **ordering the party in breach to pay the costs of the substantive proceedings irrespective of the outcome of those proceedings;**
  (d) **imposing on the party or the person in breach a fine appropriate to the breach;**
  (e) **imposing on the party's representative or representatives or the person in breach a fine appropriate to the breach.**

(2) **Any sanction imposed by the court under Rule 104(1) must be proportionate to the nature of the breach. In determining the proportionality of the sanction the court must take particular account of the fact that a breach occurred before proceedings on the merits were commenced, where that is the case.**

Comments:

1. Rule 104(1) specifies the serious, practical, consequences that may be imposed by the court where a party breaches duties relating to confidentiality and the misuse of information

10 See for instance, Arts. 6 and 8 of the IP Enforcement Directive; Recital 18 and Art. 5 of the Competition Damages Directive.

11 See, for instance, Art. 9 of the Trade Secrets Directive.

obtained as a consequence of an order to that effect under these Rules. This Rule is without prejudice to any possible criminal liability.[12]

2. The consequences set out in Rule 104(1)(a) should be reserved for only the most serious breaches. It is, however, a necessary tool in situations where monetary sanctions would not have a sufficient deterrent effect.
3. Rule 104(2) is a specific instance of the general principle of proportionality (see Rule 6).

Rule 105. Access to Evidence held by Public Authorities

(1) Except where information is protected on public interest grounds, Government and other public agencies must comply with an order made under these Rules.

(2) Where a Government or public agency seeks to refuse access to evidence on public interest grounds, they must provide the court with a reasoned explanation of the basis for their refusal and must satisfy the requirements set out in Rule 91(5).

Comments:

1. Rule 105(1) acknowledges the fact that public authorities may hold evidence that is necessary for the just determination of proceedings. It ensures that such authorities cannot simply fail or refuse to provide such information. It does so by setting out as a general rule that such authorities must comply with the evidentiary rules contained in this Part of the Rules.
2. Rule 105(2) acknowledges, however, that information held by public authorities may properly be withheld from the court on public interest grounds. It thus provides the basis on which the court should assess such a claim of privilege having regard to national, any other applicable law, and Rule 91(5)).[13]

Rule 106. Time of Applications

(1) Applications for access to evidence may be made prior to the initiation of proceedings, in a statement of claim, or in pending proceedings.

(2) If an order has been made prior to the initiation of proceedings, where appropriate, the successful applicant may be required to initiate proceedings within a specified, reasonable, period of time. If the applicant fails to comply with this requirement the court may set aside the order, direct the return of any evidence supplied to the applicant further to the order, impose an appropriate sanction on the party in default, or make any other appropriate order.

Sources:

ALI/Unidroit Principles 16.1 and 16.2.

Comments:

1. An order might be sought in anticipation of the commencement of proceedings (also see Rules 21(1), 52, 53 and 188). This is a situation common to various jurisdictions. For these cases Rule 102(3) makes it clear that the applicant should provide adequate details of the intended proceedings. Furthermore, in such a case it might be appropriate for the court to grant the order on condition that the applicant initiate proceedings within a short period of time.[14]

12 See Arts. 5 and 8 of the Competition Damages Directive.

13 Also see Art. 6 of the Competition Damages Directive.

14 See Storme Report, Arts. 4.3, 4.4. and 4.5.

2. Any failure to comply with such a condition may then result in the order being set aside and its effects undone (Rule 106(2)). A flexible and proportionate approach is necessary at this point, depending on the nature of the non-compliance. For instance, the court, at the request of an aggrieved person, may require the return of all documents, records, and objects that were subject to the order. It may also ensure that the data and information collected by or made available to the applicant cannot be used in any other process by that person or any other person to whom the information has been disclosed. The court may also set aside such an order, if it has not yet been implemented; albeit such a situation might be considered to be rare. In serious cases, the court might of its own motion (*ex officio*), issue an order for costs and declare that the applicant is liable for any damage caused to those persons who have been subject to the order.
3. It is possible that the information obtained, or not, by means of the order leads an applicant to abandon their intention to commence proceedings. In such a circumstance no sanction would appear to be necessary. The applicant should, however, be required to return any documents, records, and objects secured under the order.
4. Applications made before proceedings have commenced raise another difficulty, one that is linked with the issue of *lis pendens*. In general terms, such an application should not lead to the beginning of pendency, even if the scope of the proceedings is clearly established.[15] There is, however, a risk that in such a case the applicant's opponent might initiate a so-called "torpedo claim" in another jurisdiction. Under such a circumstance the court seised on the merits should take this situation into account when deciding on its own jurisdiction.

Rule 107. The Process for Granting Access Orders

(1) The court shall determine an application for an order under Rule 101(1) for access to evidence according to Rule 50.

(2) Orders under Rule 101(1) may be made by the court on a without-notice basis in very exceptional cases only. Where it does so it must permit parties and affected non-parties to be heard at a with-notice hearing.

(3) If applications for access to evidence are made prior to the commencement of proceedings the court should ordinarily determine the application only after giving any affected party or non-party an opportunity to respond and make representations concerning the grant of the order, its scope and proposed implementation.

(4) The party or non-party from whom access to evidence is sought may apply for the grant of a different but no less effective form or method of access. Such an application must demonstrate that the proposed alternative will be less burdensome to the party to whom it is to provide access.

Sources:

ALI/UNIDROIT Principles 16.1 and 16.2.

Comments:

1. Rule 107(1)-(3) is a specific instance of the general approach to court orders and the right to be heard applicable to individuals affected by such orders (see Rule 16).[16]

15 See the Opinion of Advocate General Saugmandsgaard Øe, delivered on 26 January 2017, in the case C-29/16, Hanse Yachts AG.

16 Storme Report, Arts. 4.3-5.

2. An order shall be made under Rule 107(2) on a without-notice (*ex parte*) basis in exceptional circumstances only, e.g., where the grant of such an order is a matter of urgent necessity. Examples of such circumstances are where any delay would frustrate the purpose of the order or where notice would enable the evidence subject to the order to be hidden or destroyed. Where such an order is made it must be reconsidered by the court at a with-notice (*inter partes*) hearing.
3. Rule 107(4) must be read consistently with the principle of proportionality (see Rules 5, 6 and 102(2)(c)). As a consequence it must ensure that any order it makes is no more burdensome than is necessary or proportionate. The following Rules amplify the factors relevant to such an application.

Rule 108. Costs and Security

(1) The cost of implementing an order for access to evidence shall be borne by the applicant. Where appropriate the court may require the applicant to make an immediate payment of costs to a party or non-party against whom the order is made.

(2) The court may, upon the application of the person against whom an order for access to evidence is made, order security to be given by the party in whose favour the order is made. The order shall be for any predictable expense to be incurred in the implementation of that order. If security is required by the court, it must be provided before any order for access can be given effect.

(3) At the conclusion of the proceedings the court may determine the incidence of costs differently from the general rule.

Comments:

1. Rule 108(1) sets out the general rule concerning the allocation of costs of access to evidence orders. The general rule may, however, be deviated from at the conclusion of proceedings through the application of the general costs' discretion under Rule 241.
2. Where security is required under Rule 108(2), the court must determine the amount. The requirement that it is given before the order can be given effect is intended to ensure that the provision of security is taken seriously and not overlooked by the applicant.
3. Implementing access to evidence orders may cause those parties or non-parties subject to them to suffer loss, apart from costs and expenses. In principle the applicant should be liable for any such damages that may arise as a result of the improper use of such orders.

Rule 109. Implementation

The court shall ensure that any such necessary and practical steps required to implement orders for access to evidence are implemented fairly and effectively. Such steps may include:

(a) issuing directions concerning the appropriate place and manner in which the order is to be carried out;

(b) directing that the applicant may be assisted by an expert; or

(c) by making any relevant order under Part X of these Rules.

Comments:

1. The court's task in administering these Rules will sometimes require detailed supervision. If necessary, an order made can include the requirement that a specific enforcement agent

or bailiff, on behalf of the applicant, be permitted to enter premises, domestic or otherwise, including specified vehicles, and the physical securing of documents or data and tangible items of property. The question of invasive access to premises should also generally be governed by the rules on protective relief (see Rule 198(2)).

2. In many cases the participation of an expert may be needed to secure the successful implementation of an order. This is clearly the case where the agreed measure consists of inspecting documents or other data. It can also be the case when it is necessary to inspect other objects and places, e.g., machinery in case of alleged infringement of intellectual property rights.
3. The reference to an expert in Rule 109 refers solely to an expert appointed by an applicant to assist them to give practical effect to the order and to be paid by them.
4. On access to evidence in respect of evidence preservation orders, see Rule 197.

Rule 110. Non-compliance with Access Orders

(1) The court may impose any one or more of the following sanctions upon any party or non-party who is subject to, and aware of, an order requiring the giving of access to evidence, and destroys or conceals such evidence, or otherwise renders it impossible to carry out the order successfully

(a) declaring as admitted the facts which form the subject-matter of the relevant order for access to sources of evidence;

(b) treating the defendant or prospective defendant as having impliedly conceded the basis or any relevant part of the claim which has been made or which was proposed by the applicant;

(c) imposing on the relevant respondent to the order (and in accordance with the relevant court's established disciplinary powers) an appropriate penalty per day of delay in implementing the order.

(2) An order made under Rule 110(1) must be proportionate to the nature of the non-compliance and may only be made on application of the party in whose favour the order requiring access to evidence was made.

(3) This Rule is without prejudice to any other sanctions or disciplinary procedural measures available to the court, including measures according to Rules 27 and 99.

Comments:

1. A party subject to an order and aware of its effect cannot be permitted to frustrate its successful implementation. Rule 110 provides a measured set of responses to such misconduct. It is without prejudice to any criminal liability which such conduct might involve. (See for instance Articles 6 to 8 of the IP Enforcement Directive.)
2. Sanctions imposed under Rule 110(1)(a) and (b) may lead to the court dismissing or declaring invalid, wholly or partially, defences or counterclaims made by the respondent to the order.
3. Rule 110 only applies where an order for access to evidence has been issued. It applies even if an order to protect or preserve evidence has been applied for or granted under Rule 107(4). If the evidence is destroyed or concealed, or the ability to implement a potential order is rendered impossible before the order is issued then the general provision of Rule 27 will apply, leading to equivalent results.

SECTION 3—TYPES OF EVIDENCE

A. DOCUMENTS

Rule 111. Documentary and Electronic Evidence

(1) Parties may offer any relevant document as evidence.

(2) Document means anything in which information is recorded or maintained in any form, including but not limited to paper or electronic form. Information may be recorded in writing, pictures, drawings, programmes, voice messages, or electronic data, including e-mail, social media, text or instant messages, metadata, or other technological means. It may be maintained electronically on, but not limited to, computer, portable electronic devices, cloud-based or other storage media.

(3) Documents that a party maintains in electronic form must ordinarily be submitted or produced in electronic form, unless the court orders otherwise.

(4) Parties may challenge the authenticity of any document submitted as evidence. In such a case, the court must order the parties to take such steps as are necessary to establish the document's authenticity.

Sources:

Transnational Rules of Civil Procedure (Reporters' Study) Rule 29.4.

Comments:

1. The particular importance of documentary evidence flows from, amongst other things, the fact that in many specific situations this form of evidence is in practice indispensable. Certain types of documents, namely in some civil law jurisdictions, are typically given a predefined probative force. Indeed, one of the most ancient restrictions relating to admissible means of evidence that still exists in a reduced form is the rule that some legal transactions may only be concluded in writing and, consequently, they cannot be proved without production of a written document.[17]
2. The definition of document in Rule 111(2) is intended to encompass those elements that are common to all legal systems. A document may typically be distinguished from other objects by the fact that it contains the embodiment of information, which has a life independently of its supporting element, i.e., the material in which it is recorded and which thus carries the information. In other words, the means by which the information is recorded or stored itself has no importance, as long as it is a suitable medium for recording its content permanently. The Rule, therefore, is open to the reality of electronic documents; although they may lack of tangible physical form of existence, they serve the same function by storing information permanently and displaying it authentically.
3. A relevant distinction, however, must be drawn between an electronic document and an electronic signature. Electronic documents may exist, which have not been electronically signed, and they may have probative value, according to their contents and to the circumstances of the case. In the case of contractual or similar documents, where signatures are relevant, the presence of an electronic signature in the electronic document will be relevant.[18]

17 See Definitions and Art. 3(12) of the IBA Rules of Evidence.

18 Directive 1999/93/EC of the European Parliament and of the Council of 13 December 1999 on a Community framework for electronic signatures. Regulation (EU) No 910/2014 of the European

4. Evidence which exists in electronic form should ordinarily be presented electronically (Rule 111(3)). This Rule will be of particular significance in procedural systems where paperless or digital proceedings have already been put in place and where, in general terms, documents, including statements of case, may or must be submitted electronically. Exceptions to this Rule might be made in cases where there are, for instance, technical problems.
5. Parties may challenge the authenticity, accuracy or completeness of documentary evidence under Rule 111(4). In some cases, it will be a matter of the free evaluation of evidence; however, if the authorship of the document is at stake, more serious steps could be taken within the procedure or affecting its development. Specific types of proceedings to test such evidence vary across European jurisdictions, e.g., the French *inscription de faux* or the Italian *querela di falso* and are not addressed in the present Rules.

Rule 112. Authentic Instruments

(1) An authentic instrument is a document, which has either been formally drawn up or the authenticity of which has been certified by a public authority.

(2) Electronically recorded authentic instruments have the same probative force as those recorded on paper.

Comments:

1. A public document is a document issued in an appropriate form by a competent authority or person acting within the scope of their authority. Public documents are typically afforded the presumption of authenticity and full probative force. In the common law system it is usually possible to speak of a public document if the document has been issued by a public officer in the course of their official duty. The institution of the "notary" as the person assigned the task of laying down legal transactions in documents exists in all continental European jurisdictions.[19]
2. While the probative force of the public document is partly founded on the authority of the person who issues it, another important ground upon which it is founded is the procedure preceding the issue of the document and relating to it. Thus, apart from the person issuing the document, it is also of crucial importance, when establishing whether a document may be evaluated as a public document, whether the person or authority entitled to issue the public document has issued it within the scope of their authority or competence. Formal requirements relating to public documents may vary from one jurisdiction to another and may equally vary depending on the type of document.

Rule 113. Documents: Language and Translation

(1) On the application of a party or on the court's own motion, any document shall be produced in or translated into a language of the court.

(2) Translation of lengthy or voluminous documents may be limited according to Rule 20(2).

Parliament and of the Council of 23 July 2014 on electronic identification and trust services for electronic transactions in the internal market and repealing Directive 1999/93/EC

19 See Art. 4(3) of the EEO Regulation.

Sources:

ALI/UNIDROIT Principles 6.1 and 6.3; Transnational Rules of Civil Procedure (Reporters' Study) Rule 8.

Comments:

1. Rule 113 is a specific application, concerning evidence by documents, of the general rule concerning translation set out in Rule 20.

B. TESTIMONIAL EVIDENCE

Rule 114. Witnesses of Fact

(1) Subject to considerations of relevance, admissibility, case management and privilege or immunity, a party may present the evidence of any witness of fact.

(2) If a witness whose evidence satisfies the requirements of Rule 114(1) refuses to give evidence, whether in whole or in part, they can be ordered to do so by the court.

(3) A witness is under an obligation to tell the truth while giving their evidence. The court may require a witness to give their evidence under oath. The court may instruct the witness accordingly prior to the examination.

Sources:

Transnational Rules of Civil Procedure (Reporters' Study) Rule 25.4.

Comments:

1. Rule 114(1) reflects the approach common to all legal systems that parties may call witnesses of fact to give evidence provided they are competent to do so and are able to convey the evidence adequately. The Rule does not address specific requirements in order to be qualified as a witness, such as minimum age or capacity, as these are matters for national legislation. Witnesses must be identified, so far as practicable, by name, address, e-mail and telephone number. Such information should be handled confidentially if the circumstances of the case justify such protection (see Rule 17(5)). Presentation of witnesses may be limited by grounds of relevance and admissibility, as is the case with evidence generally. Case management considerations may also be taken into account by the court, e.g., it may decide that it will not hear more than three or four witnesses on the same relevant factual issue (see Rules 5, 6 and 49). As far as privileges are concerned, waiver thereof may be decided by the witness or by the individual in whose interest the privilege was granted, depending on the circumstances of the case (see Rule 91).[20]
2. When the court has admitted a witness to give evidence, they are under a duty to appear and give that evidence (Rule 114(2)). The court's response to a refusal to give such evidence is context-dependent. An unjustified refusal to appear before the court may lead to a renewal of the order or, when appropriate, to more severe consequences, including sanctions and/or penalties. An unjustified refusal to give evidence before the court or to answer a relevant question may also lead to sanctions and penalties. When summoning a witness, the court shall inform them of their rights and duties.

20 See Storme Report Art. 5; Draft Unified Patent Court Rules 177 and 179.

3. Witnesses who are unable to appear before the court because of age, disease, physical disability or for some other good reason may be heard in their place of residence or through the use of communications technology, such as video-conferencing. A witness has the right to receive compensation for expenses and losses that arise directly from their participation in the proceedings. Such compensation will, in principle, be considered to be within the costs of the procedure.
4. Witnesses' statements should be the account of a witness's own recollection (Rule 114(3)). Witnesses are under a duty to tell the truth; this obligation is usually strengthened by means of an oath or by explicitly reminding the witness of that obligation and informing them of the sanctions and penalties applicable to the giving of false evidence, e.g., perjury. The nature and degree of such sanctions and penalties vary from one jurisdiction to another and are not addressed by these Rules. However, their importance should not be overlooked, as they are powerful means to ensure that the quality of evidence is not reduced.

Rule 115. Witness evidence

(1) Ordinarily, witness evidence should be received orally. The court may, however and upon having received submissions from the parties on the issue, require that such evidence be given initially in writing. Such written evidence must be supplied to all other the parties in advance of the hearing where the witness is to give oral evidence. Oral evidence at a hearing may be limited to supplemental questioning following the presentation of a witness's written evidence.

(2) Each witness shall appear in person unless the court allows the use of video-conferencing or of similar technology with respect to that witness.

(3) A person giving evidence may be questioned first by the court or the party adducing their evidence. Where a witness has first been questioned by the court or by party other than the one adducing their evidence, that party must be given the opportunity to put supplemental questions directly to the witness.

(4) Parties may challenge the reliability of witness evidence.

Sources:
ALI/UNIDROIT Principles 16.4, 19.3, and 19.4; Transnational Rules of Civil Procedure (Reporters' Study) Rule 29.4.

Comments:
1. Rule 115(1) sets out the general rule that witness evidence should be given orally, as that is the best means to enable it to be evaluated effectively. While this Rule provides that such evidence may initially be received in writing, this should be treated with caution and only be accepted exceptionally (See Rule 18). Such written evidence may however prove beneficial in complex litigation, and may promote better case management.[21]
2. Rule 115(2) is related to Rule 114(2). The use of video-conferencing or similar devices may help to reduce litigation cost and delay. It may thus also promote proportionality. It is important to stress, however, that the principle of immediacy will not be fully satisfied when a witness does not appear in person before the court. Therefore, appearance in person and via video-conferencing should not be viewed as being equivalent; the latter is subsidiary to the prior.
3. Rule 115(3) accommodates different legal traditions concerning witness examination. A party's right to put questions directly to a witness is of paramount importance. It is recognised by

21 See Arts. 4.4 - 4.10 of the IBA Rules of Evidence

many legal systems. According to the European Court of Human Rights, parties have a right to put supplemental questions to witnesses. As such the exercise of this right must not be undermined by the court through, for instance, excessive case management.[22] This has to be stressed in situations where the questioning is carried through an intermediary, for instance, when protecting children. In some jurisdictions a witness may be required to produce documents. Such provisions are not in principle incompatible with this Rule; orders for access to evidence under Rule 100 and following may also serve to this purpose.

4. Parties should have the ability to challenge the reliability of witness evidence (Rule 115(4)). They may do so even where they have called the witness or where they are connected to the witness. The Rule does not specifically address the ways in which witness credibility can be challenged, e.g., for previous inconsistent statements, for interest or bias, due to personal connections, employment relationships, an incapacity to perceive and recollect facts, prior convictions for perjury etc. A balance between the right to challenge credibility and abuse by witness harassment or distortion of the evidence must be struck by the court.

Rule 116. Witnesses: Language and Translation

(1) Where a witness is not competent in an official language in which the proceeding is being, or may be, conducted interpretation or translation must be provided by the court.

(2) Where appropriate, and with the court's and parties' consent, a witness may testify in a language other than the official language of proceedings.

Sources:

ALI/UNIDROIT Principle 6.3.

Comments:

1. As a general rule, proceedings should be conducted in the official language(s) of the State or region where the court is located (see Rule 19). Where a witness is not competent in the court's official language, the court must as a general rule provide an interpreter (see Rule 20). However, if the court and the parties are competent in the witness's language, or in a language common to all of them,[23] the witness may be permitted to give their evidence in that language if that does not prejudice the right to a public hearing, i.e., the public's constitutional right to understand the nature and content of the evidence (see Rule 19). Such an approach may, in some instances, be considered to be good practice in cross-border cases.
2. Any translation must be made by an impartial translator either selected by the parties or appointed by the court. The translation costs must be borne by the party requiring it, unless the court decides otherwise (Rules 240(1)(b) and 245(1) and (2); also see Rule 20 and Rule 113).

Rule 117. Witness Statements

(1) A party may, with the court's consent, present a written statement of sworn testimony from any person. Such a statement must be in their own words and contain their testimony about relevant facts.

22 C.G. v. the United Kingdom (Application No.43373/98), 19 December 2001 (Final 10 July 2002).

23 See Draft Unified Patent Court Rules, Rule 178.7),

(2) The court, in its discretion, may consider such written statements as if they were made by oral testimony at a hearing before the court.

(3) A party may apply for an order requiring the personal appearance of the author of such a written statement before the court. Where such an order is made, the witness may be examined by way of supplemental questioning by the court or the opposing party.

Sources:
Transnational Rules of Civil Procedure (Reporters' Study) Rule 23.4.

Comments:

1. The ability of parties to adduce witness evidence by written statement, which set out relevant facts, is commonplace.[24]
2. While the principle of orality should remain paramount (see Rule 115(1)), the ability provided by this Rule for witness evidence to be given by sworn written statement provides a degree of flexibility, and proportionality, to the trial process. It may be particularly important in cross-border cases or where the information to be provided is neutral and its accuracy may not depend upon witness credibility (e.g., the written report of a public officer concerning information appearing in their files).
3. The presentation of written statements may also prove to be helpful in respect of the promotion of settlement, as it may enable the parties to assess the strengths and weaknesses of their respect cases more effectively (also see Rules 9, 10 and 51).
4. The use of written statements should not rest exclusively on convenience. For instance, in cross-border disputes, the use of technology, such as video-conferencing and similar media may facilitate the provision of oral witness evidence without the need to resort to written statements (see for cross-border evidence-taking Rules 128 and 129).
5. Presentation of witness evidence through a written statement does not preclude a party from applying for an order requiring that witness to attend court to be examined orally; in such a case, Rules 114(2) and 115 would apply. The ability to test a witness's credibility through such oral examination should always be available.

C. EXAMINATION OF PARTIES

Rule 118. Examination of Parties and Consequences of Refusal to Respond

(1) The court may accord evidentiary effect to any statement made by a party that has been questioned before the court. Rule 114(3) applies correspondingly.

(2) Each party shall be given an opportunity to question their opponent in front of the court on relevant issues of fact.

(3) The court can draw relevant inferences if a party unjustifiably refuses to appear at a hearing or to answer any relevant question put to them by their opponent or by the court or refuses to swear an oath.

(4) If the party to be questioned is a legal person, it shall provide the identity of the natural person or persons who participated directly in the relevant course of events on its behalf, in order for them to be questioned, provided they can still be considered as a

24 See, for instance, Art. 9(2) of the European Small Claims Regulation.

representative of that legal person. The court may draw relevant inferences if a legal person fails, without justification, to provide this information.

Sources:

ALI/UNIDROIT Principles 16.1 and 16.4; Transnational Rules of Civil Procedure (Reporters' Study) Rule 25.3.

Comments:

1. The '*nemo testis in causa sua*' principle applies, if it does, in very different ways, depending on the European jurisdiction. The common law tradition is more open to the possibility of a party giving evidence in support of its contentions, while the traditional approach in civilian systems is different: a party may be questioned by the court or by their opponent, the latter aiming usually to lead that party to admitting facts or inferences, which could be harmful to their position. Rule 118 is a compromise between the two approaches, on the one hand requiring a party to be questioned before the court for evidentiary value to be given to their contentions, on the other granting each party the right to question its opponent. Regarding the way to proceed to the examination of the party, Rule 115(3) on examination of witnesses should apply accordingly.
2. Rule 118(3) should be read in context with similar provisions, such as those established in Rules 88(1), 93, or those concerning sanctions, i.e., Rules 7, 27(2) and 99(a).
3. Rule 118(4) is intended to prevent legal persons from evading the obligation to apply with Rules 118(1)-(3). As a consequence, they are required to identify a natural person or persons to be examined on their behalf. Such a person should have participated directly in the course of events. If, for the purposes of giving evidence, they can properly be considered to be representatives of the legal person (and this, in turn, will be the rule if they participated in the relevant facts or actions on behalf of the legal person), then Rule 118(3) will apply. Otherwise, such natural persons will be considered to be witnesses of fact.

D. EXPERT EVIDENCE

Rule 119. Party-appointed Experts

Parties may present expert evidence on any relevant issue for which such evidence is appropriate. They may do so through an expert of their choice.

Sources:

ALI/UNIDROIT Principle 22.4.2; Transnational Rules of Civil Procedure (Reporters' Study) Rule 26.3.

Comments:

1. Most jurisdictions identify two possible approaches to expert evidence. On the one hand, experts can be appointed by the court, *ex officio* and/or upon request of one or both parties (see Rule 120). On the other hand, parties are frequently permitted to present expert testimony furnished by an expert who they have selected. Rule 119 is concerned with the second of the two possible approaches. It is an aspect of the right to be heard (Rule 16). (See Article 5 of the IBA Rules of Evidence.)
2. Party-appointed expert evidence may give rise to the risk of expert bias, whether structural or personal. The former arises where an expert genuinely holds a specific opinion on an

issue and is instructed by the party on that basis. The latter arises where an expert either develops an animus towards the opponent of the party instructing them, or identifies with the party instructing them, such that in either case they consciously or subconsciously tailor their evidence accordingly. Given this it is in the party's interest to present party-appointed experts with proper qualification and skills, and who understand and comply with the duties imposed by Rule 122, not least their duty of objectivity and impartiality.

3. Where one or more party-appointed experts have submitted their evidence, but the court requires further clarification on the issue upon which they have given evidence, it may order the appointment of a court-appointed expert under Rule 120. It may, also, however consider the issue as not established and thus decide it according to an application of the burden of proof (Rule 25(2)).
4. This Rule must be applied consistently with the general principle of proportionality (Rules 5 and 6). It should not be understood as setting out a general right to adduce evidence from an unlimited number of experts.
5. Party-appointed expert costs are initially borne by the party who appointed the expert. As a general rule, reimbursement of such costs from a losing party may be granted in those proceedings where their appointment was necessary to determine an issue (Rule 241).

Rule 120. Court-appointed Experts

(1) The court may appoint one or more experts to give evidence on any relevant issue for which expert evidence is appropriate, including foreign law.

(2) Experts can be individuals or legal entities. In the case of legal entities at least one individual must assume responsibility for the expert's report.

(3) If the parties agree upon an expert, the court ordinarily should appoint that expert.

(4) Parties may object to the appointment of a court-appointed expert on grounds of bias. Where there is a reasonable apprehension of bias, the court must either, as relevant, refuse to appoint the expert, rescind their appointment or set aside their evidence in its entirety.

Sources:

ALI/Unidroit Principle 22.4; Transnational Rules of Civil Procedure (Reporters' Study) Rules 26.1 and 26.2.

Comments:

1. In many jurisdictions, as a general rule, experts are appointed by the court. On many occasions, such an appointment will be both proportionate and convenient. This Rule should not, however, be simply viewed as an alternative to Rule 119, such that the appointment of a court-appointed expert would preclude the appointment of a party-appointed expert. The principle of party autonomy should be given due weight, and thus where the court appoints an expert, the parties should retain the option of appointing their own expert. (See Article 6(1) of the IBA Rules of Evidence.)
2. Rule 120(1) establishes that the court has the discretion to appoint several experts if necessary. Generally, however, and consistently with the principle of proportionality (Rules 5 and 6) no more than one expert should be appointed on any relevant issue. When considering whether the appointment of more than one expert is justified, the court should bear in mind any increase in costs arising from multiple appointments. In considering the costs, the value of the claim for relief should be a relevant criterion in assessing the proportionality of the

cost of such appointments. However, the court should also consider the fundamental importance of reaching a correct decision on the merits in considering these issues.

3. Selection and choice of court-appointed experts may be performed in different ways depending on the issue for which expert evidence is required. In many European jurisdictions there are lists of potential experts and their subject-matter expertise are made available to the court. Rule 120 does not address this issue directly. The court should, however, have the power, especially in complex matters, to appoint any expert that appears suitable and to take such steps as are necessary to obtain sufficient information on potential experts.
4. Issues for which expert evidence is appropriate are those where scientific or technical knowledge is required. Foreign law may, depending on the European jurisdiction, be understood to be a matter of law or of fact. However, as the court may lack knowledge of the relevant rules of foreign law, it may appoint an expert to clarify such matters.
5. Rule 120(2) recognises the practice of entrusting expert reports to legal entities, e.g., universities, public or private laboratories, or scientific societies. In order to ensure that such entities comply with the duties imposed on experts under Rule 122, and also to secure the effective management of expert evidence-taking, such an entity must always be represented by at least one individual. That individual must take on the responsibility for producing the expert report properly. The legal entity's organisational structure should be such that it guarantees the independence of any other individual involved in drafting such a report, as well as of an individual taking on the responsibility under this Rule.
6. Rule 120(3) reflects the principle of party autonomy. The court should not interfere with the parties' consent as to the suitability of an expert lightly. However, the court must secure the neutrality and competence of the proposed expert.
7. Rule 120(4) refers to the expert's duty of impartiality. If a party has a reasonable apprehension of bias on the part of a court-appointed expert, they should apply to the court for an order under this Rule. For appeals in respect of such decisions, see Rule 179(2)(e).

Rule 121. Instructions to Court-appointed Experts

(1) The court shall instruct experts concerning the issues on which they are to provide evidence. It should set reasonable time limits within which any such expert should submit their written report or reports.

(2) In an appropriate case, the court may extend or limit the scope of its instructions to an expert. It may also vary any time limit for submission by an expert of their report.

(3) The court must inform the parties of any orders given or varied under this Rule.

(4) Where a party objects to the nature or scope of instructions given by the court to an expert, it may apply to the court to vary those instructions.

Comments:

1. Rule 121 clarifies the nature of the court's responsibility to determine the scope of a court-appointed expert's report, and to set the time period within which such a report is to be prepared and submitted.[25]
2. In order to ensure that the parties' right to be heard is respected, the court must inform them of any orders it makes under this Rule (Rule 121(3)).

25 Also see Art. 6(1) of the IBA Rules of Evidence.

3. While the primary responsibility for supervising the work carried out by a court-appointed expert resides with the court, as general rule parties may, under Rules 121(3) and (4), apply to the court to include or exclude issues from the scope of an expert's report.

Rule 122. Duties of Experts

(1) An expert, whether appointed by the court or by a party, owes a duty to the court to present a full, objective and impartial assessment of the issue addressed.
(2) No expert may give evidence outside their field of expertise. An expert may also refuse to give evidence for the same reasons a witness may refuse to give evidence.
(3) An expert must not delegate their task to third parties unless authorised to do so by the court.
(4) Where an expert, without a reasonable explanation, fails to render their evidence within time limits set by the court, the court may impose appropriate sanctions.

Sources:
ALI/UNIDROIT Principle 22.4.3; Transnational Rules of Civil Procedure (Reporters' Study) Rule 26.3.

Comments:
1. All experts owe the same duty to the court and are subject to the same consequences. The general provisions concerning sanctions apply accordingly (see Rule 27). Criminal sanctions under national law may also apply, such as prosecution for perjury.
2. Rule 122(2) reflects the duty of an expert to only provide evidence that assists the court to ascertain the truth. Consequently, an expert may only give evidence within their field of expertise and may not give evidence outside of it. Experts may also refuse to give evidence for the same reasons as other witnesses (see Rule 91). Consistently with the duty to promote proportionality both the court and parties ought to ensure that expert witnesses are not appointed if they are unable to give evidence for such reasons.
3. Rule 122(3) reflects the fact that experts are appointed for their professional competence. Therefore, a delegation to a sub-contractor is impermissible. However, preparatory work may be done by a sub-contractor under the expert's instruction provided the court agrees. Minor tasks can always be delegated if the expert cannot reasonably be expected to perform such work in person; this applies most clearly when the expert is a legal entity.
4. As an expert is under a duty to assist the court a failure to render the report or to appear in court may entail the imposition of sanctions (Rule 122(4)). Such sanctions should be proportionate. They could consist of costs or a fine. It may be useful to distinguish between court-appointed experts and party-appointed experts when it comes to sanctions. While the former are assisting the court and therefore perform a public duty, the latter act primarily on a private law basis. A failure to render expertise may therefore entail procedural consequences, as the party may not be able to discharge the burden of proof. Sanction arising where an expert provides false evidence should be directed towards the party who has engaged the expert, but, obviously, it would only apply to party-appointed experts.

Rule 123. Expert Access to Information

(1) Court-appointed experts should be provided with access to all relevant and non-privileged information necessary to enable them to prepare their written report.

(2) In particular, a court-appointed expert may ask a party to provide any information, to provide access to any documents, permit inspection of property or entry upon land for the purposes of inspection, to the extent that such are relevant and material to the proceedings.

(3) In appropriate circumstances, an expert may examine a person or have access to information derived from a physical or mental examination of that person.

Sources:

ALI/UNIDROIT Principle 16.

Comments:

1. Rule 123(1) acknowledges that court-appointed experts may require access to information in order to enable them to properly prepare their evidence. The court may do so on its own initiative or on application of the court-appointed expert. Where, however, party-appointed experts require comparable access to evidence, Section II of this Part applies.
2. Rule 123(2), read with Rules 7, 27 and 99, provides that where a party refuses to comply with a court-appointed expert's request, the court, taking account of all the circumstances of the case, may determine the most appropriate response to such non-compliance.[26]
3. Rule 123(3) may, for instance, be utilised in cases of personal injury or where the question of mental capacity is in issue in proceedings.

Rule 124. Expert Reports and Oral Evidence

(1) Expert evidence should ordinarily be given in the form of a written report. However, in simple cases, the court may order that expert evidence be given orally.

(2) An expert may give oral testimony to explain their written report either on the court's request or on the application of any party. Subject to any applicable legal provisions, such oral testimony may be given at a hearing or via any appropriate means of distance communication, such as, but not limited to, video-conferencing.

(3) The court may require an expert to give their evidence, whether that is in the form of a written report or by way of oral testimony, on oath.

(4) Where an expert gives oral testimony, parties may only ask the expert questions that are relevant to their report.

(5) If a party-appointed expert fails to appear when duly summoned to attend an oral hearing, and does so without a valid reason, the court may disregard that expert's written report.

Sources:

Transnational Rules of Civil Procedure (Reporters' Study) Rule 26.4.

Comments:

1. Rule 124(1) provides that, as a general rule, expert evidence shall be by written report.[27] This is consistent with the principle of proportionality (Rule 5), as it ensures that only where necessary is expert evidence to be given orally.
2. Rule 124(2) articulates both the court's ability to require an expert to explain or clarify their written evidence, and the parties' right to challenge such evidence at an oral hearing,

26 Also see Art. 6(3) of the IBA Rules of Evidence.

27 Also see Art. 6(4) of the IBA Rules of Evidence.

i.e., in the latter respect it is an instance of the adversarial principle. Where the court, of its own motion (*ex officio*), requires an expert to expand upon their written evidence orally, the parties shall be informed and entitled to participate in the process.[28]

3. While the general rule in Rule 124(3) provides for an expert to give their evidence on oath, as criminal sanctions for perjury apply, the court has a discretion as to whether an expert is sworn or not.
4. Rule 124(5) provides that where an expert who is ordered to attend an oral hearing to answer questions concerning their report fails to attend the hearing, the court may disregard their evidence. The court may do so either by placing less weight on the evidence than it would otherwise have done, or by disregarding it in its entirety.[29]

Rule 125. Costs

(1) The fees and expenses of a court-appointed expert shall form part of the costs of the proceedings. The court may order that a party who applies for an expert to be appointed pay their fees in advance.

(2) The fees and expenses of a party-appointed expert shall only be recoverable from the other party if the court so orders.

Sources:
ALI/Unidroit Principle 25.1.

Comments:

1. Rule 125(1) articulates the principal that experts are entitled to receive fair remuneration for the work they do. As a general rule, where a party applies for the appointment of a court-appointed expert, they ought to be responsible for such payments. That general rule is, however, subject to the application of the European Rule concern litigations costs, i.e., such remuneration should form part of the litigation costs that are subject to the loser pays principle (See Part XII and particularly Rule 241).[30] The power to order a party who applies for the appointment of an expert to make an advance payment to them is discretionary. In an appropriate case, the court may also order a party on whom the burden of proof lies on the issue upon which expert evidence is required, to make such a payment.
2. Rule 125(2) establishes the general principle that the cost of a party-appointed expert is subject to the normal costs rules (see Part XII and particularly Rule 241).

E. JUDICIAL INSPECTION

Rule 126. Judicial Inspection in General

(1) A party may apply for an order permitting the examination of persons or things. To facilitate such an examination the court may authorise access to evidence, including access to land or private premises. To ensure the adequacy of inspection, access may be subject to such conditions as the court considers just with regard to the special circumstances of the case and in accordance with applicable law.

28 Also see Art. 6(6) of the IBA Rules of Evidence.

29 Also see Art. 5(5) of the IBA Rules of Evidence.

30 Also see Art. 6(8) of the IBA Rules of Evidence.

(2) A party may apply for permission to carry out a physical or mental examination of a person. The court, in consultation with the parties, shall determine the timing and arrangements for such an examination.

(3) The court may inspect or require the inspection of evidence by a court-appointed or party-appointed expert, as it deems appropriate.

(4) Parties and their representatives may attend an inspection or examination ordered under this Rule, unless the court provides otherwise.

(5) In this Rule and in Rule 127(1), 'things' refers to any physical or electronic item, movable or immovable elements of such items.

Sources:

ALI/UNIDROIT Principle 16.1.

Comments:

1. All legal systems make provision for evidence-taking through the direct inspection of evidence by the court. It is frequently understood to be a subsidiary method of evidence-taking, used when direct inspection cannot be carried out by other means, such as via documents, photographs, video recordings, etc.
2. Rule 126(1) mirrors Rule 198(2). It should also be applied consistently with the principle of proportionality (Rule 5).
3. Rule 126(1) also provides the court with the power to order access to private premises, when that is necessary and proportionate to carry out an inspection. Both parties and non-parties may be made subject to such orders. (Also see Rule 198(2)).
4. Rule 126(3) provides the power to appoint either a court or party-appointed expert where that is necessary to assist the court in interpreting or understanding that which is being examined.[31] Such an appointment must also be made consistently with the principle of proportionality.
5. Rule 126(4) should be applied so as to take proper account of confidentiality. The examination of individuals is, generally, the most straightforward example of a situation where parties and their representatives may properly be excluded from the evidence-gathering process.

Rule 127. Non-Parties and Judicial Inspection

(1) The court may order non-parties to produce things for inspection by the court or a party.

(2) The provisions set in Section 2 of Part VII of these Rules apply to any order to be made or made under Rule 127(1).

Sources:

Transnational Rules of Civil Procedure (Reporters' Study) Rule 20.1.

Comments:

1. Rule 127 is a specification of the general provisions on access to evidence set in Section 2 of this Part, including the right of the non-party to submit arguments justifying their non-compliance with an order requiring inspection.

31 See Art. 7 of the IBA Rules of Evidence.

2. Where necessary, a court may order any thing (see Rule 126(5)) to be seised directly to facilitate their inspection. Moreover, if such an order is made, a party may also apply for the grant of provisional measures in order to preserve evidence (see Rule 198).

SECTION 4—CROSS-BORDER ISSUES

A. IN THE EUROPEAN UNION

Rule 128. Cross-border Evidence-Taking within the European Union

(1) When evidence has to be taken in another European Union Member State and when access is needed to evidence located in another Member State, the court and the parties may rely on the provisions of Council Regulation (EC) No 1206/2001 of 28 May 2001 on cooperation between the courts of the Member States in the taking of evidence in civil or commercial matters.

(2) Without prejudice to the application of Council Regulation (EC) No 1206/2001 of 28 May 2001 on cooperation between the courts of the Member States in the taking of evidence in civil or commercial matters,

(a) the court may directly summon a witness residing in another Member State;

(b) the court may appoint an expert to submit a report, the preparation of which requires the undertaking of activities (inspection of persons or premises located) in another Member State;

(c) a party or non-party, to whom an order for access to evidence is addressed, and who is residing or domiciled in the Member State of the court, is under a duty to produce the required documents and evidence, even if they are located in a Member State different to the one of the court issuing the order;

(d) a court may address an order for access to evidence to prospective parties and to non-parties domiciled in another Member State.

Comments:

1. This Rule concerns the duality of systems for evidence-taking between European Union Member States, recognised by the European Court of Justice, both for taking evidence in a Member State different from that in which proceedings are being pursued, or for asking a foreign court to order production of evidence.
2. Rule 128(1) reflects the fact that the court and parties may utilise the provisions of the Evidence Regulation. Its use is not, however, compulsory, except, possibly, for inspection of evidence that has to be performed within a different Member State from that in which proceedings are being pursued.
3. As the Evidence Regulation's use is optional, Rule 128(2) is able to provide a second route to securing evidence outside the immediate jurisdiction of proceedings. In so far as Rule 128(2)(a) is concerned, the ECJ has recognised that national courts may summon witnesses residing in other Member States directly.[32] Such a summons cannot, however, give rise to any coercive measures to secure compliance. In such circumstances, the use of video-conferencing may be of assistance.

32 Judgment of 6 September 2012, Lippens and others (C-170/11) ECLI:EU:C:2012:540.

4. Rule 128(b) reflects the ECJ's ruling that "the court of one Member State, which wishes the task of taking of evidence entrusted to an expert to be carried out in another Member State, is not necessarily required to use the method of taking evidence laid down by those provisions to be able to order the taking of that evidence".[33] This possibility, however, does not permit an expert to affect the powers of the Member State in which their activities take place, e.g., where an investigation is carried out in places connected to the exercise of such powers or in places to which access or other action is prohibited or otherwise restricted to specific individuals. In such circumstances, in the absence of any agreement or arrangement between Member States, reliance on the Evidence Regulation is the only means by which an expert investigation can be carried out in another Member State.
5. Rule 128(c) provides that an individual to whom an order for access to evidence is addressed may not refuse to comply with it on the ground that the evidence to be produced is in another Member State, provided that they are resident or domiciled in the Member State of the court.
6. Rule 128(d) concerns defendants to prospective proceedings and non-parties. In so far as the former are concerned, this Rule is a logical consequence of the general rules set in Section 2 of this Part, i.e., orders for access to evidence under that Section are permitted before proceedings are commenced; the court to which the order is applied for must determine that it has jurisdiction before issuing the order; and the possibility exists that the court will determine that it is competent, even if the prospective defendant is not domiciled in its territory. As far as non-parties are concerned, the Rule is based on the principles of mutual trust and mutual recognition. It places non-parties under the same duty to comply with orders addressed to them by the courts of other Member States and to do so on the same basis as they would be expected to comply with orders of the courts of the Member State in which they are domiciled. Securing compliance with an order may prove difficult, especially where non-parties are concerned. Where enforcement or a coercive measure is required to give effect to an order, it may be necessary to resort to the Evidence Regulation. It may also be necessary, before issuing an access to evidence order in respect of an individual who is resident in another Member State to provide advance notice to that individual of such steps as might be taken to oppose the grant of the proposed order, i.e., to bring to their attention evidentiary privileges or immunities (Rule 91). A flexible approach should be taken where a non-party seeks to make such a claim for privilege, e.g., the court should permit the claim to be made in writing as a response to the proposed order or to the order itself.

B. OUTSIDE THE EUROPEAN UNION

Rule 129. Cross-border Evidence Taking of outside the European Union

When evidence needs to be taken outside the European Union or when the addressee of an order for access to evidence has no domicile or habitual residence within the European Union, the court and the parties may rely on the provisions of the Convention on the Taking of Evidence Abroad in Civil or Commercial Matters (Hague Evidence Convention of 18 March 1970) or of other relevant international conventions.

33 Judgment of 21 February 2013, ProRail (C-332/11) ECLI:EU:C:2013:87.

Comments:

1. Neither national nor European Rules of Procedure can determine rules applicable to courts and parties outside their jurisdiction. Nor can the European Union. This Rule provides for the application of international instruments to questions of evidence-taking that need to be implemented outside of it.
2. Access to evidence, to which this Rule applies and to which Rule 101 applies may, in some circumstances, fall within the scope of Article 23 of the HCCH 1970 Evidence Convention. It should be noted that some Contracting States to the HCCH 1970 Evidence Convention have, under Article 23, made a full or qualified exclusion to the execution of Letters of Request issued for the purpose of obtaining pre-trial documentary disclosure or discovery, as it is variously known in common Law countries (practice shows, for instance, some reluctance to accept materials generated under 28 United States Code Section 1782). Implementation in such legal systems of orders for access to evidence might be beneficial in so far as it may help them to overcome, partially or fully, such reluctance.

PART VIII

JUDGMENT, *RES JUDICATA* AND *LIS PENDENS*

INTRODUCTION

1. This Part deals with judgments and judicial settlements. For the purpose of these Rules, a judgment is a decision, which finally resolves the matter by deciding the claim on either the merits, dismisses the proceedings on procedural grounds, or which decides a preliminary procedural issue or a specific legal issue on the merits.

2. A decision finally resolves the matter if proceedings in which the decision was rendered, cannot continue before the court where they have been instituted. This includes judgments that finally resolve the matter with respect to a part of the claim for relief or one or more of several, but not all claims for relief brought in one and the same proceeding. It does not encompass case management orders or orders that regulate evidence-taking. For example, a decision on the admissibility of evidence will ordinarily be made by court order, and court orders are subject to revision at the court's discretion. It is, however, a matter of the court's discretion whether to render a judgment on specific procedural issues or on specific legal issues on the merits that finally determine particularly important incidental issues, which may then be subject to the appellate process.

3. A decision on the merits is one that either grants or denies the relief sought by the claimant in full or in part for reasons of substantive law, default or consent. A decision resolving the case on procedural grounds is a full or partial dismissal of the proceedings based on a failure to satisfy a procedural prerequisite.

4. As provisional measures are dealt with in Part X of these Rules, the term "judgment" must be construed more narrowly than the definition articulated in Article 2(a) of the Brussels Ibis Regulation.

SECTION 1—GENERAL PART

Rule 130. Types of judgment

(1) The court may give

(a) a final judgment, which is a judgment deciding the whole of a claim for relief;

(b) a judgment deciding part of a claim for relief (a partial judgment);

(c) where more than one claim for relief is made, a final judgment deciding one or more, but not all, of the claims for relief;

(d) a judgment on preliminary procedural issues or on specific legal issues on the merits (see Rule 66);

(e) a judgment in default.

(2) Where the court gives a judgment that does not decide the whole of a claim for relief, the proceedings continue in respect of such parts for which judgment has not been given. If the court's judgment on a part of the claim for relief, on a procedural issue, or

ELI-Unidroit Model European Rules of Civil Procedure. ELI & Unidroit, Oxford University Press.
 DOI: 10.1093/oso/9780198866589.003.0009

on legal issues on the merits is subject to appeal the court may exercise its discretion whether to continue or stay the proceedings according to the circumstances of the case.

Sources:
ALI/UNIDROIT Principles 9.3.3 to 9.3.5, Transnational Rules of Civil Procedure (Reporters' Study) Rules 18.3.2 and 18.3.4.

Comments:

1. According to Rule 130(1)(a), a final judgment on the whole claim for relief may be based on a failure to satisfy mandatory procedural requirements (see Rules 65(2)(a), 133), or on grounds of substantive law (for the different scopes of *res judicata* see Rule 149, comment 3).
2. The court may (see Rule 130(1)(b)) give judgments that decide a claim for relief in whole or in part or, where more than one claim for relief is made, decide one or more, but not all, of the claims for relief. Such judgments finally resolve the matter with respect to that part of the claim, that claim or those claims, leaving the other part of the claim, other claim or claims to be determined at a later time in the proceedings (see Rule 130(2)). It is a matter for the court, in its discretion, to determine whether to give such a judgment, taking into account its obligation to promote the fair, efficient and speedy resolution of the dispute, as set out in Rules 2 and 4 sentence 1, and 49(7).
3. Judgments deciding part of a claim or one of several claims for relief can be made on the merits or on procedural grounds. For example, where more than one claim for relief is pursued, the procedural requirements, e.g., jurisdiction, may be met with respect to one claim for relief, but not with respect to another. Similarly, a minor who, having been granted, with the court's approval, parental permission, is considered to be an adult for the purpose of a business they direct or an employment contract they have entered into, which is permissible in many European Civil Codes, may, after a car accident, sue for damages in their own right, but may not claim damages for pain and suffering unless they are represented by their parents.
4. Judgments on part of the claim or one of several claims are regular judgments with respect to appeals and *res judicata*. However, as the judgment is limited to a part of the claim for relief or one of the claims for relief, it will not finally resolve the matter. Therefore, the proceedings must continue until a further and subsequent judgment or judgments are given on the other parts of the claim or claims.
5. The following are illustrative examples:
   a) A judgment on part of a claim for relief may be illustrated by the following example: if the claimant, in a road traffic accident case, asked for the payment of 150,000 euro (or the equivalent) for damages, the court may enter a judgment for 100,000 euro in respect of the damage to the car, leaving the determination of the remainder of the damages claim, as it concerns the cost of medical treatment or future care, for 50,000 euro to be determined at a later date. Both the judgment for 100,000 euro and the judgment for 50,000 euro are partial judgments.

      In some European legal cultures, a judgment on part of the claim is often combined with a declaratory judgment concerning the other part of the claim. In the above example, the judgment that ordered the defendant to pay 100,000 euro did so because it held the defendant to be liable for the accident. As such there will be a general declaratory judgment on liability and a partial judgment on damages, with the remainder of the damages claimed to be determined at a later date. Under the concept of *res judicata* in these Rules (see Rule 149(2)), such a judgment is not necessary to exclude contradictory results. However, it may be helpful to clarify the situation and to promote settlement.

b) A judgment that decides some but not all of a claimant's claims for relief may be given in a situation like the following: assume the claimant in an employment case asserts a claim for unpaid wages and for a failure to provide paid annual holiday leave. In such a case, the court may give a judgment on the unpaid wages claim, leaving the determination of the annual leave claim to a later judgment.

6. Rule 130(d) is addressed in the comments to Rule 66; for Rule 130(1)(e) on judgments in default see Rules 135 and following.
7. Rule 130(2) leaves it to the court, in its discretion, to decide whether to continue with or to stay proceedings upon an appeal being pursued from a partial judgment (Rules 130(1)(b) and (c)) or a judgment on an incidental issue (Rule 130(1)(d)). It may be appropriate to stay the proceedings pending the outcome of any such appeal where the *res judicata* of the preceding partial judgment could adversely affect the results of any going proceedings (see comment 5 above and Rule 66, comments 2, 8 and 9). It may, however, also be beneficial in some circumstances to continue with the rest of the proceedings while the appeal from such a partial judgment is pending where to do so properly promotes the speedy determination of the dispute as a whole (see Rule 66, comment 2).

Rule 131. Structure of a judgment

A judgment must contain

(a) the court's designation and composition;
(b) the place and date of the judgment;
(c) the names of the parties and, if applicable, of their lawyers;
(d) the relief claimed;
(e) the order of the court;
(f) the legal and factual grounds for the judgment;
(g) the signature of the judge or judges, if necessary;
(h) the signature of the court clerk, if necessary; and
(i) where relevant, information on formal requirements of any available means to challenge the decision.

Sources:

ALI/UNIDROIT Principle 23; Transnational Rules of Civil Procedure (Reporters' Study) Rule 31.2.

Comments:

1. Rule 131 contains a non-exhaustive list of a judgment's elements (also see Draft Unified Patent Court Rules, Rule 350).
2. Rule 131(a) requires the court and the judge or judges to be identified in the judgment. This is an important requirement in a democratic State and is an aspect of the principle of publicity (see Article 6(1) of the European Convention on Human Rights). A justice system in which the judge remains an anonymous figure may lead to a lack of moral responsibility or the abuse of power by the judiciary.

3. Rule 131(b) requires an indication of the place and date of the judgment. This information may become important in different situations. First, it helps to determine if a document that appears to be a judgment is really a judgment, as it is relatively easy to determine whether there was a court operating at the place and date indicated and whether the judge was a member of this court. Second, the place and date of the first instance judgment may be relevant at the appellate level, as the applicable law may depend on the date and, in some circumstances, the place of the judgment. Third, the date and place help to designate the judgment precisely.
4. Rule 131(c) requires the parties and their lawyers to be identified. Identification of the parties is crucial to know who is bound by the judgment. Identification of the lawyers is important if an issue arises as to whether a party was represented by a lawyer and whether such representation was adequate. Normally, the judgment will also contain the address and other contact details of the parties and their lawyers. However, there may be cases in which the address of a party should be kept private to protect a party. Therefore, the Rule does not require this information to be included in the judgment itself, although it does not prohibit it.
5. Rule 131(d) requires the judgment to specify the relief claimed. First, this is important to find out whether claims were dismissed on their merits and are therefore subject to *res judicata*. Second, it facilitates a determination of whether the judgment is a judgment on only a part of the claim or one or more, but not all, of several claims, or whether it decided the claim or claims in their entirety, and whether the court granted relief consistent with the relief sought (*ne infra, ne ultra* and *ne extra petita* (see Rule 23(2)). Third, it makes clear who has succeeded in the litigation, and the extent to which they did so. Such information may be relevant to questions of costs (see Rule 241).
6. Rule 131(e) is self-explanatory, as any judgment must contain the order, in other words, the court's decision in a strict sense, i.e., the judgments operative part.
7. Rule 131(f) requires the court to give the grounds or reasons for its decision. Normally, the grounds for the judgment include a summary of the parties' positions and the court's reasoning. This protects against arbitrary and partial decision-making. It also ensures that the decision is comprehensible, enabling the parties to understand why and how they succeeded or not in the litigation. As such it is also an essential means of facilitating confidence in the decision by the losing party, enhancing the prospect that all parties will accept the decision. The court's reasoning must reasonably demonstrate that the court has complied with the requirements of the right to be heard (see Rule 12, comment 2 and following). It also allows the general public to understand the reasons for the court's decision and facilitates the appeal process for both the parties and the appellate court. Finally, it is a means to facilitate the development of the law. There are, however, exceptions to this requirement, e.g., in default judgments (see Rule 12, comment 3, and Rule 135 and following), or in decisions that give effect to an agreement of the parties (see Rule 141). Parties may waive this requirement by consent upon the oral pronouncement of the outcome of the dispute, however in such a case the requirements of waiver of the right to appeal should apply (see Rule 154).
8. Rule 131(g) requires the judge or judges responsible for giving the judgment to sign it in so far as that is required by any mandatory national practice. This helps to identify them, and it also ensures that they are properly responsible for it. The signature may be written longhand or an electronic signature.

9. Rule 131(h) requires the signature of a court clerk in so far as that is required by any mandatory national practice.
10. Rule 131(i) requires the court to inform the parties if there is an applicable appeal process and if so, the relevant deadlines and formal requirements. This rule is intended to cover the steps necessary to seek permission to appeal (see Rules 166 and 172). The information may be contained in the judgment or in another document served with the judgment.
11. Ordinarily it is for the court to provide all parts of a judgment in written or electronic form. Rule 17(3) requires the public accessibility of judgments in written or in electronic form (see Rule 18(4); and see also Rule 17, comment 5). Oral judgments given in a public hearing in first instance or small claims courts are commonplace in some European jurisdictions; however, a written judgment fulfilling the requirements of Rule 131 must be served on the parties (Rule 134). Whether or not fewer formal requirements may apply in small claims proceedings is not within the scope of these Rules (see Preamble VII. 3. and VIII.3. In exceptional circumstances a judgment without reasoning may be given (see comment 7 above).

Rule 132. Contents of judgments

(1) A judgment, depending on the nature of the relief claimed, may

(a) order a defendant to do or not to do something,

(b) create, alter or terminate a legal relationship,

(c) make a declaration of rights, or

(d) dismiss the claim for relief either on procedural grounds or where it determines it to be without merit.

(2) The court may only grant a declaratory judgment, including a negative declaratory judgment, if the claimant can establish that they have a legitimate interest in obtaining the declaration sought.

Comments:

1. Rule 132(1) refers to a claimant's claim for relief. Which party is a claimant depends on the nature of the claim. Thus, in a counterclaim, a defendant bringing the counterclaim is the claimant in respect of that claim.
2. The most prominent type of judgment is a judgment containing an order upholding or dismissing the claim for relief in whole or in part and, where applicable, it either requires a defendant to perform, refrain from performing, certain actions, or tolerate certain actions being or to be carried out by the claimant. Depending on any applicable substantive law, the court may also order the creation, alteration or termination of a legal relationship, e.g., through requiring the dissolution of a legal entity.
4. According to Rule 132(2) the court may grant a declaratory judgment, including a negative declaratory judgment, if a claimant can show that they have a legitimate interest in obtaining the declaration sought (also see Rule 133(e)). It is a matter for national practice to determine the nature of an applicable legitimate interest. Examples include: where the party seeks a definitive statement concerning the law; where the claimant is unable to quantify the amount of damages; or where there is a high probability that the defendant may consent to the amount of damages upon a declaratory judgment on liability (also see Rule 66(1)(b)).
5. A judgment may also dismiss a claim for relief either in whole or in part. Such a dismissal may be due to a failure to satisfy procedural requirements (a dismissal on procedural

grounds) or a consequence of the court's finding that the claim for relief is without merit (dismissal on the merits), be it that the proven facts do not justify the relief sought or that the facts alleged by the claimant were not proven (for early final judgments also see Rule 65.)

Rule 133. Procedural requirements of judgments on the merits

The court may only give a judgment on the merits when it is satisfied that

(a) the parties have litigation capacity according to Rules 29(2)-31, 34, 35, and 45-46;

(b) the court has subject matter and territorial jurisdiction;

(c) there are no pending proceedings involving the same parties and the same cause of action in another court unless an exception provided for in the Rules on *lis pendens* applies;

(d) the cause of action between the parties is not *res judicata*;

(e) the claimant has a legitimate interest to commence the proceedings on its claim for relief; and

(f) any other procedural requirement specified in these Rules is met.

Comments:

1. This Rule generally clarifies that before giving a judgment on the merits, the court must have established that necessary procedural requirements have been satisfied. This requirement is rarely spelt out, although present, in a single procedural rule in European jurisdictions, see for instance § 261(3) no. 1 of the German CCP.
2. Rule 133(a) refers to the rules on litigation capacity of the parties as enumerated in Rules 29(2), 30, 31, 34, 35, 45 and 46. Where one or more parties lacks litigation capacity the claim may be dismissed if the defect is not cured timeously upon the court's suggestion (see Rules 33, 48, 49(8), and 65(2)(a)).
3. Rule 133(b) requires the court to have subject-matter and territorial jurisdiction. As the present Rules do not deal with jurisdiction, this must be determined by applying international treaties (e.g., 2007 Lugano Convention, HCCH 2005 Choice of Court Convention), European Union law (e.g., Brussels Ibis Regulation) and national law.
4. Rule 133(c) refers to the concept of pendency as defined in the Rules on *lis pendens* (see Rules 142 and following). Pursuant to Rule 142(1), "any court other than the court first seised shall of its own motion stay its proceedings until such time as the jurisdiction of the court first seised is established (the priority principle)". This means that no judgment on the merits is possible. Rule 143 on *lis pendens* provides an exception to the priority principle in cases of exclusive jurisdiction, and Rule 133(c) takes this into account.
5. Rule 133(d) refers to the concept of concentration of legal and factual issues as defined in Rule 22(1). Non-compliance with that Rule renders proceedings on the same claim for relief arising out of the same cause of action inadmissible (see Rule 22(2)). The concentration rule describes the negative effects of judgments becoming *res judicata* (see Rule 22, comment 1). Those persons who are bound by these negative effects of *res judicata* are determined by Rule 151. The court must take into account the preclusionary effects of *res judicata* on its own motion (*ex officio*) (see Rule 152).
6. Rule 133(e) addresses possible exceptions from the general rule that claimants who fulfil all the other requirements of Rule 133 may proceed to a judgment on the merits. Only in exceptional cases claimants may lack a legitimate interest in bringing their claim for

relief. In particular, Rule 133(e) deals with those situations where a claim is frivolous, vexatious or an abuse of process. This requirement is likely to lead to disputes because the delineation between a procedural requirement and a requirement of substantive law, the consequence of which is a judgment on the merits dismissing the claim, is not and will be never be uniform in its varying constellations across all European jurisdictions. There is, however, no European jurisdiction that does not provide a means to dismiss proceedings without dealing with the merits on the basis of the claimant acting in bad faith in bringing proceedings, or where they have no legitimate interest in doing so because of other such exceptional reasons (also see Rule 65, comment 2).

7. Rule 133(f) refers to special provisions in these Rules that establish other requirements for a judgment on the merits and which are not explicitly specified in Rule 133; see, for instance, Rules 205, 208 and 209, 213 dealing with litigation capacity in respect of collective interest injunctions and collective proceedings.
8. Whether the procedural requirements must be examined by the court on its own motion (*ex officio*) is determined elsewhere in these Rules in the context of the Rule establishing the relevant procedural requirements; see for instance Rules 32, 152, 213 and 218(1)(a).

Rule 134. Service of judgment

A judgment must be served on all parties by a method provided for in Part VI of these Rules.

Sources:

ALI/UNIDROIT Principle 5.3; Transnational Rules of Civil Procedure (Reporters' Study) Rule 31.3.

Comments:

1. It is an important part of the right to be heard (see Rule 11) that all parties are entitled to know when a judgment has been rendered in proceedings. Accordingly, notification of the judgment must be provided to the parties.
2. In many European jurisdictions service of a copy of the complete judgment, including its reasoning, is necessary. In other jurisdictions it is sufficient that the document notifying the parties of the judgment contains only certain important pieces of information, such as those specified in Rules 131(a), (b), (c), (e), (g) and (i), albeit however, every party has a right to apply for a written version, which contains the judgment's reasoning. Rule 134 prefers the clearer approach, which requires a copy of the complete judgment, including reasoning, to be served on the parties. This is further supported by the fact that full knowledge of the judgment's reasoning facilitates the decision whether to appeal from the judgment. In any event the right to public access to judgments (see Rule 17, comment 5 and Rule 131, comment 10) requires the production of a complete judgment in written or electronic form. Special rules or waiver by consent of the parties may exceptionally permit judgments to be rendered without reasons being given or with only brief reasons being given (see Rule 131, comment 6).
3. All European jurisdictions provide service of the judgment on the lawyer representing a party. Some also require service to be effected on the party in person, whereas others do so only where the party has terminated their lawyer's retainer. Rule 76 makes it clear that service on a party's lawyer suffices in the absence of any special provision modifying service of judgments.

SECTION 2—SPECIAL PART

A. DEFAULT JUDGMENT

Rule 135. Entry of Default judgment against a claimant

(1) The court must enter a default judgment dismissing proceedings where

(a) a claimant has failed to appear at a hearing at which they were required to appear; and

(b) a defendant has applied for default judgment to be entered.

(2) The court may not enter default judgment under this Rule on its own motion.

Sources:
ALI/UNIDROIT Principle 15.1; Transnational Rules of Civil Procedure (Reporters' Study) Rules 15.1 and 15.3.

Comments:

1. Parties should not be in a position to cause delay or complicate the court's task by simply not appearing at a hearing. For this reason, procedural law should provide for rules to incentivise parties to appear at hearings. With respect to the claimant, an effective incentive is a default judgment dismissing the claim if they do not appear. This rule would only apply in circumstances where parties are required to attend a hearing (see Rule 21, comment 4, on sanctions).
2. A default judgment should, however, only be given on application of a defendant, as a claimant can have such a judgment set aside under conditions that are, somewhat, less strict than the conditions required to bring an appeal (see Rules 139 and following). Moreover, setting aside such a judgment enables the proceedings to go on before the same court, thereby potentially ensuring the proceedings are conducted more efficiently and cost-effectively than if the challenge to the default judgment were to be by way of an appeal. If a defendant does not apply for a default judgment, the court may decide the case based on the court file. This means that the factual allegations and defences of both parties as well as the evidence taken so far, if any, will be taken account of by the court.

Rule 136. Entry of Default judgment against a defendant

(1) The court must enter a default judgment against a defendant, where the defendant has

(a) failed to reply to a statement of claim within the time limit for filing a defence, or

(b) failed to appear at a hearing at which they were required to appear; and

(c) a claimant has applied for default judgment to be entered.

(2) A court entering judgment on the application of a claimant shall

(a) where the facts submitted by the claimant justify it on the merits, grant the relief sought, or

(b) where the facts submitted by the claimant do not justify the grant of relief, dismiss the proceedings on the merits.

Sources:
ALI/UNIDROIT Principle 15.2; Transnational Rules of Civil Procedure (Reporters' Study) Rules 15.2 to 15.4.

Comments:

1. In respect of a defaulting defendant, a balance must be struck between the need to create incentives to engage properly with the proceedings and the fact that it is the claimant

who seeks a modification of the *status quo*. For this reason, if a defendant does not respond to the pleadings or does not appear in a hearing, a default judgment may be entered against them only insofar as the facts put forward by the claimant justify the relief sought. In other words, the claimant's factual allegations are deemed to be undisputed. Insofar as, on the basis of these facts, the claim is justified, the court shall enter a default judgment against the defendant. Where the facts alleged do not support the claimant's claim, the proceedings will be dismissed on the merits. This dismissal is not a default judgment in the strict sense, but rather a regular judgment, as the dismissal is not based on the default.

2. A default judgment can only be given on the claimant's application under this Rule. If the claimant does not apply for a default judgment, the court may decide the case based on the court file. This means that the factual allegations and defences of the defendant as well as the evidence taken so far, if any, will be taken account of by the court.

Rule 137. Default judgments on a part of a claim for relief or on one of several claims for relief

(1) The court may enter a default judgment on part of a claim for relief or on one of several claims for relief where

(a) a party fails to appear at a hearing that is dedicated exclusively to that part of the claim, or to one of several claims, for relief, or

(b) a defendant fails to reply to the statement of claim in respect of that part of the claim, or to one of several claims, for relief.

(2) Where the court is able to give, but has not yet given, judgment under Rule 130 on part of a claim for relief or on one of several claims for relief, and a party is in default, the court must

(a) enter judgment on that part of a claim for relief or on one of several claims for relief, and

(b) enter a default judgment in respect of the other part or parts of the claim for relief or other claims for relief.

Comments:

1. The purpose of this Rule is to ensure that default judgments are a proportionate consequence of a party's default in proceedings about a claim which consists of two or more parts or in proceedings about more than one claim (for the principle of proportionality, see Rules 5 and following).
2. Rule 137(1) addresses those cases in which a party's default affects the proceedings only in respect of part of the claim or of one of several claims. Default only affects part of a claim or one of several claims if the scope of a hearing was, by a procedural order communicated to the parties prior to the hearing, limited to that part or to one of the several claims. Once again, this Rule only applies in circumstances where parties are required to attend a hearing.
3. Rule 137(2) addresses those cases in which the court could have given a judgment on a part of the claim or one of several claims but has not yet done so. Generally, it is in the court's discretion whether to hand down a judgment on part of a claim or one of several claims if these are ready to be decided or to continue with the proceedings as a whole (see Rule 130).

However, when part of a claim or one of several claims is ready to be decided and a party is in default, e.g., does not appear in a later hearing, the court should not enter a default judgment on the whole claim or all of the claims, thereby giving up the opportunity to decide the case on a regular basis insofar as this may be possible. Therefore, in such a situation, the court must enter a judgment which, insofar as the case is ready to be decided, is a regular judgment subject to the regular appeal process, and insofar as this is not the case, a default judgment against which only recourse by setting aside is available.

Rule 138. Conditions precedent for granting a default judgment

(1) The Court may enter a default judgment on the basis of a party's failure to appear at a hearing only if
- **(a) notice of the date and time of the hearing was served on that party by a method provided for by these Rules, and**
- **(b) the Court is satisfied that the period between service and the hearing was adequate.**

(2) The Court may only enter a default judgment against a defendant for failing to reply to a statement of claim if
- **(a) the statement of claim was served on the defendant by a method provided for by these Rules,**
- **(b) the time limit for filing a defence has expired, and**
- **(c) where no time limit was prescribed by the rules, service was effected in sufficient time to enable the defendant to arrange their defence.**

(3) The court may enter a default judgment against a defendant even if no receipt of service has been submitted to the court if
- **(a) no proof of any other kind has been received although reasonable efforts have been made to obtain evidence that the defendant actually received the documents instituting the proceedings, and**
- **(b) a period of time not less than three months, which is considered to be adequate by the court to enable the defendant to arrange their defence has elapsed since the date of service by a method provided for by these Rules.**

(4) Notwithstanding Rules 138(3)(a) and (b), the court may grant, in case of urgency, any provisional or protective measures.

Source:
ALI/Unidroit Principle 15.3.

Comments:
1. Rule 138 specifies the procedural conditions precedent for a default judgment. If these conditions are not met, the court may not enter a default judgment but must cure the defect, e.g., by repeating service, or by dismissing the case on procedural grounds.
2. Rule 138(1) deals with default judgments against either party based on a failure to appear at a hearing. A default judgment based on non-appearance is only permissible if the defaulting party was given proper notice of the hearing, i.e., there was effective service in good time before the hearing of the notice of the hearing or the summons requiring attendance. Any such notice or summons should contain a clear warning that in the case of non appearance the court may enter a default judgment. Where no such statement is given, no default judgment may be entered.

3. Rule 138(2) concerns default judgment where a defendant fails to submit their defence in time. It requires service according to the Rules on service (see Part VI) and there has to have been sufficient time for the defendant to prepare their defence. Only if these conditions are met, will the defendant's right to be heard have been protected effectively.
4. Rule 138(3) allows a default judgment in cases in which receipt of service has not been submitted to the court. The rationale is that the claimant should have a chance to defend their rights even if service has failed. In such a situation, however, a default judgment is only possible in limited circumstances, i.e., where it can be established that service in accordance with the Rules on service was effected, that a period of at least three months has elapsed, and that the court or the party responsible for service undertook all reasonable steps to secure a receipt. The text is partly based on Article 19(1) of the ESR Regulation and the basic ideas underlying Articles 15 and 16 of the HCCH 1965 Service Convention. Furthermore, ALI/UNIDROIT Principle 15.3 has the same ethos, but is more general in its approach. These Rules are designed to apply to both domestic and cross-border service of documents. As such Rule 138(3) applies in both situations. In a cross-border setting, Rules 82 and 83 have also to be taken into account. Should the documents that are to be served on the defendant not comply with the language requirements of Rule 82, actual delivery of the documents does not cure the violation of Rule 82. Rule 138(3)(a) would nevertheless, however, allow the court to give a judgment by default, but only if the requirements of Rule 138(3)(b) are met. In this respect the court must take into account whether the lack of a translation of the documents prevented the defendant from arranging their defence.
5. In accordance with Rules 49(7), 184 and following, Rule 138(4) permits the grant of provisional measures if the general requirements are fulfilled.
6. Some European procedural codes exclude default judgments for matters in which the parties do not have the power to settle the dispute. The scope and nature of such a power is a matter of national law. Different European jurisdictions take different approaches. In some parties may practically settle all disputes, except in family matters. In others, there are a number of types of dispute, in addition to family matters, that cannot be subject to settlement, e.g., company law disputes. Determining the approach to take is outside the scope of these Rules and should be left to national law. In some situations, mandatory European or national substantive law may not permit the entry of a judgment in default in respect of certain factual contentions or claims for relief. If factual contentions form the basis for any applicable mandatory law to be considered, it ought to be left to national judicial practice whether a claimant should be asked to amend their factual contentions (see the introductory Preamble sections VI. 6 and 7, and Rule 24, comment 3 on this difficult issue).
7. In determining whether the conditions precedent of a default judgment are met, the court will rely on the claimant's allegations. If the court has concerns that proceedings are irregular, it shall investigate on its own motion (*ex officio*) in order to prevent a gross injustice, e.g., a default judgment against a person who lacks capacity (see Rule 133(e)).

Rule 139. Application to set aside a default judgment

The party against whom a default judgment has been entered may apply to have the judgment set aside on the basis that

(a) any of the conditions precedent for entry of the default judgment were not met, or
(b) the party against whom the default judgment was entered was either not responsible for the default or the default was excusable.

Sources:
ALI/UNIDROIT Principle 15.5 and comment P15-F; Transnational Rules of Civil Procedure (Reporters' Study) Rule 15.7.

Comments:
1. In all systems the defaulting party has the right to set aside a default judgment obtained without compliance with its Rules. In some European jurisdictions, such a process is carried out at first instance, in other jurisdictions it is an appellate process. This Rule adopts the first instance approach. As such it means that a regular appeal, as well as all other means of recourse, against a default judgment are excluded.
2. A party can have a default judgment set aside only when the conditions precedent of a default judgment as set out in Rule 138 were not met or they can prove that they were not responsible for the default or that the default was excusable. In such cases, the proceedings can continue in the normal way once a defence has been filed.
3. This Rule only deals with a party's recourse against a default judgment in the strict sense. A claimant who had applied for a default judgment but whose claim was dismissed, be it on procedural grounds or on the merits, may appeal from the judgment by way of a regular appeal.

Rule 140. Time limit to apply to set aside a default judgment

(1) An application to set aside must be made within 30 days of the date of service of the default judgment. In cross-border cases, the application must be made within 60 days of the date of the service of the default judgment.

(2) The court may extend the time limit under Rule 140(1) where the defendant can show good reason for their non-compliance. No application to set aside can, however, be brought more than one year and, in cross-border cases, two years after the default judgment was entered.

Comments:
1. While there may be exceptional circumstances that justify a party's failure to apply to set aside a default judgment promptly (e.g., because the reasons for the failure to defend the claim are still operative), the time frames for setting aside a default judgment, as recognised in European national procedural codes, should be short.
2. It is, however, in the interests of legal certainty and finality of litigation that a default judgment cannot be set aside after a long period of time has elapsed whatever the reason for the delay. For this reason, this Rule provides a relative deadline, starting with effective delivery or service, and an absolute deadline starting with the day when the default judgment was entered. Article 19(4) of the ESR Regulation and Article 16 of the HCCH 1965 Service Convention establish similar safeguards for the situation that a judgment by default has been given and the defendant had not been able to respond in due time or to enter an appearance. Also see Draft Unified Patent Court Rules, Rule 355.

B. JUDICIAL SETTLEMENTS

Rule 141. Judicial settlements

(1) When parties reach a consensual settlement of their dispute, either before or after proceedings have commenced or during proceedings, they may apply to the court to enter a decision giving effect to the agreement.

(2) **A decision giving effect to the agreement shall not be entered if it is contrary to law or the court would not have the power to enter a judgment in the terms of the parties' agreement.**

(3) **If the court refuses to give effect to the settlement, any party to it can appeal from the refusal. The rules applicable to first appeals apply to such an appeal (See Part XI, Section 2).**

Comments:

1. The parties may jointly ask for a decision giving effect to a settlement agreement if the preconditions for such a decision are met. Rule 141 covers all cases in which actual or potential parties have reached an agreement, be it before or during court proceedings, it does not, however, preclude the use of any other available procedure for making party-agreements enforceable, e.g., notarial authentication of the agreement or recording the agreement in the protocol on court hearings according to national law. Rule 141 is compatible with Article 6 of the Mediation Directive.

2 As a court's decision will give effect to an agreement of the parties it presupposes the existence of a valid agreement. Therefore, a court may only render the decision applied for if the parties can validly dispose of the subject-matter of their agreement and if the requirements of its correct formation are met. Thus, for instance, an agreement entered into by one party under duress cannot be a basis for a consent judgment.

3. A court upon the joint application of the parties, need not exercise any control over the correct formation of the agreement in the absence of a specific reason for so doing. According to Rule 141(2) it may particularly, however, reject the parties' application for a decision giving effect to the agreement in two cases: if the agreement is contrary to law; or if the agreement is outside the court's power.

   a) An agreement is contrary to law only if its contents are not consistent with mandatory legal rules. A court is, however, not entitled to examine the adequacy of the agreement, i.e., to assess whether the agreement is a good or a bad bargain, against the background of dispositive or mandatory law. If, for example, a bank and its client agree, by way of settlement of a consumer loan, to an arrangement for interest to be paid and that is not permitted by mandatory law, the agreement will be void. It could also not form the content of the order of a court judgment. If, instead, both parties agreed on an arrangement which had similar financial consequences but which did not infringe any applicable mandatory law the court must give effect to such a settlement agreement without exercising control over the economic adequacy of the agreement that binds the parties (see also Preamble VI. 7). It will, generally, not be necessary for a court to refuse to give effect to a settlement agreement in the interest of enforcing mandatory law if the court had participated actively in the parties' settlement endeavours (see Rule 10(3) with comment 3).

   b) An agreement is outside the court's power if it could not order the parties to do something set out in the agreement or would not have the power to make the findings set out in the agreement. Private parties are not able to unilaterally enlarge the court's powers as defined by law. However, all systems recognise the value of allowing parties to reach a settlement that include matters not strictly covered by the legal dispute before the court, e.g., matters concerning a related dispute, or to include obligations that the court could not order the parties to do, e.g., to provide an apology. Therefore, where European jurisdictions provide for such mechanisms they should be preserved.

4. The effects of a decision giving effect to the agreement are not identical with those of a regular judgment. The decision giving effect to the agreement renders it enforceable.

However, the *res judicata* effect is still a matter of dispute and, if accepted, of minor importance (see Rule 148, comment 2).

5. If the court refuses to give effect to a settlement, a regular appeal is possible without further restrictions (Rule 141(3)), as there is an interest in having the dispute resolved whenever possible in accordance with the will of the parties (see Rules 9 and following on settlement endeavours).

SECTION 3—EFFECTS OF PENDENCY AND JUDGMENTS

INTRODUCTION

1. These Rules have been drafted without making a distinction between domestic and cross-border cases for the regulation of *lis pendens* and *res judicata*. No specific need for such a distinction was identified.
2. The goals of the Rules relating to *lis pendens* and to *res judicata* are identical. In both cases, the aim is to prevent irreconcilable or contradictory judgments from being rendered. In the case of pendency, the claim brought before a second court should therefore be stayed, dismissed or in some cases consolidated in order to prevent two courts from issuing judgments in the same dispute. In respect of *res judicata*, the second proceeding in which the same claim for relief is brought again shall be barred and declared inadmissible on the ground of the existence of a previous judgment (*ne bis in idem;* see Rule 22, comment 1).
3. The Rules opt for the conception of "cause of action" for *lis pendens* as developed by the European Court of Justice. The broad conception of the European Court of Justice has been adopted and extended to domestic cases as European Union Member States' courts are now accustomed to it through using it in cross-border cases. In respect of *res judicata*, the Rules prefer a less generous conception in so far as claim preclusion is affected. Though the goals of the Rules relating to *lis pendens* and to *res judicata* are identical, full congruence of the scope of the cause of action in both cases was not recommended by the majority of the members of the Working Group responsible for this Part. The effect of a broad conception of the cause of action is much more drastic *ex post* than *ex ante*. In the pre-commencement phase of proceedings, the parties are still able to adapt their procedural conception to secure the full concentration of their dispute with one court in contrast to the situation after rendition of the judgment, where the parties may be surprised by somewhat unclear and not always foreseeable consequences. Whereas the European Court of Justice's conception has developed clear contours over the last few decades in respect of *lis pendens*, the situation in respect of *res judicata* remains unclear and under-developed. The majority of European Union Member States' apex national courts have not changed their conception of restricted claim preclusion, although very narrow conceptions seem to be diminishing in use and the compromise preferred by these Rules seems to be gaining acceptance.

A. *LIS PENDENS* AND RELATED ACTIONS

Introduction

1. Pendency has been defined by the European Court of Justice on the basis of the 1968 Brussels Convention on jurisdiction and the enforcement of judgments in civil and commercial matters (the Brussels Convention) and the Brussels Ibis Regulation (see Articles 29 – 32 of the

Brussels Ibis Regulation). The concept has also been adopted by the other, more specific, European Union instruments on procedural law. While the European Court of Justice's case law has not been adopted in all European Union Member States for domestic cases, it has been followed by national courts in international cases. The European Court of Justice's case law demonstrates that the concept generally operates smoothly.

2. The concept of the Brussels Ibis Regulation is based on two major features: priority and the *Kernpunkt* case law of the European Court of Justice. Its objective is to permit the free movement of judgments by avoiding irreconcilable judgments. Its further objectives are the sound administration of justice via the avoidance of the segmentation of a dispute by parallel litigation. The *Kernpunkt* approach has two major disadvantages: an increased race to the court and the danger of abusive lawsuits.
3. The basic concept of Articles 29-32 of the Brussels Ibis Regulation can also be used in domestic cases. Here, the basic objectives are similar: permitting the sound administration of justice by avoiding the segmentation of a dispute by parallel litigation. The case law concerning Articles 29 – 32 of the Brussels Ibis Regulation demonstrates that the operation of the concept in international cases has not entailed major difficulties for the national courts. Some European jurisdictions also apply it to domestic cases. For an international instrument or model law which covers both settings, it can serve as a common denominator.
4. Rules 142 – 146 do, however, contain a refinement of the Brussels Ibis Regulation in regard to the legal consequences of pendency: Articles 29 – 32 of the Brussels Ibis Regulation only provide for two solutions: stay and dismissal. The court second seised must stay its proceedings until the court first seised has assumed jurisdiction. At that point in time, the proceedings in the court second seised are dismissed. This is a negative approach. A third, positive, alternative might be a consolidation of the different actions in the court first seised which requires the transfer of the parallel claim. This situation is found, with variations, in many national domestic settings. The transfer of a claim requires co-operation among the courts: the court first seised must be competent to hear the whole dispute and the transfer of the parallel claim must not delay the litigation. The procedural rights of the parties must be respected. All in all, a transfer and the consolidation of the claims are only possible at the very beginning of the dispute, i.e., at first instance. At later stages of the proceedings the alternatives are a stay of the later claim and the, eventual, dismissal of the parallel claim. This solution might also be appropriate in clear-cut cases of pendency. Alternatively, a stay of the proceedings in the court second seised might appear to be the better solution. Therefore, Rule 146 provides a mechanism for the consolidation of parallel claims at the outset of the proceeding.

Rule 142. Pendency

(1) Where proceedings involving the same cause of action and between the same parties are brought in different courts, any court other than the court first seised shall of its own motion stay its proceedings until such time as the jurisdiction of the court first seised is established (the priority principle).

(2) Where Rule 142(1) applies, the court seised of the dispute may request any other court seised to provide it with information about the proceedings pending before it and the date on which it was seised in accordance with Rule 145. The court providing the information shall provide it the requesting court without delay.

(3) **Where the jurisdiction of the court first seised is established, the court shall order parallel proceedings to be consolidated in accordance with Rule 146. Where proceedings have been consolidated, any court other than the court first seised shall decline its jurisdiction in favour of that court. When the requirements for consolidation are not met any court other than the court first seised shall, as appropriate, stay or dismiss the proceedings.**

Comments:

1. Rule 142 corresponds to Article 29 of the Brussels Ibis Regulation.[1] It provides for the priority principle (Rule 142(1)). Rule 142(2) enhances the obligation placed on courts to communicate with each other in order to facilitate the consolidation of the claims, as provided for as a possible legal consequence in Rule 142(3).
2. Rule 142(1) endorses the European Court of Justice's case law on the "same cause of action". Here, the following situations must be distinguished:
   (a) Identical claims (the basketball situation: claims for the same amount of monetary damages resulting from the same facts is brought in several courts because of uncertainty about jurisdiction). Some European jurisdictions solve the issue by providing for a transfer of the claim to the competent court. Rule 142(1) provides the solution: court A decides whether it has jurisdiction, courts B and C dismiss the proceedings brought before them once court A has assumed jurisdiction, or if court A declines jurisdiction they take jurisdiction accordingly).[2]
   (b) Action for performance/action for a negative declaration. The proceedings should be continued/litigated in the court first seised, by a counterclaim by the creditor for payment.[3]
   (c) Action for performance/action for a declaration of rescission of a contract. The proceedings should be continued/litigated in the court first seised, by a counterclaim by the creditor for payment.[4]
   (d) Action for a fund limiting liability/action for damages. In such cases, the same cause of action is not present (see Maersk), but see Article 29 of the Brussels Ibis Regulation (facts are identical, the legal rule is different).[5]

1 Also see Art. 27 of the 2007 Lugano Convention.

2 See CJEU, Judgment of 22 October 2015, Aannemingsbedrijf Aertssen and Aertssen Terrassements (C-523/14) ECLI:EU:C:2015:722. Attorney General *Bobek* criticised the fragementation of claims as a result of the application of the so-called mosaic principle (which permits the recovery of partial damages in the context of Art. 7 no 2 JR) in case C-194/16, *Bolagsupplysningen OÜ*, Conclusions of July 13, 2017, EU:C:2017:554, para 81. The ECJ (Grand Chamber) took up this critique and held that the mosaic principle no longer applies to infringements of personality rights in the internet, Judgment of 17 October 2017, Bolagsupplysningen and Ilsjan (C-194/16) ECLI:EU:C:2017:766.

3 CJEU, Judgment of 9 December 2003, Gasser (C-116/02, ECR 2003 p. I-14693) ECLI:EU:C:2003:657; CJEU, Judgment of 19 December 2013, Nipponka Insurance Co. (Europe) (C-452/12) ECLI:EU:C:2013:858.

4 CJEU, Judgment of 8 December 1987, Gubisch Maschinenfabrik / Palumbo (144/86, ECR 1987 p. 4861) (SVIX/00271 FIIX/00273) ECLI:EU:C:1987:528.

5 CJEU Judgment of 14 October 2004, Mærsk Olie & Gas (C-39/02, ECR 2004 p. I-9657) ECLI:EU:C:2004:615.

3. The broad concept of the "same cause of action" entails that litigation of the dispute (action for performance) in the court first seised should be possible. In the situations noted above, transfer should take place (Rule 146(3)).
4. Rule 142(2) provides for judicial co-operation. Judges should inform each other about proceedings filed in their courts and clarify the time of pendency, which is determined by Rule 145 and any relevant provisions on issuing proceedings (see Rule 52).
5. Rule 148(3) retains the consequence of Article 29(3) of the Brussels Ibis Regulation: dismissal of the proceedings filed after the court first seised assumed its jurisdiction and has consolidated the proceedings. If the consolidation fails, the court second seised must nevertheless dismiss the proceedings. However, in exceptional circumstances the court second seised may stay the proceedings and await the outcome of the proceedings in the court first seised in order to protect the rights of the parties.

Rule 143. Exceptions from the Priority Principle

(1) When the court second seised has exclusive jurisdiction, the court first seised must decline jurisdiction in favour of that court. In such a case the court that has exclusive jurisdiction must not stay its proceedings.

(2) Rule 143(1) does not apply when both courts have exclusive jurisdiction.

(3) Without prejudice to Rules protecting weaker parties and without prejudice to jurisdiction by appearance, where a court upon which an agreement confers exclusive jurisdiction is seised, any other court must stay proceedings until such time as the court seised on the basis of the agreement declares that it has no jurisdiction under it.

(4) Where the court designated in the agreement has established jurisdiction in accordance with the agreement, any other court shall decline jurisdiction in favour of that court.

Comments:

1. Rule 143 is primarily based on Article 31 of the Brussels Ibis Regulation and, partially, on Article 29 of the 2007 Lugano Convention. The priority principle presupposes that the court second seised does not have exclusive jurisdiction. In this case, there is no need to give priority to the court first seised, which lacks competence.[6] This exception, which is found in the case law of the European Court of Justice, has been formulated positively in these Rules.
2. Rule 143(2) corresponds to Article 31(1) of the Brussels Ibis Regulation.
3. Rules 143(3) and (4) correspond to Article 31(2)–(4) but formulate the prevalence of a jurisdiction clause in a broader way without direct reference to Article 25 of the Brussels Ibis Regulation and the specific provisions for the protection of weaker parties provided for in that Regulation.

Rule 144. Related Proceedings

(1) Where related proceedings are pending in different courts, any court other than the court first seised may stay its proceedings.

(2) Where the proceeding in the court first seised is pending at first instance, any other court must also decline jurisdiction if the court first seised has consolidated proceedings according to Rule 146.

6 See CJEU, Judgment of 3 April 2014, Weber (C-438/12) ECLI:EU:C:2014:212.

(3) For the purposes of this Rule, proceedings are deemed to be related where there is a relationship between the causes of action such that it would be in the interests of justice to determine them together.

Comments:

1. The basic structure corresponds to Article 30 of the Brussels Ibis Regulation.[7] Its objective is to provide for the proper administration of justice. Causes of actions are related when the outcome of one set of proceedings influences the outcome of the parallel proceedings. In a two-party constellation, Rule 144 applies where there is a partial overlap of causes of action, i.e., when the court seised first has only limited jurisdiction. As this Part endorses the European Court of Justice's broad conception of pendency, Rule 144 mainly addresses multi-party litigation where several claimants bring proceedings against the same (co-)defendant(s) based on the same facts, e.g., in product liability, unfair standard terms etc.
2. Rule 144(1) provides for a stay of the parallel proceedings. In multi-party situations, a stay of proceedings may also entail significant adverse consequences for the parties who must await the outcome of a parallel claim without being involved.[8] Therefore, the imposition of a stay is discretionary in order to protect party interests. A stay may be terminated once a transfer of the proceedings becomes impossible.
3. Dismissal of a claim is only possible on the application of the parties and after the consolidation of the proceedings (Rule 144(2)).
4. The structure of Rule 144(3) basically corresponds to Article 30(3) of the Brussels Ibis Regulation. As the wording of that article is closely connected to the recognition of judgments under Article 45 of the Regulation, Rule 145(3) endorses a broader wording which is found in a number of European jurisdiction's national procedural rules and which concern the proper administration of justice. However, in a cross-border setting, it clearly applies to the situation addressed by Article 30(3) of the Regulation where claims are so closely connected that it is expedient to hear and determine them together in order to avoid irreconcilable judgments resulting from separate proceedings.

Rule 145. Time at which a court is seised for the purposes of pendency and relatedness

(1) The court is deemed to be seised:

(a) at the time when the statement of claim or an equivalent document is filed with the court, provided that the claimant has not subsequently failed to effect service on the defendant according to these Rules, or

(b) if the statement of claim or an equivalent document has to be served before being filed with the court, at the time when it is received by an authority responsible for service, provided that the claimant has not subsequently failed to take steps required to file it with the court.

The authority responsible for service referred to Rule 145(1)(b) is the first authority that receives the documents to be served.

7 Also see Art. 28 of the 2007 Lugano Convention.

8 See ECJ, Judgment of 26 April 2012, Invitel (C-472/10) ECLI:EU:C:2012:242.

(2) Where a statement of claim is filed during proceedings it becomes pending at the time when it is invoked in the hearing or when it has been filed with the court or served on the other party.

(3) The court, or the authority responsible for service, referred to in Rule 145(1), shall note, respectively, the date the statement of claim or the equivalent document is filed, or the date of receipt of the documents to be served.

Comments:

1. As a matter of principle, Rule 145 follows the structure of Article 32(1) and (2) of the Brussels Ibis Regulation,[9] which builds on the different ways of serving proceedings in the European national law. This Rule provides objective and automatically applicable criteria of pendency.[10]
2. There are, however, additional instances of pendency, during pending proceedings, which are addressed by Rule 145(2). Rule 145(3) establishes an obligation of the courts to assess and document the relevant date.
3. There is a considerable body of European Court of Justice case law on the moment at which pendency takes effect, albeit it is mainly concerned with family matters.[11] Recently, the Court has, however, determined the moment of pendency in the case of mandatory mediation/conciliation proceedings in the context of the Lugano Convention.[12] Provisional measures for the preservation of evidence are not relevant for the determination of pendency. This case-law is relevant in terms of assisting in the interpretation of Rule 145.

Rule 146. Consolidation of Proceedings

(1) Where the jurisdiction of the court first seised is established, it may, upon application of one of the parties, order the consolidation of several sets of proceedings under Rules 142 and 144.

(2) The court first seised may only consolidate proceedings when it has jurisdiction to hear them and when such parallel proceedings are pending at the first instance.

(3) Before ordering consolidation the court shall hear the parties and communicate with any other courts seised.

(4) When the court first seised has assumed jurisdiction over the proceedings and has consolidated them, any other court must decline jurisdiction.

(5) Consolidation does not prejudice any procedural or substantive consequences of the filing or pendency of parallel proceedings.

(6) When consolidation is not possible in the court first seised, the court second seised may, on application of any party, consolidate the proceedings, as appropriate, under Rules 146(1)- (5).

Comments:

1. Rule 146 applies to pendency (Rule 142, see the situations listed in the comment) and to related actions (Rule 144). It mainly concerns those proceedings before the consolidating

9 And see Art. 27 of the 2007 Lugano Convention.

10 See ECJ, Judgment of 4 May 2017, HanseYachts (C-29/16) ECLI:EU:C:2017:343.

11 See, Art. 16 (1)(a) Council Regulation (EC) No 2201/2003 of 27 November 2003 concerning jurisdiction and the recognition and enforcement of judgments in matrimonial matters and the matters of parental responsibility, repealing Regulation (EC) No 1347/2000 (Brussels IIbis Regulation); ECJ, Order of 16 July 2015, P (C-507/14) ECLI:EU:C:2015:512, on court vacations and the moment of pendency.

12 See ECJ, Judgment of 20 December 2017, Schlömp (C-467/16) ECLI:EU:C:2017:993.

court, i.e., the court first seised. The court second seised cannot impose proceedings on the court first seised. The court second seised must stay its proceedings and then wait until the court first seised has decided the question of consolidation. If the court first seised does not consolidate the proceedings, the court second seised may either await the outcome of the proceedings in the court first seised, which is ordinarily the case in Rule 144, or dismiss the proceedings (Rule 142).

2. Consolidation operates on the application of the parties and shall be ordered in the interests of the proper administration of justice. Consolidation is discretionary; this permits the court first seised to decline consolidation when the proceedings have already progressed too far. Such a court shall inform the other courts seised directly about its decision on the issue of consolidation. Consolidation between different instances, e.g., first instance and appellate proceedings, is not foreseen in these Rules, although it may be permitted by national law.
3. Consolidation presupposes that the court has the competence to hear the claim (Rule 146(2)). Jurisdiction or competence may also be based on submission (entry of an appearance by the parties).
4. The decision to consolidate proceedings presupposes that the parties have been heard by the court. Consolidation should be prepared in virtue of increased communication among the judiciary due to their being under a duty to inform each other both about the moment of pendency and about the different pending proceedings. In order to overcome language barriers, it may be advisable to require use of a form concerning the most important information to be exchanged (Rule 146(3)).
5. Rule 146 does not prescribe the operation of consolidation itself. In domestic settings, parties may repeat their briefs and arguments in the court first seised, and the files might be transferred to the court that will determine the consolidated proceedings. In cross-border settings, parties will usually start anew the transferred proceedings in the court first seised according to the procedural rules and in the language of that court, notwithstanding procedural rules on preclusion. Where a negative declaration is sought, a creditor may bring a counterclaim for payment in the court first seised.
6. Once proceedings have been consolidated, the court second seised may dismiss the claim or declare it moot (Rule 146(4)).
7. Rule 146(5) makes it clear that consolidation is without prejudice to any substantial or procedural right which might have been acquired by the initiation of proceedings in the court second seised, e.g., the interruption of prescription by filing the claim.
8. If consolidation is not possible in the court first seised, particularly in those cases where the court first seised declines jurisdiction, each party may apply for consolidation in the court second seised. In this situation, Rules 146(1)–(5) apply accordingly. However, the court second seised must verify whether consolidation is possible and corresponds to the proper administration of justice.
9. For consolidation in those cases where there is no voluntary joinder (see Rule 37) Rule 146 applies accordingly.

B. *RES JUDICATA*

Rule 147. Types of judgment that become res judicata

(1) **Final Judgments, including partial judgments, default judgments, and judgments that decide procedural issues or issues on the merits are *res judicata.***

(2) **Provisional measures do not have *res judicata* effects on the merits of the issues in dispute in proceedings.**

Comments:

1. Rule 147 only applies to State court decisions. It is not intended to cover either arbitral awards or settlements reached after, for example, mediation or conciliation, and which are subject to Rule 141 (judicial settlement) and are therefore enforceable. A settlement has the binding force of a contract. A prior settlement may be raised in later litigation to bar the reopening of the legal issues agreed upon. However, such a settlement should not be considered similar to a judgment and subject to the rules on *res judicata*. This approach follows the distinction of Article 2(a)–(c) of the Brussels Ibis Regulation.
2. As far as consent judgments are concerned, they are subject to different approaches. However, this kind of judgment is not known in all Member States. In some jurisdictions, they become *res judicata*, whereas in others, a *jugement de donné acte* in which the court documents the settlement of the parties is not *res judicata*. Rule 147 opts for a liberal approach and leaves open the question of *res judicata* for such consent judgments.
3. Judgments dismissing the claim on procedural issues are, for instance, based on the lack of jurisdiction of the court seised, a lack of capacity of the party, lack of *locus standi*, absence of a clearly defined claim for relief. *Res judicata* operates only with regard to the procedural issue dealt with in the judgment (also see Rule 66, comment 4 applying accordingly).
4. Rule 147(2) makes it clear that provisional measures do not have *res judicata* effects on the merits of the main proceedings. This does not mean, however, that any *res judicata* effect of provisional measures is completely lacking. It is true that the competent court may modify the provisional measure according to changing circumstances. Lacking any change of circumstances, however, the court and parties are bound by the decision rendered. This may be considered a very restricted form of *res judicata*.

Rule 148. Judgments that are res judicata

A judgment is *res judicata* when ordinary means of recourse are not or are no longer available.

Comments:

1. A judgment becomes *res judicata* when a remedy is no longer possible or is no longer available, except as may be provided for in the particular and limited situations in which an extraordinary motion for review[13] can be established (see Rule 181). As long as a judgment has not become *res judicata*, if a second identical proceeding is brought before a court, the *lis pendens* rules should apply.
2. The concept of ordinary or extraordinary means of recourse varies from one European jurisdiction to another. For example, while in some jurisdictions a second appeal in civil matters is an ordinary means of recourse, in other jurisdictions, it is defined as an extraordinary one. For the purpose of Rule 148 and adopting a functional approach, ordinary means of recourse should be understood as an autonomous concept encompassing national ordinary and extraordinary means of recourse at second and third instance, i.e., appeal, but not a motion for extraordinary recourse in these Rules, which is set out in Rules 181 and following. *Res judicata* should operate where second and third instance means of recourse are either unavailable or inadmissible in principle or no longer available or admissible.

13 E.g., *recours en révision*, *Wiederaufnahme des Verfahrens*.

3. *Res judicata* of a court decision can, however, be challenged under exceptional circumstances through an extraordinary motion for review, see Rules 181 and following.

Rule 149. Material Scope of res judicata

(1) The material scope of *res judicata* is determined by reference to the claims for relief in the parties' pleadings, including amendments, as decided by the court's judgment.

(2) *Res judicata* also covers necessary and incidental legal issues that are explicitly decided in a judgment where parties to subsequent proceedings are the same as those in the proceedings determined by the prior judgment and where the court that gave that judgment could decide those legal issues.

(3) *Res judicata* also applies where a defendant brings a defence based on set-off and
(a) the claim and that defence are upheld by the court, or
(b) the claim is admitted and the defence of set-off is rejected.

(4) Where a claim is rejected on grounds other than set-off, so that the court does not decide the set-off defence, only the judgment on the claim becomes *res judicata.*

Sources:
ALI/UNIDROIT Principle 28.2.

Comments:

1. Rule 149 deals with the positive effect of *res judicata* binding parties and courts (for the negative or precluding effect see Rule 21, and particularly comment 1). According to Rule 149(1), the *res judicata* effect should only cover what the parties have brought before court, which is the logical consequence of the "*principe dispositif*" (*Dispositionsmaxime*).
2. Rule 149(2) extends the positive effect of *res judicata* to issue preclusion, or issue estoppel. The decision on the legal relationship whose existence and validity is logically presupposed by the decision on the parties' claims for relief should also be covered by *res judicata* because it is a prejudicial legal issue, i.e., an incidental and necessary legal Issue (a *question préalable*).

   This Rule only relates to legal relationships and issues, not to facts as facts by themselves cannot be the subject of a judicial declaration covered by *res judicata.* Incidental and necessary legal issues are the necessary legal steps to the conclusion of proceedings, its logical antecedents; the decision on the claim depends upon them. For example: the claimant claims for damages on the ground of a contract; the existence and the validity of the contract are incidental and necessary legal issues to be decided if there is a disagreement on them between the parties. *Res judicata* should only apply to incidental and necessary legal issues if: there has been a debate in the proceedings on them between the parties or the opportunity of a debate existed; there is an explicit decision of the judge on the incidental and necessary legal issues; and, the issue is a necessary reason for the decision itself. No distinction is to be made in this regard between the operative part of the judgment and its reasons. It would be easier to ascertain the precise material scope of *res judicata* if all incidental and necessary legal issues that have been decided by the court would be specified in the judgment (see Rule 131(f)). However, there are important differences in the drafting of court decisions among European jurisdictions. Therefore, it should be acknowledged, even though it can create legal uncertainty, that the reasons of the judgment can be *res judicata* on the legal issues decided in them even if they are not summarised in the operative part of the court decision. This explains why some European jurisdictions reject the idea that the reasons of a judgment become *res judicata.* In those jurisdictions the parties can request the court to extend *res judicata* to the reasons corresponding to a legal, but not factual, issue which has been the object of contention between them during the proceedings.

3. An incidental and necessary legal issue should be distinguished from a preliminary one. A preliminary issue must be solved before consideration of the merits, e.g., standing, jurisdiction (see Rules 65(2)(a), 66(1)(a)). Some civil law systems acknowledge the rule contained in Rule 149(2) for incidental and necessary legal issues which fall within the subject-matter competence of the court. Some national case law applies it with regard to the validity of a contract if this is an incidental and necessary issue to be solved by the court. Other jurisdictions reach similar results by permitting a generous scope to the effect of the judgment (see above) The concept of "incidental and necessary legal issue" is close to the notion of issue estoppel in English law. Issue estoppel does, however, seem to go further for *res judicata* based on estoppel also covers facts, which is not the case in Rule 149(2). There may be some question whether this Rule may contribute to procedural economy. Although Rule 149(2) may increase the burden of litigation, it does, however, aim to improve procedural economy through the logical extension of *res judicata* to issues which have been the object of an explicit determination in the operative part or in the reasoning of a judgment. Later additional litigation can thus be avoided.
4. Rule 149(2) applies to default judgments as well as to contested judgments. Two safeguards are provided for in the Rule: first, that there must be an explicit decision of the court on the necessary and incidental issue; and, second the court must have jurisdiction to rule on the necessary and incidental issue. In the framework of these Rules, default judgments are understood as being rendered after a genuine verification of the merits of the claim by the court.
5. The requirement stated in Rule 149(2) that the court had jurisdiction to decide the incidental and necessary legal issues means that the court would have had jurisdiction if the claim had been brought before it as a main claim in the proceedings. In numerous jurisdictions, there are two types of first instance courts depending on the value at stake. If the first claim is of low value, it can happen for example that the court seised will not have jurisdiction if the total amount at stake exceeds its financial jurisdictional limits. Another example is the situation in which the incidental and necessary legal issue falls under the jurisdiction of a criminal or an administrative court.
6. In some European jurisdictions, set-off is sometimes a mere defence, in others it is dealt with as a counterclaim. In some jurisdictions, a defendant is able to and can present set-off as a defence or as a counterclaim. Rule 149(3) does not contain any statement on the procedural nature of set-off, which should be left to national law. Rule 149(3) only aims to provide for a solution for those jurisdictions in which set-off is dealt with as a mere defence.

Rule 150. Modification of judgments requiring periodical performance

(1) Where a judgment that has become *res judicata* requires periodic performance, on application by a party, the court may vary the judgment prospectively.

(2) A judgment may only be varied under this Rule where there is a substantial change of circumstances.

Comment:

Rule 150 aims to take into account a possible change of circumstances where a judgment has decided issues that concern the performance of actions or of legal situations that extend over a period in time, such as periodical payments upon tort, e.g., in personal injury cases. Where a substantial change of circumstance occurs, a party (debtor or creditor, tortfeasor) should have the right to request a new court decision. This possibility is acknowledged by statute or case law in almost all European jurisdictions.

Rule 151. Persons bound by res judicata

Only parties to proceedings, the heirs and successors are bound by those parts of a judgment that are *res judicata.*

Comments:

1. Rule 151 refers to the subjective limits of *res judicata*. Only the parties to a proceeding and their heirs or successors should be bound by the *res judicata* effects of the judgment. This does not prevent judgments, e.g., those given in affiliation or in nationality matters or in the matter of invalidity of deliberations by corporations or legal persons, from being enforceable[14] against non-parties as regards their substantial legal effects, which is different from *res judicata*. This is particularly the case of a judgment creating or altering status.[15] Moreover, under national substantive law, there can be cases where other individual persons are bound by *res judicata*. These specific substantive law issues are, however, left to national law.
2. This Rule does not deal with redress in collective proceedings in relation with *res judicata* (see Part XI, which regulates all aspects of collective proceedings).

Rule 152. Court assessment of res judicata *of its own motion* (ex officio)

The court shall take *res judicata* into account of its own motion.

Comments:

1. As the bar resulting from *res judicata* is not only in the parties' interest but also in the interest of the authority of a State's judgments and the preservation of adjudicative resources, the court should be given the power and the duty to take *res judicata* into account on its own motion (*ex officio*) (see also Rule 133(d)). This is acknowledged by some European jurisdictions as a duty of the court, whereas others conceive of it as a power, not a duty.
2. A court will, however, often be unaware of the existence of a previous judgment that is *res judicata*. Consequently, the application of this rule can be difficult to put into practice. In most cases therefore, a party will raise the *res judicata* plea before the court.

14 *"Eentgegenhaltbar"*, *"Drittwirksamkeit"*.

15 See, *"jugement constitutif"*, *"Gestaltungsurteil"*.

PART IX

MEANS OF REVIEW

INTRODUCTION

1. This Part deals with appeals and other types of recourse including extraordinary motion for review. The ability to appeal from or otherwise challenge judgments is a well-established feature amongst procedural systems, albeit it is, in principle, not recognised by the European Court of Human Rights as falling within the ambit of the right to fair trial under Article 6 of the European Convention on Human Rights.

2. The present Rules adopt the approach that there is a right to appeal, albeit one that may—not always but in important cases—only be exercised with the permission of the appellate court according to special provisions with respect to access and scope. In this way the right to challenge a procedural or substantive judgment is to a certain degree one that rests upon the appellant satisfying a test that demonstrates that there is good reason to conclude that appeal is likely to succeed as proposed. In this way the appellate process, and the right to appeal, provides an effective balance between the principles of finality in litigation, accuracy in decision-making, expedition and proportionality. It also seeks to promote the public interest by ensuring that the appellate process does not undermine public confidence in the civil process and the judiciary. It does so by seeking to ensure that the appellate process is not accessed to too great an extent, which could lead to confidence in first instance courts and judiciary being undermined as well as to significant delay in proceedings being determined finally, which could lead to the judicial system as a whole being brought into disrepute. Too great a delay caused by too great a number of appeals through too ready access to the appellate process could equally undermine the right to receive a decision in a reasonable time, contrary to the Article 6 of the European Convention on Human Rights' right to fair trial, and thereby undermine the rule of law. Requirements of permission and admission are set at a level, however, that does not unduly restrict access to appeals, which in turn could reduce the ability of the appeal process to act as an effective corrective of first instance error as well as a means to promote effective decision-making at first instance through the prophylactic effect that access to appeal can produce.

3. Principle 27 of the ALI/UNIDROIT Principles addresses the necessity of keeping the right balance between diverging aspects of the rule of law as follows: "(2) The scope of appellate review should ordinarily be limited to claims and defenses addressed in first-instance proceeding. (3) The appellate court may in the interest of justice consider new facts and evidence". This Principle sets the framework for the Rules on means of review in this Part.

SECTION 1 - GENERAL PART

Rule 153. Right of appeal or to seek recourse

Where a party, or exceptionally a non-party, has a legal interest in a judgment, subject to the provisions in this Part, they may appeal from, or rely on other types of recourse against, it.

Sources:
ALI/UNIDROIT Principle 27.

ELI-UNIDROIT Model European Rules of Civil Procedure. ELI & UNIDROIT, Oxford University Press.
 DOI: 10.1093/oso/9780198866589.003.0010

Comments:

1. Legal interest is a general criterion for legal standing. It is also a continuous test that must be fulfilled at every stage of litigation. A party has a legal interest in appealing from a judgment, or seeking other forms of recourse from one, if they have a legitimate need to challenge it. Such a legitimate need would arise in circumstances where it can be said that the judgment to be challenged was the result of a procedural error, or was based on an inaccurate assessment of relevant facts or law, such that a different result ought to have been achieved. As such a party cannot appeal from or otherwise challenge a judgment simply because they disagree with the judgment's reasoning when they obtained the relief they sought. Nor can a party appeal from or challenge a judgment because they would prefer a broader legal reasoning, which could then be applied to a broad class of potential claims or cases and could thus deter future potential claimants from bringing similar claims. Nor can they do so simply because they would like to secure a judgment from a higher court, to thus achieve a judgment of a higher or more persuasive authority than that of the first instance court. Appeals and challenges are only permitted where a party wishes to secure a different substantive result from that obtained before the first instance court. A party also cannot appeal simply on the basis that they believe the first instance court's factual reasoning in the judgment is false or not based on the evidence. (See Rules 166, 172, and 177 on the basis on which parties can appeal.)
2. Non-parties may intervene in appellate proceedings applying the criteria in Rules 39-42. Exceptionally, they may also appeal from judgments where their legal rights are affected by the decision.

Rule 154. Waiver of right to appeal or to seek recourse

(1) A party may waive their right of appeal or to seek recourse. Waiver must be informed and express. Waiver may be given to the court in writing before or during a court hearing, or given orally in a court hearing.

(2) Waiver may be effected before a first instance judgment or other decision or a first appeal judgment is made. Such a waiver may only be made where it is agreed by all the parties.

(3) Where a party is bringing or defending proceedings as a consumer, they cannot waive their right to appeal before judgment has been made.

(4) All waivers must be recorded by the court in a judgment or other official record, if any.

Comments:

1. The right of appeal or other recourse may be waived. This is an aspect of the dispositive principle, i.e., it is an aspect of party procedural autonomy. Where the option to waive the right is exercised it also promotes certainty and stability in the parties' relations. It does so because all parties, and the court, are aware of the fact that there will be no possibility of an appeal being brought. From the court's perspective this may also help reduce the duration of litigation, enabling it to manage its resources more effectively.
2. Given the importance of a waiver to appeal and the significance of its effects on parties' procedural rights, Rule 154 renders its exercise subject to the formal requirements set out in Rules 154(2) and (4).
3. The right of waiver is subject to two significant limitations set out in Rules 154(3) and (4). First, in order to ensure that the parties are aware of the consequences of a waiver given before a judgment is given, they are all required to record their agreement to the waiver.

Secondly, in order to protect consumers, given that they may not be fully informed of the effects of waiver, they cannot waive this procedural right prior to rendition of judgment. This latter protection is analogous to that provided by Article 19 of Brussels Ibis Regulation and Article 17 of the 2007 Lugano Convention. The term consumer is to be defined very broadly (see generally Preamble VI. 6).

SECTION 2—APPEALS

Rule 155. Notice of appeal - General

(1) An appeal is commenced by way of filing a notice of appeal with the relevant court of Appeal.

(2) Upon being filed with the court, notice of appeal must be served on the respondent, in accordance with Part VI of these Rules.

Rule 156. Time limits for appeals

(1) For a first appeal, the notice must be filed with the court within one month of service of the judgment.

(2) For a second appeal, the notice must be filed with the court within two months of service of the judgment.

Sources:

ALI/Unidroit Principle 27.1.

Comments:

1. Rules 155 to 158 establish a two-step approach to the initiation of appellate proceedings.
2. First, Rules 155 and 156 require a notice of appeal to be filed with the appellate court, and then served upon the respondent to the appeal. The purpose of this first step is to inform the court and opposite party of the existence of the appeal. The notice need contain no more than the means to identify the judgment to be challenged on appeal, and a declaration from the appellant that they are appealing from that judgment.
3. Second, Rule 157 for first appeals and Rule 158 for second appeals (below) set out the second step in the initiation process. On a first appeal the two steps may be combined, i.e., the appellant may set out the content and reasons for the appeal, as required by Rules 157, at the same time and in the same document as the notice of appeal under Rules 155 and 156. For a second appeal the two steps required by Rules 155, 156 and 158 must be combined. This distinction reflects the more limited scope of second appeals, and hence requiring the two stages to be combined is consistent with procedural efficiency and proportionality (Rules 5 and 6) without imposing any adverse burden upon the appellant in terms of their ability to articulate the grounds of appeal within a shorter timeframe than that applied to first appeals.
4. Short time limits for filing the notice of appeal, and the supporting reasons, are provided to ensure that the appeal process is expeditious. (Also see Rule 165 on extension of time limits.)

Rule 157. Contents of the notice of and reasons for appeal – First Appeal

(1) A notice of appeal for a first appeal must state that an appeal is being commenced and must identify the judgment subject to the appeal. It may also provide reasons for the

appeal. Reasons for the appeal if not set out in the notice of appeal should be set out in a separate document.

(2) The reasons for the appeal must specify

(a) the relief sought;

(b) the legal arguments, substantive and procedural, on which the appeal is based in respect of both its admissibility and substance;

(c) if applicable, the grounds for which any evaluation of evidence was seriously wrong; and

(d) if applicable, any new facts to be alleged and new means of evidence that will be introduced in the appeal, and the reasons why they ought to be admitted.

(3) Where reasons for the appeal are set out in a separate document from the notice of appeal they must be served within two months of service of the judgment, unless the court orders otherwise.

Sources:
ALI/UNIDROIT Principle 27.

Comments:

1. Appellants, as with claimants generally, are required to articulate the reasons upon which their appeal is based. Such reasons can either be set out in the notice of appeal or in a separate document if they wish to do so (see Rules 155, 156 and 157(1) and (3)). Also see Rule 169 on the scope of a first appeal.
2. The appellant must specify the relief sought in either the notice of appeal or the separate document. This determines at an early stage of the proceedings the scope of the appeal for the purposes of Rule 167. This enables the parties to determine their approach to the appeal at an early stage and enables the court to properly consider its approach to managing the appeal effectively.
3. Rule 157(2)(d) must be read in conjunction with Rule 168. Where an appellant intends to introduce new facts, the reasons for the appeal must not only allege those facts, but must also specify that they may only be taken account of in accordance with Rule 168.
4. In complex cases, providing reasons for an appeal may take some considerable time; in simple cases, the opposite may be the case. As such Rule 157(3) provides both a default time limit for service of reasons for appeal where they are set out in a document separate from the notice of appeal, while providing the court with a discretion to vary that time limit. Parties may thus apply for a reduction or extension of the time limit. Such applications must be supported by reasons why the variation is said to be justified. (Also see Rule 165 on extension of time limits.)

Rule 158. Contents of the notice of and reasons for appeal – Second Appeal

(1) A notice of appeal for a second appeal must state that an appeal is being commenced and must identify the judgment subject to the appeal. It must also provide the reasons for the appeal.

(2) The reasons for the second appeal must contain:

(a) the relief sought;

(b) the legal arguments, procedural and substantive, on which the second appeal is based.

Sources:
ALI/UNIDROIT Principle 27.

Comments:

1. As noted in the comments to Rules 155, 156, Rule 158 has combined the two-step approach applicable to first appeals into a single step for second appeals. The notice of appeal on a second appeal must therefore contain the reasons on which the appeal is brought. As such notice of a second appeal will always be contained within a single document.
2. The scope of second appeal proceedings is narrower than that of a first appeal. As such the appellant is expected to be able to identify the grounds of appeal so as to be able to set them out within a single document. See Rule 174 on the grounds of appeal for a second appeal.

Rule 159. Response to the notice of appeal – General

(1) The respondent to an appeal must file with the court and serve on the appellant a reply to the notice of appeal (the reply) within two months of service of the notice of appeal, unless the court orders otherwise.

(2) The appellant must respond to the reply within two weeks of service, unless the court orders otherwise.

Sources:

ALI/Unidroit Principle 27.1.

Comments:

1. Rule 159 describes how the proceedings continue after the notice of appeal and the reasons of the appeal have been filed. It provides a longer time limit, albeit one that is still relatively short, to both provide the respondent with time to consider whether they wish to defend the first instance judgment that was in their favour, to marshall their arguments, and to do so in a way that is consistent with the intention of ensuring that appeal proceedings progress expeditiously. As such it seeks to promote a fair appeal process. (Also see Rule 165 on extension of time limits.)

Rule 160. Contents of a respondent's reply

A reply may contain the following

(a) reasons why the appeal court should uphold the judgment subject to appeal; or

(b) notice of and reasons for appeal from the judgment subject to appeal, which seek to uphold the judgment for different reasons to those given in the judgment. Rule 157(2) and Rule 158(2) apply according to whether the reply concerns a first or second appeal.

Comments:

1. A respondent to an appeal may respond to the notice and reasons for the appeal in a number of ways. Rule 160 articulates two possible responses.
2. Rule 160(a) sets out what might be expected to be the general approach; that the respondent provides reasons why the first instance decision under appeal should be upheld, i.e., why the appeal court should reject the appellant's arguments.
3. Rule 160(b), which may be combined with the approach in Rule 160(a), enables a respondent to set out further reasons why the first instance decision under appeal should be upheld. These reasons could be such as had been rejected by the first instance court. They may also, exceptionally, be on fresh grounds, i.e., ones not argued before the first instance

court. In the latter case, permission from the appeal court would be needed in order to argue such new and additional grounds (see Rules 22(1) and 168; the latter where the new grounds concern additional facts and evidence).

4. Some legal systems provide the respondent with the ability to agree to allow the appeal and thus set aside the judgment under appeal. This may be done either on the respondent's own initiative or it may be done following a consensual settlement process. If the latter, the parties to the appeal ought to apply for a case management direction from the appeal court seeking a stay of the appeal proceedings pending the outcome of such a process. This issue is left to national legislation, as agreement was not reached on the question of including this form of facilitation of settlement within these Rules.

Rule 161. Derivative appeals

(1) A party that has lost their right of appeal due to the expiry of the time limit for filing a notice of appeal in Rule 156(2), may appeal if another party (the appellant) appeals from the judgment.

(2) The party bringing a derivative appeal (a derivative appellant) must serve a Notice of Appeal. Rules 156 – 159 apply accordingly.

(3) A derivative appeal lapses if the appellant's appeal is not heard on its merits.

(4) A respondent to a derivative appeal must file a response to it. Rules 159-160 apply accordingly.

Comments:

1. Rule 161 permits a party that could have appealed from a judgment to do so after the time limit for filing an appeal has expired. It does so only, however, where another party has appealed from the judgment, and hence it does not undermine the principle of finality in so far as that is given effect by procedural time limits. Such an appeal is known as a derivative appeal.
2. A common instance where a derivative appeal can be pursued is where both parties prevailed with their claims for relief in part and lost in part. In such circumstances, where an appeal has been filed and the respondent has not brought their own appeal from the judgment within the time limit for bringing an appeal, they may still bring a derivative appeal upon the other party filing their notice of appeal. Hence the appeal is derivative upon another party having already appealed from the judgment. Any appeal that is filed within the normal time-limits for appealing, set out in Rule 156(2) is outside the scope of this Rule: it is an appeal and not a derivative appeal.
3. Rule 161(3) provides for a derivative appeal to be dependent upon the "main" appeal, i.e., the one upon which it depends, continuing and being heard on its merits. If the main appeal is withdrawn or settled or otherwise does not proceed to be heard and determined on its merits, the derivative appeal lapses.
4. Once a derivative appeal has been filed with the appeal court, the general rules for appeals apply to it.

Rule 162. Provisional enforcement

(1) Unless otherwise provided for, final judgment and any appellate court judgments are enforceable immediately regardless of whether an appeal has been commenced by filing a notice of appeal.

(2) **An appellant may apply to the appellate court to stay enforcement if they have filed a notice of appeal and enforcement is manifestly excessive.**
(3) **Security may be required from an appellant as a condition of granting a stay or from a respondent as a condition of refusing to grant a stay.**

Sources:
ALI/UNIDROIT Principle 26.

Comments:
1. Judgments should be enforceable from the date that they are given. Immediate enforcement is not, however, final. Where, for instance, a judgment is reversed on appeal, enforcement must be undone. Immediate enforcement does, however, protect the legitimate interest of the party in whose favour the first instance judgment was made, i.e., it protects them from the risk of defendant insolvency or the adverse effects of delay in enforcement.
2. Immediate enforcement may, however, be inappropriate where an appeal is filed, as the possibility then exists that the first instance judgment being challenged may be reversed and it may not be possible to undo the consequences of enforcement. By way of example, if a judgment requires a defendant to demolish a building or sell a piece of art. In such cases, the court may, on the application of the party against whom enforcement is sought, order a stay.
3. In order to balance the risk of immediate enforcement or of a stay of enforcement, the court may require security to be given by one of more parties.
4. If the party against whom the first instance judgment was made cannot satisfy the judgment nor provide security, that does not affect the appeal as any stay of enforcement would not put the party in whose favour the first instance judgment was given at a disadvantage.

Rule 163. Withdrawal

(1) **A party that has commenced a first appeal can withdraw their appeal at any time.**
(2) **A second appeal can only be withdrawn by a party with the consent of the other party and the court.**
(3) **A party that withdraws an appeal must bear the costs, including any court fees, incurred by other parties because of the appeal.**

Sources:
ALI/UNIDROIT Principle 10.5.

Comments:
1. The right to withdraw an appeal or other recourse is a specific instance of the dispositive principle, of party autonomy. Withdrawal can only be effected before the decision upon an appeal or recourse has been pronounced by the court.
2. As a general rule where a party withdraws an appeal, they must bear the costs, including any court fees, incurred by other parties because of the appeal. (Also see Rule 244.)
3. In so far as second appeals are concerned, a party's right to withdraw is limited by Rule 163(3). Withdrawal may only take place with the consent of the other parties and the court. This protects the other party's interest in respect of its investment in the appeal process, and more importantly in the public interest in having the appeal decided. Withdrawal must also be carried out consistently with the obligation placed on the parties to act in good faith (see Rule 3(e)).

Rule 164. Representation in an Appeal Court

(1) If representation is not mandatory according to applicable law, a first appeal court may require a party to be represented by a lawyer if they are incapable of representing themselves in an understandable manner or if it is necessary for the proper administration of justice.

(2) Parties must be represented by a lawyer in proceedings before a second appeal court.

Sources:
ALI/UNIDROIT Principle 4.

Comments:

1. Appeal proceedings before a second appeal court only deal with questions of law. As such, they generally require expert argument, which a non-lawyer would not typically be expected to be able to provide. Rule 164(2), in contrast to Rule 164(1), thus requires parties to second appeals to be represented by a lawyer. These Rules do not contain a similar requirement for first appeals, although representation is mandatory according to many European national laws (see Rule 14 comment 1); the court may, however, require representation where the appeal raises complex issues of law or fact, or the proper administration of justice so requires it.
2. Under Rule 164(1) the court will consider a party to require legal representation where they are unable to formulate the relief sought or present their appeal's legal or factual grounds adequately. In determining whether this is the case the court must consider any submissions on the question of representation set out by other parties to the appeal. The court's decision that representation is required, as a case management decision, can itself be challenged (see Rule 178).
3. Where legal representation is required it ought to be funded from the legal aid scheme due to the public interest inherent in the circumstances set out in Rules 164(1) and (2) that mandate legal representation. (See Rule 244.)
4. Some countries restrict the ability of lawyers to act before appellate courts, and particularly Supreme courts, to specific types of or specifically qualified lawyers. This Rule is silent on this issue, and neither excludes nor prescribes that any particular type or class of lawyer may represent a client before an appeal court, and particularly before a second appeal court. It is a matter for national regulation.
5. On representation of parties generally see Rule 14, comments 1 and 2.

Rule 165. Extension of deadlines – non-domiciled parties

Where a party is not domiciled in the State whose court is seised of the proceedings, any time limit applicable to an appeal is extended by one month unless the court provides otherwise.

Comments:

1. Rule 165 acknowledges the fact that in cross-border litigation a party not domiciled in the State whose court is seised of the proceedings may need additional time to prepare a proper appeal or defence.
2. This extension should only apply to parties not domiciled in the State whose court is seised of the proceedings as they are the party at a procedural disadvantage due to their domicile. In those cases where only one of the parties is domiciled in the State whose court is seised, a broader justification of this rule is to reduce the home court advantage.

SECTION 3 – FIRST APPEALS

Rule 166. Right to appeal

(1) A party has a right to appeal against a first instance judgment if

(a) the value of the appealed claim exceeds [the value of the appealed claim as determined by applicable law, for instance twice the average monthly wage in the forum State] or

(b) the appeal court grants permission to appeal based on the contents of the notice and reasons for appeal.

(2) In deciding whether to grant permission to appeal, the appeal court shall take the following into account

(a) whether the legal issue in dispute is of fundamental significance, or

(b) the further development of the law, or the public interest in securing uniform adjudication require an appellate decision, or

(c) fundamental procedural requirements have been violated.

(3) The appeal court shall, on its own motion, assess whether the requirements of Rules 166(1) and (2) have been met.

Sources:
ALI/UNIDROIT Principle 27.

Comments:

1. A balance must be struck between the private and public interest in the right to appeal from a decision, the principle of finality of justice in a reasonable time and cost to both the parties and the State. If there was unrestricted access to the appellate process that balance would not be struck effectively. It would facilitate the growth of an approach to first instance proceedings that treated them as being no more than "test proceedings", in which the parties could rehearse their arguments and evidence. It would consequently devalue the status of first instance proceedings, undermining public confidence in the civil justice system, while also imposing a disproportionate cost burden on parties and the State. For this reason, these Rules restrict the right of appeal and the scope of the appeal. Rule 166(1) articulates those restrictions so as to balance effectively the various public interests.
2. It should be noted, however, that Rule 166 must be read together with Rules 167 to 169, which detail the scope of a first appeal. Rule 166 only concerns the first step of a detailed procedure that limits access to a first appeal to have the first instance judgment reconsidered. As a second step, Rule 167 limits such reconsideration by the appellate court to the relief sought by the parties at first instance. Exceptionally, and only with the agreement of all parties or with grant of permission by the appellate court, will amendments be allowed. Rules 168 and 169, provide a third step. They restrict consideration of new facts or new means of evidence by the appellate court: to cases where knowledge of those matters was absent at first instance notwithstanding the parties having conducted the proceedings properly; to cases where they were only available after the final hearing in the first instance court; or, to cases of procedural error or deficient management caused by the first instance court and challenged in due time, however, but not corrected at first instance.
3. The system of requirements, set out in the Rules, for a case to be reconsidered either partially or fully at a first appeal tries to combine the most promising elements of the development of the law on the appeal process in the different European procedural cultures.

While it may appear that continuing national differences provide insurmountable barriers to the identification of common ground for development in Europe, most European codes of civil procedure provide a remarkable number of elements in common concerning restrictions on access to the appellate process. Nevertheless, a careful analysis demonstrates that European national codes can be divided in three groups. On the one hand, English law, as other common law systems do, tends to limit access to appellate reconsideration by a general requirement of permission to appeal, which has to be granted by either the first instance court or the appellate court.[1] A large number of the fundamental criteria for granting permission to appeal in common law systems are similar, or even identical, to the requirements for appellate review formulated in these Rules. Judicial practice in determining applications for permission to appeal, however, provides by focusing on the question whether a proposed appeal has a real prospect of success a more restrictive approach than is currently the case in continental European jurisdictions. In the common law tradition, such decisions are not made on the basis of detailed or even sophisticated rules. On the contrary, they are exercised within a framework of broad judicial discretion, which determines in one step general admissibility and the scope of review, e.g., the issues to be subject to appellate review. In contrary to the common law approach, some countries like France[2] do not accept restrictions regarding new facts and new means of evidence, such as those contained in these Rules. As a consequence, appeals in such countries, in a remarkable number of cases, result in a full *de novo* hearing. The third approach, which is in contrast to these two clear approaches, the one restrictive the other generous in approach, is seen in an increasing number of European States.[3] This, third, approach prefers solutions that try to strike a balance. They take a middle route, as chosen by these Rules.

4. Judicial practice of appellate review can differ even between courts within the same country when they apply the same procedural provisions. This phenomenon may be increasing where courts in different countries interpret and apply the same rules in individual cases, not least as a consequence of their varying legal and judicial traditions, e.g., if they have a tradition of civil jury trials or a history of judges adopting a more active or passive approach to case management. This may be particularly true where first appeals are based on infringements of the court's duty to monitor compliance with procedural rules and failures to invite parties to correct any defects in their presentation of their cases; a situation, which may not be very rare under these Rules as they are governed by the principles of active court management and cooperation between court and parties. Differing European national judicial culture and practice concerning the nature and seriousness of such procedural errors and their consequences will, however, no doubt contribute to a slow and gentle transition towards a more harmonised approach to permission to appeal in respect of procedural errors. At the present time, remaining differences in approach should not be viewed as seriously as they would following a period of harmonisation based on the conceptions of the present Rules.

1 See, e.g., for details CPR Part 52 with PD 52 A to 52E. See, however, for the apparently smaller significance of leave to appeal and the somewhat broader scope of appellate reconsideration in the Republc of Irland Order 101 of the District Court Rules and Order 86A of the Rules of Superior Courts.

2 See especially Arts. 561, 563, 564 and following French CCP.

3 See, e.g., §§ 468, 482 Austrian CCP; §§ 529, 531 German CCP; Art. 459 and following Spanish LCP; Norwegian Dispute Act (*Lov om mekling og rettergang i sivile tvister (tvisteloven)*) § 29-21; Swedish CJP § 50:28; Art. 345 Italian CCP; Swiss CCP Arts. 310 and 317; see, however, comment 4 above.

5. Rule 166(1)(a) provides for a right of appeal in claims of significant financial value, with the value being the difference between the first instance judgment and the relief sought by the appealing party before the first instance court. Rule 166(1)(b) provides for a right of appeal in other cases where there is either no or no sufficient financial value or its financial value is difficult or impossible to determine. Rule 166(1)(b) then provides for the appellate court to consider whether it ought to grant permission to appeal having assessed the circumstances set out in Rule 166(2). Rules 166(2)(a) and (b) provide for those cases in which there is, in addition to the appellant's private interest in corrective justice, a public interest in there being an appellate decision. Rule 166(2)(c) secures both the private and public interest in ensuring that the appellate process is available where there have been significant, i.e., fundamental, breaches of procedural rights.
6. Rule 166(3) specifies that permission to appeal may only be granted by an appellate court. While it must carry out this assessment of its own motion (*ex officio*), parties have a right to be heard on the matter before a final decision is taken (see Rules 11, 12 and 16).

Rule 167. Scope of a first appeal

(1) A first appeal can be brought against the whole, or part, of a first instance judgment.
(2) In general, the relief sought is limited by what was claimed or defended at first instance.
(3) However, the relief sought may be broadened or amended within a first appeal if
(a) all parties to the appeal consent, or
(b) the court considers it appropriate for the proper administration of justice.

Sources:
ALI/UNIDROIT Principle 27.2.

Comments:

1. It is for the parties, and not the court, to decide whether to appeal and if so in respect of which issues. This is an aspect of the dispositive principle, and hence of party autonomy.
2. An appeal against part of a judgment means an appeal against an aspect of the operative part of the judgment, and not an appeal against the court's reasoning. An appeal against part of a judgment is only possible if it is separable from the remainder of the judgment. For example, an appeal against a judgment declaring that the claimant is a shareholder in a corporation may not be challenged in order to try to secure a declaration that the claimant might or could be, rather than is, a shareholder. The judgment could, however, be challenged in part if it had declared the claimant was a shareholder and held 'x' number of shares and the challenge was to the finding concerning the number of shares held.
3. Rule 167(2) limits the relief that can be sought on an appeal to that which was in issue at first instance. This protects the parties' interests on the appeal, as it is intended to ensure that the appeal process does not undermine the principle of concentration (Rule 47). Where there is good reason to permit a widening of the issues, the issues may be broadened on the appeal from that which was before the first instance court: see Rule 55(1). In considering whether to grant such an amendment the appellate court must consider the effect that that would have on the other party to the appeal in so far as it would deprive them of the opportunity to bring an appeal from its substantive decision on the new issues. In order to protect the other party's interest, Rule 167(3) allows an extension or amendment either when both parties consent to it or when such a step is required for the proper administration of justice. This is consistent with the approach taken to waiver (see Rule 154).

4. In determining whether it is in the interests of the proper administration of justice to amend the scope of the appeal beyond the issues that were before the first instance court under Rule 167(3)(b), the appellate court should take account of the following: the absence or not of negligence of the party who seeks to broaden or amend its claim, namely whether allegations could have been raised in the first instance proceedings; the procedural rights of the other party, namely the extent of the effect on them of being deprived of the right to have the issues considered at first instance; and, the existence of a close connection with what was dealt with in the first instance proceedings, namely the extent to which all necessary facts and evidence concerning the proposed new issues were considered in those proceedings.

Rule 168. New facts and taking evidence

(1) Within the relief sought, the appellate court shall consider new facts alleged by the parties
- **(a) in so far as those facts could not have been introduced before the first instance court, or**
- **(b) in so far as the first instance court failed to invite the parties to clarify or supplement facts that they had introduced to support their claim or defence under Rules 24(1) and 53(3).**

(2) Within the relief sought, the appellate court shall take evidence offered by the parties only if
- **(a) the evidence could not have been offered to the first instance court;**
- **(b) the evidence was offered to the first instance court and was erroneously rejected or could not be taken for reasons outside the party's control; or**
- **(c) the evidence concerns new facts admissible according to Rule 168(1).**

Sources:
ALI/Unidroit Principle 27.3.

Comments:
1. Appellate proceedings are generally by way of review (see Part IX, Introduction, comment 2). This Rule, however, provides the basis for the proceedings to consider new facts and, where necessary, take evidence. As such it provides a basis for the court to go beyond a strict review jurisdiction.
2. New facts may, and must, be considered only insofar as they could not have been introduced before the first instance court or insofar as the first instance court failed to invite parties to clarify or supplement facts (Rule 24(2)). This limitation ensures that parties cannot withhold facts and evidence as part of their litigation strategy. It also ensures that parties take proper account of, and comply with, the concentration principle (see Rule 22).
3. Where evidence is not readily accessible, the court will normally ensure steps are taken to adduce it (see Part VII). However, if the evidence cannot be adduced in a reasonable time period, in order to promote finality in litigation, the court may enter judgment without having taken it into account.

Rule 169. Scope of appellate review – first appeal

(1) Within the relief sought, the appellate court's review shall encompass
- **(a) the application of the law in the judgment;**

(b) the legality of the proceedings in the first instance court, provided that the appellant challenged the error complained about immediately before the first instance court if such challenge was possible;

(c) evaluation of the evidence if the appellate court determines that such a review is warranted in order to prevent serious injustice.

(2) The appellate court will reverse a first instance judgment for procedural error only if it potentially influenced the judgment or if it was so grave that such influence need not be proven.

Comments:

1. Appeals are primarily by way of review (see Part IX, Introduction 2). Rule 169 specifies the scope of such a review.
2. In Rule 169(1)(b), "challenged" must be understood in a broad sense, such that it is sufficient to encompass procedural errors. "Immediately" means that the challenge was pursued with alacrity, i.e., at the earliest possible occasion. This takes account of the fact that a party may reasonably recognise that there has been an arguable procedural error only upon receipt of the court's final judgment. In such a case, there is no need to challenge the error in the first instance court (see Rule 178).
3. Challenges to the first instance court's evaluation of the evidence is limited, by Rule 169(1)(c), to serious errors. These include violation of basic rules of logic, a failure to take account of evidence, or an arbitrary approach to evidential assessment.

Rule 170. First appeal court decisions

(1) In general, the appellate court shall decide the matter that forms the substance of the appeal.

(2) The appellate court may refer the matter back to the first instance court, if necessary, for it to decide the matter.

(3) If the parties to the appeal agree to it, the appellate court must decide the matter.

Sources:

ALI/UNIDROIT Principle 27.1.

Comments:

1. An appeal court is entitled to reverse, vary and/or confirm the judgment under appeal in part or in full.
2. As a general rule, and in order to promote procedural efficiency and proportionality, an appellate court ought to determine the matter on appeal itself. It should do so whether or not new facts are alleged, and fresh evidence is adduced in conformity with Rule 168. However, an appellate court should, exceptionally, refer a matter back to a first instance court. This may be an appropriate approach where, for instance, a first instance court would be a better forum for the assessment of evidence, where the appeal court determines that a re-trial is justified whether on grounds of efficiency, expedition, cost or due to its being the optimum forum to determine the matter, or the appeal concerned a first instance court's ruling on a procedural issue, such as the admissibility of the action.
3. Rule 170 also applies to decisions on jurisdiction, both in terms of whether the courts are competent to hear the proceedings at all, or in respect of the question whether the courts of another jurisdiction are the proper forum.

4. In specific cases, the appellate court may limit itself to declare that the judgment under appeal is null and void without referring it back to the first instance court. It may do so, for instance, where it concludes that the first instance court did not have jurisdiction to hear the proceedings.

Rule 171. Contents of the First Appeal Court's judgment

In so far as it agrees with the first instance court's judgment, the appellate court's judgment may refer to the legal and factual grounds in that judgment. It may also set out its own reasons in its judgment. In the latter case, the appellate court is deemed to have adopted the legal and factual grounds of the first instance judgment which are not contrary to its own reasoning.

Sources:
ALI/UNIDROIT Principle 27.1.

Comments:
1. Appellate court judgments must, as a general rule, conform with the requirements applicable to the contents of judgments (see Rule 131).
2. Rule 171, however, modifies the general rule. In respect of the legal and factual grounds of its judgment, an appellate court is permitted to either set out its own reasoning on them or, where it agrees with or upholds the first instance court's reasoning it may incorporate them expressly into its own judgment. This latter alternative is intended to reduce the appellate court's workload, where in effect all it would have to do would be to rephrase the first instance court's reasoning.

SECTION 4 – SECOND APPEALS

Rule 172. Right to a second appeal

(1) A party may only appeal from a first appeal judgment if such an appeal is necessary to
- **(a) correct a violation of a fundamental right,**
- **(b) secure uniformity in the law,**
- **(c) decide a fundamental question which is not limited to the case at issue, or**
- **(d) develop the law.**

(2) A second appeal court shall, on its own motion, assess whether the requirements of Rule 172(1) have been met.

Sources:
ALI/UNIDROIT Principle 27.2; Transnational Rules of Civil Procedure (Reporters' Study) Rule 33.5.

Comments:
1. Second appeals are primarily concerned with the public interest. Access to second appeals must therefore be limited to those cases that raise fundamental, important questions of general importance. As such it is limited to questions that concern fundamental rights, the need to secure uniformity in the law where, for instance, lower courts have adopted divergent approaches to legal interpretation, to legal issues the effect of which goes beyond the

immediate proceedings, and developments in the law. Were second appeals to be readily accessible, the risk would arise that this generous access too would add to legal uncertainty and undermine the proper functioning of the legal system.

2. Rule 172(1)(a) concerns the articulation and protection of fundamental rights. As such its focus is on the private interest of aggrieved parties, additionally, however, on the general public interest of ensuring the proper application of and respect for such rights as well as the providing of a corrective to lower courts and their interpretation and application of such rights. Fundamental rights, whether they are substantive or procedural rights, are, in particular, those rights guaranteed in the European Convention on Human Rights, the 1966 International Covenant on Civil and Political Rights, national constitutions, national legislation, and, insofar as applicable, the 2000 European Charter of Fundamental Rights.
3. Rules 172(1)(b) and (c) acknowledge that even in legal systems that do not adopt *stare decisis* or a binding system of precedent, second appeal court judgments are normally respected by all or at least most lower courts and the legal community in general. This arises from the need to secure legal uniformity and certainty when two or more lower courts, whether they are first instance or appellate courts, have decided a legal question in different ways. Law refers to all forms of law, constitutional, statutory and case law.
4. In Rule 172(1)(c) "fundamental" refers to matters that are important for the correct interpretation and for general public application of an existing rule. In this constellation, it is not necessary that there have already been diverging decisions of lower courts.
5. Rule 172(1)(d) provides for the situation where there is a need to develop the law if existing legal rules, be they statutory or case law, do not provide guidance for a new situation, and this situation is so important for the society as a whole that general guidance from the apex appellate court is warranted to remedy legal uncertainty.

Rule 173. Scope of a second appeal

(1) A second appeal can be brought against the whole, or part, of a first appeal judgment.
(2) The relief sought is limited by what was claimed or defended in the first appeal.

Comments:

1. Second appeals have a narrower scope than first appeals. In addition to being limited by the scope of the first appeal (Rule 173(2)), they are limited by the nature of the appellate review, which is articulated in Rule 174.

Rule 174. Scope of appellate review – second appeal

(1) Within the relief sought, as far as admissible, the second appeal court's review shall encompass
  (a) the interpretation and application of the law in the first appeal judgment;
  (b) the legality of the proceedings in the first appeal court, provided that the appellant challenged the error complained about immediately before that court.
(2) The second appeal court will reverse the first appeal judgment for a procedural error only if the procedural error has potentially influenced the judgment or if it was so serious that such influence need not be proven.

Comments:

1. The scope of second appeals is more limited than that of first appeals. Rule 174(1)(a) articulates the fundamental purpose of such appeals: to correct the interpretation of substantive or procedural law by the lower courts, and particularly by the first appellate court.

2. Rules 174(1)(b) and 174(2) concern the situation where the integrity of the first appeal judgment was undermined by a serious procedural error on the part of the first appellate court, i.e., where a judge who ought to have recused themselves failed to do so, or the publicity principle was not properly respected (see Rule 17). (Also see Rule 181 on re-opening proceedings.)

Rule 175. Second Appeal Court decisions

(1) The second appeal court shall determine the substantive issue before it if

(a) it is to reverse the first appeal judgment having held that there had been a violation of the law, and

(b) it has concluded that it can determine the issue.

(2) In all other circumstances, the second appeal court must refer the matter back to the first appeal court for it to finally determine the matter. In such a circumstance, the first appeal court is bound by the second appeal court's assessment of the law.

Sources:

ALI/UNIDROIT Principle 27.1.

Comments:

1. The second appeal court is entitled to reverse, amend and/or confirm the first appeal court's judgment. It may do so either in part or in full.
2. As a general rule, the second appeal court once it has determined the issue before it (see Rule 174), should refer the matter back to the first appeal court to finally determine it, e.g., by applying the law as stated by the second appeal court. In the limited circumstances provided for in Rule 175(1), the second appeal court must go on to determine the matter itself. This approach is justified both in terms of proportionality and efficiency in procedure.
3. When the second appeal court refers the matter back to the first appeal court, it will ordinarily be heard by the same panel or judge of that court which determined the appeal originally. The second appeal court may refer the matter back to a different panel or judge of the first appeal court in special circumstances. It could do so, for instance, where it holds there to have been a procedural error under Rule 174(2), which would render it inappropriate to refer the matter back to the same panel or judge, e.g., where bias has tainted the decision. National jurisdictional rules concerning the relations between courts should also be taken account of in determining how the jurisdiction under Rule 175(2) should be exercised.

Rule 176. Contents of the Second Appeal Court's judgment

A second appeal court must provide its own reasons in its judgment. If they are adequate, it may refer to the reasons given in the first appeal court's or the first instance court's judgment.

Sources:

ALI/UNIDROIT Principle 27.1.

Comments:

1. Second appeal judgments must, as a general rule, conform with the requirements applicable to the contents of judgments (see Rule 131).
2. Rule 176, however, modifies the general rule and provides a second appeal court with the discretion to simply adopt the first appeal court or first instance court's reasons as its own reasons where it upholds their decisions for the reasons they articulated in their judgments.

Rule 177. Leapfrog appeal

(1) Instead of a regular appeal to the first appeal court, an appeal may be brought directly to the second appeal court (a leapfrog appeal).

(2) A second appeal court may only grant permission to bring a leapfrog appeal if

(a) an appellant applies directly to it to bring such an appeal, setting out its reasons why permission should be granted, and does so within the time limits applicable to a first appeal;

(b) the appellant's application complies with Rule 158;

(c) the requirements of Rule 172(1) are met.

(3) An appeal under this rule is deemed to be a second appeal, and the Rules applicable to second appeals apply accordingly.

Comments:

1. The ability to bypass an appellate court and bring an appeal directly to the jurisdiction's apex appellate court exists in a number of jurisdictions, such as the United Kingdom. Such appeals are, however, rare. It is an example of procedural proportionality, as it ensures that where a first appeal would inevitably lead to a second appeal, neither the parties nor the court are required to expend resources unnecessarily on the first appeal.
2. Such a power, as set out in Rule 177, should be subject to a discretion provided to the second appellate court to determine whether to take such an appeal. This enables it to ensure that the appellate hierarchy is not subverted through the regular use of this process. It also enables it to ensure that the applicable national tradition concerning the relationship between the first and second appeal courts is not undermined by the process.

SECTION 5 – REVIEW OF PROCEDURAL ERROR AND MISCELLANEOUS APPEALS

Rule 178. Immediate review of procedural error

(1) If a party, or non-party affected by a procedural order, fails to challenge a procedural error that was caused by the court or another party immediately upon it being made, the error is waived.

(2) Rule 178(1) does not apply if a party acted carefully pursuant to the requirements of Rule 47 or if the rule affected is not subject to waiver by the parties. This Rule applies to non-parties *mutatis mutandis*.

(3) Upon objection and having heard the parties the court may render, revoke or vary court rulings. Rules 49 and 50 apply accordingly.

Sources:

Transnational Rules of Civil Procedure (Reporters' Study) Rule 33.3.

Comments:

1. Rules 178(1) and (2) provide parties with the ability to challenge the court's interpretation and implementation of procedural law. This ability must, however, be balanced by the need to ensure that proceedings are managed expeditiously so as to avoid unnecessary procedural delay. Consequently, this Rule requires parties to challenge procedural decisions immediately upon them being made. This enables the court to reconsider and, as the case may be, correct its decision at the earliest possible stage.

2. If necessary, it is a matter of the court's case management power to determine the effects of a successful challenge. (See Rules 49 and 62(2).)
3. Non-parties that are affected by court orders enjoy the same treatment as parties regarding their rights to challenge procedural errors combined with the requirement to do it, in principle, immediately upon threat of waiver. Such equal treatment facilitates coordinated decisions on challenges by parties and non-parties in cases of revocation, variation or replacement of court orders.

Rule 179. Separate Appeal Against the Review of Procedural Orders by the Court

(1) Unless otherwise provided for in Rule 179(2), a decision on a challenge to a procedural error cannot be made the subject of a separate appeal.

(2) A separate appeal is available against decisions made in respect of

(a) a stay of proceedings;

(b) the transfer of proceedings to another court;

(c) security for costs;

(d) the exclusion of a party from a hearing or the imposition of a fine on a party;

(e) a refusal to disqualify a judge or court-appointed expert; and

(f) if provided for in a specific rule.

(3) A separate appeal must be filed with the court within two weeks of notice of the decision.

Comments:

1. As a general rule, procedural decisions should not be subject to a separate appeal in order to promote procedural efficiency and proportionality. If the court considers it appropriate to put specific emphasis on the significance of a decision on an incidental procedural issue it may render a judgment on that issue (see Rule 66 (1)(a)) that is subject to appeal (see Rule 66, comment 4 and 5).
2. In certain situations the proper administration of justice requires parties to be provided with the opportunity to appeal from procedural decisions. Those situations are set out in Rules 179(2)(a)-(f). It should be noted that necessary immediate challenge of errors according to Rule 178 is an indispensable requirement for success.
3. In order to ensure that the ability to challenge such decisions does not undermine the proper conduct of proceedings, the time period within which such appeals may be issued is limited by Rule 179(3).

Rule 180. Appeals against procedural decisions that affect non-parties

(1) A person who is not a party to litigation but directly affected by a procedural ruling given by the court has a right of appeal.

(2) The right of appeal must be exercised in accordance with Rule 179(3).

Comments:

1. Rule 180 protects the rights of non-parties who are affected by procedural decisions. It is necessary as they are unable to challenge procedural decisions that affect them by way of an appeal from a final judgment. The right of appeal must be applied for through the same mechanism as applicable to appeals from such decisions made by parties, i.e., under Rule 179(3). Rule 178 applies to affected non-parties that must, therefore, in so far as necessary, immediately challenge procedural errors with the court that hears the case before filing an appeal according to Rule 180. If the court, exceptionally, determines procedural issues by

judgment and not by court order such judgment is subject to regular appeal (see Rule 66 (1)(a) with comments 4 and 5).

2. This Rule covers decisions such as, but not limited to, orders to produce evidence or provide information, to appear as a witness, to refuse to recognise or set aside a relevant privilege or immunity, or a refusal to permit the non-party to intervene in proceedings.

SECTION 6 – EXTRAORDINARY RECOURSE

Rule 181. Scope of an extraordinary motion for review

(1) An extraordinary motion for review re-opens proceedings that have otherwise been finally determined either at first instance or on appeal.

(2) Such a review may, if successful, rescind a judgment that has become *res judicata*. Where it does so the court will give case management directions for the future management of the proceedings.

Sources:

Transnational Rules of Civil Procedure (Reporters' Study) Rule 34.

Comments:

1. In exceptional circumstances, a party may be permitted to seek to re-open a decision that finally determined proceedings. Such decisions may be judgments that have become final, applications for permission to appeal, or appeals. If successful such an extraordinary motion for review will rescind the decision that is subject to the review. The grounds for such a review are limited, and are set out in Rule 182.
2. Where a review is successful, the decision challenged will be rescinded. The court will then need to ensure that the proceedings that have be re-opened are able to conclude appropriately. Case management directions under Rules 49 and 50 should thus be given to enable, for instance, the proceedings to be re-tried *de novo*, to enable a permission to appeal hearing to be re-heard *de novo*, or to enable an appeal to be reheard *de novo*.
3. It shall be a matter for national law to determine the appropriate court to consider applications for an extraordinary motion for review. In some European jurisdictions this is the Supreme Court, an appellate court or the court that gave the judgment that is subject to the motion for review.

Rule 182. Grounds for an extraordinary motion for review

(1) An extraordinary motion for review may only be brought against a judgment on the following grounds

(a) the court was wrongly constituted,

(b) a party's right to be heard was violated severely,

(c) a judgment was obtained by fraud or violence,

(d) after a judgment is issued, evidence that would have been decisive to it is recovered or obtained, and such evidence was not available prior to judgment being given due either to *force majeure* or improper conduct by the party in whose favour the judgment was made, or

(e) the European Court of Human Rights has ruled that the judgment given in national proceedings infringed any of the rights established in the European Convention for the Protection of Human Rights and Fundamental Freedoms and its Protocols,

provided that the infringement, due to its nature and seriousness, entails persistent effects, which can only be stopped by means of such a review; however, in no case may the review affect rights acquired in good faith by third parties.

(2) The motion shall only be admissible under Rule 182(1)(a), (b) or (c) if the applicant was unable, without any fault on their behalf, to raise the ground on which they rely before the judgment that is to be subject to review became *res judicata*.

Comments:

1. Extraordinary review can undermine finality of litigation and legal certainty. It can result in *res judicata* being set aside. As such its application must be interpreted and applied strictly. As such an appellate court should only grant an application for extraordinary review where the applicant, through no fault of their own, could not raise the issues specified in Rule 182(1) prior to the judgment that is to be challenged becoming *res judicata*: see Rule 182(2).
2. Rule 182(1) specifies the different bases for an extraordinary review. Rule 182(1)(a) concerns the circumstance where the court was constituted improperly, e.g., one of the judges was not in fact a judge, the panel of judges contained the judge whose decision was under appeal, i.e., the judge was judge in their own cause, the judge was related to one of the parties.
3. Rule 182(1)(b) permits the use of an extraordinary motion for review where there has been a severe violation of a party's right to be heard, i.e., the judgment challenged was one that failed to satisfy basic principles of procedural justice. Only severe violations should be taken account of under this Rule, e.g., there has been no attempt to provide the defendant with notice of the proceedings and as a consequence the court's jurisdiction over the defendant cannot properly be said to have been engaged or the court has, without any reasonable justification, refused to hear the defendant in the proceedings.
4. Rules 182(1)(a) and (b) may only be relied upon where there are no other available remedies, i.e., other forms of review or appeal were or are available to the applicant.
5. Rule 182(1)(c) concerns the situation where the integrity of the court process has been corrupted due to fraud (which includes corrupted evidence) or threats of violence to parties, their families or friends, members of the judiciary or court staff, or witnesses. It does not require there to have been a successful criminal prosecution for such conduct, although some national jurisdictions have taken this as a pre-requisite. In practice, a criminal prosecution will be the best evidence in support of such an application for review. Fraud is not necessarily linked with a party's conduct. It could be effected by the conduct of witnesses or other non-parties. Their conduct should, however, have been intended to benefit the party in whose favour judgment was secured. This remedy should not however be available where, as in some European jurisdictions, a separate action for relief on the basis of fraud arising from the judgment is not available.
6. Rule 182(1)(d) concerns the situation where after a judgment is rendered, decisive documents are recovered or obtained, which were not available earlier due to *force majeure* or due to the party the judgment has favoured taking steps to actively conceal them; in the latter respect this Rule overlaps with the jurisdiction set out in Rule 182(1)(c). Such material should be taken account of, however, even if no fraud can be proved, if it would lead to a different outcome and was not previously available or could not have been known through exercise of due diligence.
7. Increasing numbers of European jurisdictions permit an extraordinary motion for review where the European Court of Human Rights has ruled that a judgment given in a national

proceeding has violated the European Convention on Human Rights. To avoid an unreasonable increase in legal uncertainty, an extraordinary motion for review on this ground is only permissible where the infringement was particularly serious and entails lasting effects. Moreover, any rights acquired in good faith by non-parties should not be affected by the results of a such a motion for review.

8. These Rules do not permit an extraordinary motion for revision where there has been an infringement of European Union law public policy provisions. This approach reflects both the fact that these Rules are intended to be a model code of European civil procedure rather than a model code for European Union civil procedure, and the approach taken by the European Court of Justice that stresses the fundamental importance of the principles of finality, legal certainty and of *res judicata.*[4] EU case law furthermore does not require a legal system to provide rules allowing decisions of apex courts that have *res judicata* to be set aside in order to overcome an erroneous application or interpretation of EU law.[5] This also applies where a rule of EU public policy was not applied or was applied incorrectly.[6]

Rule 183. Time limits and withdrawal

(1) An application by a party for an extraordinary motion for review must be made within three months from the date on which that party became aware of the grounds for review.

(2) In no case may an application be made after ten years have elapsed from the time the judgment, which is to be the subject of such a review, has become *res judicata.*

(3) An extraordinary motion for review can be withdrawn at any time.

Comments:

1. A short time limit is set under Rule 183(1) in order to protect the principle of finality, legal certainty and the concept of *res judicata.* (Also see Rule 165 on extension of time limits.)
2. Rule 183(2) provides an absolute time limit to bring an extraordinary motion for review. Ten years is specified here as it strikes a fair balance between an applicant's interest in pursuing an application to rectify the harm done to its private interest and the public interest in securing a correct decision and the public interest in finality of litigation and legal certainty.

4 See, for instance, ECJ, Judgment of 1 June 1999, Eco Swiss (C-126/97, ECR 1999 p. I-3055) ECLI:EU:C:1999:269- Judgment of 13 January 2004, Kühne & Heitz (C-453/00, ECR 2004 p. I-837) ECLI:EU:C:2004:17– Judgment of 16 March 2006, Kapferer (C-234/04, ECR 2006 p. I-2585) ECLI:EU:C:2006:178– Judgment of 3 September 2009, Fallimento Olimpiclub (C-2/08, ECR 2009 p. I-7501) ECLI:EU:C:2009:506—Judgment of 6 October 2009, Asturcom Telecomunicaciones (C-40/08, ECR 2009 p. I-9579) ECLI:EU:C:2009:615

5 See, for instance, ECJ, Judgment of 30 September 2003, Köbler (C-224/01, ECR 2003 p. I-10239) ECLI:EU:C:2003:513- C-453/00, Kühne & Heitz,.

6 See, for instance, ECJ, Judgment of 21 December 2016, Gutiérrez Naranjo (C-154/15, C-307/15 and C-308/15) ECLI:EU:C:2016:980, para. 68—Judgment of 26 January 2017, Banco Primus (C-421/14) ECLI:EU:C:2017:60, para. 47.

PART X

PROVISIONAL AND PROTECTIVE MEASURES

INTRODUCTION

1. This Part concerns provisional and protective measures, which are important both in domestic and cross-border litigation to secure effective enforcement or to otherwise preserve rights and prevent (further) harm prior to the commencement of proceedings or pending final judgment (also see Rule 67). It consists of three Parts: a General Part (Section 1), which includes rules that apply to all types of measures, unless otherwise provided; a Special Part (Section 2), which includes rules on Asset Preservation, Regulatory Measures, Evidence Preservation and Interim Payments; and, a Cross-Border Part (Section 3), which primarily refers to existing legislation. Section 3 further provides a minimal number of general rules as it is not intended to provide a set of rules on the complex and multifaceted issue of cross-border provisional and protective measures.

2. Principle 8 of the ALI/UNIDROIT Principles was the starting point for the development of Rules concerning provisional and protective measures. This Principle includes three basic rules: on function and proportionality (8.1); *ex parte* measures; (8.2); and compensation and security (8.3). National approaches taken in European jurisdictions were then considered as the general approach to, and types of, provisional and protective measures, their scope, and the requirements for granting them differ substantially across them. Additionally, a number of specific EU instruments, such as the EAPO Regulation, the IP Enforcement Directive, and the case law on provisional and protective measures under the Brussels Ibis Regulation, were considered. Finally, a number of other important sources of soft law that were considered include the UNCITRAL Model Law on International Commercial Arbitration, as amended in 2006 (Articles 17-17G),[1] the 1996 ILA Principles on Provisional and Protective Measures in International Litigation (Helsinki Principles),[2] and the Storme Report (Article 10).

3. To bridge the differences between differing European traditions this Part takes a functional approach, as is clear from Rule 184. Where appropriate, diverging approaches have been accommodated by including different options. This is, for instance, clear in Rule 191 where different types of sanctions are incorporated, by reference to the general rule on sanctions (Rule 27) that have the common goal of providing an effective enforcement mechanism. In other rules, such as Rule 188, flexibility is created to facilitate tailor-made solutions for the specific situation given the wide variety of provisional and protective measures. A consequence of this approach is that

1 See <https://www.uncitral.org/pdf/english/texts/arbitration/ml-arb/07-86998_Ebook.pdf>.

2 J. Crawford and M. Byers (eds.), The International Law Association. Report of the sixty-seventh Conference held at Helsinki, Finland 12 to 17 August 1996, London: Cambrian Printers 1996. F.K. Juenger, The ILA Principles on Provisional and Protective Measures, 45 AJCL 1997, pp. 941–944, reproducing the Principles.

ELI-UNIDROIT Model European Rules of Civil Procedure. ELI & UNIDROIT, Oxford University Press.
 DOI: 10.1093/oso/9780198866589.003.0011

not all types of measures covered by these Rules exist in all European countries, while others are only available in a limited number of countries, e.g., evidence preservation measures and interim payments.

4. The Rules in this Part are drafted so as to balance the interest of the applicant in safeguarding their rights and the interest of the respondent to minimise the risk that any such measures cause unjustifiable harm. This aim is further articulated through the principle of proportionality, set out in Rule 185, which provides a particular application of the general proportionality principle (Rules 5(1) and 6).

SECTION 1 – GENERAL PART

Rule 184. Provisional and Protective Measures

(1) A provisional or protective measure is any temporary order that has one or more of the following functions:

(a) to ensure or promote effective enforcement of final decisions concerning the substance of the proceedings, whether or not the underlying claim is pecuniary, including securing assets and obtaining or preserving information concerning a debtor and his assets; or

(b) to preserve the opportunity for a complete and satisfactory determination of the proceedings, including securing evidence relevant to the merits or preventing its destruction or concealment; or

(c) to preserve the existence and value of goods or other assets which form or will form the subject-matter of proceedings (pending or otherwise); or

(d) to prevent harm from being suffered, to prevent further harm, or to regulate disputed issues, pending final judgment.

(2) A provisional or protective measure ordered should be suitable for its purpose.

Sources:

ALI/Unidroit Principle 8.1.

Comments:

1. Rule 184 describes the different functions of provisional and protective measures in these Rules. A provisional or protective measure is a temporary measure given by the court. Its temporary nature is inherent in provisional and protective measures, which will cease to have any effect, at the latest, when final judgment has been delivered. There is no requirement for proceedings to have been commenced (Rule 52) prior to an application for a provisional or protective measure to have been initiated, although Rule 188 imposes an obligation on an applicant to commence proceedings within a specified period of time or a period set by the court. It is, however, inherent in the aim of such measures that they can only properly be granted, either before the commencement of proceedings or during their pendency, if it is necessary to do so. With the exception of the special provision for interim payments under Rule 200, urgency is not a specific requirement.
2. Different terminology is used across Europe for provisional and protective measures, e.g., provisional relief, preliminary measures, preservation measures, interim relief and interim orders. The use of 'provisional and protective measures' as generic terminology to denote these variously described measures all of which serve the functions enumerated in this

Part, can, however, be traced back to the 1968 Brussels Convention.[3] As a consequence it is well-established in European law and, for that reason, adopted here.

3. A wide variety of provisional and protective measures exists in the laws and practice of European jurisdictions. Rather than giving a strict definition of what these measures entail, this Rule describes the various functions that they fulfil. In comparative procedural law doctrine, including in Article 10.1 of the Storme Report, provisional and protective measures have been divided into three broad types. First, conservatory or preservation measures to secure enforcement on the merits. Secondly, regulatory measures that cover a broad range of measures intended to maintain, what is typically referred to as, the *status quo* or to make a provisional arrangement between parties, e.g., measures requiring a party to perform or to abstain from carrying out certain acts. Thirdly, anticipatory measures that can, on a provisional and temporary basis, award either partially or in full what is or will be claimed in the proceedings. A particular example of this type of measure is an order for an interim payment (Rule 200).
4. The four categories of measure enumerated in this Rule elaborate the functions, including the preservation of evidence, they can fulfil. The Rule is intended to provide the court with the power to ensure that the applicant's interests are capable of being protected until the substantive proceedings are concluded. The first category includes measures that promote or secure the enforcement of a judgment, and typically cover, but are not limited to, asset preservation measures. The second category comprises measures that are aimed at preserving the court's ability to determine the proceedings in a complete and satisfactory manner. It includes measures to secure evidence relevant to the proceedings. The third category encompasses measures designed to preserve the existence and value of goods or other assets that are or will form the subject-matter of pending or intended proceedings. These include, but are not limited to, orders to ensure the safe custody of assets, to ensure that income is generated from assets, or to require the sale of perishable goods. The fourth category contains measures aimed at preventing harm, or further harm, to the applicant pending a final judgment. These include measures requiring interim performance, e.g., the provision of goods, providing access to premises, maintaining contractual performance, as well as restraining orders, e.g., in respect of intellectual property disputes, and interim payments.
5. The grant of any particular provisional or protective measure should only be made if, and in so far as it is, an appropriate means of achieving the purpose of the application made (Rule 184(2)). Any such measure granted must also be a proportionate means to achieve its objective (Rule 185). Additionally, any specific measure can fulfil more than one objective.
6. Provisional or protective measures granted under this Part do not include, nor should they be used as, a summary procedure to finally determine all or part of the dispute (see Rule 65 with comments 1 to 3). Nor do they have any *res judicata* effect in respect of the substantive proceedings.

Rule 185. Proportionality of provisional and protective measures

(1) A provisional and protective measure should impose the least burden on the respondent.

3 Art. 24.

(2) The court must ensure that the measure's effects are not disproportionate to the interests it is asked to protect.

Sources:
ALI/UNIDROIT Principles 5.8 and 8.1.

Comments:

1. This Rule provides that the grant of provisional and protective measures is subject to the principle of proportionality, whilst taking into account the interests of both the applicant and the respondent. This is derived from both ALI/UNIDROIT Principle 5.8 (*ex parte* orders) and Principle 8.1 (provisional measures). The former issue is further regulated by Rule 186(2). Additionally, the principle of proportionality is inherent in the law and practice on provisional and protective measures in the European jurisdictions.
2. The principle of proportionality is particularly important in assessing provisional and protective measures. This is all the more pertinent where without-notice (*ex parte*) measures are concerned (Rule 186). This is because the various procedures for obtaining them, and the required urgency involved in doing so, will often not enable a full assessment of the law and the facts in dispute, a point which is all the more apposite where the application is without-notice.
3. While Rule 184(2) requires that the court must grant such provisional or protective measures it concludes is necessary and suitable for its purpose, it must also ensure that the measure ordered imposes the least burden on the respondent and that its effects are not disproportionate to the applicant's interests. As such the court could, for instance, limit the scope or the time period of the measure or set other conditions which limit its adverse effect upon the respondent.
4. While the general burden of proof is a matter of substantive law (see Rule 25(2)), the burden of proof concerning applications for provisional and protective measures is generally placed upon the applicant. Where, however, a respondent alleges that potential negative consequences are likely to arise from the grant of such a measure, and over which the applicant cannot have any knowledge, the burden of proof will lie upon them (Rules 193, 197, 199, and 201).

Rule 186. Without-notice (Ex parte) *procedure*

(1) The court may order a provisional or protective measure without-notice ('*ex parte*') only if, in the circumstances, proceedings with-notice ('*inter partes*') would frustrate the prospect of the applicant receiving effective protection of their interests.
(2) When granting an order without-notice the court must give the respondent an opportunity to be heard at the earliest possible time, that date to be specified in the order that was made without-notice. The respondent should be given notice of the order and of all the matters relied upon before the court to support it as soon as possible.
(3) An applicant must fully disclose to the court all facts and legal issues relevant to the court's decision whether to grant relief and, if so, on what terms.
(4) The court must make a prompt decision concerning any objection to the grant of a provisional or protective measure or its terms.

Sources:
ALI/UNIDROIT Principles 8.2 and 5.8.

Comments:

1. The grant of a provisional or protective measure ought preferably to take place at a hearing where the respondent is present, i.e., at a with-notice (*inter partes*) hearing. This enables their procedural rights to be secured. It also promotes procedural proportionality as it reduces the number of hearings required to decide the matter. There are circumstances, however, where it is necessary to determine and grant such a measure in the absence of the respondent and, moreover, in the absence of notification to them. This is the case where notice is likely to frustrate the purpose for which the order is sought, and hence secrecy is needed, i.e., where the respondent, having advance notice of the application, is expected to frustrate an order protecting the applicant's financial interests by disposing of assets before an asset preservation order is made. Additionally, there may be circumstances where urgency entails that notice cannot be given.
2. In most procedural systems and particularly in relation to certain protective measures, such as asset preservation orders, the grant of such measures on a without-notice (*ex parte*) basis is commonly permitted. This is, for instance, the general rule under Article 11 of the EAPO Regulation, and equally in respect of intellectual property infringements, it is set out in Article 8 of the IP Enforcement Directive. This Rule is, however, particularly inspired by ALI/UNIDROIT Principles 8.2 (provisional and protective measures) and 5.8 (general *ex parte* proceedings), as well as Articles 17B and C(2) of the UNCITRAL Model Law.
3. The Rule requires the court to set a time within which the respondent shall be heard in respect of the measure where it was initially granted on a without-notice (*ex parte*) basis. This is to ensure that the respondent can properly exercise their right to be heard (Rules 11 and 12) and to have the matter considered in the light of a full consideration of the facts and law. To best secure the respondent's rights, a with-notice (*inter partes*) hearing should take place at the earliest possible time after the without-notice (*ex parte*) hearing. The date of the with-notice hearing must be specified in the order in accordance with Rule 186(2).This latter requirement is intended to ensure that, in the absence of such a date being set within the order made on a without-notice (*ex parte*) basis, the order does not become a *de facto* final order. It is thus intended to secure the respondent's procedural rights, particularly their right to be heard. In addition to the protection afforded to respondent's by Rule 186(2), Rule 189 enables the court to review the measure, ordinarily at the respondent's request, whereas under Rule 190 the respondent is liable if a provisional or protective measure is set aside, lapses, or if the claim is dismissed in the proceedings on the substance.
4. The Rule does not provide a set time period within which a with-notice (*inter partes*) hearing has to take place. This is both because different European jurisdictions take different approaches to the provision of timescales, and because there is need to provide the court with the flexibility to determine an appropriate date in the light of all the circumstances of the particular case. To this end the respondent must be notified of the measure immediately after it is granted. Notice includes providing both the order and any documents relied on to support the application to the respondent. A with-notice (*inter partes*) hearing will be conducted so that the court considers the application *de novo*, i.e., it considers the grant of the measure afresh and not as a review of the without-notice (*ex parte*) order.
5. On a without-notice (*ex parte*) application, consistently with the principle of proportionality, in order to protect the respondent's rights, and to enable the court to assess whether relief should be granted, applicants are required to fully disclose relevant factual and legal matters (Rule 186(3)). A similar rule is set out in Article 17F of the UNCITRAL Model

Law. Where appropriate, an applicant at a without-notice (*ex parte*) hearing should also disclose any probable defences the respondent may have, including the existence of any potential limitation defence (time-bar), or any possible right of set-off. This enables the court to make a preliminary assessment of the respondent's interests.

6. Rule 186(4) is inspired by Article 17C of the UNCITRAL Model Law. It is intended to afford the parties protection from court delay.
7. The ability to grant a provisional or protective measure on a without-notice (*ex parte*) basis is not permissible in respect of interim payments (Rule 201(3)).

Rule 187. Security

(1) When assessing whether to grant or continue a provisional or protective measure the court may consider whether security can be provided by the respondent in lieu of the order.

(2) As a condition of granting or continuing a provisional or protective measure the applicant may, depending on the circumstances, be required to provide appropriate security.

(3) Security must not be required solely on the basis that the applicant or respondent is not a national or resident of the forum State.

Sources:

ALI/UNIDROIT Principle 3.3.

Comments:

1. Rule 187 provides the basis to make the grant of a provisional or protective measure subject to the provision of security. Security may, for instance, be a bank guarantee, a guarantee by a non-party or any other type of guarantee that provides effective security (Rule 187(1)). It may also be such as to secure any payment that may become due from the applicant to the respondent, i.e., as damages for the wrongful grant of a protective measure (Rule 187(2)). In the latter case, security may also take the form of a formal undertaking to be made to the court.
2. Rule 187(1) concerns the situation where a respondent can offer security before or after a provisional or protective measure has been granted. If the respondent offers sufficient security to protect the applicant's interests, it will not be necessary to grant such an order, or an order granted already may be discontinued. Where an order has already been made, Rule 189 enables the respondent to request that the court modify, suspend, or terminate it. Also see Rule 184(2) and Rule 185 regarding the effect of a respondent giving sufficient security.
3. Rule 187(2) provides that security may be required as a condition for the court to grant the measure requested by an applicant. It is consistent with the aim of ensuring that such a measure is only ever provisional, and provides support for the liability provision set out in Rule 190. The provision of security may be of particular importance where an order to perform or refrain from performing an action is ordered under Rule 196 or an interim payment is ordered under Rule 200. It is not, however, limited to such situations. This particular Rule was drawn from Article 17E of the UNCITRAL Model Law. A similar provision can also be found in Article 9(6) of the IP Enforcement Directive.
4. While, for instance, Article 12 of the EAPO Regulation makes an order for security compulsory, in order to prevent abuse of the procedure and to ensure compensation for any damage suffered consequent to the procedure by the debtor, the present Rule is discretionary. This enables the court to determine on the individual merits of each application

whether such security is necessary. It also ensures that the question of security does not, where a respondent is unable to provide it, provide an absolute bar to an award of a provisional or protective measure.

5. In determining the nature or amount of appropriate security the court should take account of the potential harm that may be suffered by a respondent should the substantive claim be unsuccessful or the measure granted be varied, modified or set aside (Rule 187(2), and see Rule 190).
6. Rule 187(2) incorporates the non-discrimination principle that is part of European Union law, and is also set out in ALI/UNIDROIT Principle 3.3 Nationals, residents, non-nationals and non-residents should be treated equally.

Rule 188. Initiation of Proceedings

(1) Where the applicant has been granted a provisional or protective measure before initiating proceedings under Rules 21(1), 53, such proceedings must be initiated before the date set by the court. Where the court does not set such a date or it is not otherwise specified by the applicable law, the applicant shall initiate such proceedings within two weeks of the date of the issue of the decision granting the remedy. The court can extend the period on the request of a party.

(2) If proceedings have not been initiated as required by Rule 188(1), the measure shall lapse, unless the court provides otherwise.

Sources:
ALI/UNIDROIT Principle 8.

Comments:

1. European jurisdictions differ substantially when it comes to the obligation to initiate proceedings where provisional or protective measures are sought before they have commenced. In some countries there is a general obligation to commence proceedings (for instance, Italy, Spain, and Romania). In other countries there is, as is the case in ALI/UNIDROIT Principle 8, no such obligation (for instance, France, Germany, and the Netherlands). Where protective measures are conservatory, the general approach is to impose an obligation on the party obtaining the benefit of it to commence proceedings. This is the case as such measures are ordinarily granted without-notice (*ex parte*) and are intended to protect enforcement in the event of success in respect of the substantive dispute between the parties. The obligation to commence proceedings is also present in Article 10 of the EAPO Regulation, where attachment of bank accounts is concerned. Also see the obligation to commence proceedings in respect of intellectual property infringement cases (Article 50(6) of the TRIPS Agreement[4] and Article 9(5) of the IP Enforcement Directive.
2. Rule 188 diverges from the position adopted in the ALI/UNIDROIT Principles. It adopts the approach that an applicant who is granted a provisional or protective measure prior to commencing proceedings against the respondent should, unless the court orders otherwise, be required to do so. This approach is taken to ensure that protective and provisional measures do not, by default, become in effect final. It is thus intended to ensure that the substantive dispute is determined by the court consistently with the right to fair trial, i.e., both parties' right to receive a fair process is given effect. Parties may decide to settle their

4 1994 Marrakesh Agreement Establishing the World Trade Organization, Annex 1C, Trade-Related Aspects of Intellectual Property Rights.

dispute on the basis of the decision reached in an application for a provisional or protective measure. They may agree that such a decision be rendered enforceable by the court (see Rules 9(3), 141, Article 59 Brussels Ibis Regulation) or, e.g., be authenticated by a notary to become enforceable (see Article 58 Brussels Ibis Regulation and equal provisions of national law). A variety of national legal practice has developed in European jurisdictions in which contractual clauses, including enforceable contractual penalties, to punish and deter wrongdoing, replace, in part, the function of final court judgments being *res judicata* and enforceable.

3. Different approaches are taken by different international instruments to the time period within which an applicant is required to initiate proceedings following the grant of a provisional or protective measure. Article 10 of the EAPO Regulation prescribes a period of maximum 30 days after lodging the application or 14 days after the issue of the order, whichever date is the later. Article 9(5) of the IP Enforcement Directive and Article 50(6) of the TRIPS Agreement provide that the measure ceases to have effect if proceedings are not initiated within a reasonable period, which is to be determined by the judge, or in the absence of such a determination, a maximum of 20 working days or 31 calendar days after the grant of the measure, whichever is the longer. The EAPO Regulation explicitly provides that the period may be extended at the debtor's request, for example to pursue a settlement.
4. Rule 188(1) adopts the same approach as that taken by those international instruments. It provides that when a measure is granted, the applicant has 14 days to commence proceedings. As such it adopts the same approach as that set out in the EAPO Regulation. That default period may be varied by the court when granting the order, or at a later date upon the request of either party. This enables both the court and the parties to take steps to vary the time period within which proceedings must be commenced to, for instance, enable negotiations to take place. It thus enables the parties to take steps to avoid incurring the cost of commencement, where that is unnecessary. Providing a default period requiring proceedings to be commenced, in the absence of which the measure lapses unless the court orders otherwise, ensures (as noted above) that the measure does not become a *de facto* final determination of the dispute, and equally protects the parties' procedural rights.
5. Rule 188(2) provides the default rule that the provisional or protective measure shall lapse if proceedings are initiated in accordance with Rule 188(1) and Rule 21(1). However, to accommodate situations and systems where such effect is not considered desirable, the court can provide otherwise.

Rule 189. Review and Appeal

(1) The court may, either on application of a party or on its own motion, modify, suspend, or terminate a provisional or protective measure if satisfied that a change in circumstances so requires.

(2) Decisions that grant, deny, modify, suspend or terminate provisional or protective measures are subject to appeal. Rule 179(3) applies accordingly.

Sources:

ALI/UNIDROIT Principles 10.1 and 10.3.

Comments:

1. Rule 189(1) makes provision for the court to review, amend, suspend or terminate a provisional measure. It is a provision which is common in many European jurisdictions.

It enables the court to modify its order to take account of a change in circumstances, while enabling a respondent subject to such an order to protect their interests. Any such review must be carried out consistently with the principle of proportionality (Rules 5 and 185).

2. A review under this Rule would ordinarily be carried out, on-notice to the applicant, following a request from the respondent, the court, however may do so of its own motion (*ex officio*) where that is necessary (compare Rule 21, which applies to the institution of proceedings by the court and not review by the court of its own orders). While this may generally be considered to run against the principle of party autonomy and party initiative in civil and commercial cases, in exceptional cases where third-party interests (for instance those of shareholders) or the public interest requires it, the court may modify, suspend, or terminate a provisional or protective measure on its own motion (*ex officio*). This approach is consistent with that taken in Article 17D of the UNCITRAL Model Law, but also see the, partially, differing provision in Article 33 of the EAPO Regulation.
3. Rule 189(2) allows an appeal from a decision granting or refusing a provisional or protective measure as well as against decisions according to Rule 189(1). Where there is, however, a change of circumstance underlying the provisional or protective measures, parties must first apply for a review according to Rule 189(1); they cannot apply directly to the higher court.

Rule 190. Applicant Liability

(1) If a provisional or protective measure is set aside, lapses, or if the proceedings are dismissed on procedural grounds or on their merits, the applicant must compensate the respondent for such loss or damage caused by the measure.

(2) The applicant is liable to compensate non-parties for any damages, and expenditure incurred as a consequence of complying with the measure.

Sources:

ALI/UNIDROIT Principle 8.3.

Comments:

1. Rule 190 concerns the applicant's liability for damages caused to the respondent or non-parties affected by the measure. While many countries have specific rules on applicant liability in their rules on civil procedure or use the general rules on tort liability to reach similar results, this Rule, and particularly Rule 190(1) was inspired by ALI/UNIDROIT Principle 8.3. Similar rules are included in Article 13 of the EAPO Regulation, Article 9(7) of the IP Enforcement Directive, and Article 17G of the UNCITRAL Model Law. It should be noted, however, that Article 13(5) of the EAPO Regulation expressly provides that it does not deal with the question of possible liability towards any non-party. This Rule does so, given the general ability these Rules provide for protective or provisional measures to be applied to non-parties. As such, this Rule seeks to provide all those, whether respondent or non-party, with sufficient protection via the application of the compensatory principle it articulates. While some contributions discussing this provision criticised the potential high risk to applicants that they may be liable for unforeseeable significant damages, which could therefore deter applications for provisional measures, the majority stressed the necessity of not transferring the risk of provisional justice to non-parties that have no or no real influence on the development of the conflict between the parties.

2. Rule 190(1) deals with the situation where the measure is set aside, lapses (in particular when the applicant did not initiate substantive proceedings in accordance with Rule 188 and Rule 21(1)) or the substantive proceedings are dismissed either on procedural grounds or on the merits.
3. Rule 190(1) requires an applicant to compensate the respondent for loss and damage caused by the measure on a strict liability basis. This includes loss and damage directly resulting from the measure, for instance not being able to utilise goods or sell products, as well as legal costs and expenses incurred during proceedings (also see Rule 187(2)). In determining the extent of any compensatory damages, consideration should be given to the extent to which the applicant succeeded in their substantive claim, i.e., if they succeeded in part that may need to be reflected in the quantum of damages.
4. Rule 190(2) concerns damage caused to or expenses incurred by non-parties as a consequence of their compliance with a provisional or protective measure. It is not limited to the cases where the measure is set aside, lapses or where the proceedings are dismissed. Such compensation will usually relate to expenses made in implementing the measure, for instance administrative steps necessary to comply with it. However, other expenditure incurred as a consequence of compliance may have to be compensated by the applicant.

Rule 191. Sanctions for non-compliance

Except in respect of interim payments, where there is non-compliance with a provisional or protective measure the court may impose a sanction under Rule 27, as appropriate.

Sources:
ALI/UNIDROIT Principle 17.

Comments:
1. Rule 191 makes it clear that the general power to impose sanctions for non-compliance with these Rules, applies to non-compliance with provisional and protective measures, with the exception of interim payment orders.
2. The appropriate sanction will be included in the order upon the request of the applicant. The sanction, which should be proportionate to the non-compliance (Rule 185) should be an effective means to secure its aim.

SECTION 2 – SPECIAL PART

A. ASSET PRESERVATION

Rule 192. Types of Asset Preservation Measure

A court may grant, on application by a party, any of the following asset preservation orders for the purpose of protecting their claim:
(a) an attachment order, which is an order authorising provisional attachment of the respondent's assets,
(b) an asset restraining order, which is an interim order preventing the respondent from disposing of, or dealing with, their assets, or
(c) a custodial order, which is an order that the respondent's assets shall be placed in the custody of a neutral non-party (a custodian).

Sources:
ALI/UNIDROIT Principle 8.1.

Comments:
1. This Rule was inspired by Article 1 of the EAPO Regulation and Article 17.2(c) of the UNCITRAL Model Law. Orders made under Rules 192(a) and (b) would normally be granted on a without-notice (*ex parte*) basis, as advance notice of the order would be expected to frustrate its purpose (see Rule 186).
2. Rules 192(a) and (b) operate differently. Attachment orders under the former Rule confer rights on applicants with respect to assets, whereas assets restraining orders under the latter Rule impose a duty on the respondent not to dispose of, or deal with, the assets subject to the order.
3. Asset preservation orders are intended to protect the substance of an applicant's claim for relief in proceedings. It follows from Rule 188(2) and Rule 21(1) that an order will cease to have effect where an applicant fails to commence such proceedings within the prescribed time.
4. In Rule 192, the term 'a claim' means that an asset preservation order may be made to protect all types of claims, i.e., pecuniary claims and, where appropriate, claims for specific property. There may be situations, though, where an asset preservation order will not have the effect of protecting the subject matter of proceedings, e.g., it is difficult to conceive of such an order being made in proceedings seeking a declaratory judgment on the existence of a debt. Whether or not an asset preservation order may or may not be considered to be suitable to protect specific kinds of claims will inevitably vary depending on the circumstances of the case and national law.
5. Custodial orders, under Rule 192(c), are included within the ambit of asset preservation measures, although some European jurisdictions consider them to be a separate form of order. They are included here given the functional approach taken in this Part of the Rules. Such an order, like an attachment or an asset restraining order, can properly and broadly be understood to encompass the safe-keeping and preservation of any type of property, whether physical, intangible or electronic. The term "custodian" is used to refer to any non-party (whether a court officer or otherwise) who may be authorised or instructed by the court to carry such an order in the place where the relevant assets are to be kept secure. It should be noted that technology has expanded the scope for custodial intervention, i.e., it may now apply to the safekeeping of electronic data, or to prevent passwords, metadata etc. from being altered or concealed.

Rule 193. Criteria for Awarding Asset Preservation Orders

A party seeking an order under Rule 192 must show that:
(a) **their claim for relief has a good chance of succeeding on its substantive merits, and**
(b) **it is likely that, without such an order, enforcement of a final judgment against the respondent will be impossible or exceedingly difficult.**

Comments:
1. The criteria for awarding asset preservation orders under Rule 193 are inspired by Article 7 of the EAPO Regulation and Article 17A.1 of the UNCITRAL Model Law. They are intended to protect a respondent against the injustice of being subject to an order where

there is a lack of merit in the proceedings (Rule 193(a)) or where there is no pressing need for their assets to be subject to a draconian order of this nature (Rule 193(b)).

2. The two criteria, which are widely used in most European jurisdictions, are cumulative. This means that the likelihood that the applicant will succeed on the substantive merits of the dispute should not influence the assessment of whether or not there is a real risk concerning the enforceability of a final judgment unless the order is issued by the court.
3. It should be noted that, in addition to the two cumulative criteria, a third criterion must be met and that is the requirement of proportionality under Rule 185, which requires that the measure ordered by the court should be one that imposes the least burden on the respondent and, furthermore, that the measure must not be disproportionate to the applicant's interests. This means that where the requirements under Rule 193 are met, the court may not make an attachment order or asset restraining order, if such an order imposes more than the least possible burden upon the respondent or if the order is disproportionate to the interest the applicant has applied to the court to protect.
4. The standard of proof in Rule 193(a) must be met at both without-notice (*ex parte*) and any subsequent with-notice (*inter partes*) hearings (Rule 186). When granting an attachment or asset restraining order on a without-notice (*ex parte*) basis, it is also necessary to satisfy the requirement set out in Rule 184(1), i.e., a with-notice (*inter partes*) hearing would frustrate the purpose of the order.
5. Should an order be set aside, Rules 190 and 191 impose strict liability upon the applicant.

Rule 194. Limitations on Asset Preservation Orders

Asset Preservation Orders must ensure that a respondent is not prevented from receiving financial allowances, provided the amounts are reasonable, for

(a) **ordinary living expenses, and/or**

(b) **legitimate business expenses, and/or**

(c) **to enable it to fund legal advice and representation in respect of the proceedings, including such as are necessary for it to respond to the order, including seeking its variation or discharge under Rules 186(4) or 189.**

Comments:

1. This Rule contains a number of limitations that are placed upon the scope of asset preservation orders. Without such limitations, they would be oppressive.
2. The limitation in Rule 194(a) applies only to individuals, whereas those in Rules 194(b) and (c) apply equally to individuals and legal persons or entities, the latter of which might be placed in the position of having to file for insolvency if the asset preservation order rendered them incapable of meeting their business expenses.
3. Article 31 of the EAPO Regulation contains similar provisions to those set out in this Rule. Similar provisions are also present in many European jurisdictions either as restrictions on the type of assets that can be subject to such orders, quantum limitations, or through the provision of specific financial allowances to respondents.

Rule 195. Notification of Asset Preservation Orders and their effects to Respondent

(1) **At the earliest possible time after an order has been made under Rule 192, the respondent and any non-parties who are the addressees of an order must be given formal**

notice of it. Where necessary to enforce the order, non-parties may be given formal notice before the respondent.

(2) The applicant may, if it wishes, inform a non-party of an order before the respondent is given formal notice.

(3) The respondent or any non-parties who are the addressees of an order made under Rule 192 must comply with it as soon as they are notified of the order. In the event of breach, they will be subject (without limitation) to the sanctions listed in Rule 191.

Sources:

ALI/UNIDROIT Principle 8 comment P-8C.

Comments:

1. Rule 195(1) is intended to secure a respondent's procedural rights, and particularly their right to be heard.[5] It seeks to do so without jeopardising the effective enforcement of the asset preservation order. As the approach to service and notification differs across European jurisdictions, this Rule does not specify any particular approach. Service and notice ought therefore to be effected according to Part VI of these Rules.
2. Generally, asset preservation orders concern assets over which non-parties, such as banks, have control. As such an order potentially imposes obligations on parties and non-parties, it is essential that all those who are subject to the order be notified of that fact promptly, particularly where notice is required to a non-party under the substantive law to render the order effective against them. The only exception to this notice requirement is where it would render the order ineffective, in which case notice should be given at the earliest time possible.
3. Rule 195(1) is of particular importance where asset preservation orders are applied for on a without-notice (*ex parte*) basis. It should be read consistently with Rule 186(4). As a consequence, respondents should be given notice of a without-notice (*ex parte*) order as soon as possible, which includes those situations where formal notice must be given to a non-party as a pre-condition to seeking effective enforcement of the order.
4. Rule 195(2) covers those situations where non-parties are not included within the terms of an asset preservation, yet they would nevertheless under domestic law be placed under an obligation to abide by the order. The Rule acknowledges the practical reality, especially in the context of Rules 192(a) and (b), that in certain jurisdictions the applicant will be concerned to ensure that a non-party, such as the respondent's bank, should be informed of the order's existence immediately upon it being granted by the court. This is particularly important in order to ensure that a respondent cannot evade an order by acting inconsistently with its term on the basis that it did not bind a non-party.
5. Rule 195(3) provides that an order must be complied with from the moment a respondent or any non-party is given formal notice of it under Rule 195(1). Formal notice will be effected according to Part VI of these Rules. It further clarifies that the sanctions listed in Rule 191 are not the only remedy available to an applicant in the event that a respondent or non-party that is subject to the order breaches it. As such any domestic remedies for breach, additional to those in these Rules, would be available to the court, i.e., potential civil or even criminal liability may be available in addition to the sanctions herein.

5 See, for instance the approach in Art. 17C UNCITRAL Model Law and Arts. 23-24 of the EAPO Regulation.

B. REGULATORY MEASURES

Rule 196. Measures to Perform or Refrain from Performing an Action

The court may grant the applicant a measure to regulate the relationship between parties in relation to a non-pecuniary claim for relief on a provisional basis. Such a measure may require the respondent to act or to refrain from acting in a manner specified in the court's order.

Comments:

1. Rule 196 establishes the scope of orders to perform or refrain from performing an action. It enables a court, upon application by a party, to order a respondent to act or refrain from acting in a manner specified in the order. It primarily fulfils the functions described by Rules 184(1)(c) and (d). The Rule does, however, only apply to regulatory orders in respect of non-pecuniary claims. It should be noted that asset restraining orders under Rule 192(b) may compel respondents to act or refrain from acting for the purpose of protecting any claim, including pecuniary claims.
2. The Rule enables the court to regulate the relationship between parties until such time that the decision in the proceedings is given or the case is settled otherwise. In other words, such an order supports the effective administration of justice by ensuring that steps are either not taken to frustrate the court's ability to determine proceedings on their substantive merits, or are taken to achieve the same purpose. Article 17(2)(b) of the UNCITRAL Model Law articulates a similar rule.
3. Provisional measures to perform or refrain from performing an action cover a wide range of orders, including, for instance, an obligation to perform a contractual agreement, the rectification of a media publication or to refrain from carrying out or continuing to carry out acts of unfair competition or which infringe intellectual property rights. Such measures may also cover situations of imminent harm (see particularly comment 4 to Rule 184).
4. Measures ordered under this Rule are subject to the provisions set out in Section 1 (General Part) of this Part of these Rules. It is particularly important therefore to note the application of the principle of proportionality (Rule 185) and the liability provision (Rule 190).
5. The grant of a provisional measure under this Rule is subject to the criteria of Rule 197.

Rule 197. Criteria for awarding a Regulatory Measure

A party seeking an order under Rule 196 must show:

(a) it has a good chance of succeeding in the proceedings; or

(b) where there is a significant risk that damages to the respondent will not be capable of providing adequate compensation for any interference with their rights if the proceedings are dismissed, that there is a very strong possibility that the applicant will succeed in the proceedings;

and

(c) that the order is necessary to regulate the substantive issue or issues in dispute pending final determination of the proceedings.

Comments:

1. This Rule sets out two cumulative conditions that must be satisfied before a provisional measure requiring a respondent to perform or to abstain from doing something, per Rule 196, can be awarded.

2. Rule 197(a) sets out the general requirement that an applicant must show that they have a good chance of succeeding in establishing their claim, or defence, in the proceedings. For instance, where an applicant seeks a restraining order in relation to intellectual property rights, a regulatory measure should only be awarded when there is a good chance that the court will ultimately decide, in its final judgment, that the respondent has infringed the applicant's intellectual property rights.
3. Rule 197(b) is intended to provide a greater degree of protection for a respondent to an application for a regulatory measure in circumstances where there is a significant risk that the damage that such a measure would cause them (e.g. loss of reputation or of perishable goods) cannot be compensated adequately. While measures that could cause damage not being compensated adequately should generally be avoided, in specific circumstances they may be necessary to avoid irreparable harm to the applicant. In those circumstances, the applicant is required to satisfy a higher standard of proof, i.e., they are required to show that there is a very strong possibility (a high chance) that their claim will succeed on its merits.
4. In addition to the criteria in Rules 197(a) and (b), an applicant must also show that the measure is necessary to regulate the matter pending the final determination of the claim (Rule 197 (c); also see Rule 188).
5. This Rule should be read together with Rule 185 on proportionality.

C. EVIDENCE PRESERVATION

Rule 198. Evidence Preservation Orders

(1) The court has the power to secure evidence on the application of a party to proceedings through the following interim measures:
- **(a) hearing witness evidence or taking of witness evidence by a third party acting on its behalf;**
- **(b) requiring the preservation or protection of evidence by the parties or by requiring it to be placed in the custody of a custodian;**
- **(c) appointing an expert to provide expert opinion evidence.**

(2) Evidence preservation orders may, where necessary, authorise access to the evidence. Access may be subject to such conditions as the court considers just.

Sources:

ALI/UNIDROIT Principles 8 and 16.

Comments:

1. Rule 198's purpose is to facilitate the preservation of a party's ability to secure evidence relevant to material issues in proceedings. Preservation of relevant and material evidence can be a critical factor both in respect of a party's (typically the claimant's) ability to prove their case, and the court's ability to establish facts accurately and decide disputes fairly. It may be necessary for a variety of reasons, e.g., to protect evidence from perishing, to protect it from being tampered with, damaged, destroyed, or hidden. It may also be necessary where a witness is unlikely to be available at trial, i.e., due to ill-health or due to the likelihood that they may not be in the jurisdiction at the relevant time.

2. While not every European jurisdiction considers evidence preservation to be a form of interim measure, the availability of similar measures that serve the same purpose and function and which are intended to preserve the integrity of the legal process is commonplace. Preservation of evidence is also, for instance, recognised as a form of provisional (or interim) measure in Article 17 of the UNCITRAL Model Law and Article 7 of the IP Enforcement Directive.
3. This Rule emphasises the fact that evidence preservation can take a variety of forms, and that courts should be ready to grant the most appropriate form of order in any particular claim. In doing so consistently with the principle of proportionality (Rule 185), they should use the form of order which will achieve its purpose in the least invasive manner for the respondent.
4. As is the case generally with provisional and protective measures evidence preservation orders may, where necessary, be ordered on a without-notice (*ex parte*) basis (see Rule 186). They may also be ordered before the applicant has initiated proceedings concerning the dispute between parties, in which case an order under Rule 188 and Rule 21(1) would ordinarily expect to be made by the court when granting an evidence preservation order.
5. The rules on evidence and access to information in Part VII also apply accordingly.

Rule 199. Criteria for awarding an Evidence Preservation Measure

A party seeking an evidence preservation order must show that:

(a) there is a real risk that unless the order is made the evidence will not be available for determining the substantive proceedings on their merits; and

(b) if the order requires access to a party's or non-party's property the applicant has a strong *prima facie* case in respect of the merits of the applicant's claim or proposed claim for relief.

Sources:

ALI/UNIDROIT Principles 8 and 16.

Comment:

1. A preservation order may be made before proceedings have commenced, i.e., where the evidence is in danger of perishing, of being destroyed, or unavailable at trial due, for instance, to a witness's imminent departure from the jurisdiction (see Rule 188).
2. Where it is necessary in the circumstances to make a preservation order urgently or where secrecy is required in order to ensure that the order is not capable of being frustrated before it has been granted, if granted, it may be granted on a without-notice (*ex parte*) basis. Examples of steps that could be taken to frustrate such an order before it is granted are: taking action to hide or destroy evidence, to remove it from the jurisdiction. Once a without-notice (*ex parte*) order has been granted, Rule 186 applies.[6]
3. Interference with a respondent party or a non-party's private property, and hence their property rights, i.e., business premises, land etc, in order to preserve evidence is a strong measure to take. Accordingly, where that is necessary an applicant must satisfy the court to a higher standard than is required for other provisional or protective measures. This enhanced standard requires the court to scrutinise merits of the applicant's substantive claim carefully. As such the court must be satisfied that the applicant has a strong *prima facie* case on the merits of the substantive proceedings or proposed proceedings.

6 See, for instance, Art. 7 of the IP Enforcement Directive.

D. INTERIM PAYMENT

Rule 200. Interim Payment Measures

A court may grant the claimant an interim payment order in relation to a monetary claim, either wholly or in part to satisfy the claim in the proceedings, in anticipation of the expected outcome.

Comments:

1. Interim payment orders are not common to all legal systems, although they exist in about half of the European Union Member States.[7] They are not, and thus should be distinguished from, orders for payment as those exist in national procedural rules and in EU law (see the EPO Regulation). Orders for payment, unlike interim payment orders, are final orders given in specific, usually one-sided, summary proceedings in relation to uncontested claims and are excluded from the scope of these Rules (see Preamble VII.3 for proceedings on payment orders). They are specifically outside the scope of Rule 184, as provisional measures are only temporary and not final orders. Furthermore, Rule 200, makes it clear that interim payments are only to be made in anticipation of the final determination of the proceedings, and hence cannot properly be final orders.
2. Interim payment orders can be regarded as a measure to prevent further harm within the meaning of Rule 184(1)(d). They are intended to either partially or wholly satisfy the claim or claims made by a claimant, on a provisional basis, in anticipation of the expected outcome in the judgment that finally determines proceedings. The often long duration of proceedings and the absence of other tailor-made procedures to protect a claimant's interest in an anticipated final determination of proceedings, including an order for payment procedure, may jeopardise the financial position of companies or individuals.
3. Interim payment orders are provisional in the sense that there is an obligation to repay the amount if proceedings, to be initiated in accordance with Rule 188, are unsuccessful.
4. In those systems where interim payment orders are allowed as a provisional measure, the grant of such an order is often subject to more stringent requirements than required for other types of provisional and protective measures, e.g., the defendant has admitted liability, judgment on liability has been obtained by a claimant with the question of damages yet to be determine[8] (see Rule 201, for the requirements applicable to the grant of such an order under Rule 200).
5. The present Rule is not intended to suggest that interim payment orders ought to be introduced into national procedural rules. It aims to provide model criteria for this type of measures considering the interests of applicants and respondents, should they be available.

Rule 201. Criteria for awarding an Interim Payment

(1) An applicant seeking an order under Rule 200 must show that:

(a) the defendant has admitted that they are liable to pay a monetary sum to the applicant, or the applicant has obtained a final judgment on liability, or it is highly likely that the applicant will obtain at least the amount sought in a final judgment; and

(b) they are in urgent need of payment by the defendant.

7 Also see Storme Report, Arts. 10.1.2. and 10.1.3.

8 See, for instance, Rule 25.7 of the English CPR.

(2) In assessing whether to make an interim payment order the court should consider all the circumstances, including any potential or actual hardship to the applicant or the respondent as a result of refusing or granting the order.

(3) An interim payment order cannot be made on a without-notice basis.

(4) Where judgment in the proceedings is for a lesser amount than that paid, any over-payment must be repaid.

(5) An interim payment order will ordinarily be made subject to the applicant giving security. If the applicant's claim is absolutely well founded and the requirement to obtain security would frustrate the order's purpose of securing urgent relief for the applicant's economic distress, where that has been at least partially caused by the defendant's delay, the court may grant an interim payment order without or upon reduced security.

Comments:

1. Two criteria must be satisfied before an interim payment measure is ordered under Rule 200. First, the defendant must have either admitted liability to pay, judgment on liability against the defendant has been entered, or it is highly likely that the applicant will succeed on the merits at trial. Secondly, the applicant can establish that payment from the defendant is needed urgently. These requirements are intended to ensure, as far as possible, that the grant of an interim payment in anticipation of a final judgment is justified.
2. The need to show urgency, in Rule 201(1)(b) is common to those European jurisdictions that permit the making of interim payments. In assessing this requirement the court may take into account how long it would take to obtain a final judgment, what the applicant's financial needs are, and whether the applicant has made serious and expeditious efforts to otherwise obtain payment from the defendant.
3. Rule 201(2) requires the court to take account of both the applicant's and defendant's interests in deciding whether to grant an interim payment. This assessment must also be read in conjunction with Rule 185 on proportionality.
4. Rule 201(3) provides an exception to Rule 186. While other provisional and protective measures may need to be awarded on a without-notice (*ex parte*) basis on the basis of urgency or the need for secrecy, such circumstances do not apply to interim payments. Due to the close relationship such measures have with the substantive proceedings, and given the anticipatory nature of this measure, applications under Rule 201 must be on-notice to enable the defendant to be heard.
5. To protect the defendant's interests, Rule 201(4) requires over-payment made to be repaid by the applicant. This is consistent with Rule 190 on liability, but extends to the situation where part of the interim payment granted is ultimately awarded in a final judgment.
6. While Rule 187(2) provides that the grant of a provisional or protective measure may be subject to the provision of security by the applicant, Rule 201(5) provides that an interim payment measure will ordinarily be made subject to giving security. This protects against any risk that repayment may be necessary. In cases, however, where a defendant has admitted liability such security may not be appropriate. This rule is inconsistent with Van Uden v. Deco-Line,[9] where the European Court of Justice required, in the context of international jurisdiction, in favour of a court not having jurisdiction on the substance that

9 Judgment of 17 November 1998, Van Uden Maritime / Kommandit-gesellschaft in Firma Deco-Line and others (C-391/95, ECR 1998 p. I-7091) ECLI:EU:C:1998:543.

'repayment to the defendant of the sum awarded is guaranteed if the plaintiff is unsuccessful as regards the substance of his claim'.

SECTION 3 – CROSS BORDER ISSUES

Rule 202. International jurisdiction

(1) Within the scope of the European Union Regulations or international conventions, the international jurisdiction of the court in relation to provisional and protective measures is governed by those Regulations or conventions.

(2) In any event, the court having jurisdiction in respect of the proceedings will have jurisdiction to grant provisional and protective measures.

(3) Without prejudice to applicable European Union rules and international conventions, another court may grant such provisional and protective measures necessary to protect interests located within the jurisdiction or the subject-matter of which have a real connecting link with the territory of the court, or that are necessary to support proceedings brought in another country.

Sources:
ALI/UNIDROIT Principle 2.3.

Comments:

1. Rule 202(1) is primarily concerned with existing rules dealing with international jurisdiction. Within the EU, many cases will be within the scope of the Brussels Ibis Regulation (see Articles 1, 4 and 6 of the Brussels Ibis Regulation). In line with Article 35 of that Regulation, as interpreted by the European Court of Justice and particularly the Van Uden v. Deco-Line ruling (Case C-391/95), a court that has jurisdiction in respect of the substantive proceedings is also able to grant provisional and protective measures. Where a court does not have jurisdiction regarding the substantive proceedings, a real connecting link must exist between the subject-matter of the measure and the territory of that court.
2. The general requirement of the 'real connecting link' should be understood to be the place where the respondent's assets are located or will be located (e.g., debts due to the respondent from third parties). Other EU rules on international jurisdiction and provisional measures include Article 6 of the EAPO Regulation and Article 20 of the Brussels IIbis Regulation.
3. In relation to interim payments, the European Court of Justice requires that, first, repayment to the respondent of the sum awarded is guaranteed if the applicant is unsuccessful as regards the substantive proceedings and, secondly, the measure sought only relates to specific assets of the respondent that are located or are to be located within the territorial jurisdiction of the court to which application is made. While the first point can be considered primarily to be an aspect inherent in the nature of a provisional measure, the second can be considered a jurisdiction rule.
4. Rule 202(2) states the rule common to international jurisdiction regimes, including the EU rules, that the court having jurisdiction over the substantive proceedings is also able to grant provisional and protective measures. There is no requirement that such proceedings have already been brought, as is apparent from Rule 188. The court that has jurisdiction over the substantive proceedings is the 'natural' forum for granting provisional and protective measures. This rule also (implicitly) forms part of ALI/UNIDROIT Principle 2.3 and in Principle 16 of the Helsinki Principles.

5. In accordance with international jurisdiction regimes, including the EU rules, a court may have jurisdiction to grant a provisional and protective measure where it does not have jurisdiction over the substantive proceedings, i.e., the merits of the dispute. This rule is set out in in Article 35 of the Brussels Ibis Regulation amongst others. It is also included in ALI/UNIDROIT Principle 2.3 and in Principle 17 of the Helsinki Principles. However, a court will only have jurisdiction in these circumstances where local interests need protection (e.g., evidence, assets, or perishable goods are located in that jurisdiction), where there is an otherwise close connection between the measures sought and that jurisdiction (e.g., a restraining order relating to acts taking place in that jurisdiction), or where the measures are necessary to support substantive proceedings brought in another country. It is for the applicant to show that one of these situations exists.
6. There are currently few international conventions on international jurisdiction, but incidental special or bilateral conventions may include relevant rules that would fall within this Rule's scope of application. According to Article 7 of the HCCH 2005 Choice of Court Convention it does not govern interim protective measures.

Rule 203. Recognition and enforcement

(1) Within the scope of European Union Regulations or international conventions, the recognition and enforcement of provisional and protective measures are governed by those Regulations or conventions.

(2) Where no European Union Regulation or international convention applies, provisional and protective measures will be recognised and enforced in accordance with domestic law.

(3) Courts should, at the request of the parties, take into account provisional and protective measures granted in another country and, where appropriate, and in accordance with these Rules, cooperate in order to secure the effectiveness of those measures.

Sources:

ALI/UNIDROIT Principles 30 and 31.

Comments:

1. This Rule is intended to be consistent with Rule 202(1). Accordingly, it refers to existing systems of recognition and enforcement of judgments, including provisional and protective measures. Particular reference should be made to Article 2(a) of the Brussels Ibis Regulation, according to which provisional and protective measures are recognised and enforced according to its provisions where: (i) the measure was ordered by a court that has jurisdiction in respect of the substantive proceedings; and (ii) the defendant was either heard or served prior to enforcement.
2. Special conventions and bilateral conventions may include relevant provisions for the recognition and enforcement of provisional and protective measures. For instance, Article 31(3) of the CMR[10] is generally understood to cover the enforcement of provisional measures. Provisional and protective measures are, however, generally excluded from the HCCH Conventions; see Article 7 of the HCCH 2005 Choice of Court Convention, Article

10 Convention on the Contract for the International Carriage of Goods by Road (CMR) (Geneva 1956).

3(1)(b) of the HCCH 2019 Judgments Convention and Article 1(3) of the HCCH 1970 Evidence Convention.

3. Outside the scope of EU Regulations and international conventions, domestic rules will apply (Rule 203(1)). Domestic rules may also be relevant where an international convention applies in dual systems, such as in Scandinavian countries, or to implement specific rules of the convention that are left to national law. National law diverges on the recognition and enforcement of foreign judgments in general. In so far as the enforcement of provisional measures is concerned, the finality requirement may limit or prevent enforcement, as is for instance the case in England, Italy, and numerous other countries.
4. In addition, the general exceptions included in international and domestic recognition and enforcement regimes apply, notably the public policy exception and the right to fair trial. The procedural requirements included in the present Rules are intended to provide guidance in respect of such matters.
5. In respect of both Rule 203(1) and (2), the court is, at the least, required to take account of provisional and protective measures granted in another country in consequence of, and in order to further, international judicial co-operation. This may require recognition of such measures (Rule 203(2)). Where appropriate courts should also co-operate in order to enable provisional and protective measures ordered in other countries to be effective. It should be noted that Rule 203(2) is consistent with both ALI/UNIDROIT Principles 30 and 31 and Principles 18-20 of the Helsinki Principles.

PART XI

COLLECTIVE PROCEEDINGS

INTRODUCTION

1. This Part provides mechanisms for collective redress. It adopts a broad, non-sectoral approach, which is consistent with approaches across many European jurisdictions and was the approach by the European Commission in 2013.[1] It is, however, broadly consistent in approach with that taken by the European Union in 2013 and 2018.[2] It is divided into four sections, each of which deals with different mass harm situations: the first concerns collective injunctive relief (Collective Interest Injunctions) (Rules 204-206); the second concerns collective proceedings for the recovery of damages or for declaratory relief (Collective Proceedings) (Rules 207-220, 221-228); the third, provides a mechanism to declare binding a collective settlement entered into by the parties to a pending collective proceeding (Rules 221-226); and finally, a mechanism to declare a collective settlement entered into outside of collective proceedings binding (Rules 229-232).

2. Unlike the European Union's Recommendation 2013/396 and its 2018 Proposal this Part does not conclude that the use of a collective proceeding for injunctive relief is necessary. This is because the effect of such injunctive relief if brought by a single claimant acting solely on their own behalf if granted will result in the defendant having to desist from the unlawful conduct. As a consequence, the relief granted will be of general public benefit; it will not simply be of benefit to the individual claimant. In order to ensure that unlawful behaviour can be terminated whenever necessary, a broad approach to legal standing for collective injunctive relief is necessary, but also sufficient (see Section 1 of Part XI).

3. As a general rule, collective proceedings should be carried out on an opt-in basis unless the court decides that an opt-out approach would be more effective in any particular case (Rule 215). This will allow claims with large or medium-sized individual damages claims to be treated differently from claims where individual damages are low and thus the individual claimants cannot be expected to commence litigation or take an active part in any active litigation due to rational apathy. The approach taken here prefers opt-out proceedings for damages to, for instance, an account of profits where a defendant has to be held to have secured profits unlawfully. It does so in order to provide a more effective means to secure compensation for individual victims of such conduct. This approach does, however, give rise to the potential problem that some damages awarded under an opt-out mechanism may not be claimed by those entitled to them due to the fact that they may be of low value. In such cases, the Rules permit the court in an appropriate case to approve *cy-près* solutions in settlement agreements. *Cy-près* solutions imposed by the court in a judgment need a basis in substantive law, which is beyond the scope of these Rules. In

1 Commission Recommendation of 11 June 2013 on common principles for injunctive and compensatory collective redress mechanisms in the Member States concerning violations of rights granted under Union Law (2013/396/EU).

2 Recommendation 2013/396; and the Proposal for a Directive of the European Parliament and of the Council on representative actions for the protection of the collective interests of consumers, and repealing Directive 2009/22/EC (the 2018 Proposal).

ELI-Unidroit Model European Rules of Civil Procedure. ELI & Unidroit, Oxford University Press.
 DOI: 10.1093/oso/9780198866589.003.0012

a settlement parties are free to agree on an alternative distribution of the settlement fund if it is fair and adequate to do so and the court approved the settlement (Rules 224 and 232).

4. These Rules adopt a broad approach with respect to legal standing, but provide safeguards to protect defendants and group members from misuse of the collective proceeding process. Legal standing to act as a "qualified claimant" is granted to individual group members, *ad hoc* interest groups or long-standing organisations authorised by national law to represent the interests of group members in a particular field of law, such as consumer organisations or organisations representing investors. Qualified claimants must meet certain requirements (Rule 209). In order to prevent a "run to the court-house", the lead claimant acting on behalf of group members will not be determined by the court on a "first come, first served" basis. Before making a collective proceeding order the court must allow other potential qualified claimants to apply to be considered for appointment when making the decision on who is the most appropriate to be appointed the lead, i.e., the qualified, claimant (Rules 213(2) and (3)).The court may also select more than one qualified claimant to act jointly in the best interest of the group.

5. Similar rules apply with respect to legal standing to reach a settlement outside collective proceedings and a subsequent application to declare such a settlement binding. Rules 208(a) and (b) are applicable. As it is unlikely that an entity which is potentially liable for a mass harm will enter into settlement negotiations with a single individual member of the group, this has not been included in Rule 230. In practice, only entities or organisations that can claim to represent a large number of group members will have the opportunity to negotiate a settlement.

6. Efficient handling of collective proceedings requires the court to have strong case management powers and to be able to take account of the peculiarities of each particular case. In addition to the general case management rules set out in Rules 49, 50 and 62, this Part provides particular rules for the situation of complex mass damages claims for relief.

SECTION 1 – COLLECTIVE INTEREST INJUNCTIONS

Rule 204. Scope of Application

(1) The Rules in Part XI, Section 1 apply to orders, known as collective interest injunction, made by a court, which direct any person to cease any conduct or behaviour that is infringing the law.

(2) A collective interest injunction cannot be made on an interim basis under Part X of these Rules.

Comments:

1. Collective interest injunctions or cease-and-desist orders can be either provisional or final orders in proceedings. For instance, consumer law, tort law or the law concerning unfair competition in a number of European jurisdictions provide for such orders to be made as final orders in order to stop on-going infringements of the law.[3] Due to the fact that

3 See, for instance, the French Consumer Code (*Code de la Consommation*) *(CCon)*, Arts. L-621-7 and following; also see Directive 2009/22/EC of the European Parliament and of the Council of 23 April 2009 on injunctions for the protection of consumers interests (Codified version) (the Injunctions Directive).

they are concerned with collective interests they do not come under Part X, i.e., they do not come under the scope of the general rules concerning provisional measures. They are dealt with at the start of this Part of the Rules as, unlike collective proceedings for damages which focus on the provision of corrective justice for individuals who are represented before the court, the effect of a collective interest injunction is to benefit the society as a whole: they serve to put an end to conduct that is in breach of a public interest generally, i.e., consumer protection law, competition.

2. Such orders can also be sought as provisional measures. They can be brought by individuals in, for instance, personal injury cases or where an individual seeks relief against the use of an unfair contract term in a particular contract between the claimant and the defendant. They can also be brought in the collective interest where, for instance, businesses contract on standard terms that are unfair, or where there are ongoing violations of competition law. In the latter type of case a cease-and-desist order may be granted as a provisional measure on a collective basis (Rule 205). When brought in the collective interest they are likely to be brought by consumer associations or similar public interest entities that are given standing to bring such actions under the substantive law. Where such entities successfully apply for an injunction and where the defendant complies with it, the action benefits individuals and society as a whole. As a consequence such orders, as a matter of fact if not of law, apply *erga omnes*.
3. This Rule and Rule 205, as they supplement the general rules on parties in Part II and the general rules concerning provisional measures in Part X, only deal with scope, legal standing, and the binding effect of such injunctions.

Rule 205. Entitlement to apply for a Collective Interest Injunction

(1) Any entity authorised under national law to bring actions in the collective interest may apply for a collective interest injunction that requires the cessation of any infringement of the law.

(2) Where appropriate the court may order additional measures such as the publication of its decision with a view to eliminating the continuing effects of the infringement.

Comments:

1. Legal standing in respect of collective interest injunctions is a controversial issue. The right to apply for such injunctions should not, due to their nature, be limited to individuals, but should include entities that act on behalf of the public or a collective interest.
2. In the European Union, the Injunctions Directive required those entities that had been granted legal standing in one Member State to be granted the same right in other Member States. The procedural concepts behind standing, however, vary. Some Member States, such as France, apply a procedural concept according to which it is a question of admissibility whether particular entities can bring proceedings for such an injunction. In other Member States, such as Germany, Austria, by contrast, legislation implementing the Directive adopted a substantive law concept, the result of which is that only consumer associations and other entities listed in special rules are entitled to pursue such actions.
3. Irrespective of the approach adopted amongst European Union Member States the consequences are, however, similar due to the nature of such injunction orders. As a consequence, Rule 205 does not choose between the two approaches, but rather leaves it to national law to determine how to authorise entities to apply for such injunctions.

Rule 206. Effect of collective interest injunctions

A collective interest injunction binds the defendant in all future proceedings.

Comment:

Irrespective of general *lis pendens* and *res judicata* rules it seems appropriate that individuals should benefit from collective interest injunctions and should therefore be able to rely, in future proceedings, on a finding that the defendant violated the law.

SECTION 2 – COLLECTIVE PROCEEDINGS

A. GENERAL PART

Rule 207. Collective Proceedings

Collective proceedings are proceedings brought by a qualified claimant on behalf of a group of persons who it is alleged are affected by an event giving rise to a mass harm, but where those persons, known as group members, are not parties to the action.

Comments:

1. Rule 207 provides the basic rule for proceedings for collective redress (collective proceedings). It explains that group members are not and do not become parties in the proceedings, although the judgment or a settlement can be binding upon them.
2. The term "mass harm" is not restricted to particular fields of law and it can be any event which causes injury or damage to at least two persons. While this approach might seem to set the threshold for a collective proceedings at a low level, it is the approach taken by the European Union and a number of European jurisdictions. This enables courts to consider on a case-by-case basis whether a collective proceeding is the most effective mechanism to secure access to justice for group members and defendants.[4] If any other minimum requirement for group members were set out it is difficult to see what justification there could be, i.e., any other choice of number would appear to be arbitrary. It should also be noted that a low minimum numerosity threshold does not imply that collective proceedings would be the appropriate mechanism, for instance, for a road traffic accident involving three people. In such a case joinder of proceedings of consolidation of proceedings is likely to be more appropriate. The question for the court will be whether, in any particular case, collective proceedings is the most appropriate means to prosecute and defend a claim or claims for relief (See Rule 212). When assessing numerosity the court will equally have to consider the maximum number of group members within the scope of the collective proceedings.[5]
3. Collective proceedings under this Part can only be brought by and on behalf of claimants. This is the same approach taken by the European Union in Recommendation 2013/396 and the 2018 Proposal. The rationale for this choice, which is not replicated in all European jurisdictions, is practical: in general there is little practical need for a defendant group to be represented by a collective defendant. In rare cases, such as copyright infringement cases, where numerous defendants are sued at the same time, their number will normally not require particular procedural rules which go beyond the rules on joinder (see Rules 36-38).

4 See, for instance, Art. 3(b) of Recommendation 2013/396; Art. 3(3) of the 2018 Proposal.

5 In the English competition case of Walter Merricks v MasterCard [2017] CAT 27 the group membership amounted to some 46.2 million people.

4. The expression "qualified claimant" has been chosen in order to avoid the use of the term "representative". The Rules also do not use the "representative action" in the context of collective proceedings although this is the terminology used in the European Union and, for instance, in the common law tradition. There are several reasons why the use of "representation" was not adopted. First, it may be confused with the representation of parties who lack litigation capacity (see Rules 30 and 31). It may also result in confusion with references to parties being represented by a lawyer. Secondly, it avoids another possible confusion due to the use of the term "representative action" in some European jurisdictions, such as France or Italy, where it has a specific meaning, which implies that represented persons are parties to the proceedings. The core idea of collective proceedings in these Rules is, however, to have only one party, or a limited number of parties, as claimants, in order to reduce the complexity of litigation and to enable the court to manage the proceedings more effectively.
5. The qualified claimant in these Rules represents the collective interests of all the group members. As such they do not, strictly speaking, represent them.[6]

Rule 208. Claimants Qualified to Bring Collective Proceedings

A qualified claimant is:

(a) an organisation authorised, in accordance with national law, to bring collective proceedings and whose purpose has a direct relationship with the event giving rise to the mass harm,

(b) an entity which is established solely for the purpose of obtaining redress for group members and which satisfied the requirements of Rule 209; or

(c) a person who is a group member and who meets the requirements of Rules 209(a) - (c).

Comments:

1. The broad approach to legal standing taken in Rule 208 is consistent with the approach taken in a number of European jurisdictions and the approach taken in 2013 by the European Union. Three types of entities could potentially be authorised to be qualified claimants: long-standing organisations representing the interests of consumers, investors or other potential victims (Rule 208(a)); *ad hoc* organisations or private entities, which are established to represent the victims of a particular mass harm event (Rule 208(b)); and, natural persons who are themselves a member of the group of victims (Rule 208(c)). Under Rule 208 all three types of potential qualified claimants have legal standing to initiate a collective proceeding.
2. Rule 208(a) includes public regulators or public bodies authorised under national law to bring such proceedings. As rules on legal standing will often not be found in civil procedure codes, but in other regulations or statutes, no further specifications are necessary here. Some European jurisdictions, and the European Union Article 4 of the 2018 Proposal, have taken a different approach. They have confined legal standing to certain long-standing entities like consumer associations or ombudsmen. Such an approach is appropriate for collective proceedings that have a limited, sectoral scope of substantive application, such as consumer claims, and representative associations or public interest

6 Art. 3(3) of the 2018 Proposal.

bodies which have existed for decades are considered to be able to bring such proceedings (for example consumer associations). As this Part does not restrict collective proceedings to specific sectors or types of claim, it cannot be assumed that a sufficient range of such bodies exists that would justify such a restrictive approach. It is for this reason that Rule 208(b) also gives legal standing to *ad hoc* bodies that meet the requirements of Rule 209. The general term "entity" was chosen in order to make clear that legal personality is not necessary.

3. It may be difficult to establish an *ad hoc* entity in some European jurisdictions. It thus appears to be necessary to provide for the possibility that natural persons can be authorised to act as a qualified claimant. In order to prevent lawyer-driven litigation, Rule 209(d) prohibits lawyers from becoming a qualified claimant in a collective proceeding. This exception does not apply where a lawyer or anyone exercising a legal profession is a victim of mass harm and a group member. This is why Rule 208(c) refers to Rules 209(a)-(c) but not (d).

Rule 209. Requirements for qualified claimants

A person or entity shall not be a qualified claimant unless:

(a) they have no conflict of interest with any group member,

(b) they have sufficient capability to conduct the collective proceeding. In assessing this issue, the court shall take account of the financial, human and other resources available to the putative qualified claimant If appropriate, the court may require security for costs (see Rule 243),

(c) they are legally represented, and

(d) they are neither a lawyer nor exercising any legal profession.

Comments:

1. Due to the possibility for the abuse of collective proceedings, these Rules adopt the approach generally accepted in European jurisdictions and the European Union that safeguards must be in place concerning the authorisation of the qualified claimant.[7] Rule 209, in order to protect the interests of group members and defendants to such a proceeding, therefore requires both natural persons and legal entities to satisfy certain requirements in order to have legal standing to bring a collective proceeding.
2. Rule 209 does not, however, require a qualified claimant to be a non-profit making body in order to protect both interests. It rejects this approach taken by, for instance, the European Union in its 2018 Proposal, as it cannot reasonably be expected that sufficient numbers of private actors will become active in the enforcement of the interests of a group of persons affected by a mass harm event if all kinds of financial incentive are excluded.
3. Rule 209(a) ensures that a qualified claimant can only be authorised if there are no conflicts of interest between it and group members. Such conflicts are, however, only relevant if they might have an influence on the claimant's conduct of the collective proceeding, or any negotiation in, or settlement of, such proceedings. In cartel cases, for example, the group may consist of Small and Medium-sized Enterprises (SMEs) which all bought overpriced products from the defendants due to a price-fixing cartel. Although the SMEs may

7 See, for instance, recitals 13, 15, 21 of Recommendation 2013/396 and recital 4 of the 2018 Proposal.

be competitors on the same market, there is not necessarily a conflict of interest in the sense of Rule 209(a) if one of the SMEs acts as the qualified claimant. Each of the group members will have a common interest. Conflicts may, for instance, occur in product liability or pharmaceutical cases if some group members who have already suffered damage from the mass harm event intend to pursue the recovery of damages whereas another part of the group, which has not yet but may suffer injury and damage in the future, is only interested in securing a declaratory judgment. In such a situation it might be necessary to form sub-groups, each with its own qualified claimant.

4. Rule 209(b) ensures that a qualified claimant has sufficient financial resources to enable them to pursue collective proceedings properly. This also, importantly, protects defendants by ensuring that the qualified claimant is able to pay any adverse cost orders. Where the court has doubts with respect to the sufficiency of the qualified claimant's resources, an order for security for costs may be made under Rule 209(b).
5. In collective proceedings high costs may be involved for both parties. As the European or loser pays rule applies (see Rules 239 and 241) defendants face a risk that a qualified claimant cannot meet adverse cost orders. In order to prevent a high threshold for access to justice, security for costs should not be a regular requirement for such claimants. When deciding whether security for costs is necessary, the court will balance the interests of the parties, assess the qualified claimant's financial situation, and it may also take into account the prospects of the case on the merits. Where there is, based on a summary estimation of the court, a high probability of success for the group, no security should be requested as the defendant's risk with respect to an adverse cost order is low. There is also no need to protect the defendant(s) for example in follow-on actions in cartel cases where the relevant cartel authorities have already issued a binding decision that the defendant(s) participated in a cartel. Security for costs can, for example, be a deposit or a bank guarantee. Details of the nature of the security should be set out in the court order.
6. Rule 209(c) specifies that as collective proceedings always involve a certain level of complexity legal representation should be mandatory.
7. The broad wording of Rule 209(d) is intended to not only include lawyers or advocates, but also legal notaries, judges etc. It is not intended to include legal academics.

Rule 210. Collective Proceedings – Statement of Claim

(1) A statement of claim in collective proceedings must include all relevant information available concerning

(a) the event giving rise to the mass harm,

(b) the group,

(c) the causal connection between the event of mass harm and the loss suffered by the group members,

(d) the similarity of the claims of the group members in law and fact,

(e) whether compensation or other collective remedies are sought,

(f) the financial and other resources available to the qualified claimant to pursue the collective proceeding,

(g) evidence of the qualified claimant's attempt to settle the group members' claims.

(2) Before commencing collective proceedings and upon the application of a qualified claimant, the court may issue an order preventing a potential defendant from bringing an action with respect to the event of mass harm.

Comments:

1. Rule 210 requires a qualified claimant to disclose all relevant information which the court needs in order to enable it to make a collective proceeding order under Rule 212.
2. Rules 210(1)(a)-(d) specify the minimum basic information that any qualified claimant would be expected to set out to enable the court to determine whether a collective proceeding order could properly be made. It requires a description to be given of the mass harm event underlying the collective proceeding, and of the group of persons that has allegedly been affected by it. If possible, the claimant must set out the names and addresses of all group members. If the group consists of unidentified persons, it must give sufficient detail to describe the group exactly.
3. Rule 210(1)(e) assumes that the qualified claimant may seek any court order/remedy that is available in regular proceedings. This includes actions for the recovery of damages, as well as, for instance, for the reimbursement of a price paid, the repair of goods purchased, the replacement of defective products etc. As a consequence, any other form of performance by the defendant can be sought. Such a broad scope for remedies is apparent in Europe.[8] Collective proceedings may also be in the form of a declaratory judgment or a collective interest injunction. Any combination of such remedies is also possible.
4. Rule 210(1)(f) concerns the funding of the collective proceedings. Only the qualified claimant is potentially liable for an adverse cost order. As such it is highly likely that the proceeding will involve the use of some form of public funding or third-party funding. Consistently with the general approach to party co-operation and effective case management of proceedings, and to third-party funding, in these Rules, third-party funding of collective proceedings is permissible, but requires any party so funded to adopt a transparent approach to such funding (see Rules 6, 9, 49, 237 and 245). As such, a qualified claimant must provide the court and the defendant with information concerning their financial sources, particularly on any third-party funding. This is to ensure that the qualified claimant has sufficient financial resources available to pursue the collective proceedings and thus satisfy the requisite funding requirement. In so far as appropriate, the information can be restricted to the fact that third-party funding is being used and to the funder's identity. Such information should enable the court to assess whether the funding and the funder are capable of meeting any potential adverse costs award against the qualified claimant. No sensitive details on the funding terms should be given to the defendant, so as to ensure that defendants cannot use that information to build its procedural strategy based upon it (see, however, Rule 237 with comment 1). In the absence of such information, the court should not authorise a qualified claimant to act in collective proceedings. This approach differs from that of the European Union.[9] It differs as these Rules recognise the importance of such funding to render collective proceedings a practical rather than a merely theoretical procedural mechanism, the absence of available funding for such proceedings being a fundamental weakness in their development and use. The regulation of third-party funding is outside the scope of these Rules. It may, however, be necessary for European jurisdictions to regulate it. If a qualified claimant has insufficient resources

8 See, for instance, Art. 6(1) of the 2018 Proposal.

9 See, for instance, Art. 7(2) of the 2018 Proposal.

to meet any adverse cost order, the court may require security for costs from it (Rules 209(b), 243).

5. Rule 210(1)(g) is intended to prevent a "race to the courthouse" as well as unnecessary proceedings being commenced. It thus is a specific application of parties' pre-commencement duties and the duty to seek to resolve disputes consensually (see Rules 3 and 9). It thus requires any potentially qualified claimant to contact those parties that are likely to be defendants to any claim for relief before seeking to initiate collective proceedings, and to attempt to settle the dispute out-of-court (also see Rule 229). Information and evidence concerning such attempts should be included in the claim. For time limits concerning settlement attempts, see Rule 212(1)(d). This requirement could, however, increase the risk of "torpedo actions" filed by the potential defendant who becomes aware of a possible collective proceeding and may thus commence proceedings for a declaratory judgment. Depending on a broad or somewhat restrictive construction of the term "same cause of action" in Rule 142 this rule may even encourage such "torpedo actions". As a consequence, a second court seised of a collective proceeding would have to stay proceedings. This may increase the risk that a judgment for the recovery of damages would be delayed, and might finally be unenforceable in the case of defendant insolvency. Rule 210(2) therefore allows courts to issue anti-suit injunctions in order to prevent torpedo actions from the start. The necessity for such an injunction may occur in purely domestic settings, but they can be particularly important in cross-border cases where torpedo actions in another European jurisdiction, including European Union Member States, can delay collective proceedings considerably. The question of whether anti-suit injunctions should be allowed in cross-border situations actually has to be resolved in the Brussels Ibis Regulation. While current European Union case law does not allow anti-suit injunctions in proceedings to which its Regulations apply, as long as there is, however, no clear solution in the Regulation and its application is limited to those European countries within the European Union, these model rules may help in this respect. However, it should be noted that the possibility of consolidation of actions (Rule 146) can prevent the "torpedo effect".
6. For Rule 210(1)(d) see comment 4 on Rule 212(1)(c).

Rule 211. Registration of Collective Proceedings

(1) Upon the qualified claimant submitting a collective proceedings statement of claim to the court, the court must enter the proceedings into a publicly accessible electronic register.

(2) After registration any other court must dismiss any collective proceedings against the same defendant(s) in respect of the same mass harm.

Comments:

1. Rule 211 provides the basis through which information concerning pending collective proceedings can be disseminated. The easiest way to provide such information is through a partially publicly accessible electronic register, which can be consulted by all potential qualified claimants, lawyers, group members etc.
2. The effect of registration is not, however, restricted to the provision of information. Rule 211(2) helps to prevent parallel collective proceedings in respect of the same mass harm event. Traditional *lis pendens* rules cannot preclude a second collective proceeding being filed against the same defendant by another qualified claimant because the parties to the actions will be different. In small European jurisdictions, one court may have exclusive

jurisdiction to try collective proceedings, but in other jurisdictions, it is necessary to have a rule which prevents parallel actions within the same country. Rule 142(1) gives priority to the first action filed in cases where proceedings involve the same cause of action and the same parties. If the qualified claimant is not the same in a second collective proceeding, Rule 142 will not apply, and according to Rule 144 which refers to related proceedings and which does not require the identity of the parties in both proceedings to be the same, a stay of the second proceedings will not be mandatory. To protect defendants in collective proceedings Rule 211(2) bars any other collective proceeding against the same defendant with respect to the same mass harm event. An obvious counter-argument would be that such a rule encourages a "race to the court house" by qualified claimants. This is not, however, applicable in the context of these Rules. Any qualified claimant who is interested in conducting the pending collective proceeding can only be authorised to do so under the procedure set out in Rules 213(2) and (3), which is not based on a first-filed approach. Furthermore, qualified claimants must make an attempt to settle the dispute out of court before filing a collective proceeding (see Rule 210(1)(g)).

3. The register to be established under Rule 211 can be the same electronic platform provided for in Rule 220. It may be divided into publicly accessible sections and sections which are only accessible by the parties and group members. The electronic register could also be established at the European level and be used to register collective proceedings in all European or European Union jurisdictions.

B. ADMISSIBILITY OF COLLECTIVE PROCEEDINGS

Rule 212. Conditions of Admissibility

(1) The court may admit a collective proceeding if

(a) it will resolve the dispute more efficiently than joinder of the group members' individual claims,

(b) all of the claims for relief made in the proceeding arise from the same event or series of related events causing mass harm to the group members,

(c) the claims are similar in law and fact, and

(d) except in cases of urgency, the qualified claimant has allowed the defendant or defendants at least three months to respond to a settlement proposal.

(2) Upon application, the court may order any proceeding to continue as a collective proceeding.

Comments:

1. In any collective proceeding the court must determine whether the proceedings are admissible on a collective basis. Such an admissibility decision under Rule 212 may be subject to appeal.
2. Rules 210 and 212 provide criteria to be taken into account when making an admissibility decision. The court will in particular consider the number of group members (numerosity) and whether individual actions as such, to the extent they are likely to be issued, will be capable of effective case management as individual claims (see Rules 2, 3, 5 and 6). Rule 212(1)(a) therefore also applies a superiority test which is common standard for almost all types of collective proceeding across the world. When making a decision on the good administration of justice, the court should take into account the complexity of the case

with respect to its general court management powers (see Rules 49 and 50). In particular, it may consider the likely cost to group members of pursuing their claims individually and the value of each group member's claim for compensation. Group members will not be liable for procedural costs because they are not parties to the collective proceeding (see Rule 238(1)). Individual actions will therefore be more expensive and may not be a realistic option for individual group members. This is particularly likely to be the case where the amount of potential compensation for each group member is low.

3. Furthermore a collective proceeding is admissible only if all the individual claims for relief arise from the same event and therefore raise common questions of fact or law. The same event could be a so-called "single event mass harm", e.g., a mass accident such as a plane crash, a chemical plant explosion etc., or it could arise from a series of related events, e.g., a so-called "single cause mass harm" such as the use of unfair contract terms, product liability cases, or liability for misleading information in capital market brochures, etc.
4. Rule 212(1)(c) provides a requirement which is familiar to most forms of collective proceedings in European Union Member States. It deliberately does not indicate what degree of closeness is required. Most European Union approaches use 'similar' claims with some extending to 'related' claims.[10] Claims for relief that are related might still warrant collective proceedings, therefore the court should to decide on a case-by-case basis what degree of closeness suffices to authorise such proceedings. Similarity of the claims may arise from the same facts underlying each claim, but also from the applicable law. In cases in which according to the conflict-of-laws rules different sets of substantive law apply, but all claims are based on the same event, the collective proceeding should be admissible in principle (Rule 236). The court may, however, divide the group in sub-categories according to the applicable law (Rule 218(1)(d)).
5. Rule 212(1)(d) promotes the parties' duty to seek to settle disputes (see Rule 9(1)) A period of negotiation of at least three months is thus required before collective proceedings can be initiated.

Rule 213. Collective Proceeding Order

(1) An order made under Rule 212 must include the following information:

(a) the name and address, and other relevant contact details of the qualified claimant

(b) a concise description of the event of mass harm giving rise to the collective proceeding;

(c) the names or a description of all of the persons allegedly affected by the mass harm. The description must contain sufficient detail to enable any person allegedly affected by the event causing mass harm to know if they are within the group or not;

(d) the type of collective proceeding under Rule 215.

(2) Before making an order under this Rule the court shall advertise a draft of the order and set a deadline for any other potential qualified claimants to apply under Rule 207.

(3) The court shall determine which of several potential qualified claimants, if any, shall become the qualified claimant in the proceedings. It shall do so on the basis of the

10 See, for instance, in the United Kingdom, section 47B(6) Competition Act 1998 (UK) and Rules of the Competition Appeals Tribunals, rules 79(1)(b) and 73(2): "same, similar or related issues of fact or law"; and in France, Art. L. 623-1 of the CCon (in the version of the publication of the Law No. 2018-1021, November 23, 2018, replacing the old Art. L-423-1): "*une situation similaire ou identique*".

criteria set out in, among others, Rule 209. Where more than one qualified claimant is selected they must act jointly.

(4) The collective proceeding order shall be advertised in a manner which the court considers will best bring it to the attention of any person likely to be affected by the event causing mass harm on which the proceeding is based. The advertisement shall invite such persons to opt-in to the proceeding and shall give information on how to do so.

(5) The collective proceeding order or the refusal to grant such an order are subject to appeal by the qualified claimant and the defendant.

Comments:

1. To admit the collective proceeding a court order is necessary. It must clearly identify the key information required by Rule 213(1). This is particularly important for group members, as it helps enable them to decide whether to opt-in or opt-out of proceedings (see Rule 215(2)).
2. Rules 213(2) and (3) are based on experience in the Netherlands where following some mass events a large number of *ad hoc* foundations competed to secure the support of victims. This resulted in situations in which it was difficult for the group members to decide whom to support and for the defendant to choose with whom they wanted to enter into settlement negotiations. Such matters are not conducive to either effective settlement or the effective management of proceedings. In order to avoid such a situation arising under these Rules, it is for the court to determine which of several, where there are such, potential qualified claimants should be permitted to have the conduct of the proceedings.
3. The approach adopted here to determine which of several potential qualified claimants should be authorised as such is set out in Rules 208 and 209. A first come, first served approach is not adopted, i.e., the first to file is not given priority. The question is one of suitability not priority.[11]
4. Rule 213(4) requires the court secure the publication of the collective proceedings order (see Rule 219). It may choose any method of publication which it considers best to notify all persons likely to be affected. If group members are identified and their names and addresses are available, they can either be notified personally or via the secure electronic platform under Rule 220. In opt-out proceedings, Rules 215(2)-(4) apply.
5. For Rule 213(5) see Rule 179(2)(f).

Rule 214. Obligation of Qualified Claimant

A qualified claimant must at all times act in the best interests of the whole group or sub-group, if a qualified claimant for a sub-group.

Comments:

1. One of the core ideas underpinning collective proceedings is that the claimant who represents the group, or acts on the group's behalf, must act in the group's best interests at all times. Rule 214 provides an explicit rule in this respect and thus provides the court with a discretion to impose sanctions upon the claimant where they violate those interests.
2. Collective proceedings' rules, in general, must provide safeguards against misuse. Three potential conflicts of interest can arise: conflicts within the group; conflicts between the

11 See, for instance, Art. 1018e (4) of the Netherlands Code of Civil Procedure (*Wetboek van Burgerlijke Rechtsvordering*).

qualified claimant and the group as a whole; and, conflicts between the group and/or the qualified claimant on one side and the lawyer who represents the claimants on the other side.

3. The first potential conflict can be solved by establishing sub-categories according to Rule 218(1)(d). The second potential conflict is addressed in Rule 214, which imposes an express obligation on the qualified claimant to act in the interest of the group or sub-group. As the group members are absent from the proceedings, i.e., they are only present by representation, the court must supervise the qualified claimant to some extent. To enable effective supervision the court must be given the power to intervene if the qualified claimant does not act, or ceases to act, in the group or sub-group's best interests. Where intervention is necessary, the court may then substitute the qualified claimant for another one (see Rule 218(1)(a)).The third potential conflict is addressed by specific provisions, such as the need to secure court approval of any proposed settlement in collective proceedings (see Rules 224, 225 and 226) and those concerning the availability of specific litigation funding arrangements (see Rules 237, 238 and 245).

Rule 215. Types of Collective Proceeding

(1) Collective proceedings shall operate on an opt-in basis unless the court makes an order under Rule 215(2).

(2) The court may order that the proceedings will include all group members who have not opted-out of the proceedings under Rule 215(3) where it concludes that:

(a) the group members' claims cannot be made in individual actions because of their small size; and

(b) a significant number of group members would not opt-in to the collective proceeding.

(3) Where the court makes an order under Rule 215(2) it must set a deadline for group members to notify the court that they wish to opt-out. In exceptional circumstances the court may permit group members to opt-out after the deadline has expired.

(4) The court shall decide to whom and how notification under Rule 215(3) shall be given.

Comments:

1. For many years, one of the most controversial issues in debates about collective proceedings has been the question whether to use the traditional class action opt-out mechanism or an opt-in system that allows group members to better control whether or not their claim will be enforced against the defendant. Against the background of a strong principle of party autonomy governing European civil procedure, collective proceedings ought normally to be based on an opt-in mechanism. Group members will thus only be bound by the outcome of proceedings if they have expressly and actively informed the court that they have joined the collective proceeding. Such notification will ordinarily be effected through the use of a secure electronic platform under Rules 219 and 220.
2. An opt-in approach may not, however, be adequate for those cases in which the group members have suffered only minimal loss and due to their rational apathy they cannot be expected to become active and to opt-in to the proceedings. For the sake of an efficient enforcement of liability rules, which is a public good, exceptions from the opt-in approach must therefore be permitted. It is therefore in the interests of justice to enable a collective proceeding to be conducted on an opt-out basis. This is the most cost-efficient way of organising the group and which, according to insights from behavioural economics,

tends to generate a much larger group compared to an opt-in system. An often raised argument against opt-out systems is the allegedly higher potential for misuse and frivolous claims. However, in practice, those European jurisdictions that permit opt-out proceedings, such as Belgium, Bulgaria, Denmark, Norway, or Portugal have not experienced an excessively large number of those claims. Provided that safeguards like court authorisation of collective proceedings and qualified claimants, effective court case management and the European or loser pays costs rule are in place and punitive damages are not available, it cannot be expected that an excessive amount of unmeritorious collective proceedings will be promoted by way of an opt-out mechanism.

3. A concern that carries more weight is, however, that the rational apathy of group members will often prevent them from claiming compensation from a fund established as a result of an opt-out collective proceeding. The distribution of compensation funds may therefore become difficult if not impossible. In order to avoid this problem, an alternative solution could be the establishment of actions for skimming-off illegally gained profits from a defendant or disgorgement by public or private entities instead of opt-out collective proceedings. Such an approach is suggested by Article 6(3)(b) of the EU 2018 Proposal. It takes into account the fact that the distribution of small amounts of redress may be disproportionate. The conclusion it draws is that the redress shall be directed to a public purpose, which serves the collective interest of consumers (or more broadly group members). Thus, although the proceedings suggested in the Proposal are not disgorgement proceedings, Article 6(3)(b) explicitly accepts *cy-près* distributions of unclaimed compensation. Such disgorgement proceedings have the advantage that it is not necessary to distribute a compensation fund to the group members as they are not an instrument to compensate the victims of an event of mass harm. The money paid by the defendant will not, ordinarily, go to the members of the group in order to avoid enormous administrative efforts to distribute small amounts of money but may be paid to State budgets,[12] to a charity[13] or special purpose funds.
4. Compared to disgorgement proceedings opt-out collective proceedings at least offer the opportunity to secure compensation for some group members. Proposed settlements may include *cy-près* solutions, which enable the unclaimed part of a compensation fund to be paid back to the defendant, or to be paid to non-profit institutions for a special purpose, such as consumer protection, the funding of future public interest or collective proceedings. Different jurisdictions have different solutions for this issue, which is also a question of substantive law. Therefore the present Rules do not propose a firm solution here. Such settlements must be carefully scrutinised by the court under Rules 223, 224. In doing so the court may also take into account that, depending on the nature of the mass harm, the group members may not claim compensation because they may have difficulties in proving that they are actually members of the group and thus entitled to compensation, e.g., in cartel cases, consumers will often not possess documents or receipts proving that they have bought an over-priced product during a relevant period. For these cases it may be considered an adequate solution if the money paid by the defendant is used in a way, which is close to compensation of the individual group members.[14]

12 As in Germany see, Section 10 German Unfair Competition Act (UCA) (*Gesetz gegen den unlauteren Wettbewerb (UWG)*).

13 As in the UK see, Section 47C(5) of the Enterprise Act 1998.

14 See, for instance, Art. 6(3)(b) of the 2018 Proposal.

5. The decision whether opt-in or opt-out procedure is an adequate mechanism depends on the number of individual claims involved and an estimation of whether the group members have sufficient incentives to opt-in. The decision is best made by the court on a case-by-case basis, so as to enable it to take into account the features of the particular case such as the estimated amount of individual damages, the size of the group and the chance of notifying all or almost all group members, etc. The court should also consider whether group members have a realistic chance of bringing individual actions.

Rule 216. Opt-in Proceedings

(1) Where collective proceedings operate on an opt-in basis, group members must notify the court if they wish to join the proceedings in the manner specified by the court.

(2) The court shall ensure that group member notifications are properly recorded in a public register, which may be established in accordance with Rule 220.

Comments:

1. In respect of the *res judicata* effect of a judgment in a collective proceeding (Rule 227) and the binding effect of a court approved settlement (see Rules 225 and following and Rule 232 (d)), it must be clear who opted-in to the proceeding. This can become particularly relevant where a group member, or individual who could have been a group member, seeks to initiate separate, individual, proceedings. It is also important in respect of any distribution of damages arising from the proceedings.
2. Consequently, the court may provide different ways for group members to notify it that they wish to join the collective proceeding, e.g., by written statements submitted to the court or registration on the secure electronic platform. If the qualified claimant has invited group members to register with it in preparing the collective proceeding, such a list of registrations may also be submitted to the court and be an equivalent to an opt-in declaration, if the qualified claimant had informed the group members in this respect before registration. In any event, the court must ensure that there is a register which identifies the group members who opted-in (Rule 216(2)).

Rule 217. Individual Actions

(1) Group members who have opted-in under Rule 216 or who have not opted-out under Rule 215(3) cannot bring an individual court action in respect of the same event of mass harm against a defendant to the collective proceeding.

(2) In cases under Rule 215(2) any group member who brings an individual action against a defendant to collective proceedings during the opt-out period shall be treated as having opted-out of the proceedings.

(3) Any time limit provided in national law for individual actions to be brought by a group member in respect of loss caused by the event of mass harm shall be suspended from the date of commencement of the collective proceeding. The period of suspension shall end when

(a) the collective proceeding is withdrawn or dismissed; or

(b) the group member opts-out under Rules 215(2)-(4).

(4) Where Rule 217(3)(a) or (b) applies the remaining limitation period for individual claims will start six months after the withdrawal, dismissal or the date on which the opt-out was effected.

Comments:

1. In order to protect a defendant from parallel proceedings arising from the same mass harm event, Rule 217 bars group members from bringing individual proceedings. It is necessary to have an explicit rule because according to general rules on *lis pendens* individual actions may not be automatically inadmissible, e.g. as the parties to the collective and individual proceedings will not be the same, as group members are not parties to the collective proceedings. Rule 144 only permits a stay of proceedings where proceedings are related, but for collective proceedings a stricter rule seems necessary in order to protect the defendant from multiple proceedings, as well as to protect the judicial system from a disproportionate use of its resources. Parallel individual proceedings thus are barred for group members who have opted-in to collective proceedings. They can bring individual actions only if they exit the collective proceeding. Where the collective proceeding operates on an opt-out basis under Rule 215(2) the group members will not be personally known to the qualified claimant or the court seised of the proceedings. If they initiate individual proceedings without having opted-out of the collective proceeding, a defendant will become aware that the claimant in the individual proceedings is part of the group as described in the collective proceeding and may inform the court of that fact. Consequently, the claimant to the individual action shall be treated as having opted-out of the collective proceeding.
2. According to Rule 217(3) time limits are suspended. This refers to the commencement of the proceedings which can either be the filing of the claim or the service of the documents instituting the proceedings (Rule 145).
3. Rule 217(4) concerns the situation where a collective proceeding is withdrawn or dismissed or if a group member opts-out of it. In such circumstances, the time limit for the prescription of individual claims must be restarted. However, to avoid a situation where an individual may have very little time left to assert their individual claim for relief, this Rule applies a minimum six-month period.

C. CASE MANAGEMENT OF COLLECTIVE PROCEEDINGS

Rule 218. Case Management Powers

(1) In collective proceedings, the court has additional case management powers, including the power

(a) to remove a qualified claimant of a group or any sub-group if they no longer satisfy the conditions in Rule 208 and Rule 209 or fails to act in the interests of all group members,

(b) to authorise, with their consent, a new qualified claimant,

(c) to modify the description of the group,

(d) to divide a group into sub-groups and to authorise, with their consent, a qualified claimant for each sub-group,

(e) to dismiss the collective proceeding or to order it to continue as individual proceedings if there is no longer a qualified claimant

(f) to direct the correction of the group register (Rules 216(2) and 220).

(2) The court may hear any person it considers has an interest in the management of the case before making any case management order under this Rule.

Comments:

1. Rule 218(1)(a) is based on the assumption that a qualified claimant is identified by filing a collective proceeding and by fulfilling the requirements under Rule 208 and Rule 209. The court will, however, supervise the qualified claimant's activities in the interest of the absent group members. It will do so particularly in opt-out proceedings where group members have not explicitly joined the proceeding. In carrying out this supervision, it is within the court's management power to substitute the qualified claimant if they are no longer qualified or if they fail to act in the group members' best interests (see Rule 214).
2. Rule 218 provides the court with a wide power to act in the interests of absent group members. It requires the court to supervise the activities of the qualified claimant in this respect. This does not necessarily conflict with the neutral and independent role of the judge, although the court is in a different position compared to individual proceedings. The situation of the absent group members requires more active involvement on the court's part.
3. As the group members will not normally be in a position or not be willing to supervise the qualified claimant themselves, the court may substitute the qualified claimant of its own motion (*ex officio*). It is also not necessary for another qualified claimant to have applied to be substituted for the court to make such an order. If a qualified claimant is a natural person and a member of the group (Rule 208(c)), they will, for example, no longer satisfy the requirements under Rule 208 if they assign or transfer their claims during the proceedings. As they will no longer have a personal interest in the outcome of the litigation it cannot be assumed that they will act in the interest of the group any more. In order to prevent the collective proceeding collapsing in such circumstances, the court must be able to substitute a new qualified claimant. The new qualified claimant may be substituted only if they satisfy the requirements in Rules 208 and 209. If the group or the lawyer representing the group cannot identify a new qualified claimant the proceedings must be dismissed. The same applies with respect to the substitution of a qualified claimant of any sub-group.

Rule 219. Advertisements

(1) In collective proceedings the court shall advertise or shall require advertisement

(a) when a qualified claimant is removed or authorised,

(b) when the description of the group is modified or the group is divided into sub-groups,

(c) when a collective settlement is offered,

(d) when any order or judgment is made,

(e) of information about the secure electronic platform under Rule 220; and

(f) if the collective proceeding is dismissed or withdrawn.

(2) The advertisement shall be made in a manner which the court considers will best attract the attention of any person likely to be affected by the event causing mass harm and in sufficient time to allow affected persons a reasonable opportunity to participate as they see fit in the proceedings.

Comments:

1. Basic information concerning the proceedings should be available to the public and to unidentified group members. Rule 219 therefore provides a mandatory rule concerning the content of such notice via public advertisements.

2. In order to ensure that such adverts are tailored to the circumstances of specific proceedings, the court should exercise its case management powers to determine their form and content. Such information can be made available via the secure electronic platform (see Rule 220).

Rule 220. Communication – Secure Electronic Platform

The court must create or authorise the creation of a secure electronic platform for the efficient management of the collective proceeding.

Comments:

1. Rule 211 requires a collective proceeding be entered onto a register. The same register can be used as a secure electronic platform under Rule 220. Thus it can also be an easy and cost-efficient way of facilitating communication between the court, the parties and/or group members. It can also be a tool, in addition to public advertisements under Rule 219 such as publications in newspapers and on the internet or other media, to facilitate the dissemination of information concerning the proceedings. Alternatively, access to it could, if necessary, be restricted to the parties and the group members.
2. The platform should enable the court and parties to identify the group members. In particular, it could be used to provide information to the group members such as pleadings submitted by the parties, the announcement of court hearings, court orders, etc. It could also be used to register opt-in or opt-out declarations by group members.
3. Rule 220 does not specify who should be responsible for setting up and maintaining the electronic platform. Traditions across European jurisdictions vary in so far as the allocation of responsibility for distributing information concerning court proceedings is concerned. As such, responsibility for operating the platform and in respect of its content could lie with the court or, upon court authorisation of the court, with the qualified claimant.

D. SETTLEMENTS IN COMMENCED COLLECTIVE PROCEEDINGS

Rule 221. Court Approval

A group member will not be bound by any agreement settling a collective proceeding in whole or in part unless that agreement is approved by the court.

Comments:

1. It is a general standard of collective proceedings that settlements need court approval. Settlements negotiated by a qualified claimant and the defendants are not a normal settlement agreement between the parties because they intend to bind group members who are not involved in the negotiation process. Court approval is therefore necessary to protect the group members' interests and to provide a safeguard against conflicts of interests within the group or between the group and a qualified claimant or between the group and the lawyer representing the qualified claimant.
2. Court approval is necessary only if there is a collective settlement made in the interest of the group or a sub-group. If a single group member enters into an individual settlement agreement with the defendant(s) there is no need for court approval. This also applies if a qualified claimant, who is a group member, negotiates a settlement only on their own behalf.

Rule 222. Application for the approval of a settlement agreement

(1) A party to a proposed settlement agreement may apply to the court for approval under Rule 221.

(2) The application for approval shall include:

(a) the description of the group whose members will be bound by the settlement;

(b) a copy of the proposed settlement agreement. In a collective proceeding for compensation, the proposed agreement shall include the total amount of compensation payable, and the criteria for distributing the compensation to each group member;

(c) the proposed administration of the compensation fund and method of distributing the compensation payment to group members; and

(d) a concise statement of reasons showing why the terms of the settlement agreement are fair and adequate.

Comments:

1. For the court's consideration of an application for approval of a settlement, the group must be defined with clarity (Rule 222(2)). The application must also contain all the information required by Rules 222(2)(a)-(d), and particularly the information required by Rule 222(2)(d) without which the court will not be able to assess whether the proposed settlement is fair and adequate (Rule 223(1)(a)). The court may require the provision of other information to enable it to consider the proposed settlement (Rule 223(1)(a)).
2. There is no requirement in this Rule, or these Rules generally, for detailed information to be provided concerning the administration of a compensation fund. It is up to the parties to the settlement agreement to determine the mechanism through which the fund should be administered. In complex cases it may be appropriate for an administrative board to be established to manage the compensation fund. Such a board could then, as is the case in the Netherlands, include at least one legal and one economic expert.
3. Rules 208(b) and (c) should not be interpreted to prevent *cy-près* distributions of any residue of a compensation fund in opt-out proceedings under Rule 222(2)(b).[15]

Rule 223. Procedure for Approving Settlements

(1) Before approving a settlement the court may

(a) make any order necessary to obtain further information in order to assess the fairness and adequacy of the proposed settlement,

(b) appoint an expert to assist the court.

(2) The court must

(a) advertise the proposed settlement according to Rule 219, ensuring that it is clear that the court has not reached a conclusion on the fairness of the settlement,

(b) fix a period within which any comments may be made, and

(c) consider all comments made by the group members and the parties.

(3) The court may consider all other relevant comments received.

15 See, for instance, the approach in Section 47C(5) of the Competition Act 1998 (UK), which permits "damages not claimed by the represented persons within a specified period must be paid to the charity".

Comments:

1. Rule 223(1) enables the court to obtain such further information it considers useful or necessary to assess the fairness and adequacy of a proposed settlement. Court orders may, for instance, include the production of documents by the parties or by group members. In particular the court may hold an oral hearing (a fairness and adequacy hearing) with the parties and group members. It may also require the provision of expert opinions by, for instance, an economist or an accountant to assist it in assessing the settlement (see Rules 119-120).
2. The court should not approve any proposed settlement until the group members have been given an opportunity to submit comments (Rule 223(2)(c)). Therefore, when advertising the proposed settlement the court must ensure that it is clear that approval has not yet been given. It must do this in order to ensure that group members are not mislead, and hence do not submit responses.
3. All group members should have a fair chance of submitting comments on the proposed settlement. The court may use the secure electronic platform for the submission of statements (Rule 220). Legal representation must not be required for a group member to submit such a statement. Statements may also be made by any organisation or interest group, the purpose of which is closely related to the event that gave rise to the mass harm (and see Rule 43).

Rule 224. Settlement Approval Orders

The court shall not make an order approving a settlement agreement where

(a) the amount of compensation agreed for the group or any sub-group is manifestly unfair,

(b) the terms of any other undertaking by a defendant are manifestly unfair,

(c) the settlement is manifestly contrary to the public interest (*ordre public*) or

(d) the terms, whether contained in the proposed settlement agreement or not, as to the payment of legal and other associated costs of the action are manifestly unreasonable.

Comments:

1. It is a common standard in collective proceedings that settlements can be court approved only if the court considers the settlement terms to be fair and adequate for the group members. Settlements must also not violate public policy. Nevertheless it is difficult for the court to assess the terms of the settlement. The qualified claimant and the defendant having reached a settlement will not submit arguments to the court against approval. The group members will also often not be able to make an assessment themselves of the settlement terms, at least not without consulting a lawyer. Moreover, group members may well not be interested in becoming, or able to become, active in this respect if the individual compensation is low. The court must therefore be able to use all relevant sources of information to identify possible conflicts of interest or unfair settlement terms (Rule 223).
2. Rule 224(a) requires the court to consider whether the amount of any compensation under the proposed settlement is manifestly unfair considering the potential outcome of the pending litigation. In considering this the court should only make a summary assessment based on the situation at the time of the settlement. It should also consider whether

the settlement terms arose due to any collusion between the qualified claimant and the defendant.

3. Rule 224(b) is also concerned with ensuring that the settlement terms are not manifestly unfair. Settlement terms may, for example, have effects on the market in general or a defendant's competitors, for instance if a defendant agrees in the settlement to fix the prices of a product for a certain period. Particularly in respect of so-called coupon settlements or *cy-près* solutions offered in the settlement the court may consult economic experts on the consequences of such a settlement.
4. Rule 224(d) enables the court, for instance, to determine that in cases of small individual claims it would normally be considered unfair to impose costs on the group members.
5. If a court concludes that the proposed settlement is not fair and adequate or does not meet the requirements of Rule 224, before it dismisses the application it should inform the parties of its concerns and may set a time limit for them to modify the proposed settlement or present another settlement proposal.

Rule 225. Approved Settlements in Opt-in Actions

An approved settlement binds all group members who have opted-in at the time the order approving the settlement is made.

Comments:

1. Where proceedings are based on an opt-in mechanism, as a matter of logic, any settlement negotiated during the litigation will only be made on behalf of those group members who opted-in. Consequently, Rule 225 specifies that only those group members who had opted-in prior to the settlement would be bound by it.
2. While a more flexible rule could be adopted here, which would allow the court to allow further group members to opt-in after the settlement has been reached and hence extend its preclusive effect, it would have a number of disadvantages. It would undermine any incentive for a group member to opt-into proceedings from the outset. Furthermore, allowing additional group members to opt-in after the settlement would alter the basis on which the defendant has negotiated the settlement. It would, moreover, diminish the settlement amount due to the members who had opted-in prior to the settlement where the settlement figure was a fixed global sum of compensation, i.e., permitting group members to opt-in post-settlement would diminish the amount of compensation due under the settlement to each group member who had opted-in prior to the settlement. Given these issues, such a rule was not adopted.

Rule 226. Approved Settlements in Opt-out Proceedings

An approved settlement binds all group members unless they have opted-out of the collective proceedings at the time the order approving the settlement is made.

Comments:

1. Where collective proceedings are based on an opt-out mechanism a settlement approved by the court will have a binding effect on all group members who have not opted-out.
2. It is not appropriate to provide a further opportunity for group members to opt-out of the settlement. If group members were permitted to opt-out of a settlement, a defendant would not be able to calculate the risks of a settlement properly. There is a need for legal certainty for defendants with respect to the scope of claims which will be finally settled. The best way to protect the interests of group members is not to provide a second chance

to opt-out, but rather to require the court to approve the settlement and to provide it with a range of means to secure any information necessary to enable it to assess the settlement's fairness.

3. See Rule 235(2) on the effect of settlements in a cross-border situation.

E. JUDGMENTS IN COLLECTIVE PROCEEDINGS

Rule 227. Effect of Final Judgments

(1) A final judgment of the court in collective proceedings binds

(a) all of the parties, and all group members who have opted-in to the proceedings; or

(b) all of the parties, and all of the group members resident in the forum State who have not opted-out of the proceedings within the period set by the court in Rule 215(3).

(2) No other collective proceeding may be commenced in respect of any claims for relief determined in a final judgment.

(3) A final judgment may be enforced by the qualified claimant. If the qualified claimant does not enforce the final judgment within a reasonable time any group member, with the court's permission, may enforce the final judgment.

Comments:

1. Rule 227(1) prevents parties and group members who opted-in or did not opt-out of proceedings from pursuing new or a further individual claim for relief on the same grounds. The general rules on *res judicata* may not allow such an effect (Rule 151). Rule 227(1)(b) restricts the binding effect of the judgment to group members in the forum State who have not opted-out because Rule 235 sets out that with respect to foreign group members an opt-in mechanism must apply.
2. Rule 227(2) is required in order to protect defendants from the possibility that another qualified claimant could bring further collective proceedings based on the same mass harm as that which formed the basis of the immediate proceedings. General *res judicata* rules may not suffice to provide a sufficient preclusive effect because the parties to subsequent proceedings will not be the same. In so far as opt-in collective proceedings are concerned, further such proceedings may be filed by a different qualified claimant in the interest of those group members who have not opted-into the earlier proceedings.
3. Rule 227(3) provides that it is for the qualified claimant to enforce a judgment in collective proceedings. Should the qualified claimant fail to enforce the judgment the court may decide whether and when an individual group member can enforce the judgment either on behalf of the group or on their own, individual, behalf.

Rule 228. Amount of Compensation

A final judgment that sets the amount of compensation in a collective proceeding shall include

(a) the total amount of compensation payable in respect of the group or any sub-group. If an exact calculation of this amount is impossible or excessively difficult, the court may estimate the amount,

(b) the criteria for distributing the compensation to each group member, and the method of administration of the compensation fund.

Comments:

1. In collective proceedings, the exact calculation of individual group member's damages is often difficult or impossible to achieve. Substantive law, in such circumstances, can permit the court to estimate the damages to the group members as a whole, and thereafter distribute those damages according to specified criteria. Consequently, Rule 228 simply requires that a judgment set the total amount of compensation to be paid, the criteria for distributing it to the group members, and the method of its distribution. This latter point may include the appointment of administrators for the compensation fund. It may also result in the court imposing particular conditions on the qualified claimant as the administrator of the fund, e.g., making its administration subject to supervision by the court, a public regulator, or a legal or economic expert.
2. Rule 228(b) thus provides the court with a broad discretion in respect of the administration of the compensation fund. Where there is a settlement it is up to parties to the settlement agreement to agree upon the means by which the fund should be distributed and administered.
3. Where national legislation permits a court to estimate the amount of damage, that may be applied in collective proceedings.

F. COLLECTIVE SETTLEMENTS OUTSIDE COLLECTIVE PROCEEDINGS

1. In the event of mass harm, settlement without the need to engage in contentious litigation should be available to potential claimants and defendants.
2. Where a potential defendant admits liability in principle, it should not be necessary to initiate collective proceedings simply in order to settle the dispute. In such situations a special procedural mechanism is necessary to safeguard the interests of the group members, but which also allows the proposed settlement via a simplified process to become binding. In the Netherlands, the Act on Collective Settlements of 2005 (*Wet collectieve afwikkeling van massaschades*, 2005) (the Dutch WCAM) provides a successful model for such an approach. This model has, for instance, been adopted in other European jurisdictions, e.g., Belgium, Slovenia, the United Kingdom, and as of 2018 with proposals to adopt the approach being considered in Switzerland.
3. Given its utility the Dutch model was adopted as the basis for the following Rules. However, whereas existing settlement proceedings are generally based on an opt-out procedure, the approach to settlements outside collective proceedings is a matter for the parties to determine, i.e., it could be either based on an opt-in or opt-out basis (see Rules 230 and 231). Whichever approach the parties wish to adopt is subject to court approval.
4. Out-of-court settlements can be reached based on negotiations between a qualified claimant and the defendant. They may also be facilitated by a mediator or an ADR organisation. This section of the Rules only deals with proceedings for the court approval of such settlement agreements.

Rule 229. Standing to Reach Settlement

(1) Any entity fulfilling the requirements in Rules 208(a) and (b) to be a qualified claimant may reach a collective settlement agreement for a group even where a collective proceeding order has not been made.

(2) **Any such collective settlement agreement shall be negotiated in good faith for the benefit of all group members.**

Comments:

1. The Dutch WCAM allows long-standing and *ad hoc* associations to negotiate settlement agreements with persons or entities that are potentially liable for a mass tort. It does not, however, specify the requirements of representativity of the associations negotiating on behalf of, for instance, tort victims without having an explicit mandate to do so. It is up to the Amsterdam Court of Appeal which must approve the settlement to decide whether the association actually represents the interests of the mass tort victims adequately. In practice, and to provide guidance absent in the Dutch legislation, a claims code is often used to guide the approval process. This code was drafted by a group of lawyers and currently provides rules for the structure and governance of the associations and foundations. It is, however, a non-binding instrument which applies on a voluntary basis. To overcome this gap in the Dutch approach to settlement, Rule 229 applies the criteria provided in Rule 208. Therefore any person, public regulator or private entity which intends to negotiate a collective settlement in the interest of group members must meet the same requirements as a qualified claimant.
2. Rule 229 does not authorise natural persons who are group members (Rule 208(c)) to negotiate an out-of-court settlement because there is a certain risk that a defendant may select a specific group member in order to negotiate a low level of settlement. Apart from these cases of clear misuse it is not very likely that potential defendants will enter into settlement negotiations with individuals. They will prefer to settle the case with an entity or association described in Rules 208(a) and (b) which will be supported by a large number of group members.

Rule 230. Application for Approval of Collective Settlement

(1) **An application to the court for approval of a collective settlement agreement in accordance with Rule 229 must be made by all of the parties to it.**

(2) **The application shall include all of the information required under Rule 222(2). It shall also specify whether a binding settlement shall be reached on an opt-in or an opt-out basis.**

Comments:

1. Rule 230 allows a joint application to be made by the parties to a settlement. They will generally be a potential qualified claimant and the potential defendant or defendants to collective proceedings. The application must provide all information specified in Rule 222.
2. In many European jurisdictions the procedure for court approval is based on an opt-out mechanism. This provides an opportunity for a large number or all of the group members to participate and be bound by the settlement. With an opt-in mechanism the number of group members will normally be smaller. Any settlement would thus be less attractive to a potential defendant who is interested in securing global peace through the settlement and removing the potential claim from its books. Notwithstanding these points, Rule 230 adopts a different approach. It places more emphasis on the dispositive principle, and leaves it to the parties to the settlement to determine whether they want an opt-in or opt-out mechanism to be applied. There may, for instance, be good reasons to prefer an opt-in mechanism in international cases where a defendant may fear that the preclusive effect of the settlement will not be recognised in other jurisdictions if the settlement were to

be based on an opt-out mechanism. Difficulties in giving notice to all group members by public announcements may also be an argument in favour of adopting an opt-in approach.

3. Defendants may, however, often prefer an opt-out mechanism in order to maximise the extent of the settlement's binding effect, i.e., to extend it to as many group members as possible. If the court adopts a different approach and considers an opt-in mechanism to be more appropriate, it may refuse to approve a settlement. In such circumstances it should give the parties an opportunity to submit a new settlement proposal.

Rule 231. Approval Procedure

The procedure for approval of collective settlements in Rule 223 applies to any application to approve a collective settlement following an application under Rule 230.

Comments:

1. The same rules which apply for the approval of a settlement negotiated during pending collective proceedings can be applied to a settlement proceeding that fall outside the scope of such proceedings. As such the court must take the same steps necessary to obtain information in order to assess the fairness of a proposed settlement.
2. Any proposed settlement must be advertised in accordance with Rule 219, with a period fixed within which comments may be made. When advertising the proposed settlement, the court must ensure that it is clear that it has not reached a conclusion on the fairness of the settlement. Unless this is made clear, group members may be misled and thus refrain from making comments or raising objections to the settlement.

Rule 232. Approval Order and Opt-in/Opt-out Procedure

The court must approve the proposed collective settlement on the basis of Rule 224.

(a) If the court does not approve the proposed collective settlement it must give its reasons for refusing to approve it, and must remit the agreement to the parties.

(b) The court must advertise the approved settlement in accordance with Rule 219(2), give information on whether the settlement shall become binding based on an opt-in or opt-out procedure, and fix a period of at least three months for the group members to opt-in or opt-out. The court shall decide to whom and how the notification to opt-in or to opt-out shall be given. If the terms of the settlement require a fixed number or percentage of group members to accept the settlement this must also be communicated clearly.

(c) After the period fixed for opt-in or opt-out notifications and, where applicable, if the necessary number or percentage of group members have opted-in or have not opted-out, the court shall declare the approved settlement binding. Otherwise the court shall declare that the approval proceedings have been terminated without a binding settlement.

(d) An approved settlement shall bind all of the persons who have opted-in to the settlement or who have not opted-out of the settlement.

Comments:

1. Settlement approval follows the same criteria as set out for a collective settlement negotiated with a collective proceeding pending in Rule 224. If the proposed settlement does not meet the requirements of Rule 224, before dismissing the application the court must inform the parties of its concerns and may set a time limit for them to present another

settlement proposal. Otherwise the application must be dismissed. This also applies if the court considers the suggested opt-in or opt-out procedure to either be inappropriate or unfair in the circumstances.

2. Once the court has approved the terms of the settlement, and not before that, the group members who are to be bound by the settlement can decide whether or not they want to accept the settlement. As a consequence, any approved settlement must be published, giving all the necessary information on the compensation to be paid in total, the amount to be paid to individual victims or group of victims, and the mechanism through which the funds are to be distributed. If group members or victims have previously been identified by their names and addresses, the court shall ensure that the requisite information is provided to them individually. Such persons as are to be bound by the settlement shall have at least three months to decide whether they want to accept the settlement or not.
3. Some European jurisdictions specify a particular threshold for a settlement to become binding in terms of a minimum number of group members or the percentage of group members who must accept the settlement either by opting-in or by not opting-out.[16] Such regulation and any particular percentage applicable to the settlement can, however, be left to the parties of the settlement. It requires no specification in these Rules. Defendants, particularly, will have an interest in ensuring that a large number of group members will accept the settlement and will propose a provision for the settlement accordingly. If there is a minimum threshold requirement for the settlement to become binding, this should be set out clearly in the information provided to group members as it may have an impact on their decision to opt-in or opt-out of the proposed settlement.
4. Finally, after the period during which group members must notify the court that they are either opting-in or not opting-out of the proposed settlement has expired, the court must declare the settlement binding or not binding. In doing so it must take account of any minimum threshold requirement and whether it has been met or not.

SECTION 3 – CROSS BORDER ISSUES WITHIN THE EUROPEAN UNION

Rule 233. Recognition of Qualified Claimant

The recognition of a claimant as a qualified claimant by a court in an order made under Rule 213(1)(a) binds every other court in European Union Member States without the need for further application for recognition in relation to actions arising from the same event of mass harm.

Comments:

1. Rule 233 adopts the approach set out in Article 3 of the Injunctions Directive. It requires the mutual recognition of qualified claimants in European Union Member States.
2. Where multiple proceedings arise from the same mass harm event in several Member States, Rule 233 ensures that a qualified claimant is not required to seek authorisation in

16 See, for instance, Section 17 of the German Act on Model Case Proceedings in Disputes under Capital Markets Law *(Gesetz über Musterverfahren in kapitalmarktrechtliche Streitigkeiten (KapMuG))*, which requires that less than 30% of the group members opt-out.

each Member State. Consequently, it also ensures that qualification for authorisation as a qualified claimant is not interpreted differently across Member States; and, thus it avoids conflicting judgments being given in different Member States.

Rule 234. Judicial Co-ordination

(1) When a mass harm has cross-border effects, the registry entries for each collective proceeding shall be made available on the European e-justice platform or any similarly effective platform.

(2) European Union Member States' courts must use their best effort to co-ordinate collective proceedings in different Member States in order to avoid irreconcilable judgments or settlement approvals.

Comments:

1. Dissemination of information on pending collective proceedings can be very useful for group members and other potential qualified claimants in other European Union Member States. Conversely, it must be recognised that disseminating information on collective proceedings through disclosing the identity of defendants may potentially have an adverse effect on the situation of the defendant whose liability has not yet been established. As a consequence, the present Rules require publication of collective proceedings which have already been filed: intended or prospective collective proceedings cannot thus be registered. Additionally, before a qualified claimant files a collective proceeding they must try to settle the case out-of-court. Defendants thus have a chance of avoiding the action. Courts or those persons or institutions responsible for the register must also ensure that if a collective proceeding is withdrawn or dismissed, notice of that fact is published in the same way as the initiation of the proceeding.
2. Rule 234(2) requires the co-ordination of parallel collective proceedings where necessary. A superior way to manage parallel collective proceedings arising from the same mass harm event might, however, be a consolidation of the proceedings via the cross-border application of Rule 146. Irrespective of jurisdictional issues, while procedural and/or evidential and/or costs rules differ considerably across Europe, consolidation, may not be a practical possibility. Even consolidation solely for the purpose of evidence-taking following the principles of the US Judicial Panel on Multi-district Litigation (28 USC section 1407) is an instrument for the future.

Rule 235. Group Members outside the Forum State

(1) The court shall ensure that group members outside the forum State are informed of the collective proceeding in accordance with Rule 219.

(2) No order made under Rule 215(2) binds group members outside the forum State.

(3) Group members outside the forum State must, if they choose, be allowed to opt-in.

(4) Rules 235(1)-(3) also apply to collective settlement proceedings under Rules 229-232.

Comments:

1. Rule 235(1) emphasises that collective proceedings or settlement proceedings with group members outside the forum State may require additional efforts to inform such persons. It does not, however, specify the way information is disseminated. Where group members can be identified and their addresses are available personal notification or even formal service of a notification ought to be carried out. Where the group consists of unidentified

individuals any kind of publication, e.g., on websites, in newspapers or other media, which provides the most effective means of dissemination may be used. This Rule does not specify who should inform the group members, i.e., the court could be responsible for taking such steps or it could order the qualified claimant to do so.

2. Rules 235(2) and (3) recognise the fact that opt-out proceedings remain controversial and that providing information to absent group members outside the forum State may be difficult. As a consequence they ensure that the opt-out mechanism only applies to group members within the forum State. For those living outside the forum State, a judgment in collective proceedings will only have a binding effect where the group member has expressly opted-in to the proceedings (see Rules 227 and 235(2)). Against this background, the court must ensure that all group members outside the forum State have a proper opportunity to opt-in.
3. Rule 235(4) applies the principles set out in Rules 235(1)-(3) to collective settlement proceedings under Rule 229 and following. According to Rule 230 the parties to a proposed settlement must set out in their proposal whether the approval procedure should be based on an opt-in or an opt-out mechanism.
4. Within the European Union recognition of a collective settlement approval order follows from the Brussels Ibis Regulation and there is no need for further specification here. One of the most important legal consequences of a collective settlement is the preclusive effect for all group members bound by the settlement. They cannot bring individual actions against the defendant in order to receive a higher compensation. In a European cross-border setting all types of collective settlement approval orders, e.g., those made in the course of collective proceedings and those that arise from a court-approved settlement under Article 2(b) of the Brussels Ibis Regulation will be recognised in European Union Member States. According to Articles 58 and 59 only a public policy objection in respect of recognition can be raised in a Member State.
5. Where a collective proceeding was pending, and a settlement agreement was approved by the court, Rule 235(2) clarifies that group members residing outside the forum State at the commencement of the proceeding are not bound by the settlement if it is an opt-out proceeding under Rule 215(2). Nevertheless, for group members residing in the forum State the settlement will have a preclusive effect under the Brussels Ibis Regulation unless the public policy objection applies. They cannot therefore bring individual proceedings in another Member State. The same applies in respect of a collective settlement where there was no collective proceeding pending.

Rule 236. Multiple Substantive Laws

(1) Group members shall not be prevented from participating in a single collective proceeding if they are subject to different substantive laws.

(2) In any case where group members are subject to different substantive law, the court may divide the group into sub-groups under Rule 218(1)(d).

Comments:

1. Mass harm events are often cross-border. According to the Rome I and Rome II Regulations different sets of substantive law may apply to group members' claims in such circumstances. Multi-State collective proceedings can, consequently, be complex. A court may therefore conclude that collective proceedings should not be authorised if the claims of a potential group's members are not sufficiently similar, as required by Rule 212(1)(c).

2. Rule 236(1) specifies that the application of different substantive laws should not be a sufficient ground for a court to refuse to authorise or dismiss collective proceedings. A court in such circumstances should consider dividing the group into sub-groups (see Rule 218(1)(d)).

SECTION 4 – COSTS, EXPENSES AND FUNDING

Rule 237. Third-Party Funding

(1) A qualified claimant may use third-party litigation funding.

(2) Rule 245 applies to any such third-party funding agreement. A court may, however, require a qualified claimant to disclose the details of any such funding agreement relevant for the instance at stake to the court and, in so far as appropriate, to the parties.

Comments:

1. Rule 237 sets out the principle that third-party funding as such should not be prohibited.[17] However, the qualified claimant must disclose the fact that they are being funded via such means. They must also provide the identity of the funder at the start of proceedings. Details of the funding agreement are often confidential and should therefore be only disclosed upon the court's request and should not be available to the public or the defendant (see Rules 209(b) and 210(1)(f)). This seems to be a fair approach as it will enable a defendant to have a better understanding of the means of their opponent (also see Rule 51 and Rules 57 and following). Nevertheless, it is important to understand that the details of the relationship between the third-party funder and the qualified claimant must not normally be subject to disclosure to a defendant as they will normally contain sensitive information relating to the underlying procedural strategy of the party, e.g., a legal analysis of the risks of the litigation or certain limitations of the available funds, the knowledge of which would give the defendant an unfair strategic advantage.
2. The approach taken by the European Commission in 2013, and to a lesser extent in 2018, to third-party funding in collective proceedings was clearly influenced by political considerations, which took particular account of the interests of potential defendants to such proceedings, i.e. businesses. The approach taken was not well-balanced. It further applied a differential standard to public and private funding mechanisms for collective proceedings.[18] The approach taken in these Rules is intended to apply a common standard across all defendants, and to strike a fairer balance between claimants and defendants.
3. Also see Rules 238 and 245.

Rule 238. Costs and Expenses of Collective Proceedings

(1) Only a qualified claimant is liable for the costs and expenses of a collective proceeding if it is unsuccessful.

(2) If the proceeding is successful, the total amount of compensation received by the qualified claimant shall form a common fund.

17 Also see, Recommendation 2013/396, and Art. 7(1) of the 2018 Proposal.

18 Also see Recommendation 2013/396, and Art. 7(2) of the 2018 Proposal.

(3) **The qualified claimant's costs and expenses incurred in bringing the proceeding must be paid from the common fund before any distribution of compensation to group members in accordance with Rule 228. Rule 245(4) applies accordingly.**

Comments:

1. Rule 238 applies the European, or loser-pays, principle to collective proceedings. Only the qualified claimant as a party will be liable for costs. Nevertheless if the action is successful all group members must accept that the litigation costs of the qualified claimant are to be paid from the common fund, although that will be subject to any cost recovery from the losing party. The Court may, however, take into consideration any lack of fairness or appropriateness in the funding agreement.

PART XII

COSTS

INTRODUCTION

1. Litigation costs are generally considered by lawyers to be quite technical in nature. As a consequence, this subject is mostly discussed among practitioners in individual jurisdictions rather than from a comparative, policy-oriented perspective.[1] Litigation cost, in particular provisions concerning its recovery in proceedings, are much more important for procedure as a whole than may initially appear to be the case. This is for two main reasons. First, potential litigation costs, and the possibility that they may be recovered from an opposing party, are often very important incentives concerning the procedural behaviour of parties to proceedings. These incentives are not always taken into account by national legislators. In particular, cost issues are very often at the very core of parties' access to justice, as they may be decisive in respect of a decision to commence, defend, continue or settle proceedings. Secondly, claims for the recovery of costs very often form a significant percentage of parties' economic interest in litigation, that is, of the amount in dispute. Accordingly, these Rules articulate a number of uniform rules or best practices mainly concerned with, but not limited to, the recovery of costs.

2. The present Part of the Rules is relatively concise, containing seven rules. They are set at general level, due to the impact of national law and the structure of the legal profession in European jurisdictions upon this area of civil procedure in a technical sense. Issues of costs also relate to political policy choices within each jurisdiction concerning the funding of the court system, i.e., whether, and if so the extent to which, it should be funded by the parties rather than out of general taxation. While some jurisdictions have created a system where the court fees almost fully cover the state's expenses for the civil court system, other jurisdictions have opted for a system that is basically free of charge for the parties. Such differences will, inevitably, have an impact upon potential future convergence in the approach to costs in European civil procedure.

3. A further important difference across European jurisdictions that has a significant impact on litigation costs is the different approaches to fees payable in respect of legal representation in proceedings. Such rules are closely connected with the organisation of the legal profession. Even where this is not the case, there are certain national traditions concerning lawyers' fees that are deeply rooted in the respective legal cultures across Europe. These differences of legal culture cannot simply be eliminated through the provision of model Rules of civil procedure. On the contrary, such model Rules must take sufficient account of these longstanding traditions. For example, while some systems, such as that in Belgium provide flat rates for the recovery of costs

1 Although, see C. Hodges, S. Vogenauer, M. Tulibacka, (eds.) *The costs and funding of civil litigation. A comparative perspective [2010]; Study on the Transparency of Costs of Civil Judicial Proceedings in the European Union* (OUP, 2007), available at: https://e-justice.europa.eu/content_costs_of_proceedings-37-en.do; the respective sections in P. Taelman (ed.), *International Encyclopaedia for Civil Procedure*, <http://www.kluwerlawonline.com/toc.php?pubcode=CIVI >; M. Reimann (ed.), *Cost and Fee Allocation in Civil Procedure. A Comparative Study*, (Springer, 2012); and, W. van Boom (ed.), *Litigation, Costs, Funding and Behaviour: Implications for the Law*, (Routledge, 2017).

ELI-Unidroit Model European Rules of Civil Procedure. ELI & Unidroit, Oxford University Press.
© ELI & Unidroit 2021. DOI: 10.1093/oso/9780198866589.003.0013

incurred for legal representation by counsel,[2] other systems, such as that in Germany, are based on approaches that provide for flat rates for certain parts of the proceedings.[3] A further different approach is that taken, for instance, in Austria where flat rates are prescribed for individual services rendered in the proceedings.[4] Other systems have no fixed or regulated rates at all for legal representation, leaving the issue to free market competition limited only by professional regulation, i.e., legal professional ethics, and what is deemed to be a reasonable fee by the court on a case-by-case basis. All this results in completely different legal issues when it comes to the subject of the legal costs recovery in civil proceedings.

4. Finally, the rules on court organisation are also relevant to litigation costs. While some systems provide that all aspects of decisions concerning costs, including the calculation of specific amounts of individual items of work done by legal representatives, have to be carried out by the court itself, i.e., a judge, other systems transfer this responsibility, to varying degrees, to specific court officers or clerks. The Rules in this Part do not interfere with such legislative decisions. As such references to the court in this Part should be read as including a reference to such court officers.

5. One consequence of the foregoing is that the Rules in this Part are not as specific as they may be in national procedural codes. They are, however, as specific as possible. In this respect, two broad points need to be noted. A legislator dealing with costs has to decide whether and to what extent the system provides for judicial discretion in this context or whether it should provide specific, technical legal rules. Closely connected with that decision, a legislator also has to decide whether and to what extent parties are to be provided with remedies against court decisions. If a very high degree of regulation through, for instance, quite technical rules rather than judicial discretion was chosen and that was combined with the means to seek remedies against court decisions where parties believe that the rules governing costs recovery have been applied in an erroneous fashion by the lower court, the possibility of devising a uniform set of rules would be limited, for the reasons set forth above. The following rules are, however, based on the understanding that very technical rules concerning costs recovery do not increase party satisfaction with the outcome of such decisions. On the contrary, the present Rules are based on the idea that a system that provides the court with a broad discretion concerning cost recovery is optimal. Such an approach is best suited to do justice in individual cases taking account of differences arising in the broad diversity of cases. As such it is a better means to attain procedural justice in this context. As a consequence, remedies against costs recovery decisions should be, and are also, limited. This latter approach concerning remedies is not, however, driven by the insight that it provides a more effective or easier basis to achieve procedural harmonisation or unification.

Rule 239. Decision on Costs

(1) A court rendering a final judgment or terminating the proceedings in any other way shall determine which party is required to reimburse the other party or parties' costs of the proceedings, unless the parties have agreed otherwise. Any recovery of costs shall be limited to those that are reasonable and proportionate.

2 See, for example, Art. 1022 of the Belgian CCP.

3 See, for example, § 91 para. 2 of the CCP, and the respective rates pursuant to the *Rechtsanwaltsve rgütungsgesetz* (Lawyers' Compensation Act).

4 See, for example, § 41 para. 2 of the Austrian CCP and the respective rates in the *Rechtsanwaltstarifgesetz* (Lawyers' Tariff Act).

(2) **If the parties enter into a settlement, each party shall bear its own costs unless they have agreed otherwise.**

Sources:
ALI/UNIDROIT Principles 3.3, 17.3, 24.3 and 25.

Comments:

1. Rule 239 provides for the court's power to decide the extent to which one party may be able to recover the costs of the proceedings from the other. However, the rule is not limited to this; it also provides for the following additional choices.
2. Like all the other rules on costs provided here, this provision strives for maximum simplicity. As a consequence, it is anticipated that the court should only give one decision concerning litigation costs, and that should be done at the end of the proceedings. There should not, therefore, be a number of costs decisions, each taken after specific procedural steps. Such an approach promotes the efficient, economical and proportionate conduct of proceedings, as it ensures that courts are required to do less work than if they were required to make costs decisions throughout the course of the proceedings. It also enables the court to apply its discretion on the basis of an analysis of the proceedings as a whole according to Rule 241. In contrast to this approach, many national laws allow, either generally or in some cases, for multiple costs decisions to be taken throughout the course of proceedings.[5]
3. The rule also makes clear that costs can be subject to the agreement of the parties (the principle of party disposition). As a general rule, the court will render a decision concerning the reimbursement of costs at the end of the proceedings; if the parties, however, agree that no such decision shall be taken, that is binding on the court.
4. The principle of party disposition is also reflected in Rule 239(2), which deals with situations where parties enter into a settlement. As a default rule, it is intended that each party shall bear its own costs where this occurs, but this is subject to party choice. The parties can, therefore, agree to resolve questions concerning costs in a different manner, with such decision binding the court.

Rule 240. Scope and Amount of Costs

(1) **Parties may seek to recover the costs of the proceedings, in particular**
   (a) **reasonable and proportionate costs of their legal representation in the proceedings,**
   (b) **court and other fees such as those of court-appointed experts, interpreters, court reporters etc.,**
   (c) **other reasonable financial outlays resulting from the conduct of the proceedings, such as costs of party-appointed experts, travel expenses, and fees for the service of documents.**

(2) **Costs under Rule 240(1) may also include costs reasonably incurred for the preparation of proceedings before they were commenced.**

5 See for instance, the approach to costs in England and Wales, set out in its CPR generally; Art. 104 of the Swiss Federal CCP, according to which the court, 'as a general rule' will decide questions concerning the costs of proceedings in its final decision, but can also do so at certain points in the proceedings prior to the final decision ('*Zwischenentscheid*') further to Art. 237 of the Code; or, § 52 para. 1 of the Austrian CCP, which also provides for a number of cases in which the court can decide costs prior to the final decision.

(3) **Parties may only recover costs which they have reasonably and proportionately incurred for the conduct of the proceedings, taking into account the amount in dispute, the nature and complexity of the issues, the significance of the case for the parties.**

(4) **Where national law specify tariffs for the recovery of certain fees (such as, where relevant, court fees and fees for the parties' legal representation, for experts, and interpreters), any award of costs should nevertheless be consistent with the Rules of this Part.**

Sources:

ALI/UNIDROIT Principles 3.3, 17.3, 24.3 and 25.

Comments:

1. Rule 240 deals with the scope and amount of costs that can be reimbursed on the basis of a decision made under Rule 239. The two Rules do not provide for an exact mechanism to calculate the specific amount of costs recoverable. Such mechanisms are, as noted above, closely connected to a jurisdiction's specific rules concerning court fees and, where applicable, lawyers' fee tariffs. Notwithstanding that *caveat* a number of general principles governing recoverability can properly be set out within the Rules.
2. The main general principle, which is set out in Rule 240(1)(a), is that only "reasonable and proportionate costs" are subject to recovery. This wording was taken from Article 69(1) of the 2013 Unified Patent Court Agreement.It reflects the fact that the costs incurred can only be subject to reimbursement if they are in line with what could be expected to be incurred through the reasonable and diligent conduct of the proceedings by a party, i.e., that costs are not excessive in this respect, and that they are proportionate to the value in dispute. The Rule thus reflects the general procedural principle set out in Rule 8.
3. Rule 240(1) lists the costs and expenses that can typically be subject to a claim for recovery. It is indicative only, and not intended to be exhaustive hence inclusion of the wording "in particular" and, in Rule 240(1)(c) reference to "other reasonable financial outlays".
4. Rule 240(1)(b) does not refer to "reasonable and proportionate" fees because it is expected that such fees listed in that sub-rule will, by their very nature, be "reasonable and proportionate", as they are fees generated by the court itself.
5. The costs referred to in Rule 240(1) all emerge from situations where a party had to make actual payments to, e.g., its counsel (a), the court or other persons or entities (b). The same is equally applicable to "other (. . .) financials outlays" specified in Rule 240(1)(c).
6. Rule 240 does not include reference to parties' internal costs incurred in conducting litigation, i.e., in-house costs that arise from the use of in-house counsel or from work done on the litigation by other personnel employed by a party. It does not even though in some European jurisdictions, such as the Czech Republic, England, Finland and Sweden, the recovery of such costs is permissible.[6] Other jurisdictions, such as Germany and Switzerland, take a more restrictive position limiting such recovery to either the cost of time spent in court or traveling to court or to work done by parties who are not represented by lawyers in cases that are meritorious.[7] While there may be good reason for providing for the recovery of such costs, e.g., it may be no more than a coincidence that legal research on a certain

6 See, for instance, section 137 para. 1 of the Czech Code of Civil Procedure (CCP); Chapter 21, § 8 of the Finnish Code of Judicial Procedure (CJP); Chapter 18, § 8 of the Swedish CJP; Re Nossen's Letter Patent [1969] 1 WLR 638, 643, Bridge UK. Com Ltd v Abbey Pynford plc [2007] EWHC 728 (TCC) or the Litigants in Person (Costs and Expenses) Act 1975 (England and Wales).

7 See, § 91, para. 1 of the German CCP and the decision of the German Constitutional Court of 31 July 2008, 2 BvR 274/03 NJW 2008, 3207; Art. 95 para. 3(c) of the Swiss Federal CCP.

issue is conducted by a party's external or in-house counsel,[8] there has been little by way of general discussion of the issue in European jurisdiction. Given, however, the fact that recoverability of such internal costs may involve consideration and evaluation by the court of intricate questions concerning how such costs are to be calculated and where such costs can properly be said to have arisen due to the conduct of proceedings, e.g., whether the party incurred costs through a loss of profits through having to divert employees to work on the proceedings, provision for such costs has not specifically been provided for in the Rules. The general exclusion may, however, be subject to one specific exception that could properly come within the scope of Rule 240. That exception is the possibility for a lawyer to recover their costs of representing themselves.[9]

7. According to Rule 240(2), recoverable costs may also include amounts incurred in the period before the actual commencement of the proceedings. The question whether and to what extent such costs should be capable of recovery is a matter of dispute in a number of jurisdictions. The terms frequently used in national law, such as the "costs of proceedings", "procedural costs" or "costs of the legal dispute" suggest that there needs to be a certain connection to actual proceedings to justify recoverability. Such terms do, however, leave room for debate concerning how close the connection to actual proceedings needs to be, particularly in terms of time, before they can become recoverable in principle. Given the emphasis in the present Rules on the promotion of pre-commencement conduct (Rules 9(1) and 51), the better approach is that such costs being reasonably incurred in the interest of proceedings prior to their commencement, should be capable of recovery.
8. Rule 240(3) provides that costs for matters, other than those provided for in Rule 240(1) shall be subject to broad principles of recovery that are also focused on ensuring that recoverability is reasonable and proportionate.
9. The present Rules are, as noted above, not intended to set aside or replace national laws providing for certain tariffs or fees such as court fees, lawyers' fees or the fees of experts or interpreters. Consequently, Rule 240(4) includes an express reservation stating that such national rules may be applicable. Nevertheless, the existence of such national fee schedules should be reconcilable with the Rules contained in this Part. This provision is not, however, intended to encourage national lawmakers to introduce new tariffs. It simply acknowledges the fact that such systems are already extant, and that they are intricately linked to rules concerning the governance of the legal profession.

Rule 241. General Rule

(1) When determining upon which party the obligation to reimburse costs shall be placed under Rule 239, the court shall take into account the circumstances of the specific proceedings, in particular whether and to what extent the parties' claims were successful.

(2) The court may also take into account the parties' conduct, in particular, whether and to what extent they acted in good faith and contributed to the fair, efficient and speedy resolution of the dispute.

Sources:

ALI/UNIDROIT Principles 3.3, 17.3, 24.3 and 25.

8 See, for instance, Henderson v Merthyr Tydfil Urban Council [1900] 1 QBD 434 (England and Wales).

9 See, for instance, § 91 para. 2 of the German CCP.

Comments:

1. Rule 241 contains the most important provision of these rules on costs. While the approach in the United States of America (the American Rule) provides that every party has to bear their own costs, the broad European consensus (the European Rule or loser pays rule) is that the party that succeeds, in a general sense, in litigation ought to be entitled to recover their litigation costs from the unsuccessful party or parties. Given this, and in the absence of any compelling reason to adopt the American Rule, the European Rule is adopted and set out in Rule 241(1).
2. While some national jurisdictions, such as Germany or Estonia, adopt detailed provisions concerning the exact calculation of recoverable costs,[10] others such as England or France adopt an approach that provides a broad discretion for the court.[11] A broad discretion based approach is also now the norm in international arbitration.[12] It is not apparent that a strict 'mathematical' approach is preferable to a broad, structured, discretionary approach. Rule 241(2) adopts a broad, structured discretion, specifying the factors that the court must take into account in determining the assessment of recoverability. The factors to be considered relate back to, and thus emphasise the importance of, party compliance with the obligations imposed by the general procedural principles (Rules 2-3, 6, 8-9) and case management (Rules 47, 51). This approach provides a great deal of flexibility in the range of costs orders that may be made reflective of the variety of circumstances that may arise in the prosecution of proceedings. It thus enables the court to tailor costs orders more effectively than through the application of strict mathematical rules, such that the court could, for instance, order a party to pay 'a proportion of' another party's costs.
3. The starting point of any assessment under Rule 241(1) is the outcome of the proceedings, i.e., whether and to what extent a party was successful in respect of its claims for relief. This approach is not only justified in the light of its general adoption in European jurisdictions and within the European Union,[13] but also on the basis that parties have, and should have, a fair expectation that the outcome of proceedings will be of a decisive nature in respect of costs recoverability. By framing the outcome of the proceedings by reference to the extent to which the parties' claims for relief were successful, ensures that the court, when exercising its discretion, takes into account the fact that there may be counterclaims and/or multiple heads of claim and that both parties may have been "successful" on specific issues. This enables the court to take a nuanced approach to the determination of the extent to which a party's costs should be recoverable. It does so without having to resort to a mathematical calculation.
4. While the outcome is the starting point for assessing recoverability, it ought not to be the only factor that should be taken into account. The court's discretion should take into

10 See, for instance, §§ 91 para. 1 and 92 para. 1 of the German CCP; §§ 162 and 163 of the Estonian Code of Civil Procedure (CCP).

11 See, for instance, rule 44.1 and rule 44.2 of the English CPR; Art. 696 and Art. 700 of the French CCP. The present Rule does not, however, as in France provide for the parties' financial circumstances to be taken account of in determining recoverability. Such matters ought properly be considered in any assessment of legal aid, such that a party in whose favour an award of costs is made should not suffer a loss because of the other party's financial position.

12 See, Art. 38(5) of the ICC Arbitration Rules (2017).

13 See, for instance, Art. 16 of the ESC Regulation; Art. 69(1) of the 2013 Unified Patent Court Agreement.

account other factors, in particular, the behaviour of the parties in the course of the proceedings (see Rules 2-3, 6, 8-9, 47 and 51). As a consequence Rule 241(1) provides the general rule that, as a starting point, the respective success of the parties in the proceedings is relevant for the decision on the recovery of costs, while Rule 241(2) makes further provision guiding the exercise of the court's discretion and does so specifically by requiring it to take into account party conduct.

5. Rule 241(2) also refers to the question whether the parties acted in good faith and contributed to the fair, efficient and speedy resolution of the dispute (Rules 2 and 6). These are two different factors, which can, but need not, be related to each other. The question whether a party acted in good faith not only refers to its procedural choices in specific situations, such as the applications it made in respect of specific procedural steps or the evidence it presented. It also concerns the more fundamental question whether the party commenced the proceedings, or raised a defence against a claim, in good faith. It is important to note that proceedings differ significantly from each other in this respect. On the one hand, there are cases where a party knew or must have known that its claims for relief would not turn out to be successful, as is often the case in simple debt collection proceedings. In such cases, it is only fair that the European Rule applies, and that the loser pays the successful party's costs. In contrast to such situations, there are many proceedings where both parties are convinced at the outset, and even during the course of proceedings, that their position is well-founded and it only becomes apparent at a later stage of the proceedings, or when final judgment is delivered, that their good faith assumptions on legal or factual issues were misplaced. This, latter situation, may arise where the outcome of the proceedings depends upon a court-appointed expert's evidence, the content of which could not reasonably before be seen by the parties, or where legal issues that are unclear or not subject to established case law relevant to the outcome. In such cases and at least to some extent, it is often more just to split the costs of the proceedings in order to acknowledge that the "losing" party also had good reasons to originally believe that their claims for relief were well-founded.[14]
6. The issue whether the parties contributed to the fair and efficient conduct of the proceedings, as required by Rule 2, relates to the specific behaviour of the parties during the proceedings. The parties may prepare all their arguments and evidence diligently, such that they contribute significantly to the expeditious conduct of the proceedings, or they may conduct the proceedings in a piecemeal or dilatory fashion that results in procedural delay. Taking such factors into account is not only a fair way of retrospectively distributing the costs of proceedings, but it is also an important means of incentivising party conduct to promote behaviour that contributes to the fair and efficient conduct of the proceedings. This approach is found in Principle 17.3 of the ALI/Unidroit Principles, albeit there it is focused on sanctions for non-compliance with procedural obligations. In the present Rules the principle is more properly focused as a positive incentive.
7. This Rule does not incorporate a provision analogous to that provided in Part 36 of the English CPR or that set out in § 163(2) of the Estonian CCP, i.e., a rule that disentitles a

14 Some jurisdictions take a general approach that in such circumstances each party should bear their own costs: see, for instance, Chapter 18, § 3(2), of the Swedish CJP; Chapter 21, § 8(a) of the Finnish CJP; Art. 107 para. 1(a) and (b) of the Swiss Federal CCP; of Art. 394 of the Spanish LCP. The approach set out here permits such an approach to be taken on a case-by-case basis where justified on the facts.

party to cost recovery where the successful party in the proceedings refused an offer to settle the proceedings made by the unsuccessful party or suggested by the court where the final judgment was less favourable for that party than the proposed settlement. Such a Rule would be a novel development for the majority of European jurisdictions, however it was not incorporated on the basis that there may be situations where a party acted in good faith but simply was not in a position to conclude a settlement for justifiable reasons. A general principle to this effect would set out too strict an approach. Consistently with the discretion-based approach of this Rule, the court may, under Rule 241(2), take into account such behaviour in the course of its overall analysis whether the parties acted in good faith and contributed to the fair and efficient conduct of the proceedings. This approach is further supported ALI/UNIDROIT Principle 24.3, which provides that "The court may adjust its award of costs to reflect unreasonable failure to cooperate or bad-faith participation in settlement endeavours".

Rule 242. Review

(1) The court's decision on costs may be subject to an appeal.

(2) An appeal is limited to a review of whether the court exercised its discretion properly according to Rules 240 and 241.

(3) A decision on an appeal under Rule 242(2) is final and binding. It cannot be subject to a second appeal.

Sources:

ALI/UNIDROIT Principles 3.3, 17.3, 24.3 and 25.

Comments:

1. As noted above, in many cases the cost of proceedings amounts to a significant percentage of the economic impact of the judgment. Therefore, under a procedural system governed by the rule of law, there must be means of appealing from a lower court's decision on costs.
2. While some national laws provide for a decision on costs to be by way of review by a first instance court prior to an appeal to a higher court,[15] the present rules have adopted the approach that there should be a single opportunity to challenge such a decision. That challenge ought to be by way of appeal to a higher court and to be limited so that, unlike the general approach to appeals in Part IX, there should only be a single appeal. This approach was adopted to ensure effective scrutiny by way of appellate review, while preventing the possibility of time-consuming and costly disputes over costs arising.
3. As with the general approach to appeals (see Rule 155), appeals from cost decisions are limited to a review of the first instance decision. This is consistent with the provision of a broad discretion to the lower court in respect of costs, both in terms of Rule 240 and its standard of 'reasonableness' and, in particular, to the 'European Rule' set out in Rule 241. It is particularly important to take this approach to appellate review in order to prevent lengthy disputes on cost issues, and to ensure that such appellate proceedings do not second-guess the first instance court's decision in every respect. As such the review is to be limited to consideration of the question whether the lower court exercised its discretion in a proper fashion. Therefore, only a failure to apply the right standards under Rules 240 and 241 or the excessive application of those standards can result in the review leading to

15 See, for instance, Arts. 704-714 of the French CCP.

the first instance decision being set aside and a fresh decision being made by the appellate court (see Rule 170(1)), and note here as the appeal court is required to make the decision itself, it may not refer the matter back to the first instance court for it to take the decision afresh (as such this Rule excludes the operation of Rules 170(2) and (3)).

Rule 243. Security for Costs

(1) A party may apply for the other party to provide reasonable security for costs.

(2) In deciding an application for security for costs, the court shall take into account

(a) the likelihood that the applicant will be able to claim reimbursement of the costs of the proceedings,

(b) the financial means of the parties and the prospect of enforcement of the costs decision against the other party,

(c) whether such security for costs is compatible with the parties' right of access to justice and a fair trial.

Comments:

1. The question whether the Rules should include provision on security for costs is a difficult one. It could be argued that a party has a fair interest in obtaining security for costs where a decision on the recovery of the costs could be futile because the prospect of recovering such costs from the other party enforcement proceedings is questionable. It could equally be argued that requiring a party to provide security for costs as a prerequisite for the further conduct of proceedings can directly affect their right of access to justice. This is particularly apposite in cases where the respondent to such an application argues that the applicant does not have the necessary funds to reimburse its own costs after the proceedings. Reconciling these two conflicting objectives is not easy, and as a consequence some national jurisdictions, such as the French Code of Civil Procedure, do not provide any special guarantee for the payment of costs incurred in litigation.
2. This Rule aims to take account of both competing arguments, by providing the court with a discretion to award security for costs. It further seeks to balance the competing arguments by articulating a number of factors that need to be examined by the court in reaching a decision whether to make such an order.
3. An order for security for costs cannot be made in cases where it is based on the fact that the respondent party is a national or a domiciliary of another EU Member State.[16] Moreover, international treaties may prevent a court from ordering security for costs in certain situations (e.g. Article 14 of the HCCH Convention of 25 October 1980 on International Access to Justice). In any event, when considering an application for security for costs, a court must take into account whether international law and the respective national law provide a fair opportunity to enforce the costs decision against the respondent.
4. In the light of the foregoing, the prospect of obtaining security for costs will be greater in situations where the respondent's funds are located in a non-EU country and the applicant is based in an EU country and the respondent cannot demonstrate that they have sufficient

16 See, for instance, CJEU Judgment of 26 September 1996, Data Delecta Aktiebolag and Forsberg (C-43/95, ECR 1996 p. I-4661) ECLI:EU:C:1996:357; Judgment of 20 March 1997, Hayes / Kronenberger (C-323/95, ECR 1997 p. I-1711) ECLI:EU:C:1997:169; Judgment of 2 October 1997, Saldanha and MTS Securities Corporation / Hiross (C-122/96, ECR 1997 p. I-5325) ECLI:EU:C:1997:458.

funds to pay the costs of proceedings.[17] Ordering security for costs in favour of a litigant domiciled in the EU against a respondent who is also domiciled in EU but does not have the necessary funds will only be possible in exceptional cases. However, it is possible to envisage such cases, e.g., situations where the actual claimant does not have the necessary funds, but its parent company does, or where it is apparent that the respondent is a mere "process vehicle", i.e. an entity founded for the sole purpose of limiting the financial exposure resulting from potential loss by the "real" respondent.

5. Note this rule cannot address specific cases where an individual claimant may typically cause a respondent to incur significant costs in cases where the claimant is acting in the interests of other persons, collective interests and/or for the purpose of "private law enforcement", e.g., in collective proceedings arising from antitrust law or certain corporate law cases, such as challenging a shareholders' resolution. Such situations could properly be dealt with in subject-specific legislation.

Rule 244. Legal Aid

(1) Parties are entitled to legal aid, as provided by national law, if their right of access to justice and to a fair trial so requires.

(2) Such legal aid should be sufficient to cover reasonable and proportionate legal representation where legal provisions, the complexity of the case, or the vulnerability of a party so require.

Sources:

ALI/UNIDROIT Principles 3.3, 17.3, 24.3 and 25.

Comments:

1. Rule 244 does not set out a restatement of European approaches to legal aid. It provides a broad and general rule, articulating the right to receive legal aid. This approach was taken due to the right to legal aid having been subject to development under the jurisprudence of the European Convention on Human Rights as an aspect of the fundamental right of access to justice, national courts, including constitutional courts and in European Union law.[18]
2. Addressing all relevant details concerning legal aid provision in the Rules would both go beyond the scope and purpose of the Rules and, equally, tend to be both superficial and incomplete. Furthermore, given national differences in the organisation of the financing of legal aid, which go beyond procedural rules, it would not be appropriate to attempt to set out a unified approach within these Rules. For example, in many jurisdictions, such as France, Germany, the Netherlands and Italy, lawyers receive remuneration directly, as a means of legal aid, from the State for representing a party who was (partly) exempt from paying the lawyer's fee. In other jurisdictions, such as Austria, individual lawyers are required to provide representation as an obligation arising from their membership of the

17 See, for example, Order 60 of the Cypriot Civil Procedure Rules; § 196 of the Estonian CCP; or § 110 of the German CCP.

18 Council Directive 2002/8/EC of 27 January 2003 to improve access to justice in cross-border disputes by establishing minimum common rules relating to legal aid for such disputes; the third paragraph of Art. 47 of the European Charter of Fundamental Rights.

bar association and are then provided with refunds for any financial outlays incurred as a result of such representation.[19]

3. Given the above, Rule 244(1) specifies that a party is entitled to legal aid "if their right of access to justice and to a fair trial so requires". A party, however, is only entitled to legal aid on such grounds if there are no other available means of financing the litigation, i.e., self-funding, legal expenses insurance, third-party funding or success fee arrangements, are unavailable. Taxpayer funding of private litigation should always only be a subsidiary means of guaranteeing the right of access to justice and a fair trial.
4. While many national legal systems specify that legal representation is not required either generally (as in England and Wales, Finland, Sweden or Switzerland) or in specific types of claims, such as small claims, it might be thought that legal aid needs to be made available for such claims. Rule 244(2) is intended to clarify that that is not the case and that the availability of legal representation is a core feature of access to justice and fair trial as it is an essential means to secure equality of arms. It thus provides impecunious parties with a fair opportunity to finance legal representation to assist them in their prosecution or defence of a claim, and should be available generally, subject to satisfaction of the requirements set out within this Rule.

Rule 245. Third-Party Funding and Success Fees

(1) A party who receives funding for the proceedings from a professional third-party funder or from a crowd-funder shall disclose this fact and the identity of the funder to the court and the other party at the commencement of proceedings. The details of such a third-party funding arrangement are, however, not subject to this requirement.

(2) Such a third-party funding arrangement must be in accordance with applicable law and must not provide for inadequate compensation for the funder or enable the funder to exercise any undue influence on the conduct of the proceedings.

(3) Parties may enter into success fee arrangements with counsel or a third-party funder. Such arrangements must nevertheless be consistent with applicable law, the parties' access to fair legal representation and the integrity of the proceedings.

(4) A violation of the requirements of Rules 245(1), (2) and (3) does not constitute a defence against the claim of the party availing itself of third-party funding or a success fee arrangement. But, having made its decision on the claim, the court may ask for details of fee arrangements with a third party or counsel relevant for the instance at stake, and, upon consultation with the parties, it may take into account any disregard of applicable law or lacking fairness of the arrangement when it renders the final decision on costs determining the part of the claimant's costs to be reimbursed.

(5) As far as provided in Rules 237, 238 (3), Rule 245 applies to collective proceedings.

Sources:

ALI/Unidroit Principles 3.3, 17.3, 24.3 and 25.

Comments:

1. Rule 245 addresses two salient issues which have been the subject of intense international discussion in the past decades. Those issues are the availability of funding for civil

19 See § 64(1)(1)(f) of the Austrian CCP. The State then makes an annual lump sum contribution to the Bar Association's pension funds.

proceedings either by means of third-party funding or by way of a success (contingent) fee arrangement. In neither case has the debate produced a European consensus on the appropriate approach to be taken in respect of the most relevant aspects of the respective issues.

2. Against this background, Rule 245 may well be considered either too cautious an approach or too far-reaching. It does, however, seek to set out such principles that could be understood to be both generally acceptable, while providing a basis for future positive, and optimal, development.
3. Rules 245(1) and (2) addresses the issue of third-party funding. It could be argued that the source of a party's litigation funding is not a matter for the court or other parties to litigation. While the existence of professional third-party funders is a relatively new development, there have always been situations where third parties have funded proceedings. Such professional funders have been, and continue to be, insurance companies, trade unions, banks, parent companies. Legislators have never considered it necessary to subject such situations to rules governing or restricting such third-party funding. As such it could be argued that this *laissez-faire* approach should also be taken to other, and newer, forms of professional third-party funding, which, in essence, only provide financial services to litigants. This might also suggest that any such regulation ought to be a matter for financial markets regulation, thus being within the scope of financial market authorities' powers, rather than being a matter of civil procedural legislation. It could, however, equally be argued that the activities of professional third-party funders might be detrimental to procedural fairness. It could, for instance, be argued that such funders might encourage aggressive procedural strategies both at the outset of proceedings, when the decision whether to commence proceedings is made, and in situations where a decision has to be made whether a party wishes to enter into a settlement. Furthermore, it could be argued that third-party funding is unfair, because it is normally only available to claimants and not to defendants, as the latter have no financial inducement to offer such a funder in return for the funding.
4. Notwithstanding concerns regarding third-party funding, it should be welcomed as a valid means to increase parties' opportunities to secure fair and efficient access to justice. While the availability of such funding could encourage parties to commence proceedings that would otherwise not have been started, or that such funders could exercise a certain influence over the conduct of the proceedings to, for instance, prevent the funded party from entering into an otherwise reasonable settlement, such considerations can equally apply where other funding is available. There are, for instance, many other reasons why parties take a more or less aggressive litigation strategy, or why they may refuse to settle proceedings. Parties that have the means to fund their own litigation always have the choice whether to act in a more aggressive fashion without any third-party funder being involved. Equally, the availability of such funding facilitating the bringing of meritorious claims that otherwise could not be commenced or pursued promotes effective access to justice, while also reducing the prospect that a party may otherwise be induced to under-settle their claim as a consequence of the financial imbalance between the parties. Such funding thus can also promote effective equality of arms. Furthermore, the fact that it is normally only a claimant that can utilise third-party funding is not itself a reason not to permit its use. That fact is simply a consequence of it being the case that only claimants have an asset, the claim's value, to offer in return for the funding. This is simply a normal fact of the operation of financial markets, and not an inequitable and specific feature of third-party funding of proceedings.
5. A third-party funding arrangement could potentially contain unfair terms to the detriment of the party receiving such funding, i.e., where the amount promised to the funder

in return for the funding is too great (the return to the funder party is thus inadequate), or where the funder obtains an undue influence over the conduct of the proceedings (and thus could prevent the party from entering into a settlement that is in the funded party's best interests). To protect the interests of funded parties, Rule 245(2) specifies that funding arrangements must not contain such terms. It should be noted, however, that under Rule 245(4) the existence of such unfair terms does not provide a basis for the other party to litigation to raise them as a defence against the funded party's claim. To permit the terms of a third-party funding agreement to form the basis of a defence to the substantive claim would be abusive; the prohibition on such terms is no more than a means to protect the funded party.

6. Rule 245(3) concerns success (contingent) fee arrangements. Such arrangements are, as properly noted by the International Bar Association, permitted in some jurisdictions, while being prohibited in others on public policy grounds.[20] The Council of Bars and Law Societies of Europe goes so far as to expressly prohibit such arrangements.[21] While such an approach is arguably not a proper reflection of a European Union *acquis* in this respect, nor the approach taken by all European jurisdictions, e.g., England and Wales permit the use of success fee agreements.[22] The general tenor of such considerations suggests a cautious approach should be taken. While different approaches to contract law and the regulation of the legal profession differs across European jurisdictions, it appears reasonable to approach the issue of success fee agreements as not being held to be unlawful *per se* across Europe. On the contrary, most European jurisdictions adopt a selective approach, where not every success fee arrangement is lawful, with some forms of such agreements being prohibited.
7. Given this background, it might appear to be difficult to provide a specific rule on success fee agreements. Nevertheless, given the potential that such funding arrangements have for improving access to justice,[23] their endorsement in these Rules is an appropriate step to take. Given a need to reflect the differential approaches taken across Europe, the Rules, however, make provision for national law to limit the scope and content of such arrangements. This reservation is also made in order to reflect the general point, made above, that the Rules on costs ought to preserve the integrity of national regulation of the legal profession. Such provisions limiting the accessibility of success fee arrangements to the parties should, however, be based on considerations of procedural fairness, i.e., they

20 International Bar Association, *International Principles on Conduct for the Legal Profession*, (2011) at [10.3], <https://www.icj.org/wp-content/uploads/2014/10/IBA_International_Principles_on_Conduct_for_the_legal_prof.pdf>.

21 The Council of Bars and Law Societies of Europe, *Charter of Core Principles of the European Legal Profession and Code of Conduct for European lawyers*, (2019) at [3.3.1] <https://www.ccbe.eu/fileadmin/speciality_distribution/public/documents/DEONTOLOGY/DEON_CoC/EN_DEON_CoC.pdf >.

22 Courts and Legal Services Act 1990 (England and Wales) s.58.

23 See, for instance, the approach taken by the German Constitutional Court in its decision of 12 December 2006 1 BvR 2576/04 BVerfGE 117, 163, where it held that an absolute prohibition of success fees was in conflict with Art. 12 of the German *Grundgesetz*. The prohibition did not provide exceptions for cases where the specific circumstances of a client meant that without the possibility of entering into such an agreement with a lawyer they would not have been able to pursue their rights.

should in any event protect parties' access to fair legal representation and the integrity of the proceedings.

8. Rule 245 must be read in conjunction with Rules 237 and 238 concerning the application of third-party funding to collective proceedings. Such funding is typical of such proceedings. The approach adopted in Part X, on costs and funding in collective proceedings is intended to strike a reasonable balance between promoting access to justice by way of collective redress and the legitimate interests of the defendants to such proceedings. Rule 237(2) provides that details of the funding agreement should be disclosed, in confidence, to the court. While this approach is appropriate for collective proceedings, it is not appropriate as a general approach. Outside collective proceedings neither a defendant nor the court has any basis to inquire into a funded party's internal affairs, see Rule 245(1).

ANNEX

ELI – UNIDROIT Model European Rules of Civil Procedure

PART I – GENERAL PROVISIONS

SECTION 1 – Scope

Rule 1. Scope

(1) These Rules apply to the resolution of domestic and cross-border disputes in civil and commercial matters whatever the nature of the court.
(2) These Rules do not apply to:
  (a) the status or legal capacity of natural persons, rights in property arising out of a matrimonial relationship or out of a relationship deemed by the law applicable to such relationship to have comparable effects to marriage;
  (b) bankruptcy, proceedings relating to the winding-up of insolvent companies or other legal persons, judicial arrangements, compositions and analogous proceedings;
  (c) social security;
  (d) arbitration;
  (e) maintenance obligations arising from a family relationship, parentage, marriage or affinity;
  (f) wills and succession, including maintenance obligations arising by reason of death.
(3) These Rules may also apply where incidental issues arise which fall within Rule 1(2), if the principal matter in dispute is within the scope of Rule 1(1).

SECTION 2 – Principles

A. Co-operation

Rule 2. General

Parties, their lawyers and the court must co-operate to promote the fair, efficient and speedy resolution of the dispute.

Rule 3. Role of the parties and their lawyers

Parties and their lawyers must:
(a) take reasonable and appropriate steps to settle disputes amicably;
(b) contribute to the proper management of the proceedings;
(c) present facts and evidence;
(d) assist the court in the determination of the facts and the applicable law;
(e) act in good faith and avoid procedural abuse when dealing with the court and other parties.

Rule 4. Role of the Court – the General Case Management Duty

The court is responsible for active and effective case management. The court must ensure that parties enjoy equal treatment. Throughout proceedings it shall monitor whether parties and their lawyers comply with their responsibilities under these Rules.

B. Proportionality

Rule 5. Role of the Court

(1) The court must ensure that the dispute resolution process is proportionate.
(2) In determining whether a process is proportionate the court must take account of the nature, importance and complexity of the particular case and of the need to give effect to its general management duty in all proceedings with due regard for the proper administration of justice.

Rule 6. Role of the parties and their lawyers

Parties and their lawyers must co-operate with the court to promote a proportionate dispute resolution process.

Rule 7. Proportionality of sanctions

Sanctions for breach of any of the rules must be proportionate to the seriousness of the matter involved and the harm caused and reflect the extent of participation and the degree to which the conduct was deliberate.

Rule 8. Proportionality of costs

Costs of proceedings should, in so far as possible, be reasonable and proportionate to the amount in dispute, the nature and complexity of the particular proceedings, their importance for the parties and the public interest.

C. Settlement

Rule 9. Role of the parties and their lawyers

(1) Parties must co-operate in seeking to resolve their dispute consensually, both before and after proceedings begin.
(2) Lawyers must inform the parties about the availability of consensual dispute resolution methods, assist them in selecting the most suitable method, and, where appropriate, encourage its use. They must ensure that they use any mandatory method.
(3) Parties may ask the court to render a settlement agreement enforceable.
(4) When a consensual settlement as a whole cannot be reached, parties must take all reasonable opportunities to reduce the number of contested issues prior to adjudication.

Rule 10. Role of the Court

(1) The court must facilitate settlement at any stage of the proceedings. Particularly, it must ensure that the parties consider settlement in the preparatory stage of proceedings and at case management conferences. If necessary for furthering the settlement process, it may order the parties to appear before it in person.
(2) The court must inform the parties about the availability of different types of settlement methods. It may suggest or recommend the use of specific consensual dispute resolution methods.
(3) The court may participate in settlement attempts and assist the parties in reaching a consensual resolution. It may also assist in drafting settlement agreements.
(4) Where a judge mediates during a settlement process and receives information in the absence of one of the parties, that judge must not decide the case.

D. Right to be heard

Rule 11. Fair opportunity to present claim and defence

The court must manage proceedings to ensure that parties have a fair opportunity to present their case and evidence, to respond to their respective claims and defences and to any court orders or matters raised by the court.

Rule 12. Basis of Court Decisions

(1) In reaching any decision in proceedings the court must consider all factual, evidential, and legal issues advanced by the parties. Court decisions must specifically set out their reasoning concerning substantial issues.
(2) The court must not base its decisions on issues that parties have not had an opportunity to address.

Rule 13. Communications with the Court

(1) The court must not communicate with a party in the absence of other parties. This prohibition does not apply to without-notice proceedings or to routine procedural administration.
(2) All communications by parties with the court must be provided to all other parties at the time when they are made to the court.
(3) When the court becomes aware of a failure to comply with the requirement in Rule 13(2), it must promptly provide the parties with the content of the communication.

E. Representation and assistance

Rule 14. Self-representation and mandatory representation

Except when legal representation is required by law, parties have a right to represent themselves in proceeding.

Rule 15. Representation and assistance in Court

(1) Parties may engage a lawyer of their own choice. They may do so both when they choose to be, and when they are required by law to be, represented by a lawyer. This right includes the right to representation by a lawyer admitted to practice in the forum and to receive active assistance before the court from a lawyer admitted to practice elsewhere.
(2) Parties may, where the law permits it, be represented or assisted in court by an individual or organisation other than a lawyer.
(3) When representing or assisting a party the court must respect a lawyer's professional independence. This includes ensuring that lawyers are able to fulfil their duty of loyalty to their client and maintain client confidentiality.

Rule 16. Hearing Parties

(1) Parties have the right to be heard in person by the court.
(2) The court may always hear parties in person.

F. Oral, written and public Proceedings

Rule 17. Public proceedings

(1) Hearings and court decisions, including their reasoning, must, as a general rule, be public.

(2) The court may order the proceedings, or parts thereof, especially oral hearings and the taking of evidence, to be in private (in camera) for reasons of public policy, including national security, privacy, or professional secrets, including business confidentiality, or in the interests of the administration of justice. Where necessary the court may make suitable protective orders to maintain the privacy or confidentiality of hearings held or evidence taken in private.
(3) Judgments and their reasoning shall be accessible to the public to the extent that proceedings are open to the public. When hearings have been in private, publicity of the judgment may be limited to its operative part.
(4) Court files and records shall be publicly accessible at least to persons with a legal interest in them and to those making a legitimate inquiry.
(5) The identity of parties, witnesses and other natural persons mentioned in the judgment may be private where strictly necessary.

Rule 18. Oral and Written Proceedings

(1) Pleadings and applications must be presented initially in writing.
(2) The court may order parties to present oral argument and carry out the oral examination of witnesses or experts. Where a party requests it, the court must permit oral argument, and may permit oral examination.
(3) The court may order witnesses and experts to submit written statements.
(4) In so far as appropriate, proceedings may be conducted using any available means of information and communication technology.

G. Languages, interpretation and translation

Rule 19. Language of the Court

Proceedings, including documents and oral communications, must as a general rule be in a language of the court. The court may permit all or part of the proceedings to be conducted in other languages where doing that would not prejudice the parties or the right to a public hearing.

Rule 20. Interpretation and translation

(1) Interpretation or translation must be provided by the court to parties who are not sufficiently competent in the language used in the proceedings. The right to interpretation includes the right of parties with hearing or speech impediments to receive appropriate assistance. Such interpretation and translation shall ensure the proceedings are fair by enabling the parties to participate in them effectively.
(2) Where documents are translated, the parties may agree, or the court may order, that such translation be limited to such parts of the documents as necessary to ensure the proceedings are fair and that the parties are able to participate effectively in them.

SECTION 3 – **Proceedings**

A. Commencement, termination, Concentration and scope

Rule 21. Commencement and termination

(1) Proceedings may only be instituted by a party. The court cannot institute proceedings on its own motion.

(2) Parties may terminate proceedings in whole or in part by withdrawal, admission of the claim or settlement.

Rule 22. Concentration of Legal and Factual Issues

(1) Parties must bring all the legal and factual elements in support of, or in objection to, a claim for relief that arise out of the same cause of action in one single proceeding.
(2) Non-compliance with Rule 22(1) renders proceedings on the same claim for relief arising out of the same cause of action inadmissible. This preclusion does not apply if
    (a) subsequent to the earlier proceeding, there has been a change in relevant facts on which judgment in those proceedings was based, or
    (b) the non-compliant party has obtained or acquired a new right since judgment was given in the earlier proceeding.

Rule 23. Scope

(1) The scope of the dispute is determined by the claims and defences of the parties in the pleadings, including amendments.
(2) The court must decide on, and only on, the relief claimed.

B. Facts, evidence and applicable law

Rule 24. Facts

(1) The parties must put forward such facts as support their claim or defence. The court may invite the parties to clarify or supplement these facts.
(2) The court must not consider facts not introduced by the parties.
(3) The court may consider such facts not specifically addressed by a party but that are necessarily implied by matters of fact put forward by the parties or which are contained within the case file. It may only do so if they are relevant to a party's claim or defence and the parties have been given a reasonable opportunity to respond.

Rule 25. Evidence

(1) Each party is required to prove all the relevant facts supporting its case. Parties must offer evidence supporting their factual contentions. Substantive law determines the burden of proof.
(2) Each party has, in principle, a right to access all forms of relevant, non-privileged and reasonably identified evidence. In so far as appropriate, parties and non-parties must contribute to disclosure and production of evidence. It is not a basis of objection to such disclosure by a party that disclosure may favour the opponent or other parties.
(3) In so far as appropriate the court may invite the parties to supplement their offers of evidence. Exceptionally, it may take evidence on its own motion.

Rule 26. Applicable law

(1) While taking account of any applicable special provisions, the parties may present legal arguments supporting their claim or defence.
(2) The court must determine the correct legal basis for its decision. This includes matters determined on the basis of foreign law. It may only do so having provided the parties a reasonable opportunity to present their arguments on the applicable law.
(3) Where parties are free to dispose of their rights, they may agree on the legal basis of the claim or on specific issues in the claim. Such an agreement must be explicit and must,

even if it was made before commencement of the proceedings, be set out in the pleadings. The agreement binds the court.

C. Sanctions for non-compliance and relief from sanctions

Rule 27. Sanctions for Non-Compliance with Rules and court Orders

(1) The court shall disregard factual allegations, modifications of claims and defences, and offers of evidence that are introduced later than permitted by these rules or by court orders, including those concerning amendment. Preclusion does not apply if the court could have taken notice of the party's failure or mistake and itself failed to raise with the parties whether they wished to seek an amendment or relief from sanction.
(2) As a general rule, the court may continue the proceedings and decide on the merits based on the facts and evidence available to it.
(3) The court may draw negative factual inferences, order a party or their lawyer to bear the costs of non-compliance, or in serious cases of non-compliance render an *astreinte*, an order for payment of a fine, administrative sanction as provided by national law, or hold the non-compliant party in contempt.
(4) In assessing the nature of any compensation or fine under this rule, the court may require payment on the following bases: a lump sum; an amount per period of breach; or, an amount per offence. In the latter two cases the amount may be subject to a maximum as determined by the court.

Rule 28. Relief from the consequences of procedural non-compliance

Where a sanction for non-compliance with a rule or court order has been imposed, the subject of the sanction may apply for relief from that sanction. In considering whether, on application by a party, to exercise its discretion to grant relief the court must take account of the need for proceedings to be conducted consistently with the principles of co-operation and proportionality.

PART II – PARTIES

SECTION 1 – General Part

Rule 29. The Parties to Proceedings

(1) Parties to civil proceedings are all the persons by and against whom the proceedings are brought.
(2) Anyone who has the capacity to hold a right under substantive law may be a party to civil proceedings.

Rule 30. Litigation Capacity of Natural Persons

(1) Litigation capacity is the capacity to exercise rights in civil proceedings.
(2) Anyone who has the capacity to exercise rights or obligations in their own name under the substantive law shall be deemed to have litigation capacity.
(3) Anyone not within the scope of Rule 30(2) must be represented in proceedings by a representative according to the rules of the applicable law.

Rule 31. Representation of Legal Persons and other entities

Legal persons and other entities that are parties must exercise their rights through natural persons who are entitled to represent them according to the substantive law.

Rule 32. Proof of Representation

The court may, at any time in the proceedings, order the representative to prove the existence or scope of their power to act.

Rule 33. Court Review of its own motion (ex officio review)

The Court shall at all times ensure compliance with Rules 29 to 31 and make any appropriate order.

Rule 34. Persons Entitled to Bring Proceedings

Persons with litigation capacity must bring proceedings in their own name and on the basis of their own substantive rights unless either these Rules or substantive law otherwise permit.

Rule 35. Public Interest

A person who is authorised by law to act in the public interest, may act as a party or intervene in any proceedings.

SECTION 2 – Special Part

A. Multiple Parties

1. Joinder of parties

Rule 36. Voluntary Joinder of Parties

(1) Multiple parties may bring or defend claims in a single proceeding. They may do so if
  (a) their claims are closely connected, and
  (b) the court has jurisdiction with respect to all parties.
(2) The court may, where it is necessary for the purpose of properly managing the proceedings, order the claims to continue as separate proceedings.
(3) Each of the joined parties acts on their own account. Their actions or omissions in the proceedings shall not prejudice the other joined parties.

Rule 37. Consolidation of Separate Proceedings

The court may order the consolidation of separate proceedings pending before it to enable them to be managed properly in a single proceeding.

Rule 38. Necessary Joinder of Parties

(1) A proceeding must be brought by or against parties jointly where either the joint nature of the legal right or the substantive law requires a judgment to bind all of the joined parties in the same terms.
(2) A procedural act carried out by one or more of the joined parties shall affect all such parties.
(3) In the case of settlement, waiver of claim, or an admission, all the joined parties must consent to be bound by the act.

2. Intervention and Third Parties

Rule 39. Principal Intervention

Anyone not a party to proceedings who claims a right in its subject matter, may bring a claim directly against one or more of the parties in the court, in which the dispute is pending at first instance or, if the Court so permits, on appeal.

Rule 40. Voluntary Intervention in Support of a Party

(1) Anyone who has a legitimate interest in one or more parties succeeding in proceedings may intervene in support of their claim or defence. They may intervene at any time before the final hearing is concluded.
(2) The intervenor in support of a party may not object to any procedural step already taken in the proceeding. Intervenors may, however, take any procedural step that the party they support may take if this is not in conflict with any procedural step taken by that party.

Rule 41. Notice by Voluntary Intervenors

(1) Anyone seeking to participate in proceedings as an intervenor under the preceding Rules must make an application to the court. The application must state the basis on which intervention is sought. Notice of the application shall be given to the parties.
(2) The parties shall be heard concerning the proposed intervention. The court may order the applicant and the parties to attend an oral hearing.
(3) An application to intervene does not suspend the proceedings unless the court orders otherwise.

Rule 42. Third-Party Notice

(1) A party may give any person notice of the dispute if, in the event of that party's claim or defence being unsuccessful, they might have a claim against or be subject to a claim by that person.
(2) A person given notice under Rule 42(1) becomes a party to the proceedings unless the court, upon application, orders otherwise.
(3) The third-party notice must state the matter at issue and the reason why they have been given such notice.

Rule 43. Amicus Curiae

(1) Any natural or legal person, or other entity, may provide the court with submissions concerning important issues in proceedings with the consent of the court. The court may also invite such submissions.
(2) Before giving its consent, or inviting submissions, under Rule 43(1) the court must consult the parties.

B. Substitution and Succession of Parties

Rule 44. Substitution and Succession

(1) At any time after proceedings are commenced the court must permit the substitution or the succession of a party by another person where the law requires it.
(2) At any time after proceedings are commenced the court may permit the substitution or the succession of a party by another person if that is appropriate in the interest of the good administration of justice.
(3) Unless the court orders otherwise, the proceedings continue upon substitution or succession of a party from the position they had reached at the time substitution or succession was effected.

SECTION 3 – Cross border issues

Rule 45. Capacity of foreign nationals to be a party

The capacity of foreign nationals or legal persons incorporated outside the forum State shall be assessed for foreign nationals according to the law of the country of their habitual residence or their citizenship, and for legal persons according to the law of the State of their incorporation.

Rule 46. Litigation capacity

(1) A non-resident's litigation capacity shall be assessed according to the law of their habitual residence or their citizenship.
(2) A non-resident who lacks capacity to conduct litigation under the law of their habitual residence or citizenship but has such capacity under the law of the forum State may take procedural steps in proceedings on their own behalf.
(3) A legal person, incorporated outside the forum State, shall have its litigation capacity assessed according to the law of the place of incorporation.

PART III – CASE MANAGEMENT

Rule 47. Careful Conduct of litigation by the Parties

Parties must present their claims, defences, factual allegations and offers of evidence as early and completely as possible and as appropriate to the careful conduct of litigation in order to secure procedural expedition.

Rule 48. Court control of proceedings

At all stages of the proceedings the court must monitor whether parties and their lawyers comply with Rule 47 and any order made under Rule 49.

Rule 49. Means of Case management

Where necessary for the proper management of proceedings, the court shall, in particular:
(1) encourage parties to take active steps to settle their dispute or parts of their dispute and, where appropriate, to use alternative dispute resolution methods;
(2) schedule case management conferences;
(3) determine the type and the form of the procedure;
(4) set a timetable or procedural calendar with deadlines for procedural steps to be taken by parties and/or their lawyers;
(5) limit the number and length of future submissions;
(6) determine the order in which issues should be tried and whether proceedings should be consolidated or separated;
(7) determine the separation of questions concerning jurisdiction, provisional measures and statutes of limitation for early decision upon special hearings;
(8) consider necessary amendments regarding the parties' proper representation, the consequences of changes related to the parties to litigation and the participation of third parties, intervenors, or other persons;
(9) consider amendments to the pleadings or offers of evidence in the light of the parties' contentions;
(10) require a party's appearance in person or require a party's representative, who should be fully informed of all matters relevant to the proceedings, to be present at a court hearing;

(11) address the availability, admissibility, form, disclosure and exchange of evidence and, if adequate to the state of proceedings,
  (a) determine the admissibility of evidence;
  (b) order the taking of evidence.

Rule 50. Case Management Orders

(1) The court may make any case management order on its own motion or on application of a party. When orders or decisions are made without prior consultation with the parties or on a without-notice (*ex parte*) basis, parties not previously heard may apply for the order or decision to be reconsidered at a hearing or on the basis of written submissions.
(2) If the parties agree on a case management measure the court shall not determine differently without good reason.
(3) The court may vary or revoke any case management order upon a party's or its own motion.

PART IV – COMMENCEMENT OF PROCEEDINGS

SECTION 1 – Pre-commencement procedural duties

Rule 51. Duty to promote consensual resolution and effective management

(1) Before proceedings are issued, parties shall co-operate with each other in order to avoid unnecessary disputes and costs, to facilitate the early consensual resolution of their dispute and, where such a resolution is not possible, the proportionate management of future proceedings according to Rules 2-11 and 47-50.
(2) In order to further the general duty set out in Rule 51(1) parties may:
  (a) provide each other with concise details of their potential claims or defences;
  (b) clarify and, wherever possible, narrow the legal and factual issues in dispute; and
  (c) identify relevant evidence so as to facilitate effective and early assessment of the merits of their positions.
(3) Parties may also:
  (a) consider a possible timetable for proceedings;
  (b) estimate the potential cost of proceedings;
  (c) consider issues of limitation, jurisdiction, provisional measures, and of any other procedural matter.

SECTION 2 – Commencement and pleadings

A. Statement of claim

Rule 52. Submission of the Statement of Claim

To commence proceedings the claimant must submit a statement of claim to the court, as provided in Rule 53. Notice shall be given as provided in Part VI.

Rule 53. Contents of the Statement of Claim

(1) The statement of claim must state, as a minimum, the designation of the specific court and of the parties, the relief sought and the grounds therefore.
(2) The statement of claim should:
  (a) state the relevant facts on which the claim is based in reasonable detail as to time, place, participants and events;

(b) describe with sufficient specification the available means of evidence to be offered in support of factual allegations;
(c) refer to the legal grounds that support the claim, including foreign law, in a way that is sufficient to permit the court to determine the claim's legal validity;
(d) state the detailed remedy requested, including the monetary amount or the specified terms of any other remedy sought;
(e) allege compliance with any applicable condition precedent, according to applicable national law, to bringing the claim, such as parties having to engage in pre-commencement conciliation or mediation, or having to issue a formal demand concerning the subject matter of the dispute.

(3) If a claimant does not fully comply with the requirements of Rule 53(2), the court must invite the claimant to amend the statement of claim. If a claimant shows good cause why it is not possible to provide details of relevant facts or specify the means of evidence in their statement of claim but the statement of claim nevertheless demonstrates that there is plausible dispute on the merits, the court should give due regard to the possibility that relevant detailed facts will develop later in the course of the taking of evidence.
(4) Whenever possible, means of evidence on which a claimant relies, must be attached to the statement of claim, if feasible with a copy for the defendant and other parties.
(5) A claimant may apply, in their statement of claim, for access to evidence under the custody or control of a defendant or non-party and which are to be offered in support of the claimant's allegations.
(6) The claimant may respond in a statement of claim to the defendant's defence as known from any exchange of arguments before commencement of proceedings. In this case Rule 54 applies to this part of their statement of claim.
(7) If the claimant makes a third-party claim or cross-claim seeking relief from a third party or a co-claimant Rule 53 applies correspondingly.

Rule 54. Statement of Defence and Counterclaims

(1) A defendant must, within 30 consecutive days from the date of service of notice, respond to the claimant's statement of claim. In appropriate cases, the court may properly extend the time for answer by court order.
(2) Rule 53 concerning the details of statements of claims applies to the defendant's response.
(3) Any failure by a defendant, whether explicit or tacit to deny an allegation contained in the claimant's statement of claim may be considered an admission for the purpose of the proceeding and obviates proof thereof.
(4) A defendant must set out in their response to the claimant's statement of claim which allegations are admitted or contested. A contested allegation is one that is either denied, neither admitted nor denied, or for which an alternative statement of facts is alleged. Where the defendant can neither admit nor deny reasons must be given in the defence why that is the case.
(5) If a defendant relies on an affirmative defence, their response to the claimant's statement of claim must allege all facts sufficient to permit the court to determine the legal validity of the defence, and offer means of evidence in support of the factual allegations. Rules 53(2)(a)-(c), (3) and (4) applies. The claimant may answer affirmative defences.
(6) The defendant may state a counterclaim seeking relief from a claimant. The defendant may also state a claim against a co-defendant or a third party. Rule 53 applies. The parties so addressed must answer these claims as provided in the previous provisions.

Rule 55. Amendments to Pleadings

(1) A party, upon showing good cause to the court and upon notice to other parties, has a right to amend its claims or defences when the amendment does not unreasonably delay the proceeding or otherwise result in injustice. In particular, amendments may be justified to take account of events occurring after those alleged in earlier pleadings, newly discovered facts or evidence that could not previously have been obtained through reasonable diligence, or new evidence obtained from the exchange of evidence.
(2) Permission to amend must be granted on such terms as are just, including, where necessary, adjournment or continuance, or compensation by an award of costs to another party.
(3) The amendment must be served on the opposing party who has 30 consecutive days in which to respond, or such time as the court may order.
(4) Any party may apply to the court for an order requiring another party to provide by amendment a more specific statement of that party's pleading on the ground that the challenged statement does not comply with the requirements of these Rules. Such a request temporarily suspends the duty to answer.

Rule 56. Withdrawal and admission of the claim

(1) With the defendant or defendants' consent, the claimant may terminate the proceeding or any part of it by complete or partial withdrawal of the claim without prejudice save as to costs. Unilateral withdrawal without prejudice is only permitted if made before the first hearing of the court. In any case the claimant shall bear the reasonable and adequate costs of other parties.
(2) A defendant may terminate the proceeding or any part of it by admission of the whole claim or a part of the claim. The claimant may thereafter file a request to obtain judgment.

B. Joint application for party-agreed-proceedings

Rule 57. Contents of the joint application

(1) A joint application is a statement of claim in which parties jointly may submit to the court their agreement according to Rule 26, their respective claims and defences, the issues on which they disagree and which are to be determined by the court, and their respective arguments on those disputed issues.
(2) In order to be admissible, the joint application must contain:
    (a) the designation of the parties;
    (b) the designation of the court before which the proceedings are brought;
    (c) the relief sought, including the monetary amount or the specified terms of any other remedy sought; and
    (d) the relevant facts and the legal grounds, on which the action is based.
(3) A joint application must describe the available means of evidence to be offered in support of factual allegations. Whenever possible, such evidence must be attached to the application.
(4) It must be signed and dated by the parties.

Rule 58. Related agreements

In so far as procedural rules are subject to party disposition, parties may agree on any procedural matter, such as the jurisdiction of the court, provisional measures, and publicity of hearings (see Rule 26(3)).

Rule 59. Amendment

(1) Parties have a right to amend their joint application when the amendment does not unreasonably delay management of the proceedings. In particular, amendments may be justified in order to take account of events occurring after those alleged in earlier pleadings, or newly discovered facts or evidence that could not previously have been obtained through reasonable diligence.
(2) Amendments are only admissible upon agreement of the parties.

Rule 60. Termination of party-agreed-proceedings

Before party-agreed-proceedings are determined by the court, parties may terminate them or any part of them by complete or partial joint withdrawal.

PART V - PROCEEDINGS PREPARATORY TO A FINAL HEARING

Rule 61. Case management hearings to prepare for the final hearing and determination

(1) To prepare for a final hearing, the court may hold an early case management hearing and if necessary further ones as the case progresses.
(2) Case management hearings may be held in person. If appropriate the court may proceed in written form or use any available electronic means of communication.
(3) In or immediately after a case management hearing, the court should, upon consultation with the parties: set a timetable or procedural calendar with deadlines for parties to complete their procedural obligations; set the timetable for a final hearing; and, the possible date by which judgment will be given.
(4) Whenever appropriate, the court may provide parties with advice relevant to their preparation for the final hearing and judgment. Such advice should, in so far as possible, be given in the early case management hearing. Case management orders should be made in or immediately after the early case management hearing.

Rule 62. Means of Case Management during the pre-final hearing phase

(1) The court may use all the means of case management set out in Rules 49(1), (3)-(6).
(2) Appropriate measures for the disclosure of evidence and the taking of evidence before a final hearing are, particularly,
    (a) the production and mutual exchange of documents;
    (b) requests for written witness statements and their exchange;
    (c) the appointment of a court expert and expert conferences between a court-appointed expert and experts appointed by the parties, or between court-appointed experts;
    (d) requests for information from third parties, including public authorities;
    (e) personal inspection of evidence by the court.

Rule 63. The Closing of Preparatory Proceedings

(1) As soon as the court is satisfied that both parties have had a reasonable opportunity to present their case during the preparatory proceedings and that it has had an opportunity to clarify issues and take any relevant evidence before the final hearing in accordance with Rule 62(2), it will close the proceedings and refer the case to the final hearing. Once the pre-final hearing phase of proceedings is closed, no further submissions, arguments or evidence are allowed, except as provided by Rule 63(2) and Rule 64(4).
(2) Only under very exceptional circumstances may the court, on its own motion (*ex officio*) or upon a party's well-founded application, permit further statements and submissions.

Rule 64. The Final Hearing

(1) In so far as practicable, the final hearing should be concentrated. A concentrated final hearing may be adapted to the use of electronic communication techniques.
(2) The final hearing must be before the judge or judges who are to give the final judgment.
(3) Ordinarily, the court should take oral evidence and evidence on those issues that are still matters of serious dispute between the parties.
(4) All relevant evidence not received by the court in the preparatory proceedings may be taken in the final hearing. New evidence not offered in the pleadings or upon amendment in the preparatory stage may be admitted only if a party shows strong and overwhelming reasons for not having produced it earlier.
(5) The court must properly manage the final hearing according to Rules 48-49. In particular, it must
  (a) determine the order in which issues shall be tried;
  (b) require a party's appearance in person or require a party's representative, who should be fully-informed of all matters relevant to the proceedings, to be present at the hearing;
  (c) order the taking of evidence.
(6) Documentary or other tangible evidence must have been disclosed to all other parties prior to the final hearing. Oral evidence may be taken only if notice has been given to all parties of the identity of the person to be examined and the substance of their intended evidence.
(7) Parties must have an opportunity to submit their final conclusions including statements on the results of evidence-taking.

Rule 65. Early Final Judgments

(1) The court, on its own motion or on the application of a party, may give an early final judgment upon simplified proceedings.
(2) In an early final judgment the court may
  (a) determine that it lacks jurisdiction or competence to adjudicate the dispute or whether the claim is inadmissible due to a failure to comply with other procedural requirements; or
  (b) give a final judgment or a judgment on part of the claim for relief by only deciding questions of law based on non-contested facts, or on the basis that there has been a failure by the parties to assert necessary and relevant facts timeously, or there has been a failure to proffer necessary means of evidence timeously; or
  (c) give a judgment upon the withdrawal of a claim, whether that was permitted or consented to, or upon an admission by the defendant.
(3) Rules 61–64 and Part VIII of these Rules apply, as appropriate to an early final judgment.

Rule 66. Judgments on Preliminary Procedural Issues or on Legal Issues on the Merits

(1) The court on its own motion or on the application of a party may give a judgment
  (a) deciding a preliminary procedural issue, or
  (b) deciding a legal issue on the merits
(2) Rules 61–64 and Part VIII of these Rules apply, as appropriate to the issue to be determined under this Rule. Judgments on preliminary procedural requirements according to Rule 133 are subject to independent appeal.

Rule 67. Provisional Measures and Interim Payment Orders

The court may make any order for provisional measures according to Part X or for an interim payment as provided by Part X, Rules 199 and following.

PART VI – SERVICE AND DUE NOTICE OF PROCEEDINGS

SECTION 1 – General part - Service, Due Notice and the Right to be Heard

Rule 68. Service of documents and minimum content

(1) Statements of claim and any other procedural documents amending the relief sought or seeking new relief under Rule 55 should be served in accordance with Rules 74-78 and 80-81.
(2) The statement of claim or documents seeking to amend proceedings must comply with the requirements of Rules 53 and 55.

Rule 69. Information about the procedural steps necessary to contest the claim

The statement of claim must clearly state the following:
(a) the procedural requirements for contesting the claim, including where applicable: the time limit for contesting the claim; the time of any scheduled court hearing; the name and address of the court or other institution to which a response to the claim should be sent or before which to appear, and whether representation by a lawyer is mandatory; and
(b) the consequences of a failure to respond or to appear in court, in particular, where applicable, the possibility that a judgment may be entered against the defendant in default of responding to the claim and the liability for costs related to the court proceedings.

Rule 70. Where the defendant fails to enter an appearance

Where the defendant has not responded to the statement of claim or not appeared in court, default judgment shall only be given according to Rule 138(3).

SECTION 2 – Responsibility for and methods of service

A. General Provisions

Rule 71. Responsibility for service

(1) Responsibility for service of documents lies with the court/parties.
(2) If responsibility lies with the court, upon application the court may entrust a party with service of documents if appropriate.
(3) Where responsibility lies with the parties the court retains supervisory control which may include the power to set aside service.

Rule 72. Applicability of rules

The following rules on service methods apply to the documents referred to in Rule 68 and to any other documents required to be served including court decisions.

Rule 73. Priority of methods guaranteeing receipt

Documents shall be served using a method that guarantees receipt (Rules 74-76). If such service is not possible, alternative service methods apply, as specified in Rule 78. Where the address for service is unknown or other methods of service have failed, methods of last resort, specified in Rule 80, may be used to effect service.

B. Methods of Service

Rule 74. Service guaranteeing receipt

(1) Service guaranteeing receipt includes
 (a) service by physical delivery attested to by an acknowledgement of receipt signed by the addressee or by a document signed by a court officer, bailiff, post officer or other competent person who effected the service stating that the addressee has accepted the document, and the date of the service;
 (b) service via a designated electronic information system using appropriately high technical standards attested to by an acknowledgement of receipt that the system generates automatically where the addressee has a legal obligation to register with that system. Such an obligation shall be imposed on legal persons and on natural persons engaging in independent professional activities for disputes relating to their trade or profession;
 (c) service by other electronic means if the addressee has previously and explicitly agreed to use this service method or is under a legal obligation to register an e-mail address for the purpose of service. Such service must be attested to by the addressee's acknowledgement of receipt, which must include the date of receipt, and which is returned by the addressee;
 (d) postal service attested to by an acknowledgement of receipt, which must include the date of receipt, and which is signed and returned by the addressee.

(2) Where an acknowledgment of receipt, under Rule 74(1)(c) or (d), is not received within a designated time, service according to Rule 74(1)(a) or (b), if available, should be attempted before alternative service methods can be used.

Rule 75. Service on legal persons by physical delivery

If Rule 74(1)(a) or (d) applies, service on a statutory representative of a legal person can be effected at the business premises. Business premises include the principal place of business, the place of the legal person's statutory seat, the central administration, or a branch, agency or establishment if the dispute arises out of the activity of that branch, agency or establishment.

Rule 76. Service on representatives

(1) If a minor or a party that lacks legal capacity has a legal custodian or guardian, service on them is equivalent to service on the addressee.

(2) Service on a person nominated to receive service by the addressee is equivalent to service on the addressee.

Rule 77. Refusal to accept service

Service according to Rule 74(1)(a) also includes service attested to by a document signed by the competent person who effected the service and stating that the addressee refused to receive the document. The document must be deposited at a specified place for a certain period of time for the purpose of collection by the addressee who has been informed where and when to collect the document.

Rule 78. Alternative service methods

(1) If the addressee is not available for service according to Rule 74, the following alternative service methods effected by a court officer, bailiff, postal officer or other competent person are available

(a) service at the addressee's home address on persons who are living in the same household as the addressee or are employed by the addressee, and who are able and willing to accept the document;
(b) in the case of a self-employed addressee or a legal person, service at the addressee's business premises on persons who are employed by the addressee, and who are able and willing to accept the document;
(c) depositing the document at a post office or with competent public authorities and placing written notification of that deposit in the addressee's mailbox. In such a case the notification must clearly identify the document as a court document, the date by which it must be collected, the place where it can be collected and the contact details of the relevant person effecting service. Service is only effected when the document is collected.

(2) Service according to Rule 78(1)(a) and(b) shall be attested to by:
(a) a document signed by the competent person who effected service, indicating:
(i) the method of service used;
(ii) the date of service; and
(iii) the name of that person and their relationship to the addressee,
or
(b) an acknowledgement of receipt by the person served.

(3) Service according to Rule 78(1)(a) and (b) is not allowed if the recipient is the party opposing the addressee in the proceedings.

(4) Service according to Rule 78(1)(c) shall be attested to by:
(a) a document signed by the competent person who effected service, indicating:
(i) the method of service used; and
(ii) the date of collection,
or
(b) an acknowledgement of receipt by the person served.

Rule 79. Service of documents during proceedings

(1) During proceedings, if a party is represented by a lawyer, service of documents may normally be effected on the lawyer or from lawyer-to-lawyer without Court intervention. Lawyers must provide an electronic address that can be used for service of documents.

(2) During proceedings, if a party is represented by a lawyer, they must notify the Court and any lawyer who represents other parties or intervenors of any change of postal or electronic address.

(3) During proceedings, parties must notify the court of any change of residence, of place of business or of their postal or electronic address.

Rule 80. Service methods of last resort

(1) If service by methods that guarantee receipt (Rules 74-77) or alternative service (Rule 78) is not possible because the addressee's address is unknown or service has otherwise failed, service of documents may be effected as follows:
(a) by publication of a notice to the addressee in a form provided for by law of the forum State, including publication in electronic registers accessible to the public, and
(b) by sending a notice to the addressee's last known address or e-mail address, if applicable.
(c) For the purpose of subparagraphs (a) and (b), notice means information which clearly states the character of the document to be served as a court document, the legal effect of the notification as effecting service, information as to where the

addressee can collect the documents or copies thereof, and the date by which they have to be collected.

(2) The address is unknown if the Court or the party responsible for service has made every reasonable effort to discover the addressee's present address. Efforts to find the present address must be documented in the Court files.

(3) Service shall be deemed to be effected within two weeks after publication of the notice and after having sent the notice to the last known address or e-mail address, as applicable. If there is no last known address or e-mail address service shall be deemed to be effected within two weeks after publication of the notice.

Rule 81. Cure for defective service

If service of documents does not meet the requirements of Rules 74-79, such non-compliance will be cured if the addressee's conduct proves that they received the document to be served personally and in sufficient time for them to arrange their defence or in any other way respond as required by the nature of the document.

SECTION 3 – Cross border issues

A. In the European Union

Rule 82. Language requirements

(1) In the case of natural persons not engaging in independent professional activities the documents referred to in Rule 68 and the information referred to in Rule 69 must be in a language of the proceedings and, unless it is evident that the addressee understands the language of the forum, also in a language of the European Union Member State of the individual's habitual residence.

(2) In the case of legal persons the documents referred to in Rule 68 and the information referred to in Rule 69 must be in a language of the proceedings, and also the language of the legal person's principal place of business, its statutory seat or of the principal documents in the transaction.

Rule 83. Non-application of Rule 81

If service of documents does not comply with the language requirements of Rule 82, Rule 81 does not apply.

Rule 84. Modification of time periods

If the addressee is domiciled in a European Union Member State different from the forum State then the time periods provided in Rule 80(3) are four weeks instead of two weeks.

B. Outside the European Union

Rule 85. General Rule

The preceding rules also apply when the addressee has no domicile or habitual residence within the European Union, subject to Rule 86.

Rule 86. Relationship to the HCCH 1965 Service Convention

Where there is occasion to transmit a judicial or extra-judicial document for service outside the European Union, the application of the preceding rules is without prejudice to the application of the HCCH 1965 Service Convention.

PART VII - ACCESS TO INFORMATION AND EVIDENCE

SECTION 1 - General part

A. General Provisions on Evidence

Rule 87. Standard of Proof

A contested issue of fact is proven when the court is reasonably convinced of its truth.

Rule 88. Matters Not Requiring Positive Evidence

(1) The following do not require positive evidence:
 (a) admitted facts;
 (b) uncontested facts;
 (c) facts which are notorious to the court.
(2) The existence of facts can be presumed on the basis of other proven facts.
(3) When a party has possession or control of evidence concerning a relevant fact and that party, without justification, fails to produce it, the court may consider that relevant fact to be proven.

Rule 89. Relevance

(1) Relevant evidence is admissible.
(2) The court, whether of its own motion or on application by a party, shall exclude evidence that is irrelevant. Relevance is determined by the court by reference to the matters alleged in the parties' pleadings.

Rule 90. Illegally Obtained Evidence

(1) Except where Rule 90(2) applies, illegally obtained evidence must be excluded from the proceedings.
(2) Exceptionally, the court may admit illegally obtained evidence if it is the only way to establish the facts. In exercising its discretion to admit such evidence the court must take into account the behaviour of the other party or of non-parties and the gravity of the infringement.

Rule 91. Evidentiary Privileges and Immunities

(1) Effect should be given to privileges, immunities, and similar protections for all persons who are heard in order to provide information in a case or concerning the production of evidence or other information.
(2) In particular, evidence may not be elicited in violation of:
 (a) the right of a spouse, partner equal to a spouse or close relative of a party to refuse testimony;
 (b) the right of a person not to incriminate themselves;
 (c) legal professional privilege, any other professional privilege, confidence, trade secrets and other similar interests as provided by law;
 (d) confidentiality of communications in settlement negotiations unless the negotiations have occurred in a public hearing or overriding public interests so require;
 (e) national security interests, State secrets or other equivalent public interest issues.
(3) The court should consider whether these protections justify a party's failure to disclose evidence or other information when deciding whether to draw adverse inferences or to impose sanctions.

(4) The court should recognise these protections when imposing sanctions on a party or non-party in order to compel disclosure of evidence or other information.
(5) A claim of privilege, immunity or other similar protection made with respect to a document shall describe it in sufficient detail to enable another party to challenge the claim.

B. Management of Evidence

Rule 92. Management and Presentation of Evidence

(1) Whenever necessary and appropriate, the court must order the taking of relevant evidence offered by a party. Where the court makes such an order it may make case management orders concerning the sequence and timing of the production of evidence. The court may also make orders, where appropriate, concerning the form in which evidence will be produced. Rules 49(9) and (11), 50, 62, 64(3)-(6) and 107 apply.
(2) The court, while affording the parties an opportunity to respond, may suggest evidence not previously proposed by a party, which it considers may be relevant to an issue in dispute. If a party accepts such a suggestion, the court will order the taking of that evidence so that it may be offered in support of that party's contentions of fact and law.
(3) Exceptionally, the court may, while affording the parties an opportunity to respond, order the taking of evidence not previously proposed by a party.
(4) The court shall provide each party with a fair opportunity and adequate time to respond to evidence presented by another party or taken by the court.

Rule 93. Admission by a Failure to Challenge Evidence

The court may take a party's unjustified failure to make a timely response to an opposing party's contention as a sufficient basis for considering that contention to be admitted or accepted. Before doing so the court must inform the party that it is considering drawing such a conclusion concerning the evidence and provide them with an opportunity to respond.

Rule 94. Early Party Identification of Evidence

Parties must identify evidence which they intend to produce to support the factual allegations set out in their pleadings.

Rule 95. Notification of Evidence

(1) Parties must make documentary or tangible evidence available to other parties.
(2) Parties may only propose witness evidence if notice is given to all other parties of the relevant witnesses' identity and the subject-matter of their proposed evidence.
(3) The court may direct that parties keep evidence of which they have been notified confidential.

Rule 96. Additional Evidence after Amendment

The court may, while affording the parties an opportunity to respond, permit or invite a party to clarify or amend their factual contentions and to offer additional evidence accordingly.

C. Presentation and Evaluation of Evidence

Rule 97. Conduct of Hearings where evidence is to be adduced

(1) Whenever appropriate, the court will hear and receive evidence directly at a hearing before the parties unless, exceptionally, it has authorised evidence to be taken by an individual authorised to act on its behalf or at another location.

(2) Any hearing where evidence is taken shall be video recorded, provided that the necessary technical equipment is available. The video recording must be kept under the court's direction.

(3) The taking of evidence, in hearings or in camera, can involve, where appropriate, the use of technology, such as videoconferencing or similar distance communication technologies.

Rule 98. Evaluation of Evidence

The court will freely evaluate evidence.

Rule 99. Sanctions concerning Evidence

The court, whether on its own motion or on application by a party, may impose sanctions under Rule 27 when:

(a) a person has unjustifiably failed to attend to give evidence or to answer proper questions, or to produce a document or other item of evidence;

(b) a person has otherwise obstructed the fair application of the rules concerning evidence.

SECTION 2 – Access to evidence orders

Rule 100. General Framework

When making orders under the Rules in this Part the court will give effect to the following principles:

(a) as a general rule, each party should have access to all forms of relevant and non-privileged evidence;

(b) in response to a party's application, under Rule 101, seeking access to evidence, the court will, if the application is granted, direct the production of relevant, non-privileged, and sufficiently identified evidence held or controlled by another party or, if necessary, by a non-party, even if such production might be adverse to that person's interests.

Rule 101. Application for Access to Evidence

(1) Subject to the considerations and procedure contained in these Rules, any claimant or defendant, or any prospective claimant who intends to commence proceedings, can apply to the court for an order securing access to relevant and non-privileged evidence held or controlled by other parties or non-parties.

(2) An application for an order securing access to evidence may include an application for the imposition of measures to protect or preserve evidence, including an application for provisional or protective measures under Part X.

(3) Material or information supplied under this rule only becomes evidence when it is formally introduced as such into the proceedings by a party or exceptionally by the court according to Rules 25(3), 92(2) and (3) and 107(2).

Rule 102. Relevant Criteria where an application for access to evidence is made

(1) A party or prospective party applying for an order for access to evidence must

  (a) identify, as accurately as possible in the light of the circumstances of the case, the specific sources of evidence to which access is sought, or alternatively

  (b) identify closely defined categories of evidence by reference to their nature, content, or date.

(2) An application must satisfy the court of the plausibility of the merits of the applicant's claim or defence by demonstrating that
   (a) the requested evidence is necessary for the proof or proposed proof of issues in dispute in proceedings or in contemplated proceedings;
   (b) the applicant cannot otherwise gain access to this evidence without the court's assistance; and
   (c) the nature and amount of evidence subject to the application is reasonable and proportionate. For this purpose the court will take into account the legitimate interests of all parties and all interested non-parties.
(3) If an application for access to evidence is made prior to the commencement of proceedings, the applicant must indicate with sufficient precision all elements necessary to enable the court to identify the claim for relief which the applicant intends to make.
(4) The court may not grant any application under this Rule which involves a vague, speculative, or unjustifiably wide-ranging search for information.

Rule 103. Confidential Information

(1) The court shall consider whether an application under Rule 101 for access to evidence concerns or includes confidential information, especially in relation to non-parties. In so doing, the court must have regard to all relevant rules concerning the protection of confidential information.
(2) Where necessary, in the light of the circumstances of the case, the court, amongst other things, may make an order for access to evidence containing confidential information adjusted in one or more of the following ways in order to protect the relevant interest in maintaining confidentiality
   (a) redacting relevant sensitive passages in documents;
   (b) conducting hearings *in camera*;
   (c) restricting the persons allowed to gain access to or inspect the proposed evidence;
   (d) instructing experts to produce a summary of the information in an aggregated or otherwise non-confidential form;
   (e) writing a non-confidential version of a judicial decision in which passages containing confidential data are deleted;
   (f) limiting access to certain sources of evidence to the representatives and lawyers of the parties and to experts who are subject to a duty of confidentiality.

Rule 104. Sanctions for Breach of Confidentiality

(1) If a person breaches any duty of confidentiality the aggrieved party may apply to the court for an order imposing one or more of the following sanctions
   (a) wholly or partially dismissing a party in breach's claim or defence, where the substantive proceedings are still pending;
   (b) declaring the party or other person in breach liable for damages and ordering payment of such compensation;
   (c) ordering the party in breach to pay the costs of the substantive proceedings irrespective of the outcome of those proceedings;
   (d) imposing on the party or the person in breach a fine appropriate to the breach;
   (e) imposing on the party's representative or representatives or the person in breach a fine appropriate to the breach.

(2) Any sanction imposed by the court under Rule 104(1) must be proportionate to the nature of the breach. In determining the proportionality of the sanction the court must take particular account of the fact that a breach occurred before proceedings on the merits were commenced, where that is the case.

Rule 105. Access to Evidence held by Public Authorities

(1) Except where information is protected on public interest grounds, Government and other public agencies must comply with an order made under these Rules.
(2) Where a Government or public agency seeks to refuse access to evidence on public interest grounds, they must provide the court with a reasoned explanation of the basis for their refusal and must satisfy the requirements set out in Rule 91(5).

Rule 106. Time of Applications

(1) Applications for access to evidence may be made prior to the initiation of proceedings, in a statement of claim, or in pending proceedings.
(2) If an order has been made prior to the initiation of proceedings, where appropriate, the successful applicant may be required to initiate proceedings within a specified, reasonable, period of time. If the applicant fails to comply with this requirement the court may set aside the order, direct the return of any evidence supplied to the applicant further to the order, impose an appropriate sanction on the party in default, or make any other appropriate order.

Rule 107. The Process for Granting Access Orders

(1) The court shall determine an application for an order under Rule 101(1) for access to evidence according to Rule 50.
(2) Orders under Rule 101(1) may be made by the court on a without-notice basis in very exceptional cases only. Where it does so it must permit parties and affected non-parties to be heard at a with-notice hearing.
(3) If applications for access to evidence are made prior to the commencement of proceedings the court should ordinarily determine the application only after giving any affected party or non-party an opportunity to respond and make representations concerning the grant of the order, its scope and proposed implementation.
(4) The party or non-party from whom access to evidence is sought may apply for the grant of a different but no less effective form or method of access. Such an application must demonstrate that the proposed alternative will be less burdensome to the party to whom it is to provide access.

Rule 108. Costs and Security

(1) The cost of implementing an order for access to evidence shall be borne by the applicant. Where appropriate the court may require the applicant to make an immediate payment of costs to a party or non-party against whom the order is made.
(2) The court may, upon the application of the person against whom an order for access to evidence is made, order security to be given by the party in whose favour the order is made. The order shall be for any predictable expense to be incurred in the implementation of that order. If security is required by the court, it must be provided before any order for access can be given effect.
(3) At the conclusion of the proceedings the court may determine the incidence of costs differently from the general rule.

Rule 109. Implementation

The court shall ensure that any such necessary and practical steps required to implement orders for access to evidence are implemented fairly and effectively. Such steps may include:

(a) issuing directions concerning the appropriate place and manner in which the order is to be carried out;

(b) directing that the applicant may be assisted by an expert; or

(c) by making any relevant order under Part X of these Rules.

Rule 110. Non-compliance with Access Orders

(1) The court may impose any one or more of the following sanctions upon any party or non-party who is subject to, and aware of, an order requiring the giving of access to evidence, and destroys or conceals such evidence, or otherwise renders it impossible to carry out the order successfully

  (a) declaring as admitted the facts which form the subject-matter of the relevant order for access to sources of evidence;

  (b) treating the defendant or prospective defendant as having impliedly conceded the basis or any relevant part of the claim which has been made or which was proposed by the applicant;

  (c) imposing on the relevant respondent to the order (and in accordance with the relevant court's established disciplinary powers) an appropriate penalty per day of delay in implementing the order.

(2) An order made under Rule 110(1) must be proportionate to the nature of the non-compliance and may only be made on application of the party in whose favour the order requiring access to evidence was made.

(3) This Rule is without prejudice to any other sanctions or disciplinary procedural measures available to the court, including measures according to Rules 27 and 99.

SECTION 3 – Types of evidence

A. Documents

Rule 111. Documentary and Electronic Evidence

(1) Parties may offer any relevant document as evidence.

(2) Document means anything in which information is recorded or maintained in any form, including but not limited to paper or electronic form. Information may be recorded in writing, pictures, drawings, programmes, voice messages, or electronic data, including e-mail, social media, text or instant messages, metadata, or other technological means. It may be maintained electronically on, but not limited to, computer, portable electronic devices, cloud-based or other storage media.

(3) Documents that a party maintains in electronic form must ordinarily be submitted or produced in electronic form, unless the court orders otherwise.

(4) Parties may challenge the authenticity of any document submitted as evidence. In such a case, the court must order the parties to take such steps as are necessary to establish the document's authenticity.

Rule 112. Authentic Instruments

(1) An authentic instrument is a document, which has either been formally drawn up or the authenticity of which has been certified by a public authority.

(2) Electronically recorded authentic instruments have the same probative force as those recorded on paper.

Rule 113. Documents: Language and Translation

(1) On the application of a party or on the court's own motion, any document shall be produced in or translated into a language of the court.
(2) Translation of lengthy or voluminous documents may be limited according to Rule 20(2).

B. Testimonial Evidence

Rule 114. Witnesses of Fact

(1) Subject to considerations of relevance, admissibility, case management and privilege or immunity, a party may present the evidence of any witness of fact.
(2) If a witness whose evidence satisfies the requirements of Rule 114(1) refuses to give evidence, whether in whole or in part, they can be ordered to do so by the court.
(3) A witness is under an obligation to tell the truth while giving their evidence. The court may require a witness to give their evidence under oath. The court may instruct the witness accordingly prior to the examination.

Rule 115. Witness evidence

(1) Ordinarily, witness evidence should be received orally. The court may, however and upon having received submissions from the parties on the issue, require that such evidence be given initially in writing. Such written evidence must be supplied to all other the parties in advance of the hearing where the witness is to give oral evidence. Oral evidence at a hearing may be limited to supplemental questioning following the presentation of a witness's written evidence.
(2) Each witness shall appear in person unless the court allows the use of video-conferencing or of similar technology with respect to that witness.
(3) A person giving evidence may be questioned first by the court or the party adducing their evidence. Where a witness has first been questioned by the court or by party other than the one adducing their evidence, that party must be given the opportunity to put supplemental questions directly to the witness.
(4) Parties may challenge the reliability of witness evidence.

Rule 116. Witnesses: Language and Translation

(1) Where a witness is not competent in an official language in which the proceeding is being, or may be, conducted interpretation or translation must be provided by the court.
(2) Where appropriate, and with the court's and parties' consent, a witness may testify in a language other than the official language of proceedings.

Rule 117. Witness Statements

(1) A party may, with the court's consent, present a written statement of sworn testimony from any person. Such a statement must be in their own words and contain their testimony about relevant facts.
(2) The court, in its discretion, may consider such written statements as if they were made by oral testimony at a hearing before the court.

(3) A party may apply for an order requiring the personal appearance of the author of such a written statement before the court. Where such an order is made, the witness may be examined by way of supplemental questioning by the court or the opposing party.

C. Examination of Parties

Rule 118. Examination of Parties and Consequences of Refusal to Respond

(1) The court may accord evidentiary effect to any statement made by a party that has been questioned before the court. Rule 114(3) applies correspondingly.
(2) Each party shall be given an opportunity to question their opponent in front of the court on relevant issues of fact.
(3) The court can draw relevant inferences if a party unjustifiably refuses to appear at a hearing or to answer any relevant question put to them by their opponent or by the court or refuses to swear an oath.
(4) If the party to be questioned is a legal person, it shall provide the identity of the natural person or persons who participated directly in the relevant course of events on its behalf, in order for them to be questioned, provided they can still be considered as a representative of that legal person. The court may draw relevant inferences if a legal person fails, without justification, to provide this information.

D. Expert Evidence

Rule 119. Party-appointed Experts

Parties may present expert evidence on any relevant issue for which such evidence is appropriate. They may do so through an expert of their choice.

Rule 120. Court-appointed Experts

(1) The court may appoint one or more experts to give evidence on any relevant issue for which expert evidence is appropriate, including foreign law.
(2) Experts can be individuals or legal entities. In the case of legal entities at least one individual must assume responsibility for the expert's report.
(3) If the parties agree upon an expert, the court ordinarily should appoint that expert.
(4) Parties may object to the appointment of a court-appointed expert on grounds of bias. Where there is a reasonable apprehension of bias, the court must either, as relevant, refuse to appoint the expert, rescind their appointment or set aside their evidence in its entirety.

Rule 121. Instructions to Court-appointed Experts

(1) The court shall instruct experts concerning the issues on which they are to provide evidence. It should set reasonable time limits within which any such expert should submit their written report or reports.
(2) In an appropriate case, the court may extend or limit the scope of its instructions to an expert. It may also vary any time limit for submission by an expert of their report.
(3) The court must inform the parties of any orders given or varied under this Rule.
(4) Where a party objects to the nature or scope of instructions given by the court to an expert, it may apply to the court to vary those instructions.

Rule 122. Duties of Experts

(1) An expert, whether appointed by the court or by a party, owes a duty to the court to present a full, objective and impartial assessment of the issue addressed.
(2) No expert may give evidence outside their field of expertise. An expert may also refuse to give evidence for the same reasons a witness may refuse to give evidence.
(3) An expert must not delegate their task to third parties unless authorised to do so by the court.
(4) Where an expert, without a reasonable explanation, fails to render their evidence within time limits set by the court, the court may impose appropriate sanctions.

Rule 123. Expert Access to Information

(1) Court-appointed experts should be provided with access to all relevant and non-privileged information necessary to enable them to prepare their written report.
(2) In particular, a court-appointed expert may ask a party to provide any information, to provide access to any documents, permit inspection of property or entry upon land for the purposes of inspection, to the extent that such are relevant and material to the proceedings.
(3) In appropriate circumstances, an expert may examine a person or have access to information derived from a physical or mental examination of that person.

Rule 124. Expert Reports and Oral Evidence

(1) Expert evidence should ordinarily be given in the form of a written report. However, in simple cases, the court may order that expert evidence be given orally.
(2) An expert may give oral testimony to explain their written report either on the court's request or on the application of any party. Subject to any applicable legal provisions, such oral testimony may be given at a hearing or via any appropriate means of distance communication, such as, but not limited to, video-conferencing.
(3) The court may require an expert to give their evidence, whether that is in the form of a written report or by way of oral testimony, on oath.
(4) Where an expert gives oral testimony, parties may only ask the expert questions that are relevant to their report.
(5) If a party-appointed expert fails to appear when duly summoned to attend an oral hearing, and does so without a valid reason, the court may disregard that expert's written report.

Rule 125. Costs

(1) The fees and expenses of a court-appointed expert shall form part of the costs of the proceedings. The court may order that a party who applies for an expert to be appointed pay their fees in advance.
(2) The fees and expenses of a party-appointed expert shall only be recoverable from the other party if the court so orders.

E. Judicial Inspection

Rule 126. Judicial Inspection in General

(1) A party may apply for an order permitting the examination of persons or things. To facilitate such an examination the court may authorise access to evidence, including access

to land or private premises. To ensure the adequacy of inspection, access may be subject to such conditions as the court considers just with regard to the special circumstances of the case and in accordance with applicable law.

(2) A party may apply for permission to carry out a physical or mental examination of a person. The court, in consultation with the parties, shall determine the timing and arrangements for such an examination.

(3) The court may inspect or require the inspection of evidence by a court-appointed or party-appointed expert, as it deems appropriate.

(4) Parties and their representatives may attend an inspection or examination ordered under this Rule, unless the court provides otherwise.

(5) In this Rule and in Rule 127(1), 'things' refers to any physical or electronic item, movable or immovable elements of such items.

Rule 127. Non-Parties and Judicial Inspection

(1) The court may order non-parties to produce things for inspection by the court or a party.

(2) The provisions set in Section 2 of Part VII of these Rules apply to any order to be made or made under Rule 127(1).

SECTION 4 – Cross-border issues

A. In the European Union

Rule 128. Cross-border Evidence-Taking within the European Union

(1) When evidence has to be taken in another European Union Member State and when access is needed to evidence located in another Member State, the court and the parties may rely on the provisions of Council Regulation (EC) No 1206/2001 of 28 May 2001 on cooperation between the courts of the Member States in the taking of evidence in civil or commercial matters.

(2) Without prejudice to the application of Council Regulation (EC) No 1206/2001 of 28 May 2001 on cooperation between the courts of the Member States in the taking of evidence in civil or commercial matters,

   (a) the court may directly summon a witness residing in another Member State;

   (b) the court may appoint an expert to submit a report, the preparation of which requires the undertaking of activities (inspection of persons or premises located) in another Member State;

   (c) a party or non-party, to whom an order for access to evidence is addressed, and who is residing or domiciled in the Member State of the court, is under a duty to produce the required documents and evidence, even if they are located in a Member State different to the one of the court issuing the order;

   (d) a court may address an order for access to evidence to prospective parties and to non-parties domiciled in another Member State.

B. Outside the European Union

Rule 129. Cross-border Evidence Taking of outside the European Union

When evidence needs to be taken outside the European Union or when the addressee of an order for access to evidence has no domicile or habitual residence within the European Union, the court and the parties may rely on the provisions of the Convention on the Taking of

Evidence Abroad in Civil or Commercial Matters (Hague Evidence Convention of 18 March 1970) or of other relevant international conventions.

PART VIII – JUDGMENT, *RES JUDICATA* AND *LIS PENDENS*

SECTION 1 – General Part

Rule 130. Types of judgment

(1) The court may give
  (a) a final judgment, which is a judgment deciding the whole of a claim for relief;
  (b) a judgment deciding part of a claim for relief (a partial judgment);
  (c) where more than one claim for relief is made, a final judgment deciding one or more, but not all, of the claims for relief;
  (d) a judgment on preliminary procedural issues or on specific legal issues on the merits (see Rule 66);
  (e) a judgment in default.

(2) Where the court gives a judgment that does not decide the whole of a claim for relief, the proceedings continue in respect of such parts for which judgment has not been given. If the court's judgment on a part of the claim for relief, on a procedural issue, or on legal issues on the merits is subject to appeal the court may exercise its discretion whether to continue or stay the proceedings according to the circumstances of the case.

Rule 131. Structure of a judgment

A judgment must contain
(a) the court's designation and composition;
(b) the place and date of the judgment;
(c) the names of the parties and, if applicable, of their lawyers;
(d) the relief claimed;
(e) the order of the court;
(f) the legal and factual grounds for the judgment;
(g) the signature of the judge or judges, if necessary;
(h) the signature of the court clerk, if necessary; and
(i) where relevant, information on formal requirements of any available means to challenge the decision.

Rule 132. Contents of judgments

(1) A judgment, depending on the nature of the relief claimed, may
  (a) order a defendant to do or not to do something,
  (b) create, alter or terminate a legal relationship,
  (c) make a declaration of rights, or
  (d) dismiss the claim for relief either on procedural grounds or where it determines it to be without merit.

(2) The court may only grant a declaratory judgment, including a negative declaratory judgment, if the claimant can establish that they have a legitimate interest in obtaining the declaration sought.

Rule 133. Procedural requirements of judgments on the merits

The court may only give a judgment on the merits when it is satisfied that
(a) the parties have litigation capacity according to Rules 29(2)-31, 34, 35, and 45-46;
(b) the court has subject matter and territorial jurisdiction;
(c) there are no pending proceedings involving the same parties and the same cause of action in another court unless an exception provided for in the Rules on *lis pendens* applies;
(d) the cause of action between the parties is not *res judicata*;
(e) the claimant has a legitimate interest to commence the proceedings on its claim for relief; and
(f) any other procedural requirement specified in these Rules is met.

Rule 134. Service of judgment

A judgment must be served on all parties by a method provided for in Part VI of these Rules.

SECTION 2 – Special Part

A. Default Judgment

Rule 135. Entry of Default judgment against a claimant

(1) The court must enter a default judgment dismissing proceedings where
  (a) a claimant has failed to appear at a hearing at which they were required to appear; and
  (b) a defendant has applied for default judgment to be entered.
(2) The court may not enter default judgment under this Rule on its own motion.

Rule 136. Entry of Default judgment against a defendant

(1) The court must enter a default judgment against a defendant, where the defendant has
  (a) failed to reply to a statement of claim within the time limit for filing a defence, or
  (b) failed to appear at a hearing at which they were required to appear; and
  (c) a claimant has applied for default judgment to be entered.
(2) A court entering judgment on the application of a claimant shall
  (a) where the facts submitted by the claimant justify it on the merits, grant the relief sought, or
  (b) where the facts submitted by the claimant do not justify the grant of relief, dismiss the proceedings on the merits.

Rule 137. Default judgments on a part of a claim for relief or on one of several claims for relief

(1) The court may enter a default judgment on part of a claim for relief or on one of several claims for relief where
  (a) a party fails to appear at a hearing that is dedicated exclusively to that part of the claim, or to one of several claims, for relief, or
  (b) a defendant fails to reply to the statement of claim in respect of that part of the claim, or to one of several claims, for relief.
(2) Where the court is able to give, but has not yet given, judgment under Rule 130 on part of a claim for relief or on one of several claims for relief, and a party is in default, the court must
  (a) enter judgment on that part of a claim for relief or on one of several claims for relief, and
  (b) enter a default judgment in respect of the other part or parts of the claim for relief or other claims for relief.

Rule 138. Conditions precedent for granting a default judgment

(1) The Court may enter a default judgment on the basis of a party's failure to appear at a hearing only if
   (a) notice of the date and time of the hearing was served on that party by a method provided for by these Rules, and
   (b) the Court is satisfied that the period between service and the hearing was adequate.
(2) The Court may only enter a default judgment against a defendant for failing to reply to a statement of claim if
   (a) the statement of claim was served on the defendant by a method provided for by these Rules,
   (b) the time limit for filing a defence has expired, and
   (c) where no time limit was prescribed by the rules, service was effected in sufficient time to enable the defendant to arrange their defence.
(3) The court may enter a default judgment against a defendant even if no receipt of service has been submitted to the court if
   (a) no proof of any other kind has been received although reasonable efforts have been made to obtain evidence that the defendant actually received the documents instituting the proceedings, and
   (b) a period of time not less than three months, which is considered to be adequate by the court to enable the defendant to arrange their defence has elapsed since the date of service by a method provided for by these Rules.
(4) Notwithstanding Rules 138(3)(a) and (b), the court may grant, in case of urgency, any provisional or protective measures.

Rule 139. Application to set aside a default judgment

The party against whom a default judgment has been entered may apply to have the judgment set aside on the basis that
(a) any of the conditions precedent for entry of the default judgment were not met, or
(b) the party against whom the default judgment was entered was either not responsible for the default or the default was excusable.

Rule 140. Time limit to apply to set aside a default judgment

(1) An application to set aside must be made within 30 days of the date of service of the default judgment. In cross-border cases, the application must be made within 60 days of the date of the service of the default judgment.
(2) The court may extend the time limit under Rule 140(1) where the defendant can show good reason for their non-compliance. No application to set aside can, however, be brought more than one year and, in cross-border cases, two years after the default judgment was entered.

B. Judicial Settlements

Rule 141. Judicial settlements

(1) When parties reach a consensual settlement of their dispute, either before or after proceedings have commenced or during proceedings, they may apply to the court to enter a decision giving effect to the agreement.

(2) A decision giving effect to the agreement shall not be entered if it is contrary to law or the court would not have the power to enter a judgment in the terms of the parties' agreement.
(3) If the court refuses to give effect to the settlement, any party to it can appeal from the refusal. The rules applicable to first appeals apply to such an appeal (See Part XI, Section 2).

SECTION 3 – Effects of Pendency and Judgments

A. *Lis pendens* and related actions

Rule 142. Pendency

(1) Where proceedings involving the same cause of action and between the same parties are brought in different courts, any court other than the court first seised shall of its own motion stay its proceedings until such time as the jurisdiction of the court first seised is established (the priority principle).
(2) Where Rule 142(1) applies, the court seised of the dispute may request any other court seised to provide it with information about the proceedings pending before it and the date on which it was seised in accordance with Rule 145. The court providing the information shall provide it the requesting court without delay.
(3) Where the jurisdiction of the court first seised is established, the court shall order parallel proceedings to be consolidated in accordance with Rule 146. Where proceedings have been consolidated, any court other than the court first seised shall decline its jurisdiction in favour of that court. When the requirements for consolidation are not met any court other than the court first seised shall, as appropriate, stay or dismiss the proceedings.

Rule 143. Exceptions from the Priority Principle

(1) When the court second seised has exclusive jurisdiction, the court first seised must decline jurisdiction in favour of that court. In such a case the court that has exclusive jurisdiction must not stay its proceedings.
(2) Rule 143(1) does not apply when both courts have exclusive jurisdiction.
(3) Without prejudice to Rules protecting weaker parties and without prejudice to jurisdiction by appearance, where a court upon which an agreement confers exclusive jurisdiction is seised, any other court must stay proceedings until such time as the court seised on the basis of the agreement declares that it has no jurisdiction under it.
(4) Where the court designated in the agreement has established jurisdiction in accordance with the agreement, any other court shall decline jurisdiction in favour of that court.

Rule 144. Related Proceedings

(1) Where related proceedings are pending in different courts, any court other than the court first seised may stay its proceedings.
(2) Where the proceeding in the court first seised is pending at first instance, any other court must also decline jurisdiction if the court first seised has consolidated proceedings according to Rule 146.
(3) For the purposes of this Rule, proceedings are deemed to be related where there is a relationship between the causes of action such that it would be in the interests of justice to determine them together.

Rule 145. Time at which a court is seised for the purposes of pendency and relatedness

(1) The court is deemed to be seised:
  (a) at the time when the statement of claim or an equivalent document is filed with the court, provided that the claimant has not subsequently failed to effect service on the defendant according to these Rules, or
  (b) if the statement of claim or an equivalent document has to be served before being filed with the court, at the time when it is received by an authority responsible for service, provided that the claimant has not subsequently failed to take steps required to file it with the court.

The authority responsible for service referred to Rule 145(1)(b) is the first authority that receives the documents to be served.

(2) Where a statement of claim is filed during proceedings it becomes pending at the time when it is invoked in the hearing or when it has been filed with the court or served on the other party.
(3) The court, or the authority responsible for service, referred to in Rule 145(1), shall note, respectively, the date the statement of claim or the equivalent document is filed, or the date of receipt of the documents to be served.

Rule 146. Consolidation of Proceedings

(1) Where the jurisdiction of the court first seised is established, it may, upon application of one of the parties, order the consolidation of several sets of proceedings under Rules 142 and 144.
(2) The court first seised may only consolidate proceedings when it has jurisdiction to hear them and when such parallel proceedings are pending at the first instance.
(3) Before ordering consolidation the court shall hear the parties and communicate with any other courts seised.
(4) When the court first seised has assumed jurisdiction over the proceedings and has consolidated them, any other court must decline jurisdiction.
(5) Consolidation does not prejudice any procedural or substantive consequences of the filing or pendency of parallel proceedings.
(6) When consolidation is not possible in the court first seised, the court second seised may, on application of any party, consolidate the proceedings, as appropriate, under Rules 146(1)- (5).

B. Res judicata

Rule 147. Types of judgment that become res judicata

(1) **Final Judgments, including partial judgments,** default judgments, and judgments that decide procedural issues or issues on the merits are *res judicata.*
(2) Provisional measures do not have *res judicata* effects on the merits of the issues in dispute in proceedings.

Rule 148. Judgments that are res judicata

A judgment is *res judicata* when ordinary means of recourse are not or are no longer available.

Rule 149. Material Scope of res judicata

(1) The material scope of *res judicata* is determined by reference to the claims for relief in the parties' pleadings, including amendments, as decided by the court's judgment.
(2) *Res judicata* also covers necessary and incidental legal issues that are explicitly decided in a judgment where parties to subsequent proceedings are the same as those in the proceedings determined by the prior judgment and where the court that gave that judgment could decide those legal issues.
(3) *Res judicata* also applies where a defendant brings a defence based on set-off and
    (a) the claim and that defence are upheld by the court, or
    (b) the claim is admitted and the defence of set-off is rejected.
(4) Where a claim is rejected on grounds other than set-off, so that the court does not decide the set-off defence, only the judgment on the claim becomes *res judicata.*

Rule 150. Modification of judgments requiring periodical performance

(1) Where a judgment that has become *res judicata* requires periodic performance, on application by a party, the court may vary the judgment prospectively.
(2) A judgment may only be varied under this Rule where there is a substantial change of circumstances.

Rule 151. Persons bound by res judicata

Only parties to proceedings, the heirs and successors are bound by those parts of a judgment that are *res judicata.*

Rule 152. Court assessment of res judicata *of its own motion* (ex officio)

The court shall take *res judicata* into account of its own motion.

PART IX – MEANS OF REVIEW

SECTION1 - General Part

Rule 153. Right of appeal or to seek recourse

Where a party, or exceptionally a non-party, has a legal interest in a judgment, subject to the provisions in this Part, they may appeal from, or rely on other types of recourse against, it.

Rule 154. Waiver of right to appeal or to seek recourse

(1) A party may waive their right of appeal or to seek recourse. Waiver must be informed and express. Waiver may be given to the court in writing before or during a court hearing, or given orally in a court hearing.
(2) Waiver may be effected before a first instance judgment or other decision or a first appeal judgment is made. Such a waiver may only be made where it is agreed by all the parties.
(3) Where a party is bringing or defending proceedings as a consumer, they cannot waive their right to appeal before judgment has been made.
(4) All waivers must be recorded by the court in a judgment or other official record, if any.

SECTION 2 – Appeals

Rule 155. Notice of appeal - General

(1) An appeal is commenced by way of filing a notice of appeal with the relevant court of Appeal.

(2) Upon being filed with the court, notice of appeal must be served on the respondent, in accordance with Part VI of these Rules.

Rule 156. Time limits for appeals

(1) For a first appeal, the notice must be filed with the court within one month of service of the judgment.
(2) For a second appeal, the notice must be filed with the court within two months of service of the judgment.

Rule 157. Contents of the notice of and reasons for appeal – First Appeal

(1) A notice of appeal for a first appeal must state that an appeal is being commenced and must identify the judgment subject to the appeal. It may also provide reasons for the appeal. Reasons for the appeal if not set out in the notice of appeal should be set out in a separate document.
(2) The reasons for the appeal must specify
    (a) the relief sought;
    (b) the legal arguments, substantive and procedural, on which the appeal is based in respect of both its admissibility and substance;
    (c) if applicable, the grounds for which any evaluation of evidence was seriously wrong; and
    (d) if applicable, any new facts to be alleged and new means of evidence that will be introduced in the appeal, and the reasons why they ought to be admitted.
(3) Where reasons for the appeal are set out in a separate document from the notice of appeal they must be served within two months of service of the judgment, unless the court orders otherwise.

Rule 158. Contents of the notice of and reasons for appeal – Second Appeal

(1) A notice of appeal for a second appeal must state that an appeal is being commenced and must identify the judgment subject to the appeal. It must also provide the reasons for the appeal.
(2) The reasons for the second appeal must contain:
    (a) the relief sought;
    (b) the legal arguments, procedural and substantive, on which the second appeal is based.

Rule 159. Response to the notice of appeal – General

(1) The respondent to an appeal must file with the court and serve on the appellant a reply to the notice of appeal (the reply) within two months of service of the notice of appeal, unless the court orders otherwise.
(2) The appellant must respond to the reply within two weeks of service, unless the court orders otherwise.

Rule 160. Contents of a respondent's reply

A reply may contain the following
(a) reasons why the appeal court should uphold the judgment subject to appeal; or
(b) notice of and reasons for appeal from the judgment subject to appeal, which seek to uphold the judgment for different reasons to those given in the judgment. Rule 157(2) and Rule 158(2) apply according to whether the reply concerns a first or second appeal.

Rule 161. Derivative appeals

(1) A party that has lost their right of appeal due to the expiry of the time limit for filing a notice of appeal in Rule 156(2), may appeal if another party (the appellant) appeals from the judgment.
(2) The party bringing a derivative appeal (a derivative appellant) must serve a Notice of Appeal. Rules 156 – 159 apply accordingly.
(3) A derivative appeal lapses if the appellant's appeal is not heard on its merits.
(4) A respondent to a derivative appeal must file a response to it. Rules 159-160 apply accordingly.

Rule 162. Provisional enforcement

(1) Unless otherwise provided for, final judgment and any appellate court judgments are enforceable immediately regardless of whether an appeal has been commenced by filing a notice of appeal.
(2) An appellant may apply to the appellate court to stay enforcement if they have filed a notice of appeal and enforcement is manifestly excessive.
(3) Security may be required from an appellant as a condition of granting a stay or from a respondent as a condition of refusing to grant a stay.

Rule 163. Withdrawal

(1) A party that has commenced a first appeal can withdraw their appeal at any time.
(2) A second appeal can only be withdrawn by a party with the consent of the other party and the court.
(3) A party that withdraws an appeal must bear the costs, including any court fees, incurred by other parties because of the appeal.

Rule 164. Representation in an Appeal Court

(1) If representation is not mandatory according to applicable law, a first appeal court may require a party to be represented by a lawyer if they are incapable of representing themselves in an understandable manner or if it is necessary for the proper administration of justice.
(2) Parties must be represented by a lawyer in proceedings before a second appeal court.

Rule 165. Extension of deadlines – non-domiciled parties

Where a party is not domiciled in the State whose court is seised of the proceedings, any time limit applicable to an appeal is extended by one month unless the court provides otherwise.

SECTION 3 – **First Appeals**

Rule 166. Right to appeal

(1) A party has a right to appeal against a first instance judgment if
   (a) the value of the appealed claim exceeds [the value of the appealed claim as determined by applicable law, for instance twice the average monthly wage in the forum State] or
   (b) the appeal court grants permission to appeal based on the contents of the notice and reasons for appeal.
(2) In deciding whether to grant permission to appeal, the appeal court shall take the following into account
   (a) whether the legal issue in dispute is of fundamental significance, or

(b) the further development of the law, or the public interest in securing uniform adjudication require an appellate decision, or
(c) fundamental procedural requirements have been violated.

(3) The appeal court shall, on its own motion, assess whether the requirements of Rules 166(1) and (2) have been met.

Rule 167. Scope of a first appeal

(1) A first appeal can be brought against the whole, or part, of a first instance judgment.
(2) In general, the relief sought is limited by what was claimed or defended at first instance.
(3) However, the relief sought may be broadened or amended within a first appeal if
(a) all parties to the appeal consent, or
(b) the court considers it appropriate for the proper administration of justice.

Rule 168. New facts and taking evidence

(1) Within the relief sought, the appellate court shall consider new facts alleged by the parties
(a) in so far as those facts could not have been introduced before the first instance court, or
(b) in so far as the first instance court failed to invite the parties to clarify or supplement facts that they had introduced to support their claim or defence under Rules 24(1) and 53(3).

(2) Within the relief sought, the appellate court shall take evidence offered by the parties only if
(a) the evidence could not have been offered to the first instance court;
(b) the evidence was offered to the first instance court and was erroneously rejected or could not be taken for reasons outside the party's control; or
(c) the evidence concerns new facts admissible according to Rule 168(1).

Rule 169. Scope of appellate review – first appeal

(1) Within the relief sought, the appellate court's review shall encompass
(a) the application of the law in the judgment;
(b) the legality of the proceedings in the first instance court, provided that the appellant challenged the error complained about immediately before the first instance court if such challenge was possible;
(c) evaluation of the evidence if the appellate court determines that such a review is warranted in order to prevent serious injustice.

(2) The appellate court will reverse a first instance judgment for procedural error only if it potentially influenced the judgment or if it was so grave that such influence need not be proven.

Rule 170. First appeal court decisions

(1) In general, the appellate court shall decide the matter that forms the substance of the appeal.
(2) The appellate court may refer the matter back to the first instance court, if necessary, for it to decide the matter.
(3) If the parties to the appeal agree to it, the appellate court must decide the matter.

Rule 171. Contents of the First Appeal Court's judgment

In so far as it agrees with the first instance court's judgment, the appellate court's judgment may refer to the legal and factual grounds in that judgment. It may also set out its own reasons in its judgment. In the latter case, the appellate court is deemed to have adopted the legal and factual grounds of the first instance judgment which are not contrary to its own reasoning.

SECTION 4 – Second Appeals

Rule 172. Right to a second appeal

(1) A party may only appeal from a first appeal judgment if such an appeal is necessary to
  (a) correct a violation of a fundamental right,
  (b) secure uniformity in the law,
  (c) decide a fundamental question which is not limited to the case at issue, or
  (d) develop the law.
(2) A second appeal court shall, on its own motion, assess whether the requirements of Rule 172(1) have been met.

Rule 173. Scope of a second appeal

(1) A second appeal can be brought against the whole, or part, of a first appeal judgment.
(2) The relief sought is limited by what was claimed or defended in the first appeal.

Rule 174. Scope of appellate review – second appeal

(1) Within the relief sought, as far as admissible, the second appeal court's review shall encompass
  (a) the interpretation and application of the law in the first appeal judgment;
  (b) the legality of the proceedings in the first appeal court, provided that the appellant challenged the error complained about immediately before that court.
(2) The second appeal court will reverse the first appeal judgment for a procedural error only if the procedural error has potentially influenced the judgment or if it was so serious that such influence need not be proven.

Rule 175. Second Appeal Court decisions

(1) The second appeal court shall determine the substantive issue before it if
  (a) it is to reverse the first appeal judgment having held that there had been a violation of the law, and
  (b) it has concluded that it can determine the issue.
(2) In all other circumstances, the second appeal court must refer the matter back to the first appeal court for it to finally determine the matter. In such a circumstance, the first appeal court is bound by the second appeal court's assessment of the law.

Rule 176. Contents of the Second Appeal Court's judgment

A second appeal court must provide its own reasons in its judgment. If they are adequate, it may refer to the reasons given in the first appeal court's or the first instance court's judgment.

Rule 177. Leapfrog appeal

(1) Instead of a regular appeal to the first appeal court, an appeal may be brought directly to the second appeal court (a leapfrog appeal).
(2) A second appeal court may only grant permission to bring a leapfrog appeal if
  (a) an appellant applies directly to it to bring such an appeal, setting out its reasons why permission should be granted, and does so within the time limits applicable to a first appeal;
  (b) the appellant's application complies with Rule 158;
  (c) the requirements of Rule 172(1) are met.

(3) An appeal under this rule is deemed to be a second appeal, and the Rules applicable to second appeals apply accordingly.

SECTION 5 - Review of procedural error and miscellaneous appeals

Rule 178. Immediate review of procedural error

(1) If a party, or non-party affected by a procedural order, fails to challenge a procedural error that was caused by the court or another party immediately upon it being made, the error is waived.
(2) Rule 178(1) does not apply if a party acted carefully pursuant to the requirements of Rule 47 or if the rule affected is not subject to waiver by the parties. This Rule applies to non-parties *mutatis mutandis.*
(3) Upon objection and having heard the parties the court may render, revoke or vary court rulings. Rules 49 and 50 apply accordingly.

Rule 179. Separate Appeal Against the Review of Procedural Orders by the Court

(1) Unless otherwise provided for in Rule 179(2), a decision on a challenge to a procedural error cannot be made the subject of a separate appeal.
(2) A separate appeal is available against decisions made in respect of
    (a) a stay of proceedings;
    (b) the transfer of proceedings to another court;
    (c) security for costs;
    (d) the exclusion of a party from a hearing or the imposition of a fine on a party;
    (e) a refusal to disqualify a judge or court-appointed expert; and
    (f) if provided for in a specific rule.
(3) A separate appeal must be filed with the court within two weeks of notice of the decision.

Rule 180. Appeals against procedural decisions that affect non-parties

(1) A person who is not a party to litigation but directly affected by a procedural ruling given by the court has a right of appeal.
(2) The right of appeal must be exercised in accordance with Rule 179(3).

SECTION 6 – Extraordinary Recourse

Rule 181. Scope of an extraordinary motion for review

(1) An extraordinary motion for review re-opens proceedings that have otherwise been finally determined either at first instance or on appeal.
(2) Such a review may, if successful, rescind a judgment that has become *res judicata.* Where it does so the court will give case management directions for the future management of the proceedings.

Rule 182. Grounds for an extraordinary motion for review

(1) An extraordinary motion for review may only be brought against a judgment on the following grounds
    (a) the court was wrongly constituted,
    (b) a party's right to be heard was violated severely,
    (c) a judgment was obtained by fraud or violence,
    (d) after a judgment is issued, evidence that would have been decisive to it is recovered or obtained, and such evidence was not available prior to judgment being given due

either to *force majeure* or improper conduct by the party in whose favour the judgment was made, or

(e) the European Court of Human Rights has ruled that the judgment given in national proceedings infringed any of the rights established in the European Convention for the Protection of Human Rights and Fundamental Freedoms and its Protocols, provided that the infringement, due to its nature and seriousness, entails persistent effects, which can only be stopped by means of such a review; however, in no case may the review affect rights acquired in good faith by third parties.

(2) The motion shall only be admissible under Rule 182(1)(a), (b) or (c) if the applicant was unable, without any fault on their behalf, to raise the ground on which they rely before the judgment that is to be subject to review became *res judicata*.

Rule 183. Time limits and withdrawal

(1) An application by a party for an extraordinary motion for review must be made within three months from the date on which that party became aware of the grounds for review.
(2) In no case may an application be made after ten years have elapsed from the time the judgment, which is to be the subject of such a review, has become *res judicata*.
(3) An extraordinary motion for review can be withdrawn at any time.

PART X – PROVISIONAL AND PROTECTIVE MEASURES

SECTION 1 – General part

Rule 184. Provisional and Protective Measures

(1) A provisional or protective measure is any temporary order that has one or more of the following functions:
  (a) to ensure or promote effective enforcement of final decisions concerning the substance of the proceedings, whether or not the underlying claim is pecuniary, including securing assets and obtaining or preserving information concerning a debtor and his assets; or
  (b) to preserve the opportunity for a complete and satisfactory determination of the proceedings, including securing evidence relevant to the merits or preventing its destruction or concealment; or
  (c) to preserve the existence and value of goods or other assets which form or will form the subject-matter of proceedings (pending or otherwise); or
  (d) to prevent harm from being suffered, to prevent further harm, or to regulate disputed issues, pending final judgment.
(2) A provisional or protective measure ordered should be suitable for its purpose.

Rule 185. Proportionality of provisional and protective measures

(1) A provisional and protective measure should impose the least burden on the respondent.
(2) The court must ensure that the measure's effects are not disproportionate to the interests it is asked to protect.

Rule 186. Without-notice (Ex parte) *procedure*

(1) The court may order a provisional or protective measure without-notice ('*ex parte*') only if, in the circumstances, proceedings with-notice ('*inter partes*') would frustrate the prospect of the applicant receiving effective protection of their interests.

(2) When granting an order without-notice the court must give the respondent an opportunity to be heard at the earliest possible time, that date to be specified in the order that was made without-notice. The respondent should be given notice of the order and of all the matters relied upon before the court to support it as soon as possible.
(3) An applicant must fully disclose to the court all facts and legal issues relevant to the court's decision whether to grant relief and, if so, on what terms.
(4) The court must make a prompt decision concerning any objection to the grant of a provisional or protective measure or its terms.

Rule 187. Security

(1) When assessing whether to grant or continue a provisional or protective measure the court may consider whether security can be provided by the respondent in lieu of the order.
(2) As a condition of granting or continuing a provisional or protective measure the applicant may, depending on the circumstances, be required to provide appropriate security.
(3) Security must not be required solely on the basis that the applicant or respondent is not a national or resident of the forum State.

Rule 188. Initiation of Proceedings

(1) Where the applicant has been granted a provisional or protective measure before initiating proceedings under Rules 21(1), 53, such proceedings must be initiated before the date set by the court. Where the court does not set such a date or it is not otherwise specified by the applicable law, the applicant shall initiate such proceedings within two weeks of the date of the issue of the decision granting the remedy. The court can extend the period on the request of a party.
(2) If proceedings have not been initiated as required by Rule 188(1), the measure shall lapse, unless the court provides otherwise.

Rule 189. Review and Appeal

(1) The court may, either on application of a party or on its own motion, modify, suspend, or terminate a provisional or protective measure if satisfied that a change in circumstances so requires.
(2) Decisions that grant, deny, modify, suspend or terminate provisional or protective measures are subject to appeal. Rule 179(3) applies accordingly.

Rule 190. Applicant Liability

(1) If a provisional or protective measure is set aside, lapses, or if the proceedings are dismissed on procedural grounds or on their merits, the applicant must compensate the respondent for such loss or damage caused by the measure.
(2) The applicant is liable to compensate non-parties for any damages, and expenditure incurred as a consequence of complying with the measure.

Rule 191. Sanctions for non-compliance

Except in respect of interim payments, where there is non-compliance with a provisional or protective measure the court may impose a sanction under Rule 27, as appropriate.

SECTION 2 – Special part

A. Asset Preservation

Rule 192. Types of Asset Preservation Measure

A court may grant, on application by a party, any of the following asset preservation orders for the purpose of protecting their claim:
(a) an attachment order, which is an order authorising provisional attachment of the respondent's assets,
(b) an asset restraining order, which is an interim order preventing the respondent from disposing of, or dealing with, their assets, or
(c) a custodial order, which is an order that the respondent's assets shall be placed in the custody of a neutral non-party (a custodian).

Rule 193. Criteria for Awarding Asset Preservation Orders

A party seeking an order under Rule 192 must show that:
(a) their claim for relief has a good chance of succeeding on its substantive merits, and
(b) it is likely that, without such an order, enforcement of a final judgment against the respondent will be impossible or exceedingly difficult.

Rule 194. Limitations on Asset Preservation Orders

Asset Preservation Orders must ensure that a respondent is not prevented from receiving financial allowances, provided the amounts are reasonable, for
(a) ordinary living expenses, and/or
(b) legitimate business expenses, and/or
(c) to enable it to fund legal advice and representation in respect of the proceedings, including such as are necessary for it to respond to the order, including seeking its variation or discharge under Rules 186(4) or 189.

Rule 195. Notification of Asset Preservation Orders and their effects to Respondent

(1) At the earliest possible time after an order has been made under Rule 192, the respondent and any non-parties who are the addressees of an order must be given formal notice of it. Where necessary to enforce the order, non-parties may be given formal notice before the respondent.
(2) The applicant may, if it wishes, inform a non-party of an order before the respondent is given formal notice.
(3) The respondent or any non-parties who are the addressees of an order made under Rule 192 must comply with it as soon as they are notified of the order. In the event of breach, they will be subject (without limitation) to the sanctions listed in Rule 191.

B. Regulatory Measures

Rule 196. Measures to Perform or Refrain from Performing an Action

The court may grant the applicant a measure to regulate the relationship between parties in relation to a non-pecuniary claim for relief on a provisional basis. Such a measure may require the respondent to act or to refrain from acting in a manner specified in the court's order.

Rule 197. Criteria for awarding a Regulatory Measure

A party seeking an order under Rule 196 must show:

(a) it has a good chance of succeeding in the proceedings; or

(b) where there is a significant risk that damages to the respondent will not be capable of providing adequate compensation for any interference with their rights if the proceedings are dismissed, that there is a very strong possibility that the applicant will succeed in the proceedings;

and

(c) the order is necessary to regulate the substantive issue or issues in dispute pending final determination of the proceedings.

C. Evidence Preservation

Rule 198. Evidence Preservation Orders

(1) **The court has the power to secure evidence on** the application of a party to proceedings through the following interim measures:
  (a) hearing witness evidence or taking of witness evidence by a third party acting on its behalf;
  (b) requiring the preservation or protection of evidence by the parties or by requiring it to be placed in the custody of a custodian;
  (c) appointing an expert to provide expert opinion evidence.

(2) Evidence preservation orders may, where necessary, authorise access to the evidence. Access may be subject to such conditions as the court considers just.

Rule 199. Criteria for awarding an Evidence Preservation Measure

A party seeking an evidence preservation order must show that:

(a) there is a real risk that unless the order is made the evidence will not be available for determining the substantive proceedings on their merits; and

(b) if the order requires access to a party's or non-party's property the applicant has a strong *prima facie* case in respect of the merits of the applicant's claim or proposed claim for relief.

D. Interim Payment

Rule 200. Interim Payment Measures

A court may grant the claimant an interim payment order in relation to a monetary claim, either wholly or in part to satisfy the claim in the proceedings, in anticipation of the expected outcome.

Rule 201. Criteria for awarding an Interim Payment

(1) An applicant seeking an order under Rule 200 must show that:
  (a) the defendant has admitted that they are liable to pay a monetary sum to the applicant, or the applicant has obtained a final judgment on liability, or it is highly likely that the applicant will obtain at least the amount sought in a final judgment; and
  (b) they are in urgent need of payment by the defendant.

(2) In assessing whether to make an interim payment order the court should consider all the circumstances, including any potential or actual hardship to the applicant or the respondent as a result of refusing or granting the order.

(3) An interim payment order cannot be made on a without-notice basis.

(4) Where judgment in the proceedings is for a lesser amount than that paid, any overpayment must be repaid.
(5) An interim payment order will ordinarily be made subject to the applicant giving security. If the applicant's claim is absolutely well founded and the requirement to obtain security would frustrate the order's purpose of securing urgent relief for the applicant's economic distress, where that has been at least partially caused by the defendant's delay, the court may grant an interim payment order without or upon reduced security.

SECTION 3 – Cross border issues

Rule 202. International jurisdiction

(1) Within the scope of the European Union Regulations or international conventions, the international jurisdiction of the court in relation to provisional and protective measures is governed by those Regulations or conventions.
(2) In any event, the court having jurisdiction in respect of the proceedings will have jurisdiction to grant provisional and protective measures.
(3) Without prejudice to applicable European Union rules and international conventions, another court may grant such provisional and protective measures necessary to protect interests located within the jurisdiction or the subject-matter of which have a real connecting link with the territory of the court, or that are necessary to support proceedings brought in another country.

Rule 203. Recognition and enforcement

(1) Within the scope of European Union Regulations or international conventions, the recognition and enforcement of provisional and protective measures are governed by those Regulations or conventions.
(2) Where no European Union Regulation or international convention applies, provisional and protective measures will be recognised and enforced in accordance with domestic law.
(3) Courts should, at the request of the parties, take into account provisional and protective measures granted in another country and, where appropriate, and in accordance with these Rules, cooperate in order to secure the effectiveness of those measures.

PART XI – COLLECTIVE PROCEEDINGS

SECTION 1 –Collective Interest Injunctions

Rule 204. Scope of Application

(1) The Rules in Part XI, Section 1 apply to orders, known as collective interest injunction, made by a court, which direct any person to cease any conduct or behaviour that is infringing the law.
(2) A collective interest injunction cannot be made on an interim basis under Part X of these Rules.

Rule 205. Entitlement to apply for a Collective Interest Injunction

(1) Any entity authorised under national law to bring actions in the collective interest may apply for a collective interest injunction that requires the cessation of any infringement of the law.

(2) Where appropriate the court may order additional measures such as the publication of its decision with a view to eliminating the continuing effects of the infringement.

Rule 206. Effect of collective interest injunctions

A collective interest injunction binds the defendant in all future proceedings.

SECTION 2 – Collective Proceedings

A. General Part

Rule 207. Collective Proceedings

Collective proceedings are proceedings brought by a qualified claimant on behalf of a group of persons who it is alleged are affected by an event giving rise to a mass harm, but where those persons, known as group members, are not parties to the action.

Rule 208. Claimants Qualified to Bring Collective Proceedings

A qualified claimant is:
(a) an organisation authorised, in accordance with national law, to bring collective proceedings and whose purpose has a direct relationship with the event giving rise to the mass harm,
(b) an entity which is established solely for the purpose of obtaining redress for group members and which satisfied the requirements of Rule 209; or
(c) a person who is a group member and who meets the requirements of Rules 209(a) - (c).

Rule 209. Requirements for qualified claimants

A person or entity shall not be a qualified claimant unless:
(a) they have no conflict of interest with any group member,
(b) they have sufficient capability to conduct the collective proceeding. In assessing this issue, the court shall take account of the financial, human and other resources available to the putative qualified claimant If appropriate, the court may require security for costs (see Rule 243),
(c) they are legally represented, and
(d) they are neither a lawyer nor exercising any legal profession.

Rule 210. Collective Proceedings – Statement of Claim

(1) A statement of claim in collective proceedings must include all relevant information available concerning
    (a) the event giving rise to the mass harm,
    (b) the group,
    (c) the causal connection between the event of mass harm and the loss suffered by the group members,
    (d) the similarity of the claims of the group members in law and fact,
    (e) whether compensation or other collective remedies are sought,
    (f) the financial and other resources available to the qualified claimant to pursue the collective proceeding,
    (g) evidence of the qualified claimant's attempt to settle the group members' claims.
(2) Before commencing collective proceedings and upon the application of a qualified claimant, the court may issue an order preventing a potential defendant from bringing an action with respect to the event of mass harm.

Rule 211. Registration of Collective Proceedings

(1) Upon the qualified claimant submitting a collective proceedings statement of claim to the court, the court must enter the proceedings into a publicly accessible electronic register.
(2) After registration any other court must dismiss any collective proceedings against the same defendant(s) in respect of the same mass harm.

B. Admissibility of Collective Proceedings

Rule 212. Conditions of Admissibility

(1) The court may admit a collective proceeding if
    (a) it will resolve the dispute more efficiently than joinder of the group members' individual claims,
    (b) all of the claims for relief made in the proceeding arise from the same event or series of related events causing mass harm to the group members,
    (c) the claims are similar in law and fact, and
    (d) except in cases of urgency, the qualified claimant has allowed the defendant or defendants at least three months to respond to a settlement proposal.
(2) Upon application, the court may order any proceeding to continue as a collective proceeding.

Rule 213. Collective Proceeding Order

(1) An order made under Rule 212 must include the following information:
    (a) the name and address, and other relevant contact details of the qualified claimant
    (b) a concise description of the event of mass harm giving rise to the collective proceeding;
    (c) the names or a description of all of the persons allegedly affected by the mass harm. The description must contain sufficient detail to enable any person allegedly affected by the event causing mass harm to know if they are within the group or not;
    (d) the type of collective proceeding under Rule 215.
(2) Before making an order under this Rule the court shall advertise a draft of the order and set a deadline for any other potential qualified claimants to apply under Rule 207.
(3) The court shall determine which of several potential qualified claimants, if any, shall become the qualified claimant in the proceedings. It shall do so on the basis of the criteria set out in, among others, Rule 209. Where more than one qualified claimant is selected they must act jointly.
(4) The collective proceeding order shall be advertised in a manner which the court considers will best bring it to the attention of any person likely to be affected by the event causing mass harm on which the proceeding is based. The advertisement shall invite such persons to opt-in to the proceeding and shall give information on how to do so.
(5) The collective proceeding order or the refusal to grant such an order are subject to appeal by the qualified claimant and the defendant.

Rule 214. Obligation of Qualified Claimant

A qualified claimant must at all times act in the best interests of the whole group or sub-group, if a qualified claimant for a sub-group.

Rule 215. Types of Collective Proceeding

(1) Collective proceedings shall operate on an opt-in basis unless the court makes an order under Rule 215(2).

(2) The court may order that the proceedings will include all group members who have not opted-out of the proceedings under Rule 215(3) where it concludes that:
  (a) the group members' claims cannot be made in individual actions because of their small size; and
  (b) a significant number of group members would not opt-in to the collective proceeding.
(3) Where the court makes an order under Rule 215(2) it must set a deadline for group members to notify the court that they wish to opt-out. In exceptional circumstances the court may permit group members to opt-out after the deadline has expired.
(4) The court shall decide to whom and how notification under Rule 215(3) shall be given.

Rule 216. Opt-in Proceedings

(1) Where collective proceedings operate on an opt-in basis, group members must notify the court if they wish to join the proceedings in the manner specified by the court.
(2) The court shall ensure that group member notifications are properly recorded in a public register, which may be established in accordance with Rule 220.

Rule 217. Individual Actions

(1) Group members who have opted-in under Rule 216 or who have not opted-out under Rule 215(3) cannot bring an individual court action in respect of the same event of mass harm against a defendant to the collective proceeding.
(2) In cases under Rule 215(2) any group member who brings an individual action against a defendant to collective proceedings during the opt-out period shall be treated as having opted-out of the proceedings.
(3) Any time limit provided in national law for individual actions to be brought by a group member in respect of loss caused by the event of mass harm shall be suspended from the date of commencement of the collective proceeding. The period of suspension shall end when
  (a) the collective proceeding is withdrawn or dismissed; or
  (b) the group member opts-out under Rules 215(2)-(4).
(4) Where Rule 217(3)(a) or (b) applies the remaining limitation period for individual claims will start six months after the withdrawal, dismissal or the date on which the opt-out was effected.

C. Case Management of Collective Proceedings

Rule 218. Case Management Powers

(1) In collective proceedings, the court has additional case management powers, including the power
  (a) to remove a qualified claimant of a group or any sub-group if they no longer satisfy the conditions in Rule 208 and Rule 209 or fails to act in the interests of all group members,
  (b) to authorise, with their consent, a new qualified claimant,
  (c) to modify the description of the group,
  (d) to divide a group into sub-groups and to authorise, with their consent, a qualified claimant for each sub-group,
  (e) to dismiss the collective proceeding or to order it to continue as individual proceedings if there is no longer a qualified claimant

(f) to direct the correction of the group register (Rules 216(2) and 220).

(2) The court may hear any person it considers has an interest in the management of the case before making any case management order under this Rule.

Rule 219. Advertisements

(1) In collective proceedings the court shall advertise or shall require advertisement
(a) when a qualified claimant is removed or authorised,
(b) when the description of the group is modified or the group is divided into sub-groups,
(c) when a collective settlement is offered,
(d) when any order or judgment is made,
(e) of information about the secure electronic platform under Rule 220; and
(f) if the collective proceeding is dismissed or withdrawn.

(2) The advertisement shall be made in a manner which the court considers will best attract the attention of any person likely to be affected by the event causing mass harm and in sufficient time to allow affected persons a reasonable opportunity to participate as they see fit in the proceedings.

Rule 220. Communication – Secure Electronic Platform

The court must create or authorise the creation of a secure electronic platform for the efficient management of the collective proceeding.

D. Settlements in Commenced Collective Proceedings

Rule 221. Court Approval

A group member will not be bound by any agreement settling a collective proceeding in whole or in part unless that agreement is approved by the court.

Rule 222. Application for the approval of a settlement agreement

(1) A party to a proposed settlement agreement may apply to the court for approval under Rule 221.

(2) The application for approval shall include:
(a) the description of the group whose members will be bound by the settlement;
(b) a copy of the proposed settlement agreement. In a collective proceeding for compensation, the proposed agreement shall include the total amount of compensation payable, and the criteria for distributing the compensation to each group member;
(c) the proposed administration of the compensation fund and method of distributing the compensation payment to group members; and
(d) a concise statement of reasons showing why the terms of the settlement agreement are fair and adequate.

Rule 223. Procedure for Approving Settlements

(1) Before approving a settlement the court may
(a) make any order necessary to obtain further information in order to assess the fairness and adequacy of the proposed settlement,
(b) appoint an expert to assist the court.

(2) The court must
(a) advertise the proposed settlement according to Rule 219, ensuring that it is clear that the court has not reached a conclusion on the fairness of the settlement,

(b) fix a period within which any comments may be made, and
(c) consider all comments made by the group members and the parties.

(3) The court may consider all other relevant comments received.

Rule 224. Settlement Approval Orders

The court shall not make an order approving a settlement agreement where
(a) the amount of compensation agreed for the group or any sub-group is manifestly unfair,
(b) the terms of any other undertaking by a defendant are manifestly unfair,
(c) the settlement is manifestly contrary to the public interest (*ordre public*) or
(d) the terms, whether contained in the proposed settlement agreement or not, as to the payment of legal and other associated costs of the action are manifestly unreasonable.

Rule 225. Approved Settlements in Opt-in Actions

An approved settlement binds all group members who have opted-in at the time the order approving the settlement is made.

Rule 226. Approved Settlements in Opt-out Proceedings

An approved settlement binds all group members unless they have opted-out of the collective proceedings at the time the order approving the settlement is made.

E. Judgments in Collective Proceedings

Rule 227. Effect of Final Judgments

(1) A final judgment of the court in collective proceedings binds
(a) all of the parties, and all group members who have opted-in to the proceedings; or
(b) all of the parties, and all of the group members resident in the forum State who have not opted-out of the proceedings within the period set by the court in Rule 215(3).

(2) No other collective proceeding may be commenced in respect of any claims for relief determined in a final judgment.

(3) A final judgment may be enforced by the qualified claimant. If the qualified claimant does not enforce the final judgment within a reasonable time any group member, with the court's permission, may enforce the final judgment.

Rule 228. Amount of Compensation

A final judgment that sets the amount of compensation in a collective proceeding shall include
(a) the total amount of compensation payable in respect of the group or any sub-group. If an exact calculation of this amount is impossible or excessively difficult, the court may estimate the amount,
(b) the criteria for distributing the compensation to each group member, and the method of administration of the compensation fund.

F. Collective Settlements outside Collective Proceedings

Rule 229. Standing to Reach Settlement

(1) Any entity fulfilling the requirements in Rules 208(a) and (b) to be a qualified claimant may reach a collective settlement agreement for a group even where a collective proceeding order has not been made.

(2) Any such collective settlement agreement shall be negotiated in good faith for the benefit of all group members.

Rule 230. Application for Approval of Collective Settlement

(1) An application to the court for approval of a collective settlement agreement in accordance with Rule 229 must be made by all of the parties to it.
(2) The application shall include all of the information required under Rule 222(2). It shall also specify whether a binding settlement shall be reached on an opt-in or an opt-out basis.

Rule 231. Approval Procedure

The procedure for approval of collective settlements in Rule 223 applies to any application to approve a collective settlement following an application under Rule 230.

Rule 232. Approval Order and Opt-in/Opt-out Procedure

The court must approve the proposed collective settlement on the basis of Rule 224.
(a) If the court does not approve the proposed collective settlement it must give its reasons for refusing to approve it, and must remit the agreement to the parties.
(b) The court must advertise the approved settlement in accordance with Rule 219(2), give information on whether the settlement shall become binding based on an opt-in or opt-out procedure, and fix a period of at least three months for the group members to opt-in or opt-out. The court shall decide to whom and how the notification to opt-in or to opt-out shall be given. If the terms of the settlement require a fixed number or percentage of group members to accept the settlement this must also be communicated clearly.
(c) After the period fixed for opt-in or opt-out notifications and, where applicable, if the necessary number or percentage of group members have opted-in or have not opted-out, the court shall declare the approved settlement binding. Otherwise the court shall declare that the approval proceedings have been terminated without a binding settlement.
(d) An approved settlement shall bind all of the persons who have opted-in to the settlement or who have not opted-out of the settlement.

SECTION 3 – Cross Border Issues

Within the European Union

Rule 233. Recognition of Qualified Claimant

The recognition of a claimant as a qualified claimant by a court in an order made under Rule 213(1)(a) binds every other court in European Union Member States without the need for further application for recognition in relation to actions arising from the same event of mass harm.

Rule 234. Judicial Co-ordination

(1) When a mass harm has cross-border effects, the registry entries for each collective proceeding shall be made available on the European e-justice platform or any similarly effective platform.
(2) European Union Member States' courts must use their best effort to co-ordinate collective proceedings in different Member States in order to avoid irreconcilable judgments or settlement approvals.

Rule 235. Group Members outside the Forum State

(1) The court shall ensure that group members outside the forum State are informed of the collective proceeding in accordance with Rule 219.

(2) No order made under Rule 215(2) binds group members outside the forum State.
(3) Group members outside the forum State must, if they choose, be allowed to opt-in.
(4) Rules 235(1)-(3) also apply to collective settlement proceedings under Rules 229-232.

Rule 236. Multiple Substantive Laws

(1) Group members shall not be prevented from participating in a single collective proceeding if they are subject to different substantive laws.
(2) In any case where group members are subject to different substantive law, the court may divide the group into sub-groups under Rule 218(1)(d).

SECTION 4 - Costs, Expenses and Funding

Rule 237. Third-Party Funding

(1) A qualified claimant may use third-party litigation funding.
(2) Rule 245 applies to any such third-party funding agreement. A court may, however, require a qualified claimant to disclose the details of any such funding agreement relevant for the instance at stake to the court and, in so far as appropriate, to the parties.

Rule 238. Costs and Expenses of Collective Proceedings

(1) Only a qualified claimant is liable for the costs and expenses of a collective proceeding if it is unsuccessful.
(2) If the proceeding is successful, the total amount of compensation received by the qualified claimant shall form a common fund.
(3) The qualified claimant's costs and expenses incurred in bringing the proceeding must be paid from the common fund before any distribution of compensation to group members in accordance with Rule 228. Rule 245(4) applies accordingly.

PART XII – COSTS

Rule 239. Decision on Costs

(1) A court rendering a final judgment or terminating the proceedings in any other way shall determine which party is required to reimburse the other party or parties' costs of the proceedings, unless the parties have agreed otherwise. Any recovery of costs shall be limited to those that are reasonable and proportionate.
(2) If the parties enter into a settlement, each party shall bear its own costs unless they have agreed otherwise.

Rule 240. Scope and Amount of Costs

(1) Parties may seek to recover the costs of the proceedings, in particular
   (a) reasonable and proportionate costs of their legal representation in the proceedings,
   (b) court and other fees such as those of court-appointed experts, interpreters, court reporters etc.,
   (c) other reasonable financial outlays resulting from the conduct of the proceedings, such as costs of party-appointed experts, travel expenses, and fees for the service of documents.
(2) Costs under Rule 240(1) may also include costs reasonably incurred for the preparation of proceedings before they were commenced.

(3) Parties may only recover costs which they have reasonably and proportionately incurred for the conduct of the proceedings, taking into account the amount in dispute, the nature and complexity of the issues, the significance of the case for the parties.
(4) Where national law specify tariffs for the recovery of certain fees (such as, where relevant, court fees and fees for the parties' legal representation, for experts, and interpreters), any award of costs should nevertheless be consistent with the Rules of this Part.

Rule 241. General Rule

(1) When determining upon which party the obligation to reimburse costs shall be placed under Rule 239, the court shall take into account the circumstances of the specific proceedings, in particular whether and to what extent the parties' claims were successful.
(2) The court may also take into account the parties' conduct, in particular, whether and to what extent they acted in good faith and contributed to the fair, efficient and speedy resolution of the dispute.

Rule 242. Review

(1) The court's decision on costs may be subject to an appeal.
(2) An appeal is limited to a review of whether the court exercised its discretion properly according to Rules 240 and 241.
(3) A decision on an appeal under Rule 242(2) is final and binding. It cannot be subject to a second appeal.

Rule 243. Security for Costs

(1) A party may apply for the other party to provide reasonable security for costs.
(2) In deciding an application for security for costs, the court shall take into account
  (a) the likelihood that the applicant will be able to claim reimbursement of the costs of the proceedings,
  (b) the financial means of the parties and the prospect of enforcement of the costs decision against the other party,
  (c) whether such security for costs is compatible with the parties' right of access to justice and a fair trial.

Rule 244. Legal Aid

(1) Parties are entitled to legal aid, as provided by national law, if their right of access to justice and to a fair trial so requires.
(2) Such legal aid should be sufficient to cover reasonable and proportionate legal representation where legal provisions, the complexity of the case, or the vulnerability of a party so require.

Rule 245. Third-Party Funding and Success Fees

(1) A party who receives funding for the proceedings from a professional third-party funder or from a crowd-funder shall disclose this fact and the identity of the funder to the court and the other party at the commencement of proceedings. The details of such a third-party funding arrangement are, however, not subject to this requirement.
(2) Such a third-party funding arrangement must be in accordance with applicable law and must not provide for inadequate compensation for the funder or enable the funder to exercise any undue influence on the conduct of the proceedings.

(3) Parties may enter into success fee arrangements with counsel or a third-party funder. Such arrangements must nevertheless be consistent with applicable law, the parties' access to fair legal representation and the integrity of the proceedings.

(4) A violation of the requirements of Rules 245(1), (2) and (3) does not constitute a defence against the claim of the party availing itself of third-party funding or a success fee arrangement. But, having made its decision on the claim, the court may ask for details of fee arrangements with a third party or counsel relevant for the instance at stake, and, upon consultation with the parties, it may take into account any disregard of applicable law or lacking fairness of the arrangement when it renders the final decision on costs determining the part of the claimant's costs to be reimbursed.

(5) As far as provided in Rules 237, 238 (3), Rule 245 applies to collective proceedings.